LAWMEN
&
DESPERADOES

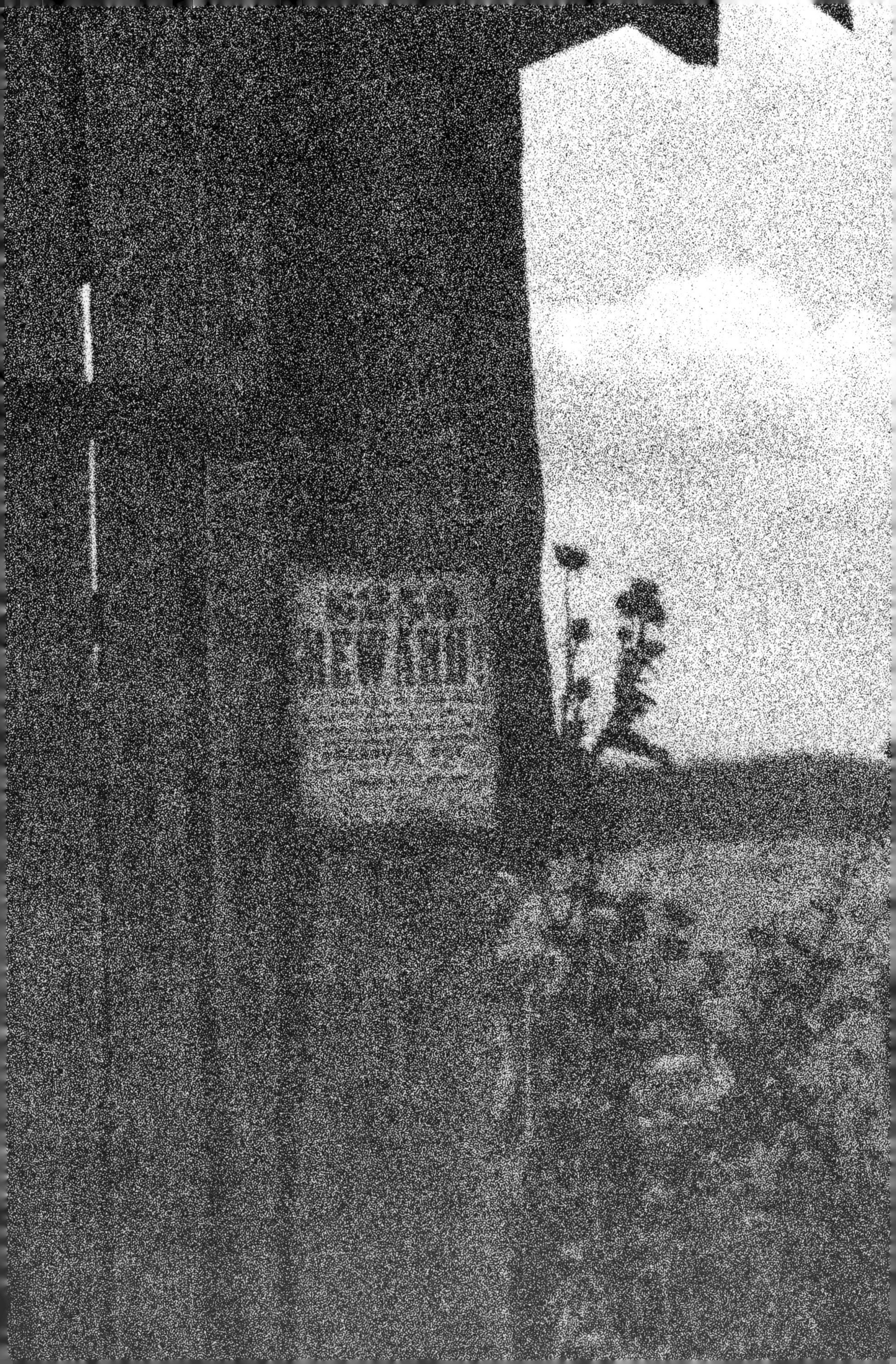

LAWMEN
&
DESPERADOES

A
Compendium
of
Noted, Early California
Peace Officers,
Badmen and Outlaws

1850–1900

by

William B. Secrest

THE ARTHUR H. CLARK COMPANY
Spokane, Washington
1994

———————

LIBRARY OF CONGRESS CATALOG CARD NUMBER 91–71133
ISBN 0–87062–209–9

The Arthur H. Clark Company
P.O. Box 14707
Spokane, WA 99214

Library of Congress Cataloging-in-Publication Data

Secrest, Bill, 1930–
    Lawmen & desperadoes   :   a compendium of noted early California
peace officers, outlaws and badmen, 1850–1900 / William B. Secrest.
    343 p.   cm. --
    Includes bibliographical references and index.
    ISBN 0–87082–209–9 : $37.50
    1. Outlaws--California--Biography--Dictionaries.   2. Peace
officers--California--Biography--Dictionaries.   I. Title.
II. Title: Lawmen and desperadoes.
HV6793.C2S42   1993
364.1'092'2794--dc20
[B]   91–71133
                                                         CIP

CONTENTS

ACKNOWLEDGEMENTS 7
INTRODUCTION 11
CHARLES AULL 25
RICHARD A. BARTER (Rattlesnake Dick) 31
TOM BELL (Thomas J. Hodges) 37
THE BLACK KID 43
CHARLES E. BOLES (Black Bart) 48
JACK BRADY (Henry Williams) 53
DAVID BROWN 59
TOMAS PROCOPIO BUSTAMENTE 64
WILLIAM WALLACE BYRNES 70
JAMES P. CASEY 76
CLODOVEO CHAVEZ 83
LAFAYETTE CHOISSER (Punch) 89
GEORGE C. CONTANT (Sontag) 95
THOMAS CUNNINGHAM 101
MASON FRAKES (Bill) DALTON 107
CHARLES H. DORSEY 113
CHRISTOPHER EVANS 121
DICK FELLOWS 127
JUAN FLORES 133
WILLIAM M. FREDERICKS 137
GEORGE E. GARD 142
LUMAN H. and SILAS E. GASKILL 147
JACK GORDON 152
WILLIAM HICKS GRAHAM 157
EMIL HARRIS 162
LEONARD HARRIS 168
JAMES HENRY 173
DR. ALEXANDER W. HOPE 177
JAMES BUNYAN HUME 181
FREDERICK EUGENE JACKSON 187

HENRY J. JOHNSON 192
ISAIAH WRIGLEY LEES 197
HENRY (Harry) LOVE 203
JAMES O. MCKINNEY 208
JOHN MASON 215
EZRA A. (Bill) MINER 219
ANATACIO MORENO 225
HENRY NICHOLSON MORSE 229
CHARLES MORTIMER (Charles J. Flynn) 235
WILLIAM MULLIGAN 241
JOAQUIN MURRIETA 246
DAVID BUTLER NEAGLE 252
ROBERT HAVLIN PAUL 257
WILLIAM HENRY HANDY PLUMMER 262
JOHN A. POWERS 268
HIRAM LEE RAPELJE 274
JOHN SONTAG 279
HENRY J. TALBOT (Cherokee Bob) 285
JOHN NELSON THACKER 291
BENJAMIN KENT THORN 295
TIBURCIO VASQUEZ 301
STEPHEN VENARD 307
JOHN DAVID WATHEN ("Wylackie John") 312
GEORGE WORK 318
BIBLIOGRAPHY 323
INDEX 329

ACKNOWLEDGEMENTS

Anyone writing a book about history winds up accumulating a substantial debt. Not merely the financial variety, but debts to people. In the end the writer does most of the work, but up to that final draft he finds himself relying on the help of many generous people. Some are close friends and correspondents of many years who share a common thread of interest. Others are staff members of libraries, historical societies, archives and various record collections in both private and public institutions. Most contribute clues or missing links or overlooked material that will help to flesh out some skeletal saga. Some merely provide encouragement. All are most helpful...and appreciated.

I must first thank my good friend and fellow bandit hunter, John Boessenecker, of Foster City, California. John provided much vital research for this project, unselfishly sharing his own years of work on the same subjects. In addition, he offered advice and opinions based on his extensive research as well as his unique personal background as a police officer and lawyer. This manuscript would have been considerably leaner, both in quality and quantity, had it not been for John's generous nature, good fellowship and expertise in an area of history where there are few experts.

Robert Chandler, of Wells, Fargo Bank, San Francisco, has been extremely helpful and generous with his time and the resources of the widely-known Wells, Fargo History Room. He has provided much valuable input for this project right from the start and his encouragement and willingness to do just a little more than was expected of him is deeply appreciated.

Laren Metzer, Joe Samora and others at the California State Archives in Sacramento will undoubteldy be relieved to know this project has finally reached fruition. Year after year Laren has provided the criminal records and pardon files utilized to document the lives of notorious California badmen and outlaws. I hope he knows just how important his help was to me.

Mrs. Sibylle Zemitis and the staff in the California Section of the State Library were consistently helpful throughout this project. Whether it was tracking down an obscure volume, or carting out stacks of photographic files, they never ceased to be cheerful, accurate and prompt.

William Roberts and the staff at the Bancroft Library in Berkeley have provided a great deal of aid over the years. Closer to home, John Jewel, Charlie Griggs, Linda Goff and Mary Castillo and their staffs at the Fresno Public Library have aided materially in the research for this work. Always cheerful, knowledgeable and delightful to work with, they long ago ceased to be public servants to become valued friends.

Mary Hanel, history librarian at the Beale Memorial Library in Bakersfield, has helped with various research projects as this work has progressed. Mrs. Lorrayne Kennedy and Judy Cunningham of the Calaveras County Museum and Archives have provided valuable documents and photographs, while Rita Hanover, of the Weaverville Public Library in Trinity County, has always responded to my calls for help. Howard Kaseburg, of the Walla Walla Valley Pioneer and Historical Society, was an important source of data on Cherokee Bob's later days. Mary Pratt, of the Los Angeles Public Library History Department, has provided much information on southern California pioneer days over the years. T.J. Smith, public information officer at Folsom State Prison, was also quite helpful, as was Mona Paine, reference librarian at the Siskiyou Public Library at Yreka.

My son, Bill Secrest, Jr., has helped me in so many ways that I hardly know where to begin to thank him. A dedicated historian and author in his own right, Bill put together the first rough outline of this work. Since then he has scanned dozens of early newspaper files, laboriously copied old documents and scrapbooks and looked up ancient records and court cases that would help shed light on the life and times of a Harry Love, Bill Miner or Tiburcio Vasquez.

My wonderful wife, Shirley has given me the most precious help of all-time. Without her doing most of my chores around the house there would never be the time needed for my never-ending research projects. I can only hope she knows how much she is loved and appreciated.

My brother, Dr. James Secrest, has come to my rescue a number of times. He provided many valuable documents and newspaper items on Mariposa County history, besides locating and photographing Punch Choisser's grave. Vern Crow, a good friend and outstanding Civil War historian, helped greatly with the final editing of this work, as did John Boessenecker.

Annie Mitchell, that premier Tulare County historian, generously provided early photographs and various bits of information over the years—particularly helping in piecing together the story of Jack Gordon. Ron Mahoney, special collections librarian at California State University, Fresno, is a valued friend who has loaned books, given me free access to his collections and otherwise always aided me in every way he could. Troy Tuggle, of King City, has also assisted in many ways, from suggesting avenues of research, to sending bits and pieces from his own research projects. Troy's interest and encouragement has helped me over many rough spots as I have rooted ever more deeply into the past.

Pat Jones, of Chicago Park in Nevada County, has provided many obscure newspaper items and other raw data over the years. As an historian, and as a friend, Pat is a rare jewel.

Other friends and acquaintances in the western history field have provided assistance in a variety of ways. My grateful appreciation is extended to Jeff Edwards, Richard Dillon, Dr. Norton B. Stern, Christian de Guigné, Harold Edwards, Jack DeMattos, Juanita Browne, Joseph G. Rosa, Mark Dugan, Jack Fleming, Robert Elder, John Kelleher, Monna Olson, Greg Martin, L.H. Hayes Jr., Carlo M. De Ferrari, Dennis Casebier, Wayne Austerman, Robert A. Olson, Cliff Davis, the late Estle Beard, Frank Latta and Colin Rickards.

I owe a special debt of gratitude to Kip Davis. Kip did the major portion of photographic printing for this project and must have been greatly relieved when it was over. Week after week he was asked to make prints from negatives made from faded, old mug books, copied in a cramped room of a courthouse or library. The negatives were often poor, but the prints were always as good as Kip could make them. Many thanks, again.

In a delightful bit of irony it was Dave Cruickshanks of London, England, who first made me aware of Bob Paul's California career as a peace officer. Thanks Dave, and thanks to you all who have been such a vital part of this project. You are hereby tendered a great share of the credit for *Lawmen & Desperadoes,* but any flaws will have to be mine alone.

WILLIAM B. SECREST
Fresno, California

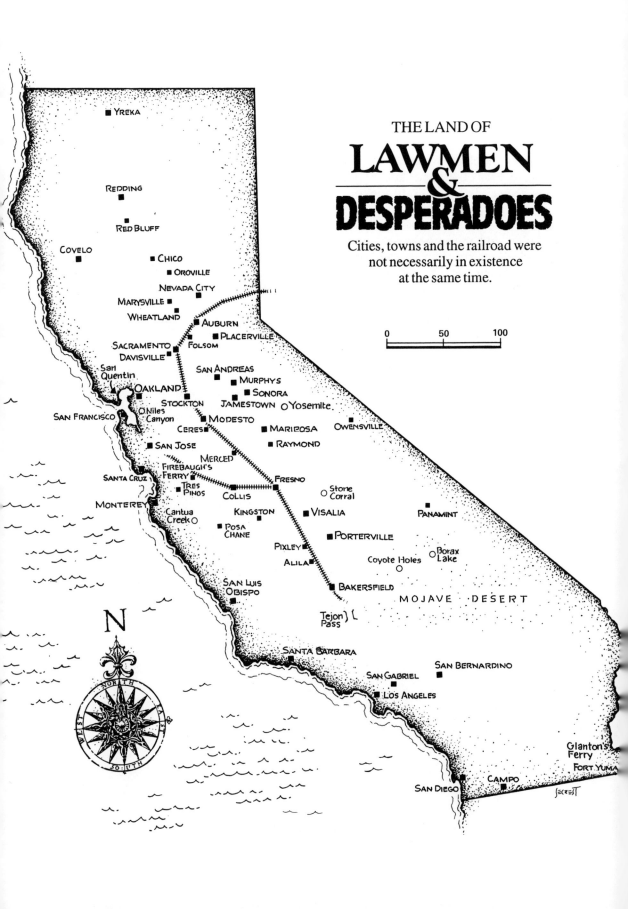

THE LAND OF

LAWMEN
&
DESPERADOES

Cities, towns and the railroad were
not necessarily in existence
at the same time.

0   50   100

YREKA

REDDING

RED BLUFF

COVELO

CHICO

OROVILLE

NEVADA CITY

MARYSVILLE

WHEATLAND

AUBURN

PLACERVILLE

SACRAMENTO

DAVISVILLE

FOLSOM

San
Quentin

OAKLAND

SAN ANDREAS

MURPHYS

SONORA

STOCKTON

JAMESTOWN

Yosemite

Niles
Canyon

MODESTO

San Francisco

CERES

MARIPOSA

OWENSVILLE

San Jose

RAYMOND

MERCED

FIREBAUGH'S
FERRY

SANTA CRUZ

TRES
PINOS

COLLIS

Fresno

Stone
Corral

MONTEREY

Cantua
Creek

KINGSTON

VISALIA

PANAMINT

Posa
Chane

PORTERVILLE

PIXLEY

Coyote Holes

Borax
Lake

ALILA

SAN LUIS
OBISPO

BAKERSFIELD

MOJAVE   DESERT

Tejon
Pass

N

SANTA BARBARA

SAN BERNARDINO

SAN GABRIEL

LOS ANGELES

Glanton's
Ferry

FORT YUMA

SAN DIEGO

CAMPO

SECREST

INTRODUCTION

From gold rush days to the turn of the century, there was no wilder, more rugged or more lawless chunk of the rapidly expanding United States than distant California. Stretching from the Yolla Bolly country of old Mendocino to the scattered gold camps along the foothills of the Sierra, gold trains were raided, gunmen shot each other down in street duels, and stagecoaches were stopped with sometimes alarming frequency.

The most startling and celebrated vigilante uprising in United States history took place in 1856 when the government of San Francisco was actually seized and maintained by citizens of the city.

Will Hicks Graham and Bill Byrnes were as fast on the draw as any of the storied gunmen of the middle west and as late as 1900 five stagecoaches were robbed at the same time by one bandit on the old Yosemite road. Few readers of Western American history, however, are aware of all this!

Although Joaquin Murrieta and Black Bart are widely known, the colorful story of California's early lawmen, badmen and outlaws seems to be a particulary lean chapter of West Coast history. This gap is abundantly emphasized by the lack of "western" novels and films utilizing early California as the locale. This may seem a trivial and minor aspect of history, but actually the fight for law and order in the far West was an important social phase of the settlement and growth of the area. As late as 1873-74, immigration to southern California was seriously hampered by the widely-publicized exploits of the notorious bandit, Tiburcio Vasquez.

With the exception of the work of such often ill-informed writers as Hubert H. Bancroft, Charles Howard Shinn and Joseph Henry Jackson, the "Wild West" aspect of California history has been a subject largely ignored by most western historians. The reasons for this neglect seems to defy all logic. Although there is ample evidence, for example, that California's lawmen, badmen and outlaws were every bit as colorful and dramatic as the Earps, the Hickoks or the James brothers, a reader looks fruitlessly for meaningful references to West Coast gunmen in such works as Prassel's *The Western Peace Officer,* or Rosa's *The Gunfighter, Man or Myth.* Yet, the period in which these Californians flourished lasted much longer than other areas of the West—from 1850 to 1900 and beyond!

But it is not just outside historians who have ignored the West Coast gunmen. California writers have, for the most part, shown the same neglect. Exactly why this has happened is difficult to understand, but since the question has been raised, perhaps an effort should be made to offer an answer.

Indications are that the 1849 gold rush largely overshadowed the criminal underbelly of California's past. This was one of the great gold rushes of history. It is not too difficult to understand how this dramatic and romantic quest for riches overwhelmed the interest and emphasis of anyone chronicling the state's past.

Even skipping past the great gold rush, however, California was richly endowed not only with economic and political annals, but in climate and natural beauty and colorful historical origins. After all, California was being settled by Spanish colonists at the same time the American Revolution was brewing in 1769. And, where else in the country could emigrants be awed by the majesty of the Sierra Nevada, the desolate wastes of the great Mojave Desert, the unparalleled richness of the vast inland valleys and the whole magnificent panorama presided over by the restless surf of the Pacific Ocean.

If California gunmen have indeed been ignored by writers in the genre, for whatever reasons, it would seem to follow that at some point the subject would be unearthed during a period of re-evaluation and re-discovery when all other aspects of far western history had been explored. Still, this has not happened. The really curious aspect of this whole subject is just how such colorful men and events could be virtually ignored by generation after generation of writers jaded by reporting and re-reporting the activities of Arizona, Kansas and Missouri badmen.

The many film, book and magazine recountings of the famed shoot-out at the O.K. Corral in Tombstone would seem to indicate this was the most deadly and dramatic encounter in frontier history. Yet, various California shooting affairs make this Arizona incident pale by comparison. In Mendocino County when the Coates and Frost families shot it out on the streets of Little Lake in 1867, six men died and three were wounded. At Mussel Slough in 1880, seven settlers and railroad men died in a bloody contest over Tulare County farm land. And, in a real life parallel to Wild Bill Hickok's fictional combat with the McCandless Gang, Captain Jonathan R. Davis fought with eleven robbers who had gunned down his two prospecting companions on a mountain trail near Placerville in 1854. As the outlaws charged upon him, Davis shot down seven of them and killed three others in a knife fight. The last bandit was only painfully wounded. The whole bloody conflict was witnessed by another group of prospectors on a nearby hill, all of whom testified as to what happened.

Although Captain Davis' adventure probably stands as one of the most sensational in frontier history, other California gunmen had an equal zest for the fray as evidenced by this eye-witness account of one of badman Billy Mulligan's scraps in 1851:

> Mulligan drew his pistol; think Rhodes fired first; they both fired; there were several shots exchanged, and I retired to the back room; in a very short time

Mulligan came running into the back room, and Rhodes after him, firing at him; after running to the back part of the room, and firing the last shot, they clenched and fought on the floor; the officers...separated them...

And who could help but cheer at Milt Duffield's classic six-gun duel with THREE badmen on the streets of old Sonora—a shoot-out he won handily to the fanfare of the local public press.

As late as 1876 the Sacramento *Daily Bee* recorded the following brawl at a time when it would seem the gun-toting days of legislators and newsmen, at least, were long past:

...[Assemblyman] Wilcox sneaked around...without being observed. The *Chronicle* reporter was busily engaged in writing, with his head bending over his desk and did not notice Wilcox. When within a few feet of the reporter's desk, the latter person gave a sudden spring forward, lifted up his cane and brought it down with tremendous force upon the reporter's head, and then immediately drew his pistol. The *Chronicle* reporter...was stunned. He staggered from his seat and drew his pistol, but it was immediately snatched from his hand...

Here we have a reporter and a state legislator, both going about armed with pistols as a matter of course, not in some inland mining camp, mind you, but in the state's capitol!

Other encounters were even more dramatic, particularly a cryptic incident reported in the Fresno *Weekly Expositor* in May of 1870. A "man from Alameda County" was riding along the west side of the San Joaquin Valley tracking several horses he had recently lost to stock thieves. At Cantua Creek he met two Mexican vaqueros who asked where he was going. After the man replied, one of the riders suggested he turn back as it would not be healthy for him to continue. The man from Alameda meanwhile, had recognized his stolen animals under the two vaqueros:

...He was carrying a Henry rifle, fully loaded, and one of the Mexicans was directly in front of the muzzle of it so, without raising it to his shoulder, he cocked it and fired it off, killing one of the Mexicans instantly, and then lifting it to his shoulder, turned and killed the other one. He then took the horses and returned...home.

In June of 1894 Merced gambler Jim Burke was mortally stabbed in a dispute with one of his patrons. When the local coroner tried to obtain an ante-mortem statement he was refused. "If I live," whispered the dying gambler, "I want to kill him, and if I die I don't want him prosecuted."

But if California's badmen were tough, the state's lawmen would match guts and accomplishments with any of the more storied western peace officers who have been so over-exposed through the years. Captain Isaiah Lees, a San Francisco police detective for 47 years, was a literal legend in his own time whom William Pinkerton called "the greatest criminal catcher the West ever knew." There were many others—some famous for a particular exploit such as Captain Harry Love who had tracked down the elusive Joaquin Murrieta. The brave and implacable Harry Morse had forty years of hairbreadth escapes and adventures as both sheriff and private detective.

Others had similarly impressive records. Ben Thorn, a Calaveras County lawman for over forty years, tracked Bill Miner and Black Bart and served almost continuously as both deputy and sheriff from 1855 to 1900. Bob Paul, later a noted peace officer in frontier Arizona, had a long and distinguished career as a California lawman and Wells, Fargo messenger. Paul was chasing the deadly Tom Bell and Rattlesnake Dick Barter when his friends the Earp brothers were mere youngsters contemplating a move west.

The California lawmen were not only tough and fearless, but progressive as well. In 1852 a San Francisco police captain had constructed a device for measuring the height of criminals. He kept a notebook recording a complete description of each offender and suggested daguerreotypes be made of all who were booked into the city jail. As early as 1856 San Francisco's title for the City Marshal was changed to Chief of Police.

Mug shots of criminals were probably introduced on the coast by the vigilantes when they controlled San Francisco in the summer of 1851. They photographed all criminals in their custody during the 1856 vigilante uprising also, and when they disbanded the municipal authorities continued the practice—as funds permitted. The city of San Jose was taking mug shots as early as 1864, utilizing a local photographer named Heering. When a prisoner continually made facial contortions during a sitting, Heering waited until his attention was diverted by a deputy giving him a lecture, then quickly made his exposure. The prisoner was furious at the trick. "He went back to his cell," commented the San Jose *Mercury* reporter, "cursing the trick whereby he had been chiseled out of his picture."

The Pony Express was no sooner established across the country than California and eastern lawmen were exchanging information on fugitive criminals. The practice was promptly accelerated with the advent of the telegraph.

Ballistics were also being utilized at an early day. The San Francisco *Bulletin* reported in November of 1870 that a Sacramento police officer had compared the bullets that had penetrated a body with those remaining in a pistol and proved them to be the same.

The police detective was yet another innovation quickly adapted by California law enforcement bodies. Francois Vidocq, the French convict turned lawman in Napoleon's time, became perhaps the first modern detective when he originated the Paris Sureté. Scotland Yard, the British detective unit, came into being in 1842 and Boston employed its own three-man detective force by 1846.

One of California's first police detectives was Isaiah W. Lees, who joined the San Francisco department in late 1853. He headed the detective unit until he became chief in 1897. Just as today, most private detectives acquired experience on the police force before going into business for themselves. Tom Ansbro, Henry Johnson and James Bovee all trained under Lees, then went into private work in the 1860s.

In Los Angeles Emil Harris and George Gard became that city's first police detectives in the early 1870s when there were only six officers in the department. Later, Harris was also a widely-known private investigator.

Wells, Fargo hired its famous Special Officer James B. Hume in March of 1872, but Henry Johnson and Steve Venard had both preceded him as company detectives. Just when the railroad companies acquired their own detective units is not clear, but Allan Pinkerton and his men had been early private investigators for the Illinois Central Railroad during the 1850s.

When the first far-west train robbery took place at Verdi, Nevada, in 1870, a Central Pacific Railroad detective named Frederick T. Burke is noted as being one of the investigators. Bill Smith and Leonard Harris were two of the more prominent Southern Pacific detectives. Ex-U.S. Marshal George Gard was appointed head of the S.P. detective force in 1894 as a reward for his capture of the notorious train robbers Evans and Sontag.

For over fifty years California had more than its fair share of outlaws and desperadoes, from Joaquin Murrieta, who was put out of action in 1853, to Jim McKinney, cut down in Bakersfield's old Tenderloin District in 1903. In between, Will Graham, Bill Owens, John Mason, Cherokee Bob Talbot, Procopio and Sam Brown left trails of bullet-bored bodies throughout the state. Some were vicious killers. Others were gunmen who attracted other killers seeking a reputation. All were colorful desperadoes and most died with their boots on.

With the possible exception of Tiburcio Vasquez, the most noted of the early California bandits were Joaquin Murrieta and Black Bart. Aside from these two outlaws, the reader will notice many Mexican or native Californian desperadoes in these pages. It is true there was substantial friction between the races in the early days—many Americans being extremely intolerant of a people they had just worsted in a war. Many a vaquero and miner turned outlaw because they were denied property and personal rights by such attitudes. The vast majority of Mexicans and Californians, however, were honest and industrious citizens and any impression to the contrary is wrong!

Although some Mexican inhabitants protected and supplied the outlaws, this was primarily a result of fear and practicality. Ranches and villages were isolated and reprisals easy. Americans behaved much the same way. It was a time when people minded their own business knowing that loose talk was sometimes repaid with blood. The lesson of the following item in the Kern County *Courier* in 1875 was distinct...and chilling:

> Murder—About two months ago a Mexican by the name of Francisco Viela came to the ranch of John Heinlan on Mussel Slough and hired out to herd horses. He subsequently stated that he had been one of the Chavez band, had resolved to leave them and was fearful he would be murdered for so

doing. On the 18th, after he had gone to work, a large, well-dressed man, whom the China cook took to be a Mexican or Frenchman, rode up and wanted breakfast. He was mounted on a large bay horse and well armed with pistols and gun. He rode away over the plain. Toward night the horse of Viela was found tied to the fence, with the saddle removed and forty or fifty rods away the dead body of the rider was found, where he had been lassoed and dragged over the plain until his neck was broken...

The Mexican vaqueros were undeniably the best potential bandits in the country, however. Born to the saddle, they could ride like the wind, live off the land and disappear from the broad plains of the San Joaquin and reappear in southern California almost overnight. Posses quickly learned that it was necessary to live on horseback if they hoped to catch up with the Mexican bandit gangs. And the best of the lawmen did just that. "We are in the saddle from early dawn until dark," wrote Sheriff Harry Morse to Governor Newton Booth during the pursuit of Vasquez. "We were quite sore from riding the first few days out, but we have got over that and can ride as far as a vaquero now."

The splendid riding abilities of these vaqueros was witnessed by a San Francisco *Bulletin* reporter in January of 1871. In a scene right out of a Roy Rogers movie script, a horse ran away while pulling a buggy driven by an old man. The horse rushed furiously down busy and crowded Montgomery Street with pedestrians scampering aside trying to avoid the terrified old man's careening vehicle. Disaster seemed inevitable at any moment. Suddenly, from a side street, a Mexican vaquero dashed full speed on his spirited mustang:

> The gallant fellow rode at the side of the runaway for a distance of several hundred feet, and finally succeeded in forming a noose out of one of the reins and placing it around the animal's nose. This feat, owing to the great speed of the runaway, required remarkable coolness and dexterity on the part of the rider. The movement was to check the animal without overturning the buggy. This was safely accomplished by crowding the steed toward the sidewalk, and bringing him to a halt near a drug store. The vaquero actually rode into the store before he could check the horse upon which he was mounted. The occupant of the vehicle was rescued...and heartily congratulated upon the successful termination of his wild ride. The vaquero, a native Californian, petted his horse a few moments, then lighted the inevitable cigarette and rode away...

It seems clear from research and the perspective of time that being a bandit in early California was seldom a full-time job. Many Murrieta men were mustang runners, packers and vaqueros and only occasionally engaged in crime. Others would supply the gang and sometimes travel with it, but for the most part worked at legitimate occupations.

Tiburcio Vasquez was noted for having two or three men as the nucleus of his gang, then recruiting members for particular raids. The isolated villages of Los Angeles, Posa Chané, Las Juntas, the California Ranch, Panama (near Bakersfield) and New Idria could always be counted on for adventurous souls looking for some easy money. Too, the large scattered ranchos of the time made excellent hideouts for outlaws waiting for a "job" opening, or for a trail to get cold. Adopting this on-again-off-again bandit lifestyle enabled many a desperado to die with his boots off.

Judicial machinery was quickly established in California, although miner's courts and vigilantes were common throughout the 1850s. The Mexican alcalde was the civil magistrate in the villages of pre-gold rush days. Serving primarily as a justice of the peace, the alcalde was at times a combination mayor, judge, policeman and city council. With the coming of statehood in 1850, California assumed all the civil and judicial machinery of the rest of the country.

By an act of May 19, 1853, it was provided that the judicial system of the state should consist of the supreme court, the district courts, the San Francisco superior court, the county courts, the courts of sessions, the probate courts, the justice courts, the recorder's courts and mayor's courts. The courts of sessions were the forerunner of the present day county board of supervisors and were also involved in legal matters, besides being a court of first instance in criminal cases. These minor courts were abolished with the adoption of the superior courts created by the constitution of 1879.

Those who enforced the laws were county sheriffs and their deputies, city marshals and their policemen, private police, constables and often justices of the peace. U.S. marshals and their deputies handled federal matters. Although lawmen's salaries were frequently low, they obtained fees for serving papers, obtaining jurors, escorting prisoners, as well as travel mileage. Lawmen, especially sheriffs, frequently became quite wealthy from tax collecting alone.

California's prison system evolved as the need arose. Although there were a few scattered Mexican jails in California when the Americans took over, there was no central prison where felons could be isolated to serve out their sentences. General Mariano Vallejo and a political hack named James M. Estell took charge of the new state's convicted felons in late April of 1851. They had offered to house, clothe and feed them in exchange for the use of the convicts' labor, and state legislators, faced with a steadily draining treasury, jumped at the offer. Although there was some muttering about slave labor, most seemed satisfied with the arrangement.

At first there were so few prisoners that they were subcontracted out to San Francisco Sheriff Jack Hays who put them to work quarrying stone on Angel Island. The prisoners were housed in an old ship named the *Wabau*. Hays promptly discovered that with escapes and other problems he was losing his shirt on the deal and began scrambling to get out of the arrangement.

The eventual need for an actual prison was obvious and the legislature purchased twenty acres of land at a place called Point San Quentin. The site was strategically located across the bay from San Francisco, in Marin County. In mid-July of 1852 the *Wabau* was towed to Point San Quentin and the forty or fifty prisoners were put to work preparing the ground for building. Presumedly the three or more women prisoners were put to gentler tasks.

The convicts continued to live in the *Wabau* until a stone cellblock was completed in January of 1854. The "Stones," as it was called, consisted of a two story structure 180 feet long by 24 feet wide. There were 48 cells in the upper story, while the lower level consisted of a long dormitory with the turnkey's office at one end. By this time, however, the convict population had increased to some two hundred and fifty. By the end of the year the number had jumped to over three hundred.

A legislative report in 1855 specified that the enclosure surrounding the cellblock was to be a square with five hundred foot long walls on each side . . . "to be four feet in thickness at the base . . . and to be carried up to the height of ten feet above the ground with stone, laid in cement, and then ten feet more in height, to be built of brick . . ." The wall was to be several more years in construction, with various outbuildings and guard towers.

There was massive fraud in most of the early prison operations as Estell and other administrators bled the state for all they could get. Despite the fact that ten dozen hickory shirts were listed as being purchased in 1855, visitors to the prison noted that the convicts were invariably dressed in rags, being forced to wear the clothes they were convicted in. A report made to the legislature in 1858 stated:

> The general clothing of the prisoners seems too scant for winter weather [and is] in such a tattered, torn, forbidding and filthy condition that the commonest street beggars sleeping by the wayside and begging their daily bread would by comparison have the appearance of newly Parisian-clad gentlemen. The bedding (if bedding it can be called) of the prisoners [is] insufficient to protect them from absolute suffering from the cold. The cells being six feet by ten, with something like two shelves on each side, about two feet in width each, upon which is a kind of straw mattress and one coarse, shaggy, double blanket, which is all that is found [and] has become a mass of dirty, filthy rags, the lice being so plentiful as to be easily seen crawling about the so-called bed and bedding . . .

The guards wore no uniforms, and except for the guns they carried differed little in appearance from their wards. It wasn't until 1865 that the grey and black striped uniforms were introduced to the prison.

The principal work of the prisoners was quarrying at nearby sites, brick-making at a sixteen-acre steam plant adjoining the prison, and woodcutting to fuel both the brickyard and the prison. Other convicts loaded and unloaded schooners supplying brick and rock to the San Francisco market. They worked long hours, usually sunrise to sunset, seven days a week.

Supply warrants issued in late 1855 show food purchased to have been potatoes, flour, coffee, sugar, vinegar, pepper, molasses, onions, butter, salt, lard and beef. Just how much food reached the convicts is not known since

Estell was engaged in so much fraud, but investigating committees generally concluded the prisoners were being given enough to eat.

The state took over management of the prison in 1861, but both before and after this occured, escapes were many and bloody. The last mass escape attempt was in 1864, the previous ten years accounting for the escape of some 654 convicts. The next ten years saw only seventeen breakouts. San Quentin had evolved into an important social institution housing a steadily growing number of inmates.

A second state prison was seen as an eventual necessity in the late 1850s and in 1868 a site was selected at Folsom, in the foothills east of Sacramento. Folsom State Prison was opened in July 1880 with the transfer of a group of inmates from San Quentin. Designed as a maximum security prison, Folsom housed inmates serving long terms, as well as incorrigibiles and repeat offenders.

The subjugation of crime in the far west was due as much to rewards as to the officers and courts that enforced the laws. Rewards were the incentives that kept posses riding and outlaws looking over their shoulders. There seems to have been few rules where rewards were concerned. Sheriffs operated freely in neighboring counties and throughout the state during the second half of the nineteenth century.

For a $1,000 reward private detective Jim Bovee pursued a Fresno County fugitive some 1,500 miles, from San Francisco to the deserts of Arizona, through snow storms and blistering heat. But he got his man! Sheriffs and bounty hunters from all over the state swarmed over Tulare County in the early 1890s hunting for outlaws Chris Evans and John Sontag. When the pair were finally ambushed and gunned down by a posse in the foothills, men who had not arrived on the scene until long after the shooting stopped later submitted reward claims unashamedly.

But there were obvious problems. Officers were sometimes accused of not responding promptly enough unless an incentive was offered for the capture of a criminal. Too, there were occasions when lawmen accepted rewards for merely doing their duty. Often officers would ask for a reward before acting in a case, as bizarre as this may seem today.

Most private detectives were primarily concerned with recovering stolen property. Unless there was a reward for him, capturing the thief was usually secondary. Often detectives would bargain with a thief for the return of stolen property. It was a period when one San Francisco police chief could legitimately send a boatload of officers several hundred miles down the coast to retrieve a boatload of scuttled Mexican silver, all on city time. He then claimed the booty as salvage and was praised for his good work in the local press!

In justice to the lawmen, however, it was also a time when expenses were often paid out of their own pockets and they depended on being reimbursed by the rewards. Detective Tom Burns had spent months tracking Evans and Sontag and was one of the small posse that finally ambushed and captured them.

19

Another deputy sheriff, who had arrived after the battle, put in for a portion of the reward and infuriated Burns during a court appearance. Later the two men met while on a train returning to Tulare County, and Burns shot and badly wounded the bogus claimant.

In San Francisco at least, Police Judge Henry Coon finally found it necessary to come to grips with the reward problem. He ruled that fees paid by prisoners to officers must be strictly supervised by superiors and that only standing rewards, such as those offered for escaped convicts should unquestionably be paid to officers. Judge Coon further suggested that most rewards be paid into a police benevolent society such as was being done in New York and other large cities. The judge's ruling, made in 1858, was only adhered to when convenient, however.

Perhaps the most celebrated, if not always the most just, means of curbing crime were the vigilance committees. When the thugs and thieves got out of hand in San Francisco in 1851, the citizens took the law into their own hands. They captured criminals, held brief trials, and either hanged or threw the rascals out of town. The initial cleansing did not "take," however, and in 1856 the greatest vigilance committee in history rose up and once more took over the city. While historians may disagree as to the motives and necessity of the San Francisco vigilantes, one can hardly argue with the awesome proportions of the popular uprising. Surely something had to be wrong for nearly 7,000 men to flock to the vigilante banner.

Looking back at the vigilante phenomena it becomes increasingly clear that men frequently took the law into their own hands, not because of a lack of law, but because of an overabundance of it. One of the plagues which struck California in the course of the gold rush was the horde of politicians and attorneys who flocked to the new land hoping to make a name for themselves, get rich or to get in on the ground floor of the developing state power structure. Lawyers were everywhere. They stumbled over each other to obtain clients and there was plenty of business. Anyone reading over the criminal trials of those days is struck by one significant fact. There were as many legal loopholes and technicalities for a criminal to escape punishment in early California as there are today!

When murderer David Brown was lynched in Los Angeles in 1855 it wasn't the result of a lack of law, but because the mob knew he would never hang legally despite the brutal murder he had committed. And when a Monterey County deputy sheriff hanged a convicted murderer despite a postponement from the governor, an exasperated editor penned the reasons:

> In the County of Monterey, within the last three years, over forty murders have been committed, and we believe this is the first legal conviction followed by punishment that has ever been had since the organization of the county; and may well be considered a triumph of law and order, although

20

attempts have been made in certain quarters to construe the fact of the case differently.

In San Francisco young Sam Clemens, a reporter on the old *Morning Call* in 1864, complained bitterly that when a brutal criminal named Mortimer was convicted of a vicious beating and robbery, "our lenient court...as usual, only gave him a year in state prison."

To be sure, there were some vigilante groups which were little more than lynch-mad mobs of drunken thugs and vagabonds who were so far removed from home and civilizing influences that they had lost all touch with decency. When a drunken Fourth of July crowd in Downieville lynched a Mexican woman after the barest hint of a rump trial, a spectator characterized the crowd as the "hungriest, craziest, wildest mob standing around that I ever saw anywhere!"

The Humboldt *Times* criticized the people of Shasta for lynching the murderous Ruggles brothers in 1892, noting that "such an advertisement of their lawlessness will in the long run prove far more expensive than the most costly of criminal trials." A Shasta newspaper dismissed the criticism with the terse comment—"Yes, and those men who are murderously inclined will avoid Shasta County if these lynchings are kept up."

In May of 1874 John Overend, his wife and four children were all found murdered on their farm near San Diego. It was a particulary heinous crime; all were beaten to death, the youngest child having it's head cloven in two as it lay in the cradle. Three Indians were sought for the crime, only two of whom were captured. One of the suspects, Clemente Monteca, confessed that he had been the lookout when the crime had been committed and that the other prisoner, Jose del Carme, was one of the principal murderers. Del Carme was an old offender, already indicted for yet another murder. Since there was no other evidence against the pair, a plea bargain was made to secure the confession of Monteca. He was swiftly sentenced to a ten year term and that same day was hastily taken aboard a ship bound for San Quentin Prison.

San Diegans were furious! "Certain it is," snarled the editor of the San Diego *Union*, "that had the people entertained the least suspicion of what had been done at the courthouse in the afternoon, the prisoner would not have been taken to the steamer."

The fact that the case could have been dismissed without the confession (which was useless unless a plea of manslaughter was accepted) made little difference to the public. They were outraged! Just the thought of the child with its head cleaved in two and one of the killers charged with only *manslaughter* was enough to make a statue cry out in horror.

Pioneer Californians struggled desperately for answers to the vigilante and lynching manner of justice and the question is still being argued today. When all else has apparently failed—when the laws and justice system have broken down,

21

or work more for the criminal than the victim, do people have the right to take the law into their own hands? After all, in a Democracy, are not the people the final arbiters of their own society—particularly a frontier society?

Strangely enough, contrary to popular conception and despite the vigilantes, the gunsmoke and the lynching of our "Wild West" days, it was socially a period when crime was in a considered decline. Alarmed by the high crime rates of the 1830s and '40s, Americans began stressing character development from the pulpit, in the press and in both popular literature and school books. And it worked! This decline in the crime rate was to continue for about a century until the 1920s and '30s when new moods and morals began emphasizing "personality development," rather than character. Readers may judge for themselves what has happened since then.

In mid-August of 1899 California sheriffs held a convention in San Francisco where methods were compared and suggestions made toward better and more effective cooperation among lawmen. The twenty sheriffs present also took a tour of San Quentin and the San Francisco jails. Frontier days were rapidly coming to a close.

In offering these brief biographies of California's noted lawmen, badmen and outlaws, it is hoped they will not only prove of interest, but will serve as a valuable research tool and help establish, at last, California's place in our "Wild West" history. The reader will bear in mind, I hope, that this is not intended as a social commentary or scholarly study of any kind. Rather, it is a harsh and unvarnished documentary of the lawmen and desperadoes who made early California the first, and last, of the frontier West.

As for the choices for inclusion in this compendium, the word "noted" in the title has been the guide. Obviously this did not always apply. Various characters did not comfortably fit this criteria, but were so interesting or otherwise appeared important that inclusion seemed mandatory—to the author, at least. Others, although little-known today, were quite renowned in their lifetimes. There will be disagreements with the selections, of course, but it is hoped any disappointment will be tempered with curiosity and interest in the selected characters.

The trail of these men has been a long one. Despite prolonged research and constant digging in California and other states, some discoveries were pure chance. Old Bill Miner, for example, claimed to have performed heroic feats as a dispatch rider during the Civil War. No one really believed that he had ever been in the army until an old 1864 muster roll for the California Volunteers was turned up in the California State Archives. When Miner's military record in the National Archives was obtained, it turned out to be typically Miner. Far from containing any heroics, the documents disclosed that after obtaining a cash bounty for his enlistment, Bill promptly deserted some three months later to pursue his lifelong love affair with crime.

The story of Cherokee Bob's California career was particulary difficult to unravel. When I first stumbled across his name in an early Santa Cruz newspaper while researching another subject, I felt sure this was quite likely the same character who later was so prominent in Washington and Idaho history. After all, how many men could there be in the same area and time period with a nickname like "Cherokee Bob?" Actually, besides the original Bob, I found a stagecoach robber by that name who was reported killed near Jackson in 1859. Another "Cherokee Bob" reportedly helped stick up a stagecoach with Jim Driscoll near Folsom in 1858, then disappeared with the loot when Driscoll was caught. Still another "Bob" appeared in a reminiscence in the old San Francisco *Argonaut* in 1877. All of these characters were eliminated one by one as being the original Bob Talbot, but for awhile it seemed as though "Cherokee Bobs" were popping up everywhere!

The story of Harry Love is a good example of how some of these subjects have suffered from historians continually relying on previous, written accounts and arriving at erroneous conclusions. One prominent California writer and historian characterized Love as a "cruel and vindictive" wife-beater. When his record is carefully reviewed, this conclusion hardly seems warranted. His Texas army records indicate he was a brave man, highly valued by his superiors. Moreover, he was assigned important exploring projects for which he received high praise from both the army and the press.

In California he was a pioneer builder of dams and roads who participated in the pursuit of outlaws when duty called. Because of his prominent record in Texas and California, he was a natural choice to head up the California Rangers for the chase after Murrieta.

There was indeed much trouble between Love and his wife in the later years of their marriage, but it seems highly unlikely he was a wife-beater. In the first place, he would have been hard-pressed to beat a three hundred pound wife who was noted throughout California as a woman who could take care of herself. Research seems to indicate that Love's troubles with his wife stemmed primarily from her domineering personality. Business affairs further alienated the couple as did her hiring a young man to help her out when she and Harry were no longer living together.

To base a judgement of Harry Love's whole life solely on the drunken jealousy and exasperation of a man who had been repeatedly disappointed in love and livelihood in the late years of his life, seems quite unfair.

This personal side of these biographies has been the most difficult to establish. Newspaper articles, court records or prison registers seldom reveal character. We are generally made well aware of a noted lawman's bravery and other virtues, but seldom exposed to his frailties. Similarly, we are left to wonder about the qualities of a Cherokee Bob who refuses to give the court or prison authorities his real name so as not to disgrace his aged father in the east.

Many of these biographies are fairly complete, while others must remain sketchy for a variety of reasons. George Contant, Harry Morse and Jim Hume left books, interviews, records and scrapbooks to document their lives and actions. The story of others had to be dug out painfully, bit by bit, from the old newspapers and documents—guided frequently by the barest of clues. While Harry Morse and Jim Hume might often write up their experiences for publicity purposes, others were not so obliging to the historian. "Too many people," commented detective Isaiah Lees, "would be hurt by a book telling the complete story of my life in San Francisco."

In these stories of bad men and good I have relied heavily on early newspaper accounts, bolstered with other contemporary sources wherever possible. Pioneer reminiscences, both published and unpublished, have been utilized, as well as census records, government reports, prison records, city directories and court documents. The author has, in the text, quoted liberally from contemporary sources so as to establish validity and add substance to characters and events that have become dimmed and out of focus over the years. I wanted to emphasize that these were real people who had lived, fought and died, and underscore the raw evidence of their existence.

But even in the more detailed studies there were gaps that could not always be filled. Some may be fleshed out eventually but many must remain incomplete. Prison records and government documents have been lost or discarded years ago, before modern techniques, organization and concern assured their safety. Even runs of old newspapers have disappeared or are in private collections. Much history has been destroyed in early fires and floods or otherwise blown away by the relentless winds of time.

With apologies for any shortcomings, here they are, the heroes and villains whose stories provide a portion of the meat and marrow of California's past. For better or worse, these are the builders and wreckers, the drifters and men of substance, the lawmen and desperadoes by whom we judge our progress.

CHARLES AULL

Courtesy Folsom State Prison.

Born near Liberty, Missouri, in 1849, young Charles Aull was brought to California by his physician father during the gold rush in 1852. While growing up in Stanislaus County, the boy received a good education and engaged in the mercantile business at an early age. He moved to Modesto in 1870 and two years later accepted an appointment as undersheriff by Sheriff John Rodgers.

Modesto was the county seat of a booming farm and ranching area and many criminals, toughs and gamblers mingled with the farm hands and cowboys who filled the saloons and dance halls. The local newpaper editor wailed, "Citizens of Modesto...are you not ashamed of the fact that there is so much violence, rowdyism and law-breaking thus chronicled against the fair name of this community?" It was a good training ground for a young lawman and Aull quickly learned that he was playing for keeps.

In the summer of 1874 Aull arrested a thug named Ramon Quiroz for larceny. When he tried to escape, the lawman fired on him and when Quiroz was caught he vowed never to let Aull arrest him again. On November 4th Aull was again compelled to serve a warrant on Quiroz for assault and larceny. Constable A.H. Davis accompanied him and they found their quarry at breakfast with some friends. When Aull told him he was under arrest, the badman asked to see the warrant, as reported in the Modesto *Stanislaus News* of November 6th:

> ...He looked at it for a short time, and then tore it into pieces and started

25

rapidly to raise from his seat, at the same time reaching behind him for a weapon...The [under]sheriff retreated rapidly backward as he saw that it was the aim of Quiroz to run under him and throw him. The officer retreated towards the door where he succeeded in drawing his revolver... [He] fired over the Mexican's head, the ball taking effect between the shoulders and ranging downward into the lungs...The wounded man then threw up his hands...When he was disarmed by constable Davis it was found that in addition to his knife he was armed with a five-shooter...

Quiroz lingered for five days before dying from his wound. He had a long criminal record and was well known to the police of San Francisco and Sacramento.

In the fall of 1875 Aull was appointed turnkey at San Quentin, California's state prison. At that time the prison was under the control of the lieutenant governor and Aull learned much about the supervision and control of the 1,400 inmates. In 1880 he resigned his position when a Republican administration made sweeping new appointments of prison officials.

Aull's next position was as a Wells, Fargo detective, working under his good friend James B. Hume. As chief special officer of the express company, Hume supervised several other detectives, besides being responsible for the shotgun messengers who guarded the treasure being shipped by railroad, steamer and stagecoach.

Modesto, California, was a tough railroad town and farming center when Aull was deputy sheriff there in the 1870's. *Courtesy McHenry Museum, Modesto.*

Ramon Quiroz [inset] as he appeared in a Sacramento police mug book of the 1870's. *Courtesy Sacramento City Archives.*

During the summer and fall of 1881 a series of stagecoach holdups were believed to be the work of a recently released convict named Dick Fellows. Aull's steady and patient detective work was instrumental in tracking down the bandit and Fellows was ultimately captured and sentenced to another long prison term.

When the stage from Sonora to Milton in Tuolumne County was held up on November 7, 1881, Aull was on the scene the next day. He quickly determined that the bandit leader was a notorious ex-convict named Bill Miner, although it wasn't thought he was in the state at the time. In company with local lawmen, Aull scoured the countryside and finally traced Miner and several companions to San Francisco. Bill Miller, one of the outlaws, had a ranch near Woodland and Aull's posse headed there. A well-known desperado named Jim Crumm was captured at Miller's ranch and two other men were seen to run away as the lawmen approached. Aull sensed that the fleeing men were Miner and Miller and after trailing them for some distance the fugitives were captured. All three of the outlaws entered San Quentin in December.

In early February of 1882 two masked men held up a stage between Chinese Camp and Copperopolis. There had been only $200 in the Wells, Fargo box, but Aull quickly was put on the case. Accompanying Deputy Sheriff Whitlock of Tuolumne County, Aull rented a buggy and proceeded to Sycamore on the San Joaquin River where the outlaws had last been reported. From there they proceeded to the California Ranch, a notorious outlaw hangout, then to White's Bridge where the two bandits had camped for several days. Learning their quarry had taken a sheepherder's wagon and headed for the coast range, the two lawmen were joined by a Merced deputy named L.C. Davis. It was raining hard when the trio again resumed the chase and by the time they entered the hills it was a pitch black evening. While Davis walked ahead with a lantern, Aull and Whitlock followed in the buggy. About 4 o'clock in the morning the buggy suddenly went over a ten foot embankment, ending up in a heap and bruising both lawmen considerably. Obtaining another buggy, the men kept up their dogged pursuit. Finally, they caught up with the two outlaws who were surprised and captured. The San Francisco *Call* noted:

> ...The prisoners, who proved to be Frank H. Rolfe and Joe Hampton, were taken by wagon to Hollister, and brought to this city last night by Detective Aull and lodged in the Central Police Station enroute to Tuolumne, the scene of the robbery. Rolfe...completed his last term on the 26th of December last and came to this city and purchased a rifle. This fact became known to Detective Aull, who immediately drew the inference that he had gone on the warpath and he conducted the pursuit with the belief that Rolfe was one of the robbers.

Later this same year Aull learned that a man named Collins was being held on a burglary charge in St. Louis. Working with Captain Isaiah Lees of the San Francisco police, the two officers concluded that Collins was wanted on a

27

robbery and murder charge in Nevada County dating from 1879. The two detectives headed east and after talking to the local police determined that Collins was the right man and had a partner living under an assumed name in Indiana. Lees then picked up the partner and both prisoners were returned to California where they were convicted of murder and robbery under their names of Patterson and Dorsey. The Grass Valley *Union* of October 24th reported:

> On Sunday night's train Patterson and Dorsey, the noted criminals who robbed and murdered Wm. Cummings . . . were brought up from San Francisco by Captain Aull of Wells, Fargo & Co.'s detective force and lodged in the county jail at Nevada City.
> . . . The history of this crime, the disappearance of the criminals, and their discovery after three years of time is a strange chapter of criminal history and the manner in which the case has been worked up by Aull and Lees is one of the most creditable pieces of detective skill of the time . . .

Over $5,000 in rewards had been offered for the men, of which Aull received $3,400 as his share and Lees the balance.

When Paul Shirley was appointed warden of San Quentin in 1883, Aull accepted the position of deputy warden. He held this post for four years until assuming the warden's post at Folsom Prison in January of 1888. Because of his tour of duty at San Quentin, he was always referred to as Captain Aull.

A tough and dedicated lawman, Aull nonetheless felt a keen responsibility for the prisoners in his charge. A noted case was that of a burglar named William Schmidt, convict No. 999. Schmidt was an incorrigible serving a ten-year term when Aull took office. He had served nearly all his time in solitary confinement and had nearly carved his way out at one point. After numerous escape attempts, an assault on a guard and an attempt to kill the warden, Schmidt's case was described to various prison authorities around the country in an attempt to either break his spirit or reform him. Nothing worked.

When Aull took over at Folsom, Schmidt was still in solitary. The case had received a great deal of publicity and Aull decided on an unprecedented course of action. Calling Schmidt to his office, the warden told him of the comforts he was losing because of his attitude. He must obey the rules and give up any further escape attempts. The prisoner complained he had been unfairly treated by the former warden, but that if he was released from solitary he would make every effort to reform. Aull believed him and cautiously had him returned to normal activity. When his strength had been restored, Aull put him to work at his trade as a mason. He worked steadily on a dam at the prison, never losing a day's work. Though he often had the opportunity, he never again attempted to escape. He worked on the dam for nearly a year when in May of 1889 a derrick fell and killed him. "The death of Schmidt," commented the San Francisco *Bulletin,* "will be a severe disappointment to those penologists who, ever since his release from the Folsom dungeon, have hoped to see in his case the establishment of the rule of kindness over the rule of cruelty."

Folsom state prison as it appeared when Aull served as warden.
Courtesy California State Library.

Many noted criminals were under Aull's supervision at Folsom which had been established as a second state prison in 1880. When convict William Fredericks was paroled in late May of 1893, Aull was convinced he was involved in an escape plot and questioned him closely. Fredericks would say nothing, however, and upon his release secured several guns which he then hid in the prison quarry. On June 27th George Contant (Sontag) and several other prisoners seized a guard as hostage and obtained the hidden guns in the quarry. As the group of convicts moved toward a ravine which would shelter them, the hostage guard suddenly jumped down an embankment. The other guards now opened fire as Contant and several of his men tried desperately to protect themselves in a clump of rocks. Warden Aull took his place on the firing line and directed a withering fusilade into the convict's position. In a short time a hat appeared on a rifle barrel and Aull ordered a cease fire. Contant and another convict limped into view, covered with blood. The San Francisco *Chronicle* described the closing scenes of the tragedy:

     ...Seeing that the men were practically helpless...Warden Aull, Captain

Murphy and several guards walked towards the convicts. Contant pointed behind some rocks to indicate where his companions were.

The men advanced and on turning a corner beheld a sight so ghastly that it tried even their nerves of steel. There, lying, piled on one another, in a little hollow that was splashed with their lifeblood, lay the dead bodies of Dalton, Wilson and Williams...

Aull was widely praised for his handling of the daring escape attempt.

When his wife died in August of 1897, Captain Aull became despondent to the point that his health was impaired. He died at the prison on October 9, 1899, and was buried at Oakland, next to his beloved wife. "The breath of scandal never tainted his administration of the penitentiary," noted the San Francisco *Examiner*, "while the prison had become, under his management, famous throughout the country for the almost perfect manner in which it was kept and managed."

Aull was deeply affected by the death of his lovely wife in 1897 and was still in mourning at the time of his own death two years later. *Courtesy California State Library.*

PRINCIPAL SOURCES ───────────────────────

Dillon, Richard, *Wells Fargo Detective*, N.Y., Coward-McCann, 1969; Lamott, Kenneth, *Chronicles of San Quentin*, N.Y., David McKay Co. Inc., 1961; Rickards, Colin, "Bill Miner—50 Years a Hold-Up Man," *English Westerners Brand Book*, Jan., 1966; San Francisco *Bulletin*, July 5, 1889; San Francisco *Daily Morning Call*, Jan. 28, Feb. 18, 1882; Fresno Weekly *Expositor*, Feb. 22, 1881; *Pacific Coast Commercial Record*, Aug. 20, 1888; San Francisco *Examiner*, Oct. 12, 1899; The Modesto *Stanislaus News*, Nov. 6, 13, 1874; Wells Fargo Bank History Room, San Francisco.

RICHARD A. BARTER
(Rattlesnake Dick)

A native of Canada where he was born about 1833, Dick Barter was reportedly the son of an English army colonel living in the area of Quebec. Little is known of his early life, but young Dick was later described as a "roving, reckless sort of boy." When news of the California gold discoveries was received, his adventurous nature responded. In 1850 Dick, an older brother and another relative headed west for the land of gold.

The trio took up mining at Rattlesnake Bar, on the North Fork of the American River. Having little success, Dick's partners decided to return home, while he determined to stay and make a living as best he could. In 1853 Dick was accused of stealing some clothing from a store, but at his trial he was pronounced "not guilty" by the jury. Later it was reportedly proved he did not commit the crime. Dick had begun traveling in fast company, however, as noted in the Sacramento *Daily Union* of September 15, 1854:

> GRAND LARCENY—The young man named Richard Barter, who was arrested a few days since for stealing a mule from Rattlesnake Bar, was examined before the Recorder yesterday...The mule was the property of W.H. & R.H. Pratt of Placer City, Colusa County, and was stolen on Sunday night during a visit of the former at the Bar...Upon being interrogated Barter said he had purchased it about five weeks since at Auburn, for $80, and after his arrest admitted to Capt. Deal that it had been stolen, not by him, but by his partner...he would not reveal his partner's name and thereby implicate him. Barter is a fine looking youth and can scarcely have attained his majority.

On December 18th Dick was sentenced to one year in the state prison by the Sacramento Court of Sessions. He was received at San Quentin on December 20, 1854, and became No. 516. A newspaper described life at "Point San Quentin" at that time as being hard and monotonous:

> Get up at daylight, march to a stone quarry, tug and lift heavy stones, propel a heavy wheel-barrow over a rough road and up a plank, break the rock... stand by the hour together in a suffocating dust, carry heavy loads of brick and follow other amusements till the breakfast hour, hurry down your food, go to work again till dinner, work again till supper, get to bed in a small stone tomb called a cell, up again at daylight...

31

Dick was delighted to be released on December 18, 1855, and according to tradition headed for Shasta County where he was not known. When a former acquaintance identified him as an ex-convict, he is quoted as saying, "...my conviction hounded me at every turn until I could stand it no longer." He reportedly robbed a stagecoach in Shasta County before heading south for his old Placer County stamping grounds.

Dick was described at this time as being "nearly six feet in height, and weighed about 160 pounds, slight of build, but rather broad-shouldered...very muscular. He was very handsome...his hair was black...while his flashing black eye betrayed every passion that animated his mind."

Back on the American River, Barter reportedly formed a gang composed of George and Cyrus Skinner, Adolph Newton, a young Mexican named Nicanora Rodriguez, and William Carter. The Skinner brothers, alias Walker, Williams and Williamson, were ex-convicts and robbers. While in Shasta Dick had learned of a regular treasure train which carried gold between Yreka and Shasta. Tradition insists that Dick planned to rob this mule train near Trinity Center, change the gold packs to unbranded mules and take the loot south. George Skinner was to be in charge of the robbery, while Dick and Cyrus Skinner were to steal new mules and meet the gang as they fled south. Reportedly the treasure train carried some $17,000 in gold, while several packers with the group carried thousands of dollars more.

The robbery went off without a hitch on March 12, 1856. The outlaws waited in vain at the rendezvous point for Dick and Cyrus and the new mules, however, and finally had to bury the gold and skedaddle. Posses were trailing them closely by now and Bill Carter was picked up in Marysville. He needed little encouragement to inform on his comrades and with his aid much of the treasure was recovered. Dolph Newton was picked up near Folsom, while a Sacramento officer and two private citizens located George Skinner, using the name Walker, Rodriguez and another of the gang named Bill White, alias Gristy, at a cabin near Folsom on April 22. One of the posse, Robert Harrison, later recalled what happened when the lawmen burst into the cabin:

> ...He jerked the door open and Marshal Anderson and myself entered with our guns cocked; I said "Now we have got you, surrender!" ...before I had time to speak more, the deceased, Walker sprang at Marshal Anderson ...at the moment I discharged one or both the barrles of my gun at deceased; I thought the whole contents of the gun went into his heart...

White managed to escape, but young Rodriguez was also gunned down after firing several shots. Carter, Newton and Rodriguez were returned to Shasta and convicted of the robbery. Meanwhile Dick and Cy Skinner had been caught trying to steal the mules at Bear River and were languishing in the Auburn jail. Dick managed to escape before long and reportedly fled to San Francisco. Cy Skinner received a fourteen year sentence, but escaped in 1860 and was later lynched in Montana.

Dick escaped several times from the Auburn jail, shown at left. To the right is the courthouse where he made various appearances, also. *Author's collection.*

Jim Driscoll, a reported confederate of Barter, had a long prison record. *Courtesy Wells Fargo History Room.*

Dick, now using the alias "Richard Woods," soon found the bay city also too hot for him. A great vigilante uprising was in full swing and he quickly decided the foothills were a much healthier climate. The next notice of him was in the Nevada *Journal* of October 10, 1856:

> THIEF CAUGHT—A chap named Richard Woods was caught under suspicious circumstances at the Virginia House on Monday. His person was searched and two purses were found...A breastpin was taken from him which was recognized...A watch chain was also found...Woods was brought before Justice Van Hagen and committed to jail to await his trail.

Dick found himself in jail with a notorious thief and gunman named Jim Webster. It was just a matter of days before the two managed to dig their way to freedom and disappeared. Dick later circulated the rumor about himself that he had been killed when he fell into a mine shaft. Meanwhile he reportedly put together a gang to engage in something more than his recent petty crimes. A friend named George Taylor was recruited, along with Aleck Wright, Billy Dickson and Jim Driscoll. Just what crimes they committed is not clear, but the robbing of teamsters and travelers, stealing from sluice boxes and the pilfering

33

of homes and cabins were a steady source of plunder. Teamsters, carrying gold with which to purchase the supplies they hauled, were a particular target.

In early April of 1858 Dick and George Taylor robbed three men who promptly swore out warrants for their arrest. Constable John Boggs was given the warrants to serve and took along John Mitchell as a back-up. They already had word that Dick and Taylor were on the Folsom stage and they intercepted the coach near the Franklin House. Boggs told the two desperadoes to get down off the coach and as they did so they bantered him about showing his warrant. Boggs later testified that the two opened fire on him a moment before he fired and hit Taylor in the arm. The two then scampered off into the woods as Boggs headed back for reinforcements.

Constable Boggs now charged Dick with attempted murder and began looking for him in earnest. Meanwhile Dick and his men were blamed for the holdup of the Telegraph stage running between Nevada City and Auburn on May 3, 1858. The Placer *Herald* of the 8th gave some of the details:

> Daring Stage Robbery. Yesterday morning, between one and two o'clock ...the...stage, which connects by railroad with this city, was stopped by six men armed with guns and pistols, and a box of treasure belonging to Wells, Fargo & Co., containing $21,000 stolen. The contents were two bars, one numbered 1683, valued at $7,607.28 and the other numbered 1685 valued at $7,217.01, and dust and coin making up the balance...

Dick had little time to enjoy his loot, however. Deputy Sheriff Van Hagen of Nevada County, with a small posse, located the fugitive at a place called Greenhorn Crossing in mid-May of 1858. "I went up with him and a couple of others," recalled pioneer Thomas Marker in 1906, and "Dick was there. He made his way up the hill, but dropped his gun while going over a log. I headed him off and we brought him to town..."

Lodged in the Auburn jail, Dick began casting about for a method of escape. Somehow he obtained a knife and working with another inmate named "Curly Bill" they succeeded in prying the locks off their cells late one night. They were working on the outer wall with a crowbar and making "promising headway" when they were discovered by the jailors. The Placer *Herald* of June 12, 1858 commented:

> ...Rattlesnake Dick took the disappointment good naturedly, but Curly cursed his luck "powerful." The sheriff has put extra weight on these restless gentry, that will prevent further operations of the kind on their part.

On August 24, 1858, Dick filed for a continuance with the court claiming that his counsel still had not located several witnesses. The outlaw maintained that he had not fired at Boggs that day on the stage and that "...A. W. Bee, G.B. Taylor, Mrs. Ghayer and others who were on the stage as passengers" were needed as material witnesses. Dick even had his attorney try to locate the passengers through the stage agent, but he had no luck. Actually, Taylor was already in San Quentin on an attempted murder rap in Nevada County and A.W. Bee was on a trip to the Atlantic states. Dick filed for another continuance on November 19th, but before he could come to trial he had once again managed to escape. Lawman Boggs hadn't realized how much Dick had hated him after this incident. When he came home early one morning the constable found a note scribbled on his gatepost; "Have been waiting for you nearly all night!"

Dick managed to elude capture well into the following year, but his luck was fast running out. A letter from his sister Harriet in late March of 1859 must have given him food for thought. "Years have passed away since your last letter," she pleaded, "...I have grieved, but never despaired, for I have prayed the Father that he would restore you to the path of rectitude..." But Dick had no intention of changing his ways or going back to San Quentin.

Late on the afternoon of July 11, 1859, Dick and a companion were seen some four miles below Auburn on the stage road. A posse composed of Deputy Sheriff Bill Crutcher, Deputy Tax Collector George Martin and Undersheriff George Johnston quickly assembled and rode to intercept the outlaws. The Nevada *Democrat* reported:

> ...The robbers fought desperately, Mr. Martin, of the sheriff's party, was shot dead, the ball passing entirely through his body. Officers Johnston and Crutcher were both shot in the hand, the former quite severely, the ball passing though the knuckle-joint of the forefinger. The robbers both made their escape, but the officers were certain that Dick carried away a shot from each of their pistols.

Auburn as it appeared in 1857. *Courtesy California State Library.*

Although officers searched most of the night, it was not until the following morning that Dick's body was found near the Junction House stage station. He had two wounds in the body and one in the head. In his right hand was a scrap of paper on which the outlaw had scrawled "Rattlesnake Dick dies, but never surrenders, as all true Britons do." On the reverse was written, "If J. Boggs is dead, I am satisfied." Apparently Dick had mistaken Martin for the man against whom he still held a grudge for the stagecoach incident.

Whether Dick had committed suicide rather than be captured, or asked his companion to finish him off is not known. Just who Dick's partner was that fatal night was another subject for conjecture. George Taylor was already in San Quentin and Jim Driscoll was also in jail on a stage robbery rap. Aleck Wright was a likely candidate, but he did not turn up until September of 1860 when he shot a man over some horses. He was sent to San Quentin for ten years and, when he was released in May of 1869, the Placer County sheriff was waiting to take him back and try him for the murder of Dick Barter. There was little evidence, however, and Wright was turned loose to promptly disappear.

Dick was buried in the fine clothes he was wearing at the time of his death. His first grave marker in the Auburn cemetery has long since disappeared. In 1893 the gravesite was moved and today it is marked by a beautiful, polished black marble monument erected some thirty years ago by a local history group. A portion of the inscription reads:

> No further seek his merits to disclose
> Nor draw his frailties from their dread abode.
> There they alike in trembling hope repose,
> The bosom of his father and his God.

PRINCIPAL SOURCES ——————————————————————————

Angel, Myron (editor), *History of Placer County, California,* Oakland, Thompson and West, 1882; Boggs, Mae Helene, *My Playhouse was a Concord Coach,* Oakland, Howell-North, 1942; Harlow, Alvin F., *Old Waybills,* N.Y., London, D. Appleton-Century Co., 1934; Jackson, Joseph Henry, *Bad Company*, New York, Harcourt, Brace and Co., 1949; Calif. State Senate, 1856 sess., (Doc. No. 9) *Report of the Directors of the State Prison & Accompanying Documents* (Sacramento) James Allen, State Printer (1856); Placer County court records, copies in collection of John Boessenecker; San Francisco *Bulletin,* Mar. 25, Oct. 13, 1856; Nevada *Democrat,* July 13, 20, 1859; Placer *Herald,* May 8, June 12, Nov. 6, 1858, July 16, Aug. 13, Sept. 10, 1859; Auburn *Journal,* Jan 5, 1967; Wells Fargo Bank History Room, San Francisco; Prison records in California State Archives, Sacramento.

TOM BELL
(Thomas J. Hodges)

Tom Bell's given name was Thomas J. Hodges and he was apparently born in or near Rome, Tennessee, about 1830. During the Mexican War he joined a volunteer regiment from his state and served as a medical attache. According to his own statement he came to California in 1849 and began mining in Mariposa County.

Although Hodges located a rich claim, he gambled away his money as fast as he made it and soon found himself with neither a claim nor funds. An old Texan named Wiley talked him into stealing some mules and several such ventures proved quite successful. "Doctor" Hodges claimed that he originally stole only from foreign miners, but in any case he was soon picked up and tried for grand larceny in the fall of 1851. He was sentenced to five years in the state prison where his record lists him as being convict No. 24. He was received on October 8, 1851, but just where he was confined is not clear. It was probably in a temporary prison fitted up in one of the old abandoned ships in San Francisco Bay since a state institution had yet to be built.

While plans were being made for a new prison at some undecided point, Sheriff Jack Hays of San Francisco was given the contract to care for all state prisoners in late 1851. He fitted up the old bark *Wabau* and had it towed out to Angel Island in the bay where the forty-odd convicts, Tom Hodges among them, were put to work in some rock quarries. In early July of the following year, twenty acres of land were purchased by the state at Point San Quentin, in Marin County just across the bay from San Francisco. Hodges and his convict companions were put to work preparing the site for building. At the end of the year the prisoners were still living in the *Wabau,* but their number had increased three-fold. The first cell block was completed in January of 1854, but the forty-eight cells were woefully inadequate for the two hundred and fifty inmates.

In prison Hodges made the acquaintance of George and Cyrus Skinner, two convicts also known as the Williamson brothers. Ned Connor was another crony, along with Jim Smith, a young Prussian, and Bill White, alias Gristy. White later claimed that a prison official made a deal with him to take five or six other convicts and escape because the management was losing money on the prison contract. Accordingly, when White led prisoners Hodges, Asa Carico, Cherokee Bob, Stewart, Ned Connor and Jim Smith on a wood-chopping detail on May 12, 1855, they all broke and ran at the appointed signal. With a guard firing *blank* cartridges at them, the convicts disappeared into the Marin countryside.

Using the name Tom Bell, Hodges formed a gang composed of White, Connor and Jim Smith. They performed a few robberies and in time acquired other members named Juan Fernandez, English Bob Carr and Monte Jack Lyon. Like all such criminal organizations, members came and went. The Skinner brothers, Jack Phillips, Nat Green and many others belonged to the gang at various times. One early-day lawman later wrote that Bell's group consisted of some thirty members operating in different areas. Jack Phillips, owner of the Mountaineer House near Auburn, was a lookout for the gang and appraised them of likely victims staying at his hotel. The gang was unwieldly enough to make the use of a countersign practical and members carried a bullet with holes drilled through it and marked, as a sign of recognition.

Once in operation the gang was blamed for nearly every crime committed in the northern mines and it is difficult to pinpoint their actual robberies. When George Skinner, now using the name of Walker, helped engineer the robbery of a gold-laden pack train in the Trinity Mountains, in March of 1856, he and several gang members were located in a cabin near Folsom. In a shoot-out with officers, Skinner was killed and Bill White was identified as having escaped after firing several shots.

Later that spring the gang went into operation with a vengeance. They held up travelers of every description, but teamsters were a favorite target since they

James P. "Jim" Smith escaped from San Quentin with Bell and others in May of 1855. He participated in the Camptonville stage attack, but was back in prison late the following year. He was an outlaw most of his life and died in the Napa State Asylum in 1886. *Courtesy John Boessenecker.*

Freighters, who often carried large sums of gold with which to purchase the goods they hauled, were frequently the targets of road agents such as Tom Bell. *Courtesy California State Library.*

often carried valuable goods or the gold to purchase supplies for a contractor. When Jack Phillips pointed out a peddler named Rosenthal who had money and was staying at his place, Bell, White and several others followed him. Rosenthal was later discovered in the woods, half-eaten by wild animals. Bill White later recalled what happened:

> ...We took him about one hundred yards from the road and found on his person twelve hundred and fifty dollars. We then took his sash and tied him to the tree...The day he was robbed we all noticed that Tom Bell remained behind a few minutes. We came to the conclusion that he had killed the man...

Near Oroville, Bell and White chased a lone horseman who had refused to give up his gold. White finally got him to stop after shooting him in the leg. The San Francisco *Bulletin,* quoting White, reported:

> By this time Tom Bell came up; after taking all the money he had, Tom took his pocket handkerchief and tied up the wound...By this time a teamster drove up; we stopped him and found he had about two hundred dollars... After robbing the teamster, we put the wounded man in the wagon with instructions that he should be well treated...

Returning to the Mountaineer House on July 25, 1856, Bell and White stopped peddler David Lash on the road, taking $40 in cash and several hundred dollars worth of goods. About one o'clock in the morning Bell and several of his men pounded on the door of the Grizzly Store near Nevada City. When W.W. Argrave opened the door he was knocked down with the butt of a pistol and the place plundered. By this time the gang was also being aided by a Mrs. Elisabeth Hood who ran the Western Exchange Hotel on the Sacramento-Nevada City road. Times were good for Tom Bell.

Flushed with success, Bell now plotted to stop and rob one of the gold-heavy stagecoaches operating between the mining towns and the supply centers. The coach running between Camptonville and Marysville was selected and an accomplice named Smith Sutton was sent to Camptonville to alert the gang to the next big gold shipment. On August 12, 1856, Bell and six of his men were mounted and waiting along the road. As the stage approached, the bandit leader commanded the driver to deliver up the treasure. The guard opened fire instead. There was a general exchange of gunfire, before the bandits retreated. "I fired the rifle one time, and my pistol...three times," White later recalled. "The party, with the exception of Bell and myself, ran after the first fire; Bell acted very cool throughout..." The Marysville *Daily Herald* carried a full account of the incident in its issue of August 13:

> ...As many as forty shots were fired on both sides. The robbers finding themselves so stoutly opposed, retreated, leaving the passengers masters of the field and treasure.
>
> The driver, Mr. John Gear, was shot through the right arm, above the elbow. Mrs. Tilghman, wife of a barber in this city, was shot in the head, the ball entering over the right eye and penetrating the brain.
>
> Mr. John Campbell, another of the passengers, received a glance shot over the eye. Another passenger was shot in both legs... The stage is riddled with bullet holes...

The whole state was outraged at this latest foray and lawmen fanned out into the countryside, pressing the bandits hard. On the 14th a posse came upon three of the outlaws' worn out horses, one of which had a bloody bridle. Later it was discovered Monte Jack had been shot in the hand. A rancher named Ramirez was shot when he resisted some possemen who were searching for Jack. The Folsom *Granite Journal* gave one of the best descriptions of Bell in early September:

> Tom Bell is in stature nearly six feet, well proportioned, combining in his frame strength with action; of a sanguine temperment—quick in his motions, he is described as never at rest—sandy hair, and a full crop of it—light goatee to match his hair in color. His nose which was originally well formed and large has been mashed in the bridge so as to be almost level with his face...His eyes are a very light blue...nearly to a gray...

Bill White would later recall that "...the country was too hot for us (and) we concluded to go south..." Picking up Mrs. Hood and her two young daughters, Bell and some seven of his men headed south and located a stock ranch on the San Joaquin River, a few miles from Firebaugh's Ferry. Two brothers named Farnsworth were left to look after the ranch, while Bell and some of his men went off in search of cattle with which to stock it. Bill White and Juan

Fernandez headed north again and took to the road on September 9th. After robbing several teamsters, they stole two horses at a road house and were arrested at Knight's Ferry on the 16th. During his questioning of Juan Fernandez, Calaveras County Deputy Sheriff Bob Paul was given the bullet countersign and told how it was used. It was the first big break for the lawmen and Paul went right to work. Elsewhere, Placer County deputy Ben Moore had been trying to get a black badman named Charley Hamilton to tell of his association with Bell. Hamilton would not talk, but he finally agreed to work with the lawmen if they would pay his expenses and release him. It was a long shot, but it paid off. On the night of September 30th Hamilton telegraphed the Placer County sheriff that Bell and two others had just crossed the Folsom bridge. A posse of five lawmen rode to meet them as described in the Placer *Herald* of October 4, 1856:

> About half past twelve the sheriff's party were galloping along the road...a little below the Franklin House...Deputy Boggs...was in advance and had already passed them when the guide remarked that "that was a party."
> ...The robbers were now between the sheriff's men, they dismounted and at once commenced shooting and retreating...In the confusion some fifteen or twenty shots were exchanged, the effect of which was to wound one of the horses of the officers, and to kill Ned Conway, one of the robbers...

Bell and Perris Owen, alias "Texas", made their getaway. Meanwhile, Bill White, to save his own hide, had made a full confession and been returned to San

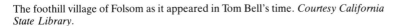

The foothill village of Folsom as it appeared in Tom Bell's time. *Courtesy California State Library.*

Quentin. Juan Fernandez agreed to guide a citizen's posse headed by George G. Belt, a former Stockton alcalde, to Bell's San Joaquin River ranch. They arrived on September 29th, but the sheriff's posse had beaten them to it. While the officers continued to scour the countryside, Belt and his men remained in the area of Bell's camp in the hope that at least some of the outlaws might show up. On October 4th a rider was discovered talking to a vaquero along the river. When Belt and his men surrounded him with cocked weapons, Bell admitted his identity. Although a message was sent to the sheriff, Belt and his men had no intention of waiting for his arrival. The Stockton *Argus* chronicled Bell's last few hours on earth:

> He was generally calm during the five hours of his confinement, conversing freely and often with a smile on his countenance. Just before leaving for the gallows he prayed fervently. Bell was a man of easy, pleasant manners and had been educated with a view of becoming a physician. At the outset he stated distinctly that he had no revelations to make as far as concerned others.

Just before he was hanged the doomed outlaw was allowed to write several letters, but was told to make it fast. One was to Mrs. Hood and the other to his mother in Rome, Tennessee:

> Dear Mother: As I am about to make my exit to another country, I take this opportunity to write you a few lines. Probably you will never hear from me again. If not, I hope we may meet again where parting is no more. In my prodigal career in this country I have always recollected your fond admonitions, and if I had lived up to them probably I would not have been in my present condition; but, dear mother, although my fate has been a cruel one, yet I have no one to blame but myself. Give my respects to all my old and youthful friends. Tell them to beware of bad associations...
>
> Your only boy, Tom

Just what happened to the body is not known, but Judge Belt probably left it hanging or had it buried in an unmarked grave.

PRINCIPAL SOURCES ─────────────────────────────────

Boggs, May Helene Bacon *My Playhouse was a Concord Coach,* Oakland, Howell-North, 1942; Jackson, Joseph Henry, *Bad Company,* N.Y., Harcourt, Brace and Co. 1949; Lamott, Kenneth, *Chronicles of San Quentin,* N.Y., David McKay Co. Inc., 1961; Calif. State Assembly, 1855 Sess. (Document No. 26) *Report of Committee Relative to the Condition and Management of the State Prison* (Sacramento) B.B. Redding, State Printer, (1855); San Francisco *Daily Alta California,* May 14, 1855, Sept. 19, Oct. 3, 12, 1856; San Francisco *Bulletin,* Sept. 24, Oct. 6, 13, 1856; Nevada *Democrat,* Oct. 15, 1856; Marysville *Herald,* Aug. 12, 13, Oct. 9, 25, 1856; Placer *Herald,* Oct. 4, 1856, Feb. 28, 1857; Wells Fargo Bank History Room, San Francisco; Prison records in California State Archives, Sacramento.

THE BLACK KID

The San Francisco *Chronicle* published this sketch of a photo found in the robber's effects. It was thought at the time to be a photo of the Black Kid. *Author's collection.*

One evening in mid-May of 1900 a stagecoach was held up and robbed as it rattled along the Big Oak Flat Road towards Yosemite Valley. The passengers were plundered by a lone highwayman who ordered the coach to move on just as another stage approached on its way out of the hills. The second coach was also stopped and the occupants robbed, both holdups netting the bandit something less than $250. The double robbery caused quite a stir—not even Tom Bell or Black Bart had contemplated stopping two coaches at once in their palmiest days. Of course Tom and Bart had to contend with armed guards and at this late date the stage company forbade its employees to carry guns.

Just two weeks later a private stage out of Raymond was taking a party up to a grove of the big redwood trees on the Yosemite road. It was June 2, 1900, already a hot and dusty morning as the coach pulled through a sandy stretch of road two miles west of Grub Gulch. Again, a masked man holding a shotgun stepped out from behind a tree and stopped the coach. As the driver pulled off the road he noticed the bandit had blackened his face and hands and appeared to be disguising his voice. The passengers were lined up along the road and told to put their valuables in a passed hat. They were then told to return to the coach, the driver—as was the custom—not being robbed.

When the driver asked to sit beneath a tree, the robber let him do so. As he passed by the bandit gave him a card on which was lettered, *The Black Kid.* "Here's my card," said the masked man," in case we ever meet again." A.H. Foster, the driver recounted the meeting to a Fresno *Republican* reporter:

> While the desciple [*sic*] of Black Bart was waiting for the other stages to come up he passed the time bantering the men he had just relieved of their money. It was then that he handed Foster the card. The latter was quite close to him and he noticed that under his mask his face had been blackened with

43

A stagecoach in Yosemite Valley about 1906. *Author's collection.*

burnt cork or charcoal. He could not see the color of his eyes. The robber avoided the scrutinizing glance of the driver and later when he saw him casting furtive glances at him warned him not to do so again...

Mr. Foster describes him as weighing 140 or 150 pounds and being about 5 feet 10 inches in height.

A short time later a wood team and a freight wagon approached and were stopped by the highwayman. These two drivers were told to park their wagons next to the coach while they too were robbed. Two soldiers, advance members of an approaching cavalry troop on maneuvers, were cantering along the road and were also stopped. After being disarmed the soldiers were told to stand over by the other victims. The next vehicle to arrive was a coach full of Yosemite tourists going into the valley. This stage also was pulled over and the passengers lined up and robbed. The bandit took only cash—no watches or jewelry. The passengers noted later that he was quite calm and polite during the whole proceedings.

A fifth vehicle now wheeled into view and was also directed to pull over. The passengers were some fifteen Chinese and the robber had an animated time trying to explain that they were being robbed. Finally, the last holdup accomplished, the bandit told everyone to get back in their respective vehicles and proceed in the same order in which they had arrrived. Strangely enough, about the same amount of money was obtained as had been taken in the previous month's robbery. The Wells, Fargo box was not opened.

The two soldiers were told to get in one of the coaches and two passengers were ordered to mount the army horses. The two animals promptly ran away with their new and unfamiliar riders. The main military group, a unit of the 6th U.S. Cavalry, was a mere three hundred yards down the road by this time and several members quickly secured the two runaway horses. When advised of what had happened, the troopers were ordered to the attack, but the bandit quickly made his getaway into the heavy, surrounding brush. It was just as well. The troopers had no ammunition for their weapons due to their habit of continually shooting at anything that moved along their line of march. An article in the Fresno *Republican* on June 4th gave details of the resulting search for the highwayman:

> THE NERVY LONE BANDIT—Madera Sheriff Thurman and posse are hard upon the track of the fleeing robber, who broke the record for stage holdups. There is not the slightest doubt that the "Black Kid" as he calls himself, will be captured before the week is out unless he shuns the roads and is content to wait in some of the innumerable mountain fastnesses which are within half a days travel from the scene...

Two Madera County lawmen of the period when the Black Kid prowled the old Yosemite Road. *From Pidgeon Collection, courtesy Special Collections, Library, California State University, Fresno.*

Despite the optimism of the press and the hard riding of the sheriff's posse, the bandit was not apprehended. The army version of the affair was written up some days later by Dr. A.J. Pedlar, a Fresno physician on duty with the unit:

> . . . Of course you have had your laugh over the robber incident. So have we. Nothing of the kind ever before furnished so much that was truly ridiculous.
>
> . . . Two passengers excitedly galloping down the grade brought word of the robbery to the cavalry . . . The major, his son, and I pushed forward and at 75 yards sighted a freight wagon stopped in the road . . . I had no weapon of any kind. As I faced to the right, I came face to face with the 'Black Kid.' He was 60 yards off coming my way through dense brush . . . He covered me instanter, and his appearance as well as his promptness I shall never forget. Bareheaded, his face blackened, a narrow uncolored ring around his eyes, his cloth mask gone, he would have made a good Kodak picture . . .

On August 15, 1905, a stagecoach was heading into Yosemite carrying one of the many groups of sight-seers visiting the valley that season. Anton Vieth was

Found in the collection of an early Fresno County sheriff, this photograph is thought to show an actual stagecoach holdup in progress around the turn of the century. *From the collection of early Fresno County Sheriff J.D. Collins, in June English Collection, courtesy Special Collections, Library, California State University, Fresno.*

editor of the Milwaukee, Wisconsin, *Herald* and Austrian consul at that city. He was on a western tour taking scenic and agricultural photographs for his publication. Six women and three other men were also in the coach when it was stopped just the other side of Grub Gulch. The lone bandit got little cash, but he did allow Veith to photograph the robbery. A $700 reward was offered for the robber, but again he avoided capture.

On July 7, 1906 five coaches were held up on the same road between Ahwahnee and Wawona. A private wagon was stopped also and some forty people robbed. This bandit also escaped and was never caught. The *Republican* noted:

> From the place of the holdup and the coolness displayed by the knight of the road, the officers believe that it was committed by the same man that held up a Yosemite stage last August, and that this nick of the woods contains a Black Bart not less daring than the original. At that time the robber permitted himself to be photographed by one of the passengers as he was actually engaged in the holdup...

No one was ever caught and convicted of these robberies and it was never known whether all were the work of the "Black Kid" or if others were involved.

PRINCIPAL SOURCES ————————————————————

Secrest, William B., *The Great Yosemite Holdups,* Fresno, Saga West Publishing Co., 1968; Fresno Morning *Republican,* May 19, June 3, 5, 9, 12, 1900, Aug. 16, 17, 18, 20, 1905, July 8, 1906; Fresno *Bee, Aug. 29, 1954; Yosemite Tourist,* July 19, 1906; Yosemite Natural History Association and Museum.

CHARLES E. BOLES
(Black Bart)

A mug shot of Black Bart from the San Francisco police Rogues Gallery portrait made at the time of his capture. *Courtesy San Francisco Police Credit Union.*

California's greatest stage robber was born about 1828. His place of birth, according to a family friend, was England, but he was brought to this country by his parents in 1830. The Boles (sometimes spelled Bowles) family settled in Jefferson County, New York, where the father farmed some 100 acres near the town of Plessis. Charles was the next to youngest of ten children—three daughters and seven sons. A neighbor later recalled:

> Charley, as we usually called him, received a common school education and when grown up became better known than any other young man in this section on account of excelling in athletic sports, and was probably for his weight the best collar and elbow wrestler in Jefferson County. He was a young man of excellent habits and greatly esteemed by all who knew him . . .

Young Charley and his brother David joined the gold rush to California in 1850 and mined on Union Bar for a time. The boys returned home in early 1852, but again went to California where David died in July of 1852. Another brother, Robert, died in the mines a short time later. Charley mined for a time, but is thought to have returned home again before drifting to the mid-west about 1854. He married and settled down in Decatur, Illinois, but in 1862 joined a Union infantry regiment and served during the Civil War. He saw much action and was wounded several times. Discharged near Washington, D.C. in early June of 1865, Charles returned home to Decatur.

Perhaps acquiring a wanderlust during the war, Charley Boles soon left his family and sought his fortune in the mines of Idaho and Montana. He wrote home several times during the next few years, but never returned to his family. His last such letter was written in 1871 when he was leaving Montana for Salt Lake City. Before long he was back in California where he reportedly taught school and engaged in other types of work. From this point on nothing is known of his movements until he surfaced again some years later.

On July 26, 1875, John H. Shine was driving one of the John Olive and

48

Company stages travelling daily between Sonora and Milton, California. Heading up a grade after crossing the Stanislaus River, Shine was startled when a masked man jumped out in front of his horses and shouted—"Please throw down the box!" As he reined up Shine noticed the bandit leveling a shotgun. He was wearing a linen duster with a flour sack as a mask. "If he dares to shoot," called out the highwayman, "give him a volley, boys!" In the brush alongside the road Shine now noted a half dozen rifle barrels aimed at his coach. After emptying the box, the bandit commanded Shine to drive on which he did. Returning to the scene a few minutes later, Shine saw that the six rifle barrels were in reality only blackened sticks of wood.

The reward poster circulated after Black Bart's first holdup in 1875. *Author's collection.*

REWARD

WELLS, FARGO & CO.'S EXPRESS BOX
on SONORA AND MILTON STAGE ROUTE, was ROBBED
this morning, near Reynolds' Ferry, by one man, masked and
armed with sixteen shooter and double-barreled shot gun. We
will pay

$250

for ARREST and CONVICTION of the Robber.

JNO. J. VALENTINE, Gen. Supt.

San Francisco, July 26, 1875.

The same bandit held up the Marysville stage in December, then on June 2, 1876, stopped the coach running between Roseburg and Eureka. On August 3 of the following year he robbed the Point Arenas coach and left behind one of the most famous bits of doggerel in Western frontier history. It read:

> I've labored long and hard for bred
> For honor and for riches,
> But on my corns too long you've tred
> You fine haired Sons of Bitches.
>   Black Bart, the Po8

As the robberies continued, Wells, Fargo's Special Officer James B. Hume was able to gradually assemble bits of information, but there were few clues as to the robber's identification. Whoever he was, he apparently walked everywhere he operated, carrying a bedroll and tools for opening the treasure boxes. He took meals at farmhouses and local inns as he familiarized himself with the country.

Black Bart had successfuly robbed 21 stages by the time he hid alongside the road on July 13, 1882, waiting for the Oroville and Laporte coach to come into view. When the stage finally made its appearance, Bart once again politely asked for the box, but was startled at the response he received. Wells, Fargo guard George Hackett recalled:

> ...He ran out in front of the team with a shotgun in his hands. As soon as I saw him I shot, hitting him on the head. He then pointed his gun at the driver, but before he could shoot I fired at his gun, knocking it out of range. He then turned and ran away and fell down, losing his hat and mask. Before I could reload he was out of reach...

Clutching his head, Bart ran for his life and again vanished into the surrounding hills. Hume and Hackett picked up what clues they could and added them to the bandit's dossier. A Wells Fargo circular of the time detailed what information Hume had assembled on the troublesome outlaw:

> He is always armed with a double barreled shotgun which he unbreeches and rolls in his blankets as soon as he is safe from immediate pursuit. Always brings an old ax to the scene of the robbery which he uses to open the box...In opening the mail sacks he cuts them with a sharp knife, thus T on top of the sack, near the lock. He has never manifested any viciousness and there is reason to believe he is averse to taking human life. He is polite to all passengers and especially so to ladies. He comes and goes to the scene of robberies on foot...a good walker as he sometimes covers long distances in a day—getting food from houses in out-of-the-way places...never allows himself to be seen in the vicinity of a robbery...the only baggage visible when traveling is a roll of blankets...

The now famous lone highwayman held up four more coaches before striking another sour note. On November 3, 1883, he stopped the Sonora to Milton coach again and sent the driver, Reason McConnell, off some distance while he broke open the box. A boy out hunting came up and both he and McConnell took several shots at Bart as he worked at opening the box. Again, the bandit scampered off into the brush and disappeared. This time, however, he left a number of valuable clues that were soon being examined by Sheriff Ben Thorn and Wells, Fargo detectives. The most promising lead seemed to be a simple handkerchief.

Private detective Harry Morse, who had been employed by Hume for some six months, promptly began checking out the handkerchief's San Francisco laundrymark-F.X.O.7. After calling on many of the city's 90 odd laundries, Morse finally struck paydirt. A mining man named Charles E. Bolton owned the handkerchief and his alibis were quickly proven to be false by Morse and Detective Hume. Charles E. Boles proved to be the suspect's correct name. Under the heading "Black Bart, the Noted Stage Robber Captured at Last," the San Francisco *Alta* chronicled the exciting news in its issue of November 14, 1883:

50

Reason McConnell [inset] was one of the more noted stage drivers and guards and was driving the last coach Bart tried to rob. That stagecoach was this mud wagon, now restored and in a private collection. *McConnell sketch from San Francisco* Call, *Feb. 19, 1899. Stagecoach photo courtesy of Meade Simpson.*

Black Bart, the famous highwayman...was captured in this city at 7 o'clock last Monday evening, by James B. Hume, the special detective of Wells, Fargo & Co., who was assisted by Captain A.W. Stone of the regular police and Harry Morse. In the incarceration of this audacious highwayman, the express company and the Postal Department of the United States have rid themselves of one who has been a terror to stage drivers and passengers and a most expensive hamper to the safe delivery of valuables and treasure...

Captain Hume claimed that the company has lost by his depredations but $2,000, in addition to the $4,700 he took on the 3rd. If this be the case, then many a stage passenger can tell a wonderful tale of the loss of a well-filled purse and a heavy belt, for Mr. Bolton while in this city lived in luxury and never was known to perform a days work.

In not quite two weeks from the time of his last robbery, Bart found himself in jail. Good witnesses and strong evidence convinced him that he had better plead guilty and make the best deal he could. After a hearing on November 16 at San Andreas, in Calaveras County, Bart was sentenced to six years in San Quentin. "He seemed rather pleased with the sentence," commented the Calaveras *Weekly Citizen*. He was admitted to the state prison on November 21, 1883 as prisoner No. 11,046.

Left, the Calaveras County courtroom in San Andreas where Black Bart had the hearing after his final holdup and capture. Bart, at right, looked every inch the prosperous mining man he claimed to be in this photo taken after his capture. *Calaveras County courtroom from author's collection. Bart photo courtesy Wells, Fargo History Room, San Francisco.*

A model prisoner for his entire term, Bart was released in January of 1888, then promptly dropped from sight. He was suspected of later stage robberies and was reportedly seen in California on various occasions. He was reported in other parts of the country also, but the truth is he never surfaced publicly again. By 1892 Bart's wife, who then lived in Hannibal, Missouri, was listing herself as the "widow of Charles E. Boles" in the local directories. An unconfirmed report noted Bart's death in New York in 1917, but he may have died in California.

Black Bart's long string of successful robberies made him a romantic figure, but Detective Hume was more pragmatic in his opinion of the famed highwayman. "If anyone thinks that a man who lets his wife struggle along in poverty for years while he lives comfortably off our express boxes, . . . is acting as a husband should toward his wife, why, we differ in opinion, that's all."

PRINCIPLE SOURCES ————————————————————————

Dillon, Richard, *Wells Fargo Detective,* N.Y., Coward-McCann, 1969; Harlow, Alvin F., *Old Waybills,* N.Y., D. Appleton-Century Co., 1934; Hume, James B. and Thacker, John, *Report of Jas, B. Hume and Jno. N. Thacker, Special Officers, Wells Fargo & Co's Express, Covering a period of Fourteen Years, Giving Losses by Train Robbers, Stage Robbers and Burglaries, and a Full Description and Record of all Noted Criminals Convicted of Offenses Against Wells, Fargo & Company Since November 5th, 1870,* San Francisco, H.S. Crocker and Co., 1885; Jackson, Joseph Henry, *Bad Company,* N.Y., Harcourt, Brace and Co., 1949; San Francisco Daily *Alta California,* Nov. 14, 1883; San Francisco *Chronicle,* Jan. 6, 1884; San Francisco *Examiner,* Aug. 6, 1889, Jan. 25, 1899; Wells Fargo Bank History Room, San Francisco; Prison records in California State Archives, Sacramento.

JACK BRADY
(Henry Williams)

Henry Williams' (alias Jack Brady) mug shot was taken at the time of his admittance to Folsom prison in late 1895. *Courtesy California State Archives.*

Reportedly born in Illinois about 1871, nothing is known of Henry Williams' early life, but he probably came to California sometime in the late 1880s. He worked at various odd jobs and in early 1891 was hostling in a San Francisco stable. His employer recalled that Williams neither smoked nor drank, seldom swore and liked children. Tiring of his job, Williams left town and met a young man named Oscar Brown at a Stockton hotel in May of 1891. Brown, who sometimes used the name Browning, was from Missouri and about the same age as his new friend. He had spent some time in the Indian Territory and was a tough character. The pair traveled to Amador County where they secured work at the ranch of a man named Little. They had only worked there a short while when they disappeared along with four horses belonging to their employer. Two of the animals had already been sold when Williams and Brown were picked up by officers in San Francisco. Promptly tried, the two were convicted of grand larceny and sentenced to a year apiece in the state prison at San Quentin. They began serving their terms on July 11, 1892.

The two horse thieves were apparently model prisoners. Williams, No. 15028, was described in the prison register as aged 21, a salesman, 5 feet, 7½ inches tall, florid complexion, hazel eyes, dark hair, full forehead, large features, square chin and with good teeth. Both men were discharged on May 11, 1893, and lost no time in heading back to the foothills. They found employment at a small town near Fresno where they worked in a mill for several months. Tiring of this they moved on, laboring at a number of jobs. While employed on the Jack Berry ranch the two would spend their free time in either Sacramento or Marysville. Apparently they resumed their life of crime with the holdup of a Sacramento saloon on August 25, 1894. A few nights later they robbed the occupants of a

Oscar Brown, alias Browning, was a lady-killer as well as a thug and robber. *Courtesy John Boessenecker.*

brewery and saloon. They did not get a lot of money, but with some experience under their belts they were planning bigger things. After some celebrating in San Francisco, they held up Haggerty's saloon at the Cliff House, shooting and wounding the proprietor.

The boys were now ready for big game. On October 11, 1894, Williams and Brown stopped an express train just west of Sacramento, at Davisville. The robbery went off without a hitch. Taking a safe from the express car, the bandits put it on the engine, uncoupled the other cars and chugged some miles down the track operating the engine themselves. After unloading four sacks of money from the safe, the bandits reversed the throttle and sent it back down the tracks while they disappeared into the countryside. The San Francisco *Chronicle* reported:

> . . . They ran the locomotive close up to the town of Washington, he said, took off their treasure, reversed the lever and then sent the engine on the back track. At that time they had no idea they had captured a fortune of $53,000. They imagined the great bulk of coin was silver.
> After taking out and dividing $1,600 they buried the remainder of the booty. Then they made their way to the river . . .

The following month the two outlaws turned up in San Francisco. Williams, who was now using the alias Jack Brady, took a room at 305 Grove Street, while Brown, calling himself Browning, rented a room on Van Ness. When they ran out of money they visited the spot where they had buried their stolen loot, but were never able to find it. Out of funds, they planned new robberies.

Just after midnight on March 3, 1895, Brady and Browning stopped the eastbound train No. 3 at Ben Ali, near Sacramento, but the robbery was unsuccessful. Frustrated, they held up Scheld's Brewery, robbing the bartender and several patrons, then driving off in a cart towards Stockton. On March 8th they again stopped train No. 3 near Lodi, but were unable to open the express safe and contented themselves with stealing the shotgun and pistol of the guard. On March 16th they reportedly held up the Ingleside House in San Francisco and killed the owner.

Living in San Francisco the two outlaws frequently went bicyling and adapted the vehicles to their robbing operations. In late March of 1895 Brady and Browning put on their bicycle riding costumes, tying overalls and linen dusters

A newspaper sketch made from a tintype showing Brady and Browning posing with their bicycles. The photo was found by the San Francisco police while searching the outlaw's rooms. *San Francisco* Chronicle *of April 2, 1895.*

behind the seats of their vehicles. They rode east out of town and just after midnight on March 30th boarded the Oregon Express at Wheatland, just south of Marysville. After forcing the engineer to stop the train, the robbers obtained a package from the express car, then proceeded to rob the passengers in a coach. The conductor, James E. Shortridge, later recalled what happened:

> They gave the fireman a bag made of the leg of a pair of overalls sewed up at the small end, and as they entered the door of the coach they sternly commanded the passengers to throw up their hands and to deposit in the sack...whatever valuables they had about them. The passengers readily complied with the order, but one of them, a man named Sampson, from Redding, made a show of refusing to give up his money. His rebellious spirit was tamed by one of the robbers beating him on the head with a large revolver, cutting a gash in Sampson's scalp about four inches long...
>
> The same order was given in the smoker and the passengers threw up their hands...While the robbers were finishing...Sheriff Bogard, who was in another car [appeared], just as the robbers were receiving a money contribution from their first victim, and at once opened fire on them. The first shot struck the taller robber...the sheriff fired again, and almost at the same instant the shorter robber fired, the bullet striking Bogard in the right side of the back...

Sheriff John J. Bogard, of Tehama County, was dead when he hit the floor, but Browning was mortally wounded also. As he lay on the floor he looked up at Brady and pleaded, "Don't leave me Bill, take me with you." Forgetting all about the sack of valuables, Brady fired several wild shots down the aisle, then panicked and fled into the night. Fireman Nethercott was badly wounded by one of these shots but later recovered. The sheriff was given a handsome casket by Wells, Fargo, then shipped home to Red Bluff. A massive manhunt was initiated for the fugitive bandit.

Brady made his way to northern California trying to avoid posses as herds of lawmen began assembling clues to the outlaw's identity. With some of California's greatest lawmen involved in the case, Brady had little chance of escape. Sheriff Tom Cunningham, of San Joaquin County, John Thacker, of Wells, Fargo, George Gard, chief of the Southern Pacific detective force, and San Francisco's Captain of Detectives Isaiah Lees, were all working on the case and the outlaws' identities were established by April 1st. The bicycles of the train robbers were found and traced back to San Francisco, enabling Captain Lees to locate the desperado's rooms. Questioning their landladies and a search of their belongings yielded further information and the officers soon had Brady's and Browning's prison records.

Brady meanwhile was trying to stay under cover. Once, Shasta officers wounded him with buckshot, but he managed to escape again. He kept to rugged mountain country, eating what food he could steal from farms. George Gard seems to have followed the bandit most closely and it was one of his men,

William Ahern, who cinched the capture. Ahern dogged Brady's trail and when a particular horse was stolen near Sacramento, he knew he was on the right track. Brady had formerly worked on the ranch and was the only one who could ride the animal. Alerting local officers, Ahern had all roads in the area carefully watched and when a suspicious character was spotted under a bridge, he was arrested by Deputy Sheriff Alexander McDonald and William Johnson. The man was promptly locked up in the Sacramento jail and at first denied being Brady. Photographs produced by the sheriff forced the fugitive to admit his identity, although he steadily denied being involved in the Bogard killing. "Bandit Brady Safe in Jail," headlined the San Francisco *Chronicle* on July 27, 1895:

> The tale of his wanderings that the bandit relates would fill a volume. Nights in the open air when the rain was pouring down, days in which there was nothing to eat but a scanty supply of green fruit, long intervals without water and constant watching for his pursuers form a chapter that accounts for the sallow complexion and the sunken cheeks of Brady.

Enough evidence had been produced by the officers to induce Brady to finally confess to the Davisville train robbery. He even took his captors to the spot where the loot was buried, but no trace of the money could be found. It was not until the following February that a tramp named Harmen was picked up and admitted to having found the money. He had spent some $11,000 in riotous living in San Francisco and told lawmen he regretted being caught before he could spend all the loot.

John Harms, alias "Carl the Bum," who discovered Brady and Browning's stolen loot and lived high on the hog. . . for a time. *Courtesy California State Library.*

57

Brady had his preliminary examination in Marysville on August 12th. Captain Lees came over from San Francisco to aid in the prosecution and to take him into custody on other charges should he be acquitted. It seemed for a time that the evidence was indeed too weak for a conviction, but he was pronounced guilty on November 18, 1895. On the 26th he was sentenced to life imprisonment at Folsom Prison where he was received the following day as prisoner No. 3647.

Brady's prison case file revealed that his real name was Henry Ury. Born in Croten, Illinois, Henry's mother died when he was still a boy and he was unhappy when his father remarried. He ran away to the midwest where he changed his name to Williams so he would be difficult to find. He mostly worked on farms, then headed west to California about 1889.

Brady's prison life seems to have been relatively trouble-free. When he came up for parole in late 1913 several newspapers campaigned against it. The prosecutor at his trial noted that he had missed the death penalty by only one vote and he should therefore serve his full sentence. Nevertheless, Brady's prison mug shot notes that he was paroled on April 4, 1914.

Nothing is known of the ex-convict's later life. He reportedly died on May 19, 1940, while still on parole. His final resting place is unknown, but Jack Brady will be remembered as a transitional outlaw, a man who introduced the bicycle to train robbery in the far west.

PRINCIPAL SOURCES ———————————————————

Dillon, Richard, *Wells Fargo Detective*, N.Y., Coward-McCann, Inc., 1969; Duke, Thomas S., *Celebrated Criminal Cases of America*, San Francisco, James H. Barry Co., 1910; Sweeny, J.D., "Thrilling Crime Chapter in Early Tehama History When Train Robbers Shot to Kill, Rode Away on Bicycles," Typescript in Tehama County Library, Red Bluff, Calif.; Boessenecker, John, "The Browning-Brady Gang," *Real West*, Oct. 1973; Edwards, Harold L., "Bullets and Bicycles," *Real West*, Mar. 1988; San Francisco *Daily Morning Call*, Feb. 13, 1896; San Francisco *Chronicle*, Mar. 30, 31, Apr. 1, 2, July 27, 30, 31, Aug. 13, Nov. 19, 26, 1895; San Francisco *Post*, August 19, 1895. Scrapbooks of James B. Hume, Wells Fargo History Room, San Francisco; Prison records in California State Archives, Sacramento.

DAVID BROWN

Born about 1825, Brown appears in the 1850 Los Angeles census as being a former resident of Texas, 25 years of age and with no occupation. On February 12, 1850, he had arrived at the Colorado River with John Glanton and his band of desperadoes and scalp hunters who had been chased out of Mexico for trying to pass off Mexican scalps as Apache. Brown was traveling in fast company. Glanton was an ex-Texas Ranger who had killed several men in personal encounters and probably dozens of Indians. Besides Brown, Glanton's gang was made up of John A. Johnson, Bill Prewitt, John Dorsey, John Jackson, Tom Harlin, Henderson Smith, John Gunn, Sam Chamberlain, Tom Watson, Jim Miller, Bill Carr, Marcus Webster and Joe Anderson.

Finding a lucrative ferry being operated on the river by Dr. A.L. Lincoln, Glanton horned in on the enterprise. He forced Lincoln to accept him and his men as partners in the ferry operation. The great gold rush was in full swing and business was brisk. Charging exorbitant rates the ferry operators made a great deal of money. They also made trouble by taking local Indian women as concubines and otherwise mistreating the natives. When the Indians established their own ferry downstream, Glanton killed one of their men and destroyed their boat. In April, taking Dave Brown and several others with him, Glanton traveled to San Diego where he deposited a large amount of cash and purchased supplies. The San Francisco *Alta* noted the trip on January 8, 1851:

> ...While in San Diego, one of Glanton's men, Brown by name, killed a soldier. Brown was arrested by the military, but connived with a sentry to escape. Glanton furnished $500 which Brown paid to the sentry who deserted at the time Brown broke jail. Then the desperado robbed the deserter and fled north...

Brown was living in Los Angeles in early May of 1850 when three of Glanton's men arrived in town. In a deposition made before the Alcalde, they told how Glanton and most of his men had been killed by the Yuma Indians and how they had barely been able to make a getaway. Glanton had just returned from his San Diego trip when the Indians caught them sleeping off a drunk and massacred all but the three who had escaped. Not knowing the true character of Glanton and his thugs, southern Californians immediately organized an expedition to punish the Indians. Dave Brown volunteered as scout and guide of a force of some sixty men under state militia quartermaster, General J.C.

The Los Angeles of David Brown's time was a rude collection of flat-roofed adobes in a desert wilderness. *From the Williamson Railroad Survey Report of 1853, courtesy California State Library.*

Morehead. Along the way Brown discovered that he was in danger of being arrested for his San Diego escapade and fled back to Los Angeles. Morehead's troops accomplished little other than some inneffective mischief.

When a city marshal and several deputies proved unable to combat crime in Los Angeles during mid-1851, Dr. Alexander Hope was appointed police chief with a large force of volunteer deputies to assist him. Although not a member of the original group as listed in the local press, Brown later became one of these volunteer officers. When John Thornpen, a desperado from the mining country, was arrested in town, the Los Angeles *Star* reported the capture:

> . . . The police are entitled to great praise for their efforts in arresting this criminal. Of those who were particularly vigilant in the search it is proper to mention. . . J.P. Bailey and David Brown.

Brown offered himself as a candidate for city marshal in August of 1851, but was defeated in the election.

In 1852 Brown is reported to have been approached by two prominent residents of the city to participate in a robbery. John Temple, a wealthy local merchant was leaving for Mexico with a large amount of cash. Brown and his two accomplices planned to waylay him on the road, bury the money until the heat was off, then divide the spoils. One report has it that Temple changed his route and thwarted the robbers. Another more probable story states that the night before the projected robbery Brown shot himself in the foot while cleaning his pistol. His two partners were furious when they had to cancel their plans at the last minute. John Temple meanwhile safely caught his boat and Dave's two fellow conspirators lived in constant fear that Brown would mention the conspiracy during one of his frequent drinking bouts.

Brown gambled for a time, then worked as a vaquero for the prominent cattle rancher, John Rains. On October 13, 1854, Brown was in Los Angeles and drinking heavily. He was quite drunk when he asked his friend Pink Clifford for a loan which was refused. Enraged, Brown stabbed his friend to death. He was quickly taken into custody and nearly lynched by a mob the following day. Mayor Stephen Foster dispersed the crowd only by promising to lead them in a lynching if Brown escaped justice. The local Mexican and native Californian population was greatly disturbed that another American would escape hanging through legal maneuvers, while Mexicans invariably hanged for their crimes.

On November 30th Brown was tried in the District Court and sentenced to hang on January 12, 1855. Another convicted murderer, Felipe Alvitre, was also to hang on that date. It would be a good test of the law and the locals

Steve Foster was married to a prominent native California woman, and although mayor of Los Angeles, led the mob that lynched Dave Brown. *Courtesy California Historical Society, Los Angeles.*

watched and listened closely to see what would happen. Brown's lawyers worked hard and on January 10th were rewarded with a stay of execution for their client. "Last night," noted a dispatch from Los Angeles, "one of the largest and most excited mass meetings ever convened in our city was held in the immense dining room of the Montgomery (saloon)." The committee issued a resolution stating that "whereas the time for the execution of Brown and Alvitre will have arrived by tomorrow. . .and as by some means Brown had received a respite and Alvitre none; and as they are both equally guilty—we the committe think they should both be executed at the same time and on the same day." Despite the pleadings of prominent citizens for Sheriff Barton to give up the prisoner, the lawman made out his will and refused to compromise the law. A dispatch from Los Angeles on the day scheduled for the hanging was alarming:

Although this 1870 lynching took place in Los Angeles some years after the Brown incident, the events were quite similar. Shown is the death of murderer Miguel Lachenaise, last victim of the Los Angeles vigilantes. *Courtesy California Historical Society, Los Angeles.*

62

1 o'clock P.M. - Two thousand men have gathered from all portions of the county, well-armed and determined. One hundred dollars has been paid this morning to the proprietor of the shooting gallery, by Californians, for loading their revolvers. Masses of people are congregating from all quarters. Stores closed...

When Alvitre was hanged on schedule at 3 o'clock in the afternoon, Mayor Stephen Foster resigned his office to lead the mob. Foster was married to Maria Merced Lugo and had close ties to the Mexican portion of the community. And he had made a promise. When Alvitre was hanged, the mob promptly broke down the jail doors and dragged Brown from his cell. The Los Angeles *Southern Californian* reported what happened from that point on:

> There being no scaffold prepared, he was taken across to a large gateway opposite the court house, to the heavy crossbeam to which a rope was fastened, and a chair being placed beneath, Brown was elevated thereon and the rope fixed about his neck. Some time was allowed him, during which he evinced the utmost coolness, recognizing and speaking to his acquaintances in the crowd and reflecting in jocular terms upon the crowd who were engaged in his execution... Perceiving that those about were ignorant of the method of preparing the rope, he called to an acquaintance and requested him to get some Americans who understood it to hang him.
>
> Throughout the scene he manifested the most careless indifference and finally jumped off into eternity with the same coolness and hardihood as had characterized him through life. His body was taken down and placed in the jail buildings, and on the succeeding day buried by some of our citizens.

And so died Dave Brown, escorted to hell by the mayor and other eminent residents of the town as well as the mob of Californians. Foster was re-elected mayor by a large majority a few days later. It was said in later days that two of the prominent members of the mob were Dave's two former partners in crime who could now at last rest easy in the knowledge that their scheme to rob John Temple would never be known.

PRINCIPAL SOURCES

Bell, Major Horace, *On the Old West Coast*, N.Y., Grosset & Dunlap, 1930; *Illustrated History of Los Angeles County*, Chicago, Lewis Publishing Co., 1889; Newmark, Harris, *Sixty Years in Southern California*, N.Y., Houghton Mifflin Co., 1930; Guinn, J.M. "Yuma Indian Depredations and the Glanton War," *Annual Publication of Historical Society of Southern California*, Los Angeles, 1903; San Francisco *Daily Alta California*, Jan. 8, 1851, Jan. 23, 1855; Placerville *Democrat*, Jan. 20, 1855; Los Angeles *Star*, Aug. 9, 1851; 1850 census of the City and County of Los Angeles.

This mug shot of the noted Procopio
was probably taken at the time of his
capture by Sheriff Harry Morse in
early 1872. *Courtesy San Jose Historical
Museum Collections.*

TOMAS PROCOPIO BUSTAMENTE

Although his birthdate is not known, Procopio was probably born near San Jose de Guadalupe, Mexico, about 1840. His father was killed by Indians while driving stage between Ures and Hermosillo in 1852. Procopio's mother, Vicenta, was an older sister of Joaquin Murrieta and was living with her husband's relatives when her brother came home for a visit that same year. When Joaquin returned to California he took his widowed sister and her young son with him.

In California young Procopio and his mother lived in Niles Canyon, Alameda County, near the ranch of Joaquin and his wife. According to one authority, Murrieta was not killed at the celebrated Cantua Creek fight as reported, but was later wounded by officers and died from loss of blood and shock at this home. Young Procopio was reportedly present when his outlaw uncle was buried in a room of his home in the late summer of 1853. After Joaquin's death the widow Bustamente married a sometime member of his gang, Francisco Valenzuela.

Procopio and his step-father did not get along, causing a separation between his mother and her husband. Little is known of the boy's early years, but he seems to have inevitably drifted into a life of crime. Leaving home at an early age, Procopio became a vaquero and was associating with thieves and cut-throats before he was out of his teens. When a prominent southern California rancher was murdered near San Bernardino on November 17, 1862, Procopio and others were taken into custody as noted in a letter of Robert Carlisle who was investigating the crime:

Old San Jose was the home of many friends of Procopio and he spent much time there. *Courtesy California State Library.*

Well, we have got some of the murderers of John Rains, Manuel Cerradel, one Tal Eugenio and one who calls himself Lewis Sanchez...The balance Procopio Bustamente, Jesus Astares and one "Tal Juanita." Cerradel, being the first caught, says that Don Ramon Carrillo paid him $500 to do the deed. Cerradel...says Procopio told him all about it...

Cerradel, convicted of another crime, was lynched while being taken to prison, but the others were released for lack of evidence. Procopio and his companions quickly fled north as reported by a dispatch published in the San Francisco *Alta* on April 6, 1863:

Firebaugh's Ferry, April 5.—Juanito, one of the men concerned in the murder of John Rains near Los Angeles, was mortally wounded near this place yesterday evening. He was trying to steal a horse belonging to an Indian, and shot at the Indian, wounding another man named Nuenes. The Indian then shot Juanito three times, also cut him severely. Both Nuenes and Juanito are mortally wounded. Procopio, another of Rains' murderers, is in the vicinity.

When prominent Southern California rancher John Rains was murdered in 1862, Procopio was one of the principal suspects. *Courtesy Ingersoll Collection, Los Angeles Public Library.*

65

Livermore was a favorite hangout of Procopio. This street scene shows the old town as it appeared in the 1880's or 90's. *Courtesy John Boessenecker.*

Just when Procopio arrived in the Livermore Valley is not known, but he immediately took up with Narciso Bojorques, Chano Ortego and other known thieves and highwaymen. When Aaron Golding, his wife and child and a vaquero were found murdered at the rancher's burned home in early 1863, Procopio and his new friends were prime suspects. Taken in for questioning, the trio were released for lack of evidence, although local lawmen knew Ortego had quarreled with Golding over money. Procopio may have been in the south at the time of the murders, but Ortego and Bojorques had been seen in the area and may well have committed the crime.

That summer Procopio and Bojorques stole a herd of cattle from a rancher named Pope in Alameda County. When Procopio was being paid off after having sold the cattle to a butcher at Alvarado, Constable O.B. Wood stepped from a hiding place with a leveled pistol. Surprised, the rustler surrendered and stated that he was unarmed. As the lawman lowered his own weapon to shackle his prisoner, Procopio swiftly drew his pistol and shot Wood in the arm. The outlaw then ran down the street as a posse of citizens formed and gave pursuit. There were some shots fired, but when he was cornered on a creek bank Procopio surrendered. At his trial he refused to identify his companions and was convicted and sentenced to San Quentin for nine years.

At state prison Procopio was listed as No. 2603, under the alias of Tomas Rodundo. He was received there on September 4, 1863; "age 21; occupation, laborer; 5'11¾" tall; dark complexion; hazel eyes; brown hair..."

When he was discharged on March 1, 1871, Procopio lost no time in returning to his old life—"as a dog to his vomit," one newspaper phrased it. He stole two steers from a rancher named Arnett, but was quickly traced to Juan Camargo, a notorious fence. With a noose around his neck a group of vigilantes convinced Camargo he had better discuss the matter with them, but Procopio had already felt a pressing need to ride over to Monterey at a rather fast gait.

On the coast Procopio joined with Tiburcio Vasquez, and several others to form a gang of highwaymen. On August 17, 1871, the five bandits stopped and robbed a man in a buggy while they waited for an overdue stage. When the coach finally did roll into view, it was driven into a field where the five passengers were robbed of some $500 cash and jewelry, then tied up. Another traveler was robbed before the bandits rode off into the hills. The last victim secured some help and chased the robbers, but was unable to catch them. Sheriff's posses proved just as ineffective. The following month, however, a gang member named Francisco Barcenas, was killed in a shootout with officers. A wounded outlaw who managed to escape was thought to be Procopio.

With the proceeds of their recent escapades, Procopio and Vasquez fled to Mexico where they rusticated in debauchery for several months. By the end of the year both were anxious to return to California. They spent some time in San Francisco before Vasquez left to assemble another bandit gang. Procopio, enjoying himself in the Mexican deadfalls of the bay city, was finally recognized by a police detective who notified Sheriff Harry Morse of Alameda. Two local police officers assisted Morse and a deputy when they closed in on the desperado as reported in the *Bulletin*:

> ...They shadowed his haunts for about 24 hours, and Saturday afternoon found that he was in a house on Morton street. The officers made entrances simultaneously by different doors. Procopio was sitting at a table eating and seeing the officers enter at the front door he jumped to draw his revolver, but before he could pull it, Sheriff Morse, who had entered at the rear, had him pinioned by the throat, and in a moment he was handcuffed and on his way to...the San Leandro jail.

On April 25, 1872, Procopio was tried in Alameda County on the Arnett crime, which seemed the strongest case against him. "The defendent is a fine-looking young man," noted the *Bulletin,* "of about 32 years of age, rather tall. He has a well-built frame, with a countenance that one would scarcely believe could belong to a man of such bad instincts." The jury promptly found him guilty and on May 4th he was again admitted to San Quentin for a term of

A photograph, probably taken in the 1880's, underscores a newspaper comment that Procopio had "a countenance that one would scarcely believe could belong to a man of such bad instincts." *Courtesy Monna Olson.*

seven years. This time he was No. 5247, a description of the time noting "...a small scar on back of left hand and arrow wounds on left arm above elbow and on left breast."

Discharged on June 6, 1877, Procopio reportedly lost no time in resuming his old way of life. He seems to have settled on the west side of Fresno County and was suspected of various bandit raids in the area. On the evening of November 12, 1877, a party of five masked Mexicans robbed Brownstone's store at Grangeville. About a month later the same number of men robbed a store at Caliente, in Kern County. Moving south the outlaws rustled some stock then headed for the Tejon Pass. They were captured in the mountains and brought to Bakersfield where all five were lynched. Although Procopio was suspected of being the leader, he managed to avoid capture. On December 26th another group of outlaws entered the Phillips & Weinshench store in Hanford and after tying up the clerks in approved Vasquez fashion, made off with some $300 and jewelry. "We hear it rumored," noted the Tulare *Times,* "that if they are caught their fate will be similar to those robbers who were hanged at Bakersfield last week."

A posse of five men began tracking the outlaws the following day. One suspect was located at Posa Chané, a small Mexican settlement near present-day Coalinga. The suspect was surprised while sleeping and told to dress. While pulling on his overcoat he suddenly grabbed two revolvers and started shooting. Deputy Sol Gladden was killed and the other lawmen driven from the shack. Running to his horse, the killer rode off, but the posse, with one man dead and two horses wounded, returned to Hanford. There seemed to be no doubt as to the identity of the killer as noted in the Fresno *Expositor:*

> The Mexican who killed Gladden. . . was a recent graduate from San Quentin College of Arts. He is known by the name of Procopio, and is a nephew of the renowned bandit, Joaquin Murrieta. Posa Chané, where the killing was done, is but a short distance from Joaquin's old headquarters. Procopio is supposed to have led the bandits that raided Caliente.

New posses quickly formed and pursued the fugitive to the San Luis Obispo area, but they showed little disposition to get within gunshot range according to newspaper accounts. A letter from Firebaugh's published in the Fresno *Republican,* noted that Procopio had been at that place during both the Hanford raid and the Gladden murder.

There is little record of the noted outlaw's movements after the incident at Posa Chané, but there are many indications that he fled to Mexico. Historian Frank Latta's interviews with Procopio's wife revealed the outlaw was killed at La Lista Blanca, northeast of Hermosillo, although dates and circumstances are lacking. His wife did say that he died as an outlaw and the following article in the San Diego *Union* of August 4, 1882, perhaps is his death notice:

> Tucson, August 2—Advices from Guaymas, Sonora, say that on Monday last Aureillo Cantatran, an actor, was shot and killed by Procopio Murietta in a house of ill fame. The slayer is a nephew of the notorious California outlaw, Joaquin Murietta. He has killed two men in Los Angeles and made his escape from prison to New York, where he was again incarcerated. From there with a Chinaman, he again escaped, and has been here since. He was shot on Tuesday morning by order of the Governor.

Indications are he died about 10 years later, however. Although a shadowy figure in California outlaw annals, Procopio must rank close to the top as one of the more colorful of the early day desperadoes.

PRINCIPAL SOURCES

Black, Esther Boulton, *Rancho Cucamonga and Dona Merced,* Redlands, San Bernardino County Museum Assoc., 1975; Greenwood, Robert, *The California Outlaw, Tiburcio Vasquez,* Los Gatos, Talisman Press, 1960; Latta, Frank F.,*Joaquin Murrieta and his Horse Gangs,* Santa Cruz, Bear State Books, 1980; San Francisco Daily *Alta California,* Apr. 6, 1863; San Francisco *Bulletin,* Aug. 19, 28, Sept. 15, 1871; Feb. 12, Apr. 26, 1872; San Francisco *Daily Morning Call,* May 14, 1882, Feb. 28, 1886; Visalia *Delta,* Nov. 17, Dec. 29, 1877, Jan. 5, 11, 1878; Alameda County, *Gazette,* May 2, 1872; Fresno *Republican,* Dec. 22, 29, 1877; Interview with Joe Whitesides in H.G. Schutt Collection, Special Collections, California State University Library, Fresno; Prison records in California State Archives, Sacramento.

WILLIAM WALLACE BYRNES

The only known likeness of Bill Byrnes is a newspaper sketch made from a photograph once owned by his daughter. *From the San Francisco* Call *of April 3, 1892.*

Apparently born in Maine about 1824, Bill Byrnes moved to Missouri with his family when he was still quite young. He reportedly studied for the priesthood at Saint Louis University, but a check of existing records failed to disclose his name. He joined Sterling Price's Regiment of Missouri Mounted Riflemen in May of 1846 and served throughout the Mexican War. In June of 1847 he was mustered out at Santa Fe, New Mexico.

After the war Byrnes took up scalp hunting with the noted Jim Beckwourth and several other mountain men. At that time Apache scalp prices ranged from $100 to $200, with the Mexican government paying even more for chiefs. A strange dream reportedly caused Byrnes to see the depravity of his occupation and he came to California with Thomas "Pegleg" Smith during the gold rush of 1849.

In 1850 Byrnes was mining at Placerville when he had a dispute with a man named Marple in a local saloon. When Byrnes reached for his pistol, Marple told him he would bet he could knock him down before he could cock his weapon. Byrnes decided it would be more prudent to buy drinks for the house, instead.

During the second El Dorado County Indian War, Byrnes was in Tracy's company, stationed at Mormon Station, just over the California line in what was then Utah Territory. Returning to Placerville in July of 1851, Byrnes and his men had a brisk fight with Indians and lost one man.

Byrnes returned to Carson Valley later in the year and was a member of the committee which formed the first civil government of the area. In November of 1851 he was elected sheriff of the area—the first sheriff in what is now the state of Nevada. In the spring of 1852 Sheriff Byrnes was invited to shoot at targets with a local trading post operator named N.R. Haskill. After Byrnes had taken the first turn and emptied his pistol, Haskill suddenly began shooting at the sheriff instead of the target. Byrnes was badly wounded and when a hastily assembled court considered a neck tie party for the murderous merchant, Haskill skipped out for California. Sheriff Byrnes made a remarkable recovery, however, and soon began leaving Mormon Station on mysterious trips. When he returned one day and stated that no more trips would be necessary, it was assumed he had located Haskill and settled with him.

In early 1853 Byrnes was back in California, mining in Mariposa County. In May he signed on as a lieutenant in Captain Harry Love's freshly organized California Ranger organization. The rangers had been authorized by the state legislature to track down a group of Mexican bandits led by one Joaquin. The outlaws had been terrorizing the gold rush country and Byrnes claimed to have known the bandit leader when they had gambled together in one of the gold rush camps. The ranger muster roll describes Byrnes at this time as being 29 years of age, over six feet tall with brown hair and gray eyes. Byrnes was a particularly valuable member of the group since he at least had known one of the five Joaquins who were named as leaders of the bandits by the legislative action.

Byrnes mined and gambled at Placerville, California, in the early 1850's. *Courtesy California State Library.*

Byrnes was stationed at Mormon Station during the second Eldorado County Indian War and later served as first sheriff of the area. *Courtesy Nevada Historical Society.*

After over a month of hard riding, the rangers located the bandits in the coast range, camping on Cantua Creek in what is now Fresno County. Following a sharp fight in which some six bandits were killed and two captured, the dead outlaw leader was identified by Byrnes as Joaquin Murrieta. Joaquin's head was then cut off by Byrnes, along with the head and hand of his lieutenant, Three-fingered Jack. Byrnes and John Sylvester were then detailed to take the trophies to nearby Fort Miller where they could be preserved in alcohol. Their arrival was noted in the Stockton *San Joaquin Republican* of July 30, 1853, just five days after the battle:

Capture of the Bandit Joaquin

Headwaters of the San Joaquin, July 26th

Sir—As an express is going to start from these diggings I hasten to inform you of the death of Joaquin, the robber, who has been such a curse in the country for sometime. Capt. Burns [*sic*], of the Rangers, and Mr. Sylvester arrived here yesterday evening with the heads of Joaquin and one of his band ... The remainder of the party are expected here this evening with two prisoners. Captain Burns has preserved the heads in spirit in order that they may be the more readily recognized ...

Byrnes' wife was later to write that her husband could only secure whiskey at Fort Miller and was told that this was inadequate to store the heads. Leaving the ghastly trophies with a soldier friend, Byrnes instructed him to change the whiskey frequently until he returned from Mariposa with some pure alcohol. When he did return it was to discover that this friend had drunk the whiskey which was supposed to be used with the heads and Three-fingered Jack's head had been damaged beyond repair and discarded. What actually happened was that the rangers had taken along alcohol in which to store any captured heads, but had drunk it all in the course of the campaign. Jack's head had several bullet holes through it and by the time it reached Fort Miller after a ride of some 80 miles in 100 degree plus weather, it was virtually unrecognizable. Jack's head was discarded and just his hand retained.

Many affidavits were gathered testifying to the authenticity of the head of Joaquin and since Byrnes himself claimed to have been the only ranger to have known him, he made out his own document before a notary:

Quartzburg, August 8th, 1853

I do hereby certify that the Mexican head now in the possession of Capt. Harry Love is Joaquin Muriati [sic], I having known him ever since the spring of 1850, personally.

Wm. Byrnes ...

After collecting his share of the reward, Byrnes looked about for other opportunities. Probably as a result of his service to the state, he obtained a job as prison guard at the state penitentiary being built at Point San Quentin. He went to work in the fall of 1853 and at the same time filed on some land a short distance from San Quentin. Discipline at the prison was very lax at the time due to the small number of prisoners and guards. Another prison employee named Tom Young later testified that Byrnes used convict labor to build a cabin on his claim:

... In the fall of 1853 some of the guards (one by the name of Byrnes) squatted on some land seven miles from prison, and took some four or five prisoners out to assist them to build their cabin; I met them on the way, with axes, three miles from the prison ...

The guards and the prisoners dressed in regular clothes at this time and both could frequently be seen drinking at the bar of cook G. W. Woods, who was also a guard. Even at this early date Byrnes was a heavy drinker, Tom Young noting that "William Byrnes frequently got on a spree ..." The prison was riddled with corruption and Byrnes soon tired of the area. Sometime in 1855 he moved to

73

Monterey where, according to his daughter, he married a woman named Mary A. Ross. Byrnes hired on as a bodyguard for Lewis Belcher during the bitter and bloody feuding over the Sanchez estate. When Belcher was assassinated in June of 1856, "Burns" is mentioned as one of the those accompanying the body to San Jose.

In 1859 Byrnes was in northern California where he participated in the Indian campaign of State Adjutant General William C. Kibbee. Elijah Potter was a member of the same command and later wrote:

> We elected our own officers. Two noted men contested for the office of captain. One was William Byrnes, who was once a Texas Ranger, a noted gunfighter and also had the distinction of being the man who killed Joaquin Murrieta . . . Byrnes won by three votes. I wanted to see Jones elected, as I had been in an Indian war with Byrnes in El Dorado County in 1851 and knew he was not cautious enough to be a good Indian fighter . . .

The campaign was a brief one and Byrnes was soon off prospecting in Nevada during the Washoe silver mining excitement. He was mining near Virginia City when the Paiute War of 1860 erupted. "There are three men in command of volunteers at Washoe who have had much experience in Indian fights," reported the Santa Cruz *Sentinel,* "Col. Jack Hays, commander-in-chief, Captain Wm. Fleeson, and Capt. Wm. Burns [*sic*]. Three more effective men would be hard to find."

After the close of the war Byrnes had various narrow escapes from Indians and was shot by a woman in a mining claim dispute. Byrnes' daughter claimed he was in seven shooting scrapes and had been wounded some 32 times. He had always been a hard drinker, but the pain of these wounds made him even more dependent on the relief of the bottle.

Byrnes spent several weeks in the Sacramento County Hospital in early 1873 trying to obtain some relief from his pain. In late March his mind seemed affected and it was thought best to confine him to a police cell while preparations were made to send him to the state asylum at Stockton. He was visiting San Jose at the time and the *Mercury* of March 26, 1873, commented on his deteriorating condition:

> His mind is terribly shattered, and he is seldom able to recall a single circumstance that has occurred in his life. Singular as it may seem, on meeting Joseph Patton, assistant jailor, he recognized him as an old acquaintance, and remembered to have met him twenty years ago. A few minutes afterward the circumstance passed from his memory, and he had no recollection of having ever seen him. We saw the unfortunate man in his cell on Monday. He stands about six feet high, and has been a man of rather prepossessing appearance, but scarcely a vestige of his former self remains now.

Byrnes reportedly died the following year in the Stockton asylum, although no records have been located. His burial place is unknown. He remains one of the more colorful and enigmatic figures of old California.

PRINCIPAL SOURCES ───────────────────────

Angel, Myron T., *History of Nevada,* Oakland, Thompson & West, 1881; Latta, Frank F. *Joaquin Murrieta and his Horse Gangs,* Santa Cruz, Bear State Books, 1980; Templeton, Sardis W., *The Lame Captain,* Los Angeles, Westernlore Press, 1965; Upton, Charles E., *Pioneers of El Dorado,* Placerville, privately pub., 1906; Wren, Thomas, A. *History of the State of Nevada,* N.Y., Lewis Publishing Co., 1904; (Calif. State Senate, 1856 Sess.) (Doc. No. 10) *Report of Special Committee Appointed to Ascertain the Amount of Controllers' Warrants Issued During the Year 1855, on Act of State Prison* (Sacramento:) James Allen, State Printer, (1856); Potter, Elijah Renshaw, "Reminiscences of the Early History of Northern Caifornia, and the Indian Troubles," ms. in the Bancroft Library, Berkeley, Calif.; San Francisco *Daily Alta California,* Apr. 2, 1873; San Francisco *Daily Morning Call,* Apr. 3, 1892; San Francisco *Examiner,* May 30, 1873; National Archives, Washington D.C.

JAMES P. CASEY

James P. Casey was a thug and politician who shot the wrong man, in the wrong place and at the wrong time. *Courtesy California Historical Society.*

Born in New York about 1817, young Jim Casey had little or no education other than that which he received in the streets. He grew up in the back alleys and shadows of the city's political underworld and although illiterate he made himself popular with the local democratic bosses. Small, wiry and tough, he became a thug and ballot box stuffer hanging around saloons and political halls all day and living with a prostitute. When he had a falling out with his girl friend, Casey decided to sell some of the funiture he had given her. It was a bad move. The woman put the law on him and he was convicted of grand larceny and sentenced to a two year term at Sing Sing. He entered prison on September 5, 1849.

Prison records describe Casey as "32 years old, 5'5" high, dark complexioned, dark brown hair, very dark blue eyes, middle joint of forefinger on right hand is crooked, above right temple, near hair, is large, angular scar. Small scar on side of nose..." He was discharged on September 4, 1851.

Casting about for new opportunities, Casey learned that many of his cronies and local politicians had gone to California during the gold rush. He, too, soon headed west, turning up in San Francisco in 1853. In the bay city Casey looked up his old pals and quickly became a thug and organizer for the party bosses. He obtained a political appointment and served two years as assistant county treasurer. San Francisco at this time was controlled by the worst kind of money-grubbing politicians and Casey was right at home...and usually in trouble.

A group of the local politicians, along with Casey and his coterie of goons, had a meeting at the Mercantile Hotel in February of 1854. When the meeting turned into a drunken brawl and the proprietor called the police, the lawmen were badly mauled. Casey and five or six others were finally dragged off to jail, but the politicians would not stand for their pet thugs being locked up. Judge

Alexander Wells, of the state Supreme Court, soon had them all released on a writ of habeus corpus. Later Wells was seen drinking with these same rioters in a saloon. The police force threatened to resign in a body and the incident was only smoothed over with great difficulty by the mayor. The *Daily Alta California* grumbled:

> ...Under this view of the case we call upon all good citizens to look well to their lives and property. The conservators of the peace are stopped in their work. The police are about resigning, and we shall soon be adrift at the mercy of a lawless mob and a cowardly set of officials who have not the courage or the honesty to do their duty.

Casey himself was just getting warmed up. The *California Chronicle* noted his being fined $70 for assault and battery in July of 1854 and the following month he attempted to fight a duel at Mission Dolores, but was stopped by the police. The *Times and Transcript* reported yet another scrap in early September:

> A fight took place...at the Union Hotel in San Francisco at 11 o'clock on Monday night between James Casey, Esq., and another gentleman, name unknown. They fought from the shoulder first, in which Mr. Casey succeeded in flooring his antagonist, and after separation pistols were drawn, but Mr. Casey had the "Dead wood" on his antagonist. No shots were fired.

Casey's aborted duel at the mission had been with J. W. Bagley, a dissident of the same party. About the time of the duel, Casey and Robert Cushing, a Bagley cohort, met on Kearney Street and both reached for their guns as reported by another thug and politician, "Dutch Charley" Duane:

Gold rush San Francisco was just the right place for a Jim Casey to rise to the top, or sink to oblivion. *Courtesy California State Library.*

...I heard a report and turning I saw Cushing and Casey in the middle of the street with their pistols drawn, exchanging shots...They were about twenty feet apart and they had each fired several shots when I sprang between them...Just then some policemen could be seen coming towards us, so both men pocketed their weapons and went off in different directions...

Bagley, Cushing and three others sought to ambush Casey during a primary election in August of 1855. When Casey dropped into his precinct to obtain the election results, he was attacked by all five men wielding fists, knives and pistols. Unarmed at the time, Casey was creased by several bullets, but managed to seize a knife and badly wound one attacker. He then grabbed a pistol and shot it out with the others. Both Bagley and Cushing were wounded, leaving Casey triumphant on the field.

Although illiterate, Casey dredged up an editor and founded a newspaper called the *Sunday Times*. It was a scurilous sheet in which he aired his pet peeves and operated from offices in William T. Sherman's bank building. Sherman, the future-famed Civil War general, summed up Casey's latest endeavor in a letter written in April of 1856:

> I...send you a leaf from the *Sunday Times* in which you will observe he pitches into us...having repeated the same abuse of all bankers...The fellow wanted blackmail and so far as I know has not made a cent. His printing office was in our building, but before he put us on the list he had the good sense to move out...I would have...[tossed]...him and his press out of the window...

The *Evening Bulletin,* a new newspaper, made its appearance in October of 1855. James King, a former banker who was convinced the people of San Francisco no longer controlled their city, was the editor. He launched an all-out attack on the crooked politicians, banks and election-riggers of the city. His motives will be argued forever, but he stirred his audience and gained a large following of residents who gradually came to see the corrupted state of their city. When Bagley sent for Casey's prison record and gave it to King, Casey begged that it not be published in the *Bulletin*. King just told him to get out. That evening, May 14, 1856, as King began his walk home down Montgomery Street, Casey caught him by surprise and shot him down. The gunman was quickly taken into custody by police and his political cronies and whisked off to jail amid growing crowds of excited people.

King was known to always be armed. He had made many enemies and even if he died Casey expected to be tried and easily acquitted. But he had misjudged the temper of the times. Judge Murray Morrison, a local attorney, noted the events in a letter to a cousin on May 21st:

> The excitement was beyond anything I ever beheld...Mr. King was very popular; his murderer, a man by the name of Casey, was a desperado and the

JAMES P. CASEY

Left: Editor James King of William misjudged the desperate character of Casey and paid for it with his life. *Courtesy California State Library.*

Below: Editor King was shot as he emerged from the alley between the four-story Montgomery Block building and the express office with the fringed awning. *Courtesy collections of George Eastman House, Rochester, New York.*

leader of a crowd of desperate men. The citizens gathered in their strength soon after the shooting and organized a Vigilance Committee; about 3,000 persons joined it and on Sunday last they demanded of the civil authorities the person of Mr. Casey and also the person of one Charles Cora who stands charged with the murder of our late Marshal Gen. Richardson. The sheriff, seeing about 2,000 men drawn up in front of the jail with two heavy brass field pieces, well shotted bearing full upon the building, concluded that it would be discreet in him to do as they directed . . .

The vigilantes, close to 7,000 in number by some estimates, were commanded by merchant William T. Coleman who had headed the 1851 vigilance committee, also. When the vigilantes demanded the surrender of Casey and Cora by the sheriff, witnesses described Casey as glowering in his cell like a caged lion. He was wielding a large bowie knife and shouted "Dave, I made you sheriff, now God damn you, take care of me." But Sheriff Scannell could not protect him.

The governor had pleaded with Coleman to let justice take its course, but the vigilantes were adamant. When editor King died on May 20th, Casey and Cora were being tried at the vigilante headquarters, Fort Gunnybags. Casey well knew that the tolling of firehouse bells throughout the city were not only signalling King's death, but his own as well.

On May 22, 1856, James P. Casey and Charles Cora were hanged from windows of the vigilante headquarters. Vigilante troops stood at attention in formation as thousands of spectators viewed the spectacle. Although the hero of dozens of personal brawls and gunfights, Casey broke down completely at the end. Muttering about "mercy" and his "poor mother," he was barely able to stand when he plunged to his death. Cora had watched him with contempt. Buried under Catholic auspices at the old Mission Dolores, Casey's body was followed to the grave by some eighty-four carriages and over four hundred people on foot, mostly working class Irish of the city. His impressive tombstone, erected by the fire company he belonged to, may be seen in the old mission cemetery today.

Casey and Cora were hanged from the upper windows of vigilante headquarters. Fort Gunnybags, as it was known, is shown as it appeared that eventful summer of 1856. *Courtesy California State Library.*

A contemporary lithograph depicting the deaths of Casey and Cora and the huge crowds that witnessed the terrible scene. *Courtesy California State Library.*

Although Casey is not known to have left a family, a strange story surfaced in 1903. In late July a group of convicts escaped from Folsom Prison after killing a guard. Five convicts aided the guards in trying to prevent the break and were later rewarded by the governor. Joe Casey, one of the inmates, had been serving a life term for a murder committed in Colusa County in 1890. Governor Pardee granted Casey a full pardon for his brave action, but with the stipulation that if he was ever again convicted of another crime, he would have to serve that sentence on top of his pardoned term. On October 17, 1903, the San Francisco *Chronicle* reported the story and added this curious epilog:

> ...Casey is a native of Louisiana and 50 years old. He had resided in Williams at intervals since 1878. He had been employed as a bartender. Casey's father figured prominently in the early days of California. He was hanged out of a third-story window on Montgomery Street, San Francisco, in 1856, by vigilantes, for killing James King, of William, editor of the *Bulletin*.

PRINCIPAL SOURCES ───────────────────────

Clarke, Dwight L., *William Tecumseh Sherman: Gold Rush Banker,* San Francisco, Calif. Historical Society, 1969; Coblentz, Stanton A., *Villains and Vigilantes,* N.Y., Thomas Yoseloff, 1957; Lotchin, Roger W., *San Francisco, 1846-1856,* N.Y., Oxford Univ. Press, 1974; Williams, David A. *David C. Broderick, A Political Portrait,* San Marino, Huntington Library, 1969; Huggins, Dorothy H., "Continuation of the Annals of San Francisco," *Calif. Historical Society Quarterly,* June, 1937; Morrison, Murray, "A Glimpse of San Francisco in the 50's as it appeared to Judge Murray Morrison," *Calif. Historical Society Quarterly,* Mar. 1937; San Francisco *Daily Alta California,* Feb. 19, 1854; Sacramento *Union,* Sept. 14, 1854; San Francisco *Bulletin,* May 15, 1856; San Francisco *California Chronicle,* July 1, Aug. 26, 1854.

CLODOVEO CHAVEZ

Chavez grew up in the mission town of San Juan Bautista where he was born about 1846. Issac Mylar, a friend of boyhood days, described him as a "hardlooking boy, almost like an Indian, not a bad boy, but rough, thick-necked, dark and heavy set.". Another childhood friend was Luis Raggio, son of an Italian father and a native Californian mother. Chavez grew up to be a sheep herder and vaquero and, as an adult, was described as being "about 5'11" in height...muscular, weighing over two hundred pounds. His complexion is rather light for a Mexican and he has grey eyes, short whiskers...small goatee...hair worn rather long..."

Chavez was working for Estanislaus Hernandez in early 1873 when he became acquainted with Tiburcio Vasquez. The "wily and oily-tongued Vasquez" was a notorious outlaw with a long prison record. He corrupted young Chavez and the two soon rode off together despite the warnings of Hernandez. They reportedly robbed a stagecoach and a number of teamsters, then fled to Soledad where they spent their loot in riotous living. When funds ran low, the two outlaws headed north again to the ranch of Abdon Leiva where

Chavez is generally thought to have been an honest vaquero until corrupted by the "wily and oily-tongued Vasquez," shown here the year he was hanged for his crimes. *Courtesy California State Library.*

they planned the robbery of the store at Firebaugh's Ferry. Vasquez, Chavez, Leiva and several others made the raid on February 26, 1873. With a new gang member named Teodora Moreno, the outlaws next sacked the small village of Tres Pinos the following August. Here many victims were tied up and robbed, several stores were looted and three men were shot down in cold blood. The whole state was outraged and with posses fanning out over the countryside, the killers managed to make their escape to southern California.

In November Vasquez and his men re-appeared near Millerton in Fresno County where they robbed Jones' store on the San Joaquin River. The day after Christmas they struck again, capturing and robbing the entire village of Kingston, on the Kings River west of Visalia. They tied up and robbed some thirty people in three separate stores before word of the raid leaked out to some surrounding homes. Local cattleman Jack Sutherland and several others crept up and opened fire, driving the outlaws back across a toll bridge and out of town. There were some eight or ten in the gang, one being killed and several injured in the brief gunbattle. Chavez was badly wounded in the leg as noted in a letter from Sheriff Harry Morse dated March 21, 1874:

> ... Three of the Vasquez party were wounded at the Kingston robbery, one of them Refugio Montejos, has since died. Another named Lopez was shot through the neck, and the worst man of the gang, to wit, Chavis [*sic*] was shot through the leg, the bone was splintered ...

Chavez apparently hid out at a ranch in the Posa Chané area until his wound healed and he could rejoin Vasquez. On February 25, 1874 the two bandits held up the stage station at Coyote Holes in the Mojave Desert. After taking everything of value from the inhabitants and the station, the two outlaws robbed the incoming stage before fleeing to a hideout near Soledad.

With Sheriff Morse and a strong posse pressing from the north, and Los Angeles posses nipping at his flanks, Vasquez staged a few more holdups before he was trapped and captured at a cabin near Los Angeles in mid-May of 1874. Chavez, however, managed to keep under cover. When Governor Newton Booth offered a $2,000 reward for his capture a few days later, Chavez headed for Mexico.

Just when he returned to California is not known, but Monterey County Sheriff Jim Smith was searching for Chavez the following September. In early 1875 the Bakersfield *Californian* announced his return under dateline of February 10th:

> A report comes to us that Chavez, the renowned companion and lieutenant of Vasquez, has made his appearance in the eastern part of this country. On Sunday night last he with his band of outlaws appeared at the store of Mr. Scobie on the South Fork of the Kern River. They captured five horses, a large amount of store goods and $800 in money. Sheriff Bowers... telegraphed to the sheriff of Los Angeles County as Chavez was evidently shaping a course in that direction.

Coyote Holes stage station as it appeared a few years after Chavez and Vasquez conducted their robbery there. *Courtesy Dennis Casebier.*

The bandits were heading east, however, and embarked on a series of hit-and-run raids through the Mojave Desert country. Lone travelers, teamsters and isolated locations were all fair game and newspapers throughout the state began clamoring for something to be done. "Let us if need be," penned an irate reader of the Los Angeles *Star,* "turn out, horse, foot and dragoons with thirty days rations, with powder and ball...and scout the country from Oregon to Cape Horn, if necessary, until Chavez and his league of plunderers are chained to the walls of some dungeon..."

On March 24th Chavez and his men pillaged the stage station at Little Lake in Inyo County. Two days later they pounced on the Granite Springs Station as reported in a letter from the owners published in the San Bernardino *Guardian:*

> Yesterday we were visited by Chavez and two of his gang who robbed us of $100, including cash, arms, goods, etc... The robbers offered no violence to any one except the Indian who didn't relish the idea of having his hands tied...
>
> Now, since we pay an Internal Revenue Tax for the privilege of keeping a station, then to be taxed with an Infernal Revenue, we ask, is there no protection? Yours truly,
>
> Nichols & Littlefield

On April 30th the bandits stopped a party of teamsters near Borax Lake, robbing all five and stealing everything they had. After compelling the cook at a water station to bake them a supply of bread, the outlaws disappeared into the desert. "The robbers," noted an article in the Panamint *News,* "said they were attacked by soldiers at Big Lake, ten days ago; one of them was wounded and some of their horses killed. The leader of the party told the cook his name was Cruz Lopez, but his appearance and especially a large scar on the right side of his face, answers to the description of Chavez..."

On May 5th they robbed another station and a stage, and in mid-month plundered the Cottonwood Station as well. Waving his hat as he rode away, the bandit chief suddenly wheeled his horse and shouted, "I'm Chavez," then once again vanished into the desert. With posses swarming all around him, Chavez suddenly felt a compelling need for another visit to Old Mexico.

By a curious coincidence, Luis Raggio began working on the King Woolsey ranch in Arizona in October of 1875. While out chasing cattle one day he suddenly came upon his old boyhood friend, Clodoveo Chavez, camped on the Gila River. They talked briefly, the fugitive warning his old acquaintance not to identify him. He told Raggio that he had been in Mexico, but was now returning to California. Promising to visit him later, Raggio returned to the ranch and quickly checked to see if the rewards for the outlaw were still in effect. In a letter to his father the following month, Raggio related the events which followed:

> ...On my return to the ranch I told the two men working with me about it and they agreed to go with me and capture him. So on the 25th of November we started and got close to where he was, and we camped...Next morning we rode over, and I told my men to ride ahead and go to the house and wait for me. But as soon as they saw Chavez they told him to surrender and he ran and my partner shot him in the back and he fell dead...

Raggio's partners, Harry Roberts and Clark Colvig, accompanied Raggio and the body in a wagon to Yuma. First notice of the incident was published in the Yuma *Sentinel* on November 27, 1875:

> Harry Roberts will be in Yuma tomorrow with the dead body of Chavez, the noted highwayman of California. He was killed at Baker's ranch today [Nov. 25th]. No doubt of his identity. Two persons are with Roberts who have known him for years.

In Yuma there was a brief rhubarb when several Mexicans who had known Chavez under an alias claimed the body was that of a man named Espinosa. The identity was promptly reconciled and a coroner's jury found the killing justifiable. The body contained seventeen buckshot in the left side, several slugs passing through the lungs.

A physician from Fort Yuma removed the head from the body and Harry Roberts then began the long trip back to California with his trophy in a 5 gallon can of alcohol. Roberts first stopped off at San Juan Bautista as he later explained in a letter to his brother-in-law:

> ...I had the head identified at San Juan by all the principal men in town and presented their affadivits to the governor. I think now I shall have the head placed in a glass case and exhibit it in San Francisco and try and make a portion...of my expenses out of it.

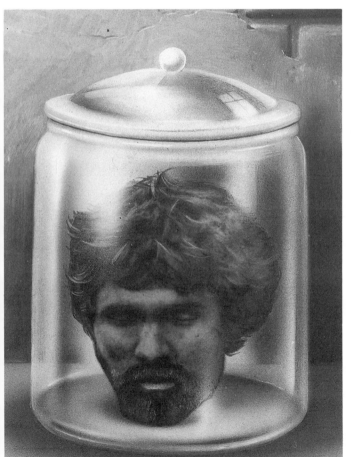

Above: Yuma, Arizona, as it appeared when the body of Chavez was brought into town. *From an original stereo view in author's collection.*

Left: This is thought to be the head of Chavez as it appeared when being displayed in various areas of California. *From author's collection, print obtained from Vincent Mercaldo.*

Although there was no immediate money available to pay the reward, on March 2, 1878, a warrant in the amount of $2,199.42 was issued to Roberts, Raggio and Colvig.

Various stories of the bandit's survival were current for some time after his death, but there was little real doubt that the head was genuine. An article in the San Diego *Union* in December of 1875 was particularly sad:

> The mother of Chavez resides in Hollister and when informed of the death of her son at the hands of the Raggio brothers, said she had no doubt it was true as the Raggio boys were brought up in San Juan with Chavez and knew him well...the old lady wept over the death of her misguided son, but said she would rather he should die in this way than be dragged over the state and then hanged as Vasquez was.

A purported photograph of the bandit's head survives, but the final disposition of the terrible trophy is not known.

PRINCIPAL SOURCES ───────────────

Greenwood, Robert, *The California Outlaw, Tiburcio Vasquez,* Los Gatos, Talisman Press, 1960; Hoffer, Dominga L. Cervantes, *Tiburcio Vasquez — Bandit,* Puyallup, Wash., Historic Memories Press, 1964; Nadeau, Remi, *City Makers,* N.Y., Doubleday & Co., 1948; San Francisco *Daily Alta California,* Mar. 21, Apr. 12, 1875, May 20, 1876; San Francisco *Bulletin,* Feb. 11, 1875; San Francisco *Daily Morning Call,* Jan. 11, 1876; San Francisco *Chronicle,* Mar. 20, 21, 24, 27, Apr. 11, 1875; Visalia *Weekly Delta,* Feb. 18, 25, 1875; Yuma *Sentinel,* Dec. 4, 1875; San Diego *Union,* Nov. 28, Dec. 4, 24, 1875; California State Archives, Sacramento.

LAFAYETTE CHOISSER
(Punch)

Punch Choisser was as good a lawman as old Mariposa ever knew, but it hadn't always been the case. *Courtesy John Condrey.*

Of French descent, Lafayette "Punch" Choisser was born on October 22, 1834, in Saline County, Illinois. He was a high-spirited youth and at the age of 15 he and his brother Talleyrand, ran away from home and joined the gold rush to California. They arrived at the Bear Valley headquarters of General Fremont in 1849 and engaged in local mining.

Far from home and civilizing influences, the Choisser brothers drifted into bad company. Punch apparently mined and worked at odd jobs, but by the time he was 20, saloons and gambling halls were getting a good deal of his attention. When bad-man Sam Brown and a partner named Bunty Owens killed two Chilenos over a Monte game in a small Calaveras County mining camp in June of 1855, they fled with a crowd of the dead men's friends at their heels. After killing one of the pursuing mob, Brown and Owens sought shelter at a friend's cabin where they were captured by Deputy Sheriff Ben Thorn. The killers were tried before a local justice of the peace, the two Choisser brothers being present as witnesses for Brown. After the hearing, Lafayette tried to slip a loaded pistol to Brown, but Thorn intercepted the move and knocked Choisser to the floor. Brown received a term at San Quentin, while Punch and his brother drifted back to Mariposa County.

Just how he acquired his nickname "Punch" is not known, but Choisser was known by that name when the following article appeared in the Mariposa *Democrat* on October 29, 1857:

> FATAL SHOOTING AFFAIR—...On Sunday last a man named "Punch" entered a saloon kept by a man named Joseph Bigler, and asked for liquor which was served to him. After drinking he was walking away from the bar without paying for the liquor when Bigler asked for the money. Some angry words then passed between Bigler and Punch, when the latter struck the

former on the head with his pistol. After some further altercation, Punch went out, in a moment returned and in the scuffle which ensued, Bigler was shot with a pistol in the hands of Punch. The ball entered the right breast and passed out the left side, causing death in about twenty minutes...

Bigler's Bear Valley saloon was near Mariposa and the shooting caused considerable excitement. There was much trouble and litigation over the Fremont mining properties and estate at that time and other accounts of the incident state that an argument over these matters had been the cause of an accidental shooting. Whatever happened, Bigler had been a popular family man and Punch thought it best to make himself scarce for awhile. He was captured by Sheriff J.D. Crippen late the following month, however, and lodged in the Mariposa County jail. There were lynching rumors, but Punch safely languished in his cell before commencing his trial. He was convicted of manslaughter and on July 24, 1858, was sentenced to five years at the state prison.

Choisser was received at San Quentin on November 7th as prisoner No. 1508. He is described in the register as a farmer, aged 24 and 5'3½" tall. His attorney was applying for a pardon as early as May of 1859 and petitions were being circulated by Talleyrand. Bearing the signatures of many Mariposa residents, including the judge who sentenced him and officials at the state prison, the petitions finally paid off. Punch was pardoned on May 3, 1861 on condition that he leave the state "where his associations are likely to tempt him to evil-doing," noted the judge who had tried him.

Back home in Illinois, Punch must have realized he had a second chance and took advantage of it. He worked in a photography studio for some years and was married in July of 1865. He never forgot the West, however. Talleyrand wrote frequently and described his activities in the early oil development in the San Joaquin Valley. In the spring of 1871 Punch brought his wife and children back to Bear Valley where they established their home.

Talleyrand was killed in an accident in the summer of 1872. Punch kept busy at mining and ranching, but in the mid-1870's he joined the staff of Sheriff John C. Clark as a deputy. In early May of 1878 a rancher living some nine miles from Mariposa was shot and killed as he worked about his home. The following month a local Indian named Willie Ross was captured as he prowled suspiciously around another rancher's cabin. Brought to town and lodged in jail, Ross was a prime suspect in several recent murders and robberies since he had a local criminal record.

A vigilante organization had been formed after this latest murder. Calling themselves the Chowchilla Rangers they looked in vain for clues to the crime and during the election of June 19th they tried to break down the jail door and lynch the prisoner. The sheriff and district attorney were finally able to disperse the rangers and restore order.

Ross was tried and convicted the following January on purely circumstantial

A portion of the town of Mariposa as it looked at the time of the Willie Ross excitement. *From Mariposa Historical Society.*

evidence. Terrorized by the rangers, Willie finally confessed and the sheriff asked for an immediate sentencing to avoid any more trouble. Chowchilla Rangers lined the corridors leading from the courthouse, but Sheriff Clark had Punch pick up the prisoner through an outside window. Riding his own "Black Bess," Choisser settled Ross in the saddle of another horse and galloped out of town before the rangers knew what was happening. A light snow was falling as the two riders headed for Merced where they would catch the train for San Quentin. The rangers, composed of E.G. Laird, his two sons, John Hale, Charlie Grow and others, quickly realized what had happened as chronicled in the Mariposa *Gazette* on January 29, 1879:

> ...Then commences a rustling and running in all directions, some to convey the intelligence, others for the horses of those who were bent upon pursuit and shedding the blood of the Indian. About twenty minutes after the departure of the deputy sheriff and his prisoner, the parties who were seeking the life of the Indian dashed by the courthouse, mounted on the best horses in the county...

91

Punch and his prisoner rode for their lives. Once the pursuers caught sight of their quarry and fired several times, but without effect. The deputy obtained fresh horses at Hornitos and told the liveryman to stall the pursuers as best he could. He made the forty-five mile ride to Merced in the record time of four hours. Most of the pursuing rangers gave up the chase, but the leader galloped up to the Merced jail door just fifteen minutes after Punch had lodged Ross safely in a cell. The two left for San Francisco on the six o'clock train the following morning and were interviewed upon arrival by a *Chronicle* reporter. After detailing circumstances of the case, Punch discoursed on the Chowchilla Rangers:

> ...This body of men, Mr. Choisser said, controlled the upper portion of Mariposa County and made it one of their duties to punish perpetrators of crime by driving them out of their district. The society was a secret one and composed of all the wealthy landowners in that part of the county...
>
> Mr. Choisser stated that these rangers were so determined to catch Ross that many of them before they started on the pursuit made their wills not knowing what would be the result of the chase...

Punch was the hero of the hour, even though in the scramble to leave he had rushed off without Willy's committment papers. He returned home a few days later, just in time for the appalling climax to his brave ride. Laird, a prominent rancher with property in both Mariposa and Merced Counties, had brooded bitterly over the escape of Willy Ross. He and the other rangers were convinced that Ross and other Indians were responsible for various crimes and terrorism in the area and they determined to do something about it. On Sunday morning, January 26th, a group of rangers rode over to the Indian camp about five miles below town. After a series of screams, shouts and gunshots, the rangers galloped off into the surrounding hills. In the camp three young Indians named Sam, Charlie and Amos lay dead. "Close by," noted the account in the *Gazette,* "was an old decrepit Indian about seventy years of age who had been hung up by a rope til dead...[He was] said to be the father of Willie Ross."

A coroner's jury found that the Indians came to their death at the hands of Laird, his two sons and others of the rangers. Some of Laird's men had actually gone to church after the massacre to establish alibis!

Sheriff Clark and another deputy went about rounding up the rangers, while Punch and a deputy named French sought Laird and his sons in Merced County. Sheriff A.J. Meany of Merced County helped trace Laird to Mormon Bar where he and his sons had driven a herd of hogs. When Laird walked up to the hotel where his sons were staying, Meany stepped out on the porch to greet him. As the rancher turned to flee, Punch and Deputy French made their appearance to block his way.

District Attorney George Goucher felt sure of an easy conviction when Laird's trial began in late April of 1879. He had five Indian witnesses who had seen the murders committed. Even when the noted attorney David Terry joined the defense staff, Goucher only smiled. When the defense objected to the witnesses on the grounds that they did not understand the nature of an oath, Goucher was startled. When the judge sustained the objection, Goucher's case went out the window. The jury brought in a verdict of not guilty and all the rangers went free.

Punch gave up his deputy's star some time later and went to work for a large Mariposa mining corporation. Later he served as assistant superintendent of the Mariposa Grant. On November 17, 1884, his horse returned riderless to his Bear Valley home. A young son went out to see what happened and found his father's body in the Merced River Canyon. There were two large gashes in his head.

A coroner's jury on November 21st was unable to establish just how Choisser had come to his death. Strangely enough, when Punch's son had returned home after finding the body, a neighbor named Maurice Newman volunteered to ride to Mariposa for the doctor. Newman was the second husband of Margaret Bigler, the widow of the saloon keeper Punch had shot and killed so long ago in 1857.

Willie Ross died in the San Quentin hospital in 1888.

PRINCIPAL SOURCES

Representative Citizens of Northern California, Chicago, Standard Genealogical Pub. Co., 1901; Chamberlain, Newell D., *The Call of Gold,* Mariposa, Gazette Press, 1936; San Joaquin Valley *Argus,* Jan. 26, Feb. 1, 8, 15, May 3, 1879; San Francisco *Chronicle,* Jan. 18, 1879; Mariposa *Democrat;* Oct. 29, Nov. 26, 1857; Merced *Express,* Feb. 8, 15, 1879; Mariposa *Gazette,* May 11, 15, 18, 22, 1878, Jan. 18, 25, Feb. 1, Apr. 6, 19, 1879, Nov. 22, 29, 1884; San Joaquin *Republican,* Nov. 24, 1857; Trial records in Mariposa County Courthouse, Mariposa; Correspondence with John B. Condrey, grandson of Lafayette Choisser, Dec., 1964; Prison records in California State Archives, Sacramento.

The grave of Punch Choisser as it appears today. *Photo by Dr. James Secrest.*

GEORGE C. CONTANT (SONTAG)

Minnesota was still Indian country when George Contant was born at Mankato in 1864. His brother John had been born three years earlier and the two had grown up in the small town, later moving to a farm in the country. When their father died, the boys' mother re-married a man named Sontag, but George kept his original name. John left home and headed west in 1878, while George found employment as a mule skinner. Later he worked as a carriage painter and railroad brakeman, always spending all his free time in saloons and drifting ever further away from home influences. He was employed in a grocery store when he became infatuated with a young woman and embezzled some money. Tried and found guilty, George promptly found himself serving a ten year term in the Nebraska State Prison as inmate No. 828. He escaped while a trusty, but his mother prevailed upon him to return and finish his term. He was released in 1887.

Returning to Mankato, George married and went into the painting business. His brother John visited home in 1891 and told George that he and a friend named Chris Evans had robbed trains in the San Joaquin Valley of California. John soon returned to the West where he and Evans bungled a train robbery at Ceres on September 3, 1891, barely managing to escape capture. Shortly after this John returned again to Mankato where he and George made plans to rob a Chicago train in November of 1891. The robbery was successful, George claiming later that they obtained nearly $10,000, although another $100,000 had been overlooked in the express car.

Traveling to California, George met John's friend Chris Evans at Visalia. According to George's story he returned to Minnesota on business where Evans later joined him. The two men held up a train at Kasota Junction in June of 1892. They obtained no money in the robbery, but detectives were now on their trail and followed them back to the coast. In California George, John and Evans made plans to rob yet another train.

Shortly before midnight on August 3, 1892, Southern Pacific train No. 17 was stopped at a location near Collis, about 15 miles west of Fresno. George himself later told how the train was robbed:

> . . . John was lame and he was left with the team while we boarded the train. He drove the team back to the school house while we ran the train out and robbed the express car. I got off on the right hand side and shot three or four times; Chris got off on the left hand side and blew in the express car with dynamite bombs . . .

Upon his release from prison, George tried a number of jobs before deciding on a career in show business. Ultimately, he was a pioneer film producer. *From Contant's book,* A Pardoned Lifer.

After obtaining some $2,000 the trio drove off towards Fresno, John and Chris continuing on to Visalia while George followed on the train. Quite pleased with himself after the night's adventure, George began drinking and telling stories of the robbery, claiming to have talked to passengers on the trip to Visalia. In his cups he suggested that he knew even more of the events. Word of his babbling soon reached the ears of interested lawmen who began checking on Evans and John Sontag, also.

Picked up and grilled by a contingent of local officers, railroad and express detectives, George managed to keep his story reasonably straight. When two lawmen went out to the Evans home to pick up John and corroborate George's story, there was a shooting scrape and Evans and John fled to the mountains. The two lawmen, both wounded, rushed back to town and jailed George. That night Chris and John returned home and killed a deputy sheriff in another shootout, before returning to the mountains. After failing in an escape attempt, George was taken to Fresno where he was indicted and put on trial for the Collis robbery. George was a good looking prisoner and cut quite a figure in court as recorded in the *Republican* of October 26, 1892:

> George C. Contant . . . has achieved that kind of notoriety that is mistaken for chivalry by the average fool woman, and his path through imprisonment is being strewn with roses and choice samples of Fresno's fine fruit.
>
> George is a fine looking man and appears handsome by contrast with his homely attorneys and the unkissable counsel who appear on behalf of the people . . .
>
> Fresh fruit and fragrant flowers are sent to him every day. There is more fruit than one man can eat and more flowers than one man can smell, so the suspected train robber kindly divides these offerings of sympathy . . . among his fellow prisoners . . .

The trial lasted for five days and George was easily convicted on a mass of circumstantial evidence. Although not generally known, in trying to save

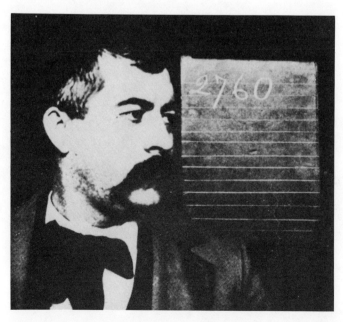

George Contant's prison mug shot shows him to have been a good looking rogue who easily attracted the ladies. *Courtesy California State Archives.*

Although made a few years later, this view of the Folsom quarry is just as it appeared during the Contant escape attempt. The convicts tried to escape up the rocky cliffs to the right, below the guard tower. *Courtesy California State Library.*

himself at one point he mentioned that he "had strong suspicion from the manner of my brother and Chris Evans that they were in the robbery. . ." In any case, George was sentenced to life imprisonment at Folsom State Prison.

Received at Folsom on November 3, 1892, George was listed as prisoner No. 2760. He was described as "age 28, painter, 5′9″, dark complexion, hazel eyes, dark hair with gray. . ." With his head shaved and wearing the striped convict's uniform, George's future looked grim indeed. Meanwhile he heard bits of news of his brother and Evans who were still at large in the mountains. They had killed two more lawmen in September and managed to elude posses all that winter. They were badly wounded and captured by a posse on June 10, 1893. Although losing an eye and arm as a result of his wounds, Evans recovered, but John died a painful death in the Fresno County jail on July 3, 1893.

Elderly Mrs. Sontag was in California now and had nursed John up to the time of his death. George dreaded her projected visit to Folsom, but he had already made his escape plans. A recently paroled convict named Fredericks had secreted two Winchesters, some cartridges, a pistol and a knife in the prison quarry. Fredericks then passed the word to George that everything was ready.

On June 27, 1893, Contant, Frank Williams, Anthony Dalton and several others obtained the guns in the quarry. Guard Frank Briarre was seized as a hostage and the convicts formed behind him and began moving away from the prison over a rocky ledge. Taking a desperate chance, Briarre jumped over the ledge, dragging one of the convicts with him. Although it was nearly a 75 foot drop, neither was hurt until Briarre slugged the dazed convict with a rock.

97

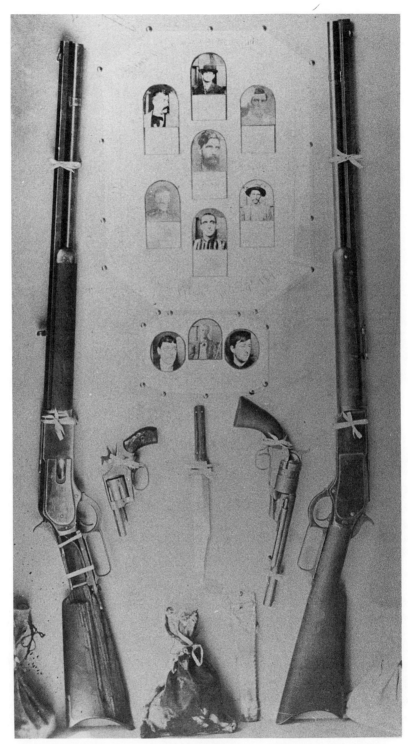

The guns used in the Contant break were displayed in the Folsom warden's office for many years. *Courtesy California State Library.*

Contant and the others were now exposed to the deadly Gatling gun tower and fire from the other guards. In a moment the rocky area was a hell of whining and richocheting bullets. Hiding as best they could in rocky crevices, the convicts returned the fire, but in less than an hour were shot to pieces. Warden Charles Aull was on the firing line and yelled for a cease fire when the convicts signalled a surrender. The San Francisco *Examiner* noted the bloody scene:

> ...When the firing ceased Sontag crawled out in the open more dead than alive, followed by Abbot. Neither of them could walk. The warden, Captain Murphy and several guards advanced towards them at once, when a ghastly spectacle met their view.
>
> Williams, Wilson and Dalton were dead in the hole, lying on top of each other, their bodies completely riddled with bullets.
>
> Sontag had been hit three times, in the thigh, the shinbone and the lower part of the body, each shot breaking bones...

George was badly wounded with some seven bullets in his body. It was at first thought he would die, but he rallied and slowly recovered. His mother visited the prison shortly after John had died. "If she keeps her reason after John's death," noted a newspaper, "it will be due to a wonderful mental vitality, for she gets no sleep and her eyes are like coals of fire..." When his mother told him she had been badly treated by the Evans family, George decided to blow the whistle on the whole train-robbing episode. Late in September he called in Warden Aull, J.B. Wright of the Southern Pacific and Jim Hume of Wells, Fargo. The wounded convict made a full confession of all he knew of the robberies. He also testified against Evans in court. The Fresno *Expositor* printed the full confession, along with George's stated reasons for "singing:"

> I realize the position I am in at the present time. I am all shot to pieces, my legs all wounded up and I have got a life sentence. I have got a family, my wife and two little children, destitute, that I think a good deal of.
>
> My mother came out here and these people slighted her in such a manner that I really cannot express myself as to how I feel about it...I have done what is right and I should ask a favor of you [and] I have the hopes that possibly you would assist me...

George seems to have genuinely seen the error of his ways and worked with friends to achieve his freedom. His sentence was finally commuted and he was discharged on March 20, 1908. After working at various jobs he eventually moved to San Bernardino where he found work as a painter. His small book, "A Pardoned Lifer," appeared in 1909 and he traveled on the lecture circuit speaking on the evils of crime and selling his publication. The Bakersfield *Echo* gave him a good review when he appeared there in 1914:

> Mr. Sontag gives a very interesting lecture entitled "The Folly of a Life of Crime," which is illustrated with numerous stereoptican views showing the train robberies, the chase...the hut that Evans and Sontag hid in for two days, the capture, life in Folsom...

99

When he lectured in Madera, the local paper commented that "Sontag is doing a good work and his lectures will have much to do with turning many a wayward boy from the path that leads to degradation and the prison."

George made a living from his lecture tours, but also saw the future of the new moving pictures. With others he formed the United States Feature Film Company and put together the story of Evans and the Sontag brothers. The film was made in 1914 around Chico and Oroville, rather than Visalia, with locals and George as the actors. Titled "The Folly of a Life of Crime," the film was first shown at an Oroville theater which "was filled for the first performance long before the hour at which a start was to be made at showing the picture," noted a press review. "And outside the theater was a big crowd that blockaded the sidewalk and overflowed into the street." Although first reviews were good, it was an amateur effort and couldn't compete with Dustin Farnum and the more sophisticated films being released.

Last notice of George was in 1928 when he signed his second wife's death certificate in San Francisco. He apparently died in the mid-1930's, one writer penning that his death was the ultimate result of a "loathsome disease."

PRINCIPAL SOURCES ———————————————————

Smith, Wallace, *Prodigal Sons,* Boston, Christopher Pub. House, 1951; Warner, Opie L., *A Pardoned Lifer,* San Bernardino, Index Print, 1909; San Francisco *Chronicle,* June 27, 1893; Oroville *Daily Register,* Aug. 22, 1914; Visalia *Delta,* June 29, 1893; Bakersfield *Echo,* Mar. 17, 1914; San Francisco *Examiner,* June 27, 1893; Fresno *Weekly Expositor,* Oct. 4, 1893; Madera *Mercury,* Mar. 19, 1910; Fresno *Morning Republican,* Oct. 26, 28, 30, 1892; Oct. 1, Dec. 2, 1893; Jan. 14, 1915; Correspondence with Troy Tuggle, King City, Cal.; Prison records in California State Archives, Sacramento.

A poster used during Contant's lecture tours.
Copied from the original in California State Library.

As the long-time sheriff of San Joaquin County, Tom Cunningham was respected as a tough lawman who treated his prisoners fairly. *Courtesy John Boessenecker.*

THOMAS CUNNINGHAM

The youngest of seven children, Thomas Cunningham was born in Ireland on August 17, 1838. Several sisters emigrated to America and when he was ten years old young Tom followed them to the new land. He was apprenticed to a brother-in-law in the harness-making business and worked at that trade in Brooklyn. In 1855 he came to California by steamer, arriving in San Francisco on June 16th. He went directly to Stockton where two of his sisters lived.

After working in the harness trade for several years, Cunningham went into business for himself in 1860. He was married the following year and became prominent in civic affairs. Besides being elected chief of the Stockton Fire Department during 1864-66, he served several terms as alderman, during which time his harness business thrived.

He was the Republican candidate for San Joaquin County sheriff in 1871 and after winning the general election, took office in March of 1872. Although the "harness-maker" was scorned by some as not lawman material, Cunningham quickly proved the doubters wrong. He was a tough enforcer of the law, but believed in humane treatment to all criminals and vowed never to take a life unless it was unavoidable. He was tough, but kind, and criminals learned they could trust him. Del Keagle, a deputy, later recalled how the sheriff seldom used a gun in making an arrest. "Mr. Cunningham just said, 'You come along with me,' and the man always came."

When the bandit Tiburcio Vasquez and his gang robbed various small villages and killed several people in 1873, he seemed immune to capture by local lawmen. In early January of 1874 California Governor Newton Booth summoned Alameda County Sheriff Harry Morse to his office. Morse was put in charge of an expedition to kill or capture Vasquez and the man selected to be his lieutenant was Tom Cunningham. With seven other possemen, Morse and Cunningham left Firebaugh's Ferry on March 13th to begin the manhunt. Nearly a month was spent searching the coast range and although much stolen stock was recovered, there was no word of their quarry. The company followed up every lead, crossing Kern County to Fort Tejon and covering much of that wild area. When Morse received word on where Vasquez was hiding, he informed the Los Angeles sheriff who dismissed the information as unreliable. After being out sixty-one days and traveling some 2,700 miles, the Morse party ended its campaign on May 12th. The Los Angeles sheriff later captured Vasquez, but Cunningham had proved himself a tough campaigner.

Stockton in the 1870's was a booming supply center for the mines and the thriving surrounding agricultural area. *Courtesy California State Library.*

In recognition of his participation in the Vasquez pursuit, Cunningham's friends presented him with a beautiful horse and a hand-tooled, silver-mounted saddle.

Prior to his taking office, Cunningham's county had been a haven for law-breakers and escaped convicts, but he promptly made it known that this was no longer the case. Always an active, hard-riding lawman, Cunningham was fast to join with other officers to track down criminals. He helped round up Bill Miner and his gang when they held up the Sonora-Milton stage in 1881 and he was prominent in the search for, and capture, of Black Bart in 1883.

When former State Supreme Court Justice David S. Terry was killed by Dave Neagle at Lathrop in August of 1889, Sheriff Cunningham played a minor role in resulting events. Neagle, a bodyguard hired to protect a federal judge who had been threatened by Terry, was held in the Stockton jail for some time. Cunningham journeyed to San Francisco to arrest Justice Stephen Field, the man Neagle had been protecting, but had to return empty-handed when the jurist posted a $5,000 bond.

A series of train robberies were initiated in the San Joaquin Valley beginning in 1889 and Sheriff Cunningham again rode tirelessly with the posses seeking the bandits. When a train was stopped at Ceres on September 3, 1891, Cunningham was promptly on the scene as noted in the Merced *Star* of the 10th:

> ...After making an excursion of the ground, Cunningham found the tracks
> of two horses leading toward the San Joaquin River. He followed them for
> about four miles and lost the trail in a field where there were loose horses...

After another train robbery at Collis in early August of 1892, two Visalia residents became prime suspects. Chris Evans and John Sontag were at the Evans home when two local lawmen tried to arrest them and were driven from the scene. The two suspects killed another deputy before fleeing to the nearby mountains. The Fresno *Republican* commented on the incident as follows:

> ...After the Collis train robbery Detective Thacker and Hickey and
> Sheriff Cunningham of Stockton traced the robbers to this city and before
> noon today Detective Will Smith asked Deputy Sheriff Witty to accompany
> him to Evans' home...
> The opinion is general that if Smith had waited until the arrival of Sheriff
> Cunningham and Detective Thacker the men would have been arrested...

Cunningham reportedly brought his new pair of bloodhounds down with him, but they proved to be more of a hindrance than help and the manhunt proceeded without them.

In early September of 1897 some railroad ties were placed on the track near Ripon in what was thought to be a robbery attempt. Cunningham suspected another holdup effort would be made and stationed several deputies aboard the express. When the train was again stopped on September 8th and the deputies investigated, they were fired on by several men hiding behind a fence. Returning the fire, the lawmen forced the would-be bandits to flee across a field where they quickly disappeared. Cunningham put together a posse and was soon on the scene. Stanislaus County Sheriff R.B. Purvis, along with Wells, Fargo detective Thacker and four others, made up the posse and promptly located the fugitive's trail. Forming two groups, Cunningham and his men pressed the chase from behind while Thacker's group headed them off. George Williams and George Schlagel were finally cornered in a field and captured without a fight. Both received life sentences in San Quentin.

Cunningham had numerous narrow escapes during his long career. Once he was returning to Stockton with a murderer named Winters. As the two men stepped off the train after dark, Winters dropped down and rolled under the car hoping the sheriff would run back over the platform to the other side. Instead, Cuningham dove after his prisoner and grabbed him by the collar. "They wrestled and twisted beneath the car," reported an account in the Stockton *Record.* "Had the train moved both of them would have been maimed or killed. The sheriff exerted his strength to drag Winters out. A moment after he rolled him from under the car, the train pulled out."

Another time the sheriff was pursuing an escaped convict named Lopez in a light buggy. He had instructed his driver to sharply turn the vehicle when they spotted their quarry so as to allow Cunningham to jump out and fight on foot. When they suddenly confronted the convict, however, the driver turned the wrong way and the lawman had to jump at the wrong time and fell to the ground. Undaunted, Cunningham rolled across the ground and came up shooting. He managed to kill the fugitive's horse, keeping Lopez too busy to shoot. In a moment the sheriff had his man shackled and in custody.

Sheriff Cunningham was a meticulous record keeper and by 1898 had a Rogues Gallery of criminal portraits numbering nearly 42,000, assembled at a cost of $10,000. In addition, his private museum at the sheriff's office contained over one thousand weapons and other articles of crime he had collected over the years. Fresno County Sheriff J.D. Collins toured the Stockton sheriff's office in August of 1899 when returning from a convention in San Francisco. The Fresno Morning *Republican* reported on the trip when the sheriff returned home:

> ...The sheriff's office in Stockton, owing to the efforts of ex-sheriff Cunningham, is one of the best regulated in the state. There is a complete record kept of every criminal in the state. Three sets of books are kept, all indexed so that any name can be turned to in a moment. A record of local offenders is kept, also of San Francisco crooks and then the San Quentin record...

When he retired after over 26 years of service in January of 1899, there was speculation that Cunningham intended opening a large private detective agency. "No," he told a reporter, "I have been fairly successful in my long career as sheriff and I do not intend to engage in the man-hunting business for private gain. There is a great deal of difference between being actuated by a sense of duty and a sense of personal gain."

Sheriff Cunningham and several deputies are shown in their Stockton office about 1895. *Courtesy Holt-Atherton Center for Western Studies, University of the Pacific.*

The old lawman was campaigning for a friend running for Congress when he was struck down by a fatal heart attack. He died at Tuttletown, Tuolumne County, on November 26, 1900, and is remembered as one of the very best of the old time peace officers.

PRINCIPAL SOURCES ——————————————————

Gilbert, Frank T., *History of San Joaquin County, California,* Oakland, Thompson & West, 1879; Greenwood, Robert, *The California Outlaw,* Los Gatos, Talisman Press, 1960; Tinkham, George Henry, *History of San Joaquin County, California,* Los Angeles, Historic Record Company, 1923; Benjamin, Theodosia, "Sheriff Thomas Cunningham," *San Joaquin Historian,* June, 1971; Ruse, R. Tod, "Thomas Cunningham, Man and Sheriff," *Valley Trails,* Dec., 1966; San Francisco *Daily Morning Call,* Nov. 4, 1883, Oct. 23, 1898; San Francisco *Chronicle,* Sep. 3, 15, Oct. 20, 1897; Stockton *Independent,* Nov. 27, 1900; Stockton *Daily Record,* Nov. 28, 1900; Fresno *Daily Republican,* Aug. 6, 1892, Mar. 28, 1899; Merced *Star,* Sept. 10, 1891; Wells Fargo History Room, San Francisco.

MASON FRAKES DALTON
(Bill)

He should have been an honest rancher and family man, but the happy-go-lucky Bill Dalton had a darker destiny. *Courtesy Western History Collections, University of Oklahoma Library.*

Lewis Dalton married Adeline Younger in Jackson County, Missouri on March 12, 1851. Dalton kept a saloon for a time and usually had a piece of land to farm, but most of his life was spent roaming the country as a horse race promoter. In between racing seasons he managed to father fifteen children, all of whom were raised by the mother. Two of the Dalton children died in infancy and all but three were boys.

Of the ten Dalton boys, Ben, Lewis and Cole were the oldest. Littleton was born in 1857, Grattan in 1861 with Mason—known to history as Bill—arriving in 1863. Franklin was born next and Robert in 1869. In 1871 Emmett was born at Belton, Missouri, while the youngest, Simon, came along in 1878. All this time the family kept on the move, finally settling in the Indian Territory.

Lewis Dalton began taking his older boys along on his racing circuit and in 1877 took Ben, Cole and Frank with him when he covered California's great San Joaquin Valley. Ben stayed and went to work skinning mules. Littleton and Frank came out in April of 1878 and went to work on farms, while Grat followed in 1880. When the father brought Emmett to California for the first time in 1887, he found Littleton running a saloon in San Miguel, near where brother Bill was renting farm land in the Cholame Valley.

Bill was the talker of the family—some said he had even attended college at one time. If he had it did not do him much good. He had traveled with his father, worked the mines in Montana, then in 1881 returned to California. He obtained

106

work as a farm hand when he returned for good in 1884, working for the Bliven ranch in Merced County. Later, he had married the boss's daughter Jane, and went into partnership with his brother-in-law, Clark Bliven in 1887. Their property adjoined each other on the Estrella River, near San Miguel.

Bill worked hard to prove himself on his small farm. Jane's parents had been against the marriage and had wanted something better for their daughter than a drifter ranch foreman. Nevertheless, the father had given Bill some good horses and cows to start with and Bill planned to buy his rented land as soon as the property started paying. Meanwhile his love of talk led him into politics and he became active in the Democratic Party in Merced County and in San Miguel.

Some of the other Dalton boys returned to Indian Territory. Frank became a deputy U.S. marshal and was killed in the line of duty in 1887. Grat, Bob, and Emmett followed in their lawman brother's footsteps, but found sidelines such as rustling more profitable. When they pushed their luck too far they had to flee to California in late 1890. Grat, Bob and Emmett all stayed at Bill's small cabin but did little work and drank heavily in the saloons of San Miguel, Paso Robles and San Luis Obispo.

When the boys went through their rustling money, they began talking about robbing a train. Cole and Bill tried to talk sense to their brothers, but Lit advised them to stay clear of Bob, Grat and Emmett or they would be dragged down with them. Bill managed to get them a job on another ranch and in lieu of wages gave them two of his own work horses. The boys rode off, but not to work on a ranch. The Visalia Weekly *Delta* of February 12, 1891 devoted three, front page columns to Bob and Emmett's "work":

Littleton Dalton did all he could to straighten out his brothers, but knew when to give up before they dragged him down with them. Lit spent most of his life in California, passing away in 1942. *Courtesy California State Library.*

107

> South-bound Southern Pacific train No. 17 was held up about one mile south of Alila last Friday night at about eight o'clock. The train robbers' bold attempt to rob the train was frustrated by the warm reception accorded them by Express Messenger Haswell. In the fusilade of shots, Fireman Radcliffe was mortally wounded and died the next day. The train robbers surprised by the bold resistance, gave up the attempt and mounted their horses and disappeared...

> Sheriff Kay of Tulare County and Sheriff Borgwardt of Kern, accompanied by a large posse, left Saturday in hot pursuit of the train robbers...

The boys had been drinking heavily at the time of the robbery, with Grat scouting for them and Bob and Emmett staging the holdup. Emmett later admitted shooting the fireman. They left plenty of clues, but because of disagreements among the lawmen as how best to proceed, the outlaws were able to safely return to Bill's ranch. One of the lawmen remembered that "the robbers rode good horses which were not shod, and their tracks were easily followed... If the advice of Sheriff Kay had been followed and a posse sent by train to Huron that night, the fellows could have been headed off before they got into the hills..."

When the San Luis Obispo County sheriff and railroad detective Will Smith visited Bill on the chance he was harboring his suspected brothers, they wound up spending the night there. Bob and Emmett were safely hidden away in the attic above them. As soon as the lawmen departed the next day, Bill left to help spirit his brothers out of the state. Sheriff Kay and a deputy chased the two fugitives some 6,000 miles over seven states, but were finally compelled to return home empty-handed. Jane Dalton later recalled:

Grat Dalton saw much of the San Joaquin Valley of California, mostly from the windows of saloons in the railroad towns of the area. *Courtesy Special Collections, Library, California State University Fresno.*

A Southern Pacific train at Porterville in 1888, near the site of the Dalton robbery at Alila. *Courtesy Jeff Edwards Collection.*

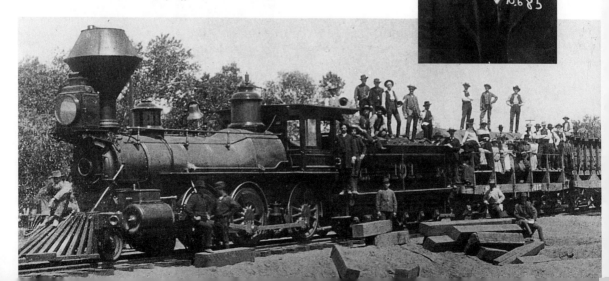

...He was gone two weeks and it seemed two years to me. I walked the floor night and day in anguish of anticipation. Perhaps he was dead, perhaps wounded or taken prisoner along with his brothers.

When the neighbors called I had to entertain them with smiles and light words while my heart was breaking. They were not to know why he was absent. I could not write home about my trouble, for I had not pleased my parents in my choice of a husband and my pride kept me from seeking their consolation.

Bill no sooner returned home than he was arrested and indicted, along with Bob, Grat and Emmett, for the Alila robbery. Grat stood trial in June of 1891 and was convicted, while Bill managed to be acquitted at his trial the following October. The boys' mother came out from Indian Territory with some $2,000 she had managed to scrape up to help with attorney's fees. But as Jane Dalton later recalled, this was only the beginning:

These court proceedings continued for one year. In the meantime farming implements, household furniture and the stock—a wedding present from father—had been sold at a sacrifice to pay the lawyer's fees. Nothing was left...

Bill was out on bail when another train was robbed on September 3, 1891. He and a companion named Riley Dean were armed and acting suspiciously when captured by Sheriff Eugene Kay a few days later at the old Cross Creek stage station. A week later they had just been released for lack of evidence when a reporter cornered Bill:

...Dalton was very willing to be interviewed, and by the way is a good talker. He is 32 years old, measures five feet eight inches and weighs 186 pounds. He is a fine-looking man and no one would take him for a train robber. When questioned as to the charge against him he at once replied:

"Of course I am innocent... Had I been guilty... and if I had the courage to stop a train or shoot a detective, do you for a moment believe I would have hesitated to kill both Sheriff Kay and Deputy Witty?... Emmett and Bob are somewhere, I don't know exactly, and it is said they held up trains on the Missouri, Kansas & Texas road... I don't pretend to defend them, but I tell you they are brave boys..."

When Bill's bondsmen withdrew he was once again slapped in the Visalia jail where Grat was being held pending his one-way trip to San Quentin. On the night of September 28th, Grat and two other prisoners escaped by sawing a window bar and replacing it with a blackened broomstick. Chris Evans, later a fugitive desperado himself, provided a waiting horse and Grat disappeared into the night. A $500 local reward was quickly coupled with a Wells, Fargo and Southern Pacific offer of $3,000 more. The fugitive Dalton had meanwhile holed up in the mountains east of Fresno. It was several months before Sheriff Kay learned where Grat was hiding.

A combined Tulare and Fresno County posse was searching a landmark now known as Dalton Mountain on December 23, 1891. Grat and Riley Dean were surprised by Fresno County Sheriff John Hensley and Deputy Ed McCardle on the side of the mountain and Dean was taken prisoner. When Grat appeared a moment later, McCardle remembered it the rest of his life:

> Dalton was carrying his Winchester rifle over his shoulder. He threw it forward and to his shoulder in one quick motion and fired instantly. I fired at almost the same instant. My bullet went over Dalton's head and whistled over the heads of the rest of the posse down the hill. The bullet from Dalton's rifle entered the oak tree about six inches from, and above, my face.

Grat had had enough of California. He promptly headed for the Indian Territory to find his brothers. Cole went along with him, all the way trying to talk him out of joining his outlaw kinsmen. He could have saved his breath. On October 5, 1892, just a year after Bill's trial had begun for complicity in the Alila holdup, Grat and Bob Dalton were killed at Coffeeville, Kansas, while trying to rob two banks at the same time. Two other gang members were killed also, while Emmett was badly wounded and captured.

Back in California Bill Dalton had been acquitted of the Alila charge, but it was a hollow victory. He had lost everything he owned and his neighbors now avoided him. Leaving his wife and two children with her brother, Bill visited his mother in Indian Territory and began seeing more and more of Bob, Grat and Emmett. When his brothers were killed at Coffeeville, Bill began riding with Bill Doolin, George Newcomb and other notorious outlaws. He brought his family to Kingfisher and tried to farm nearby, but he often left on mysterious trips. When she read about various robberies, Jane Dalton probably guessed the truth. "If I had but known," she recalled sadly, "the life he intended to follow when he sent for me to join him, I would have remained here [California], not because I did not love him, but because of that love which I knew would have brought him back to us some day."

Grat and Bill Dalton both did time in the Tulare County jail at Visalia. Grat escaped during his term, then fled the state to his date with the grim reaper at Coffeyville, Kansas. *Courtesy Tulare County Historical Society.*

SOUTHERN PACIFIC COMPANY.

(PACIFIC SYSTEM.)

$3,000 REWARD.

Supplementing circular letter of W. E. Hickey, Special Officer S. P. Co., dated San Francisco, Feb. 26, 1891, wherein is offered a reward of $5,000 for the arrest and conviction of all parties concerned in the attempted robbery of train No. 17, on the night of Feb. 6th, 1891.

The Grand Jury of Tulare County have indicted **Bob and Emmett Dalton** as principals in said crime, and William Marion Dalton and Gratton (or Grafton) Dalton, as accessories; the two latter named being now in jail in Tulare County awaiting trial.

The Southern Pacific Company hereby withdraw said general reward in regard to Bob and Emmett Dalton, and in lieu thereof offer to pay $1,500 each for the *arrest* of said Bob and Emmet Dalton, described below, upon *their delivery to a duly authorized Agent or representative of the State of California, at any jail in any of the States or Territories of the United States.*

In addition to the foregoing, the State and Wells, Fargo & Co. have each a *standing reward of $300* for the arrest and conviction of each such offender.

About 8 o'clock in the evening of Feb. 6th, 1891, two armed men attempted, unsuccessfully, to rob the south-bound train, No. 17, near Alila, Tulare Co., California. The Express Messenger offered a gallant resistance, and during the interchange of shots the fireman, G. W. Radliff, received a wound, from the effects of which he died the following day.

It is now known that the attack was made by two brothers, viz: Bob and Emmet Dalton, described as follows:

BOB DALTON: About twenty-three years of age (but might be taken for 25); height, 6 ft. 1½ inches; well built and straight; light complexion, but florid and healthy looking; boyish beard and mustache; light hair and eyes; weight, 180 to 190 lbs.; large, bony, long fingered hands, showing no acquaintance with work; large nose and ears; white teeth; long, sunburned neck, square features. Was wearing square, box-toed, custom made, new, calfskin boots with morocco legs, size 8½. Is a good poker and card player; drinks whisky in moderation, but does not chew tobacco; smokes brown paper cigarettes occasionally.

EMMETT DALTON: Between 20 and 21 years of age; nearly 6 feet in height; weight, about 180 lbs.; well built; hair lighter than Bob's; no mustache nor whiskers; looks the counterpart of Bob; has scar on forehead, over eye; also plays cards and drinks in moderation, but does not use tobacco.

On the 2d inst. they left San Luis Obispo County, on horseback, and on the 8th disposed of their horses at Ludlow, a station on the A. & P. Railway, about 100 miles east of Mojave, and there took passage on an East-bound train, since which time no trace of them has been obtained.

The Daltons are brothers, and it is believed that Bob and Emmett came to California from Indian Territory in the latter part of 1890, and Grat. in January, 1891, and that they now have relations and friends in that region.

Any communications regarding them, addressed to E. W. Kay, Sheriff Tulare County, Visalia, Cal.; Jas. B. Hume, Special Officer, Wells, Fargo & Co., San Francisco, Cal., or the undersigned, will receive prompt attention, and if so desired, will be treated confidentially.

Railroad and Express Agents receiving a number of these circulars, are respectfully requested to place them in the hands of local officers, or citizens who will take an interest in the matter.

W. E. HICKEY,
Special Officer, S. P. Co., S. F.

San Francisco, March 26th, 1891.

After a series of robberies, a posse of marshals trapped the Doolin-Dalton gang in the village of Ingalls, Oklahoma. Bill killed Marshal Lafe Shadley when the gang shot its way clear, two other lawmen being killed in the fighting, also. Splitting off from Doolin, Bill led his own gang in a series of raids, culminating in the bloody bank robbery at Longview, Texas in late May of 1894. Piling their families in two covered wagons, Dalton and several gang members headed south seeking relief from the relentless posses. Stopping near Ardmore, Jane was sent into town to buy supplies while Bill and the two children remained at a secluded cabin. But the outlaws had already been located. Lawmen surrounded the place and Bill was killed as he tried to flee on June 8, 1894. The last of the outlaw Daltons was taken home to California by his wife who was interviewed by a Fresno *Expositor* reporter on the last leg of the train trip:

Mrs. Dalton received an *Expositor* reporter this morning. She wore the sombre dress of the mourning. It was her face, however, that told the story of her sorrow. Its lines were mute witnesses, more powerful than words, that the man whose body she was bringing to her home to be buried was no other than the notorious outlaw...

Mrs. Dalton will live with her people. She has no connections in the Indian Territory now that her husband is dead, and has returned to her old home in Merced County. The funeral of Dalton will be held tomorrow.

Dalton was buried at the Bliven home in Livingston. Jane later remarried a childhood friend who helped raise her two young children. Emmett Dalton, after spending many years in prison, died in Los Angeles on July 13, 1937. He had been much more successful selling real estate than he and his outlaw brothers had ever been during their career of crime.

PRINCIPAL SOURCES

Dalton, Emmett, *When the Daltons Rode,* N.Y., Doubleday, Doran & Co., Inc., 1931; Latta, Frank F., *Dalton Gang Days,* Santa Cruz, Bear State Books, 1976; McCullogh, Harrell, *Selden Lindsey, U.S. Deputy Marshal,* Oklahoma City, Paragon Publishing, 1990; Samuelson, Nancy, *The Dalton Gang Family,* privately published by the author, 1989; San Francisco *Call,* Feb. 5, 1899; San Francisco *Chronicle,* March 20, 1896; Visalia Weekly *Delta,* Feb. 12, 19, 1891; Fresno Daily Morning *Expositor,* Sept. 7, 14, 1891, June 18, 1894; Tulare *Register,* Sept. 28, 1891; Fresno Morning *Republican,* Dec. 25, 1931; Merced *Star,* Sept. 10, Oct. 1, 1891, June 14, 1894.

Bill Dalton in death. *Courtesy Western History Collections, University of Oklahoma Library.*

112

CHARLES H. DORSEY

Charley Dorsey—alias Thorne, alias Moore, alias George Lee, and half a dozen other aliases— was one of the most dangerous highwaymen of old California. *Courtesy John Boessenecker Collection.*

"I was born in Kentucky in 1841," stated Charles Dorsey in an interview in 1890. "My parents were well-to-do people. From birth I was a victim of circumstances, a creature of fate, a victim for other people to make money on. I was a boy on my father's farm when the war broke out and entered the rebel army with a gang of raiders. After serving four years, during which time my two brothers were killed and my father's home broken up, I came to California in 1865, without a trade, money or friends." Falling in with bad company, Dorsey was arrested on a burglary rap in Nevada County and sent up for two years at San Quentin. He served several other prison terms and at various times used the names Charles H. Thorn, Dorsey and A.D. Moore. "My true name," he once stated, "I have never divulged."

Dorsey undoubtedly met John C. Collins, alias Patterson, sometime in the late 1870s when both were doing time in prison. When he was discharged in early 1879, Dorsey kept in touch with his new pal. After Collins' release in May of that same year, the two met near Marysville and looked about for opportunities. Together with a notorious ex-convict named Jim Crumm, they held up a stage in Tuolumne County, but Crumm didn't trust his partners and soon disappeared. Dorsey and Collins set up a camp near Grass Valley close to the home of another ex-con named Ben Frazee. Pretending to be camping outdoors for their health, the two plotted another holdup.

On September 1, 1879 the Eureka stage was coming down from Moore's Flat with ten passengers. About three and one half miles from Nevada City a masked man stepped into the road and shouted for the driver to stop. As the coach pulled up, another masked man holding a shotgun appeared, also. The passengers were told to get out and line up in the road while Collins proceeded to search the coach. The last article found was a leather valise under a seat.

113

John C.P. Collins was Dorsey's partner during the robbery in which Cummings was killed. Later Collins would die for the murder Dorsey had committed. *From San Francisco Police mug book, courtesy Special Collections, Library, California State University Fresno.*

Banker William Cummings had been riding next to the driver. He was lined up with the others when the valise was discovered and grabbed it as Collins dragged it from the vehicle. "That's mine," he shouted. "It's all I have and you can't have it!" As the two men struggled for the valise, Collins' pistol was discharged and the two fell to the ground. Dorsey then stepped forward and as Cummings scrambled to his feet the bandit shot him in the neck, killing him instantly. Proceeding to rob the passengers, the highwaymen then ordered the coach to move on. Cummings was left lying in the road. He had died for a bar of gold worth some $6,700. Under the heading, "An Awful Crime," the Grass Valley *Union* reported:

Banker William Cummings was brutally murdered by Dorsey during a robbery near Nevada City, California. *Courtesy California State Library.*

...As soon as the stage arrived in town...Sheriff Montgomery rallied an armed force of thirty or forty citizens and followed. Telegrams reporting the deed were sent to all parts of the adjacent country so that the people might be on the lookout and...arrest the highwaymen who will be made short work of if captured...

Rewards totaling more than $5,000 were quickly placed on the bandit's heads as Dorsey and Collins split up to make tracking more difficult. In a few days Dorsey returned to Frazee's house with a shotgun he had borrowed. Collins

REWARD!

STATE OF CALIFORNIA,
EXECUTIVE DEPARTMENT.

WHEREAS, on the first day of December, A. D. 1887, one

C. H. THORN, alias DORSEY,

Sentenced to life imprisonment from Nevada County, State of California, for murder in the first degree, succeeded in escaping from the State Prison, at San Quentin.

Now, therefore, I, R. W. Waterman, Governor of the State of California, by virtue of the authority in me vested by the Constitution and laws of this State, do hereby offer a reward of

Three Hundred Dollars

For the re-arrest and delivery to the Warden of the State Prison, at San Quentin, of the said C. H. THORN, alias DORSEY.

IN WITNESS WHEREOF, I have hereunto set my hand and caused the Great Seal of the State to be hereunto affixed this third day of December, A. D. 1887.

[SEAL.]

R. W. WATERMAN,
Governor of California.

By the Governor:
W. C. HENDRICKS, Secretary of State.
By H. B. DAVIDSON, Deputy.

DESCRIPTION:

Age, forty-four years; five feet ten and five-eighths inches in height; brown, almost black, eyes; square features; very prominent, high cheek bones; pale, florid complexion; dark, straight hair; prominent, projecting forehead; cheeks noticeably hollow; has the appearance of having Indian blood in him.

Courtesy California State Archives.

appeared some time later and after asking about his partner, soon left. The two met later near Sacramento and from there traveled east to New Orleans. In the Crescent City Collins deposited some of the bullion at the U.S. Mint after melting down the gold bar. The two then traveled to Louisville, Kentucky, where they posed as miners from Arizona. Here more of the bullion was deposited and exchanged for coins. After dividing their spoils, the outlaws separated. Collins traveled around the country for a time, while Dorsey settled in Union City, Indiana. He attracted attention in town when he obtained change for a $1,000 bill in one of the local banks. The action had the desired result and Dorsey was soon a partner in a saloon and lumber business.

In the summer of 1882 Collins was picked up on a felony charge in St. Louis, Missouri. He was later convicted and while still in jail on appeal, talked too much to one Roger O'Meara, a former San Quentin cellmate. O'Meara told the police that Collins had admitted participating in a stage robbery and murder in California. A photograph of the prisoner was forwarded to San Francisco where it was compared to a police mug shot of Collins in the collection of Detective Captain Isaiah Lees. After meeting with Wells, Fargo detective Charles Aull, Lees and his fellow lawman agreed that the St. Louis prisoner might very well be one of the men involved in the Cummings murder. They traveled to St. Louis and were convinced they had the right man.

When Lees and Aull discovered that a "lawyer" named C.P. Thorn had provided depositions containing alibis for Collins, they smelled a rat. Thorn lived in Union City, Indiana and the two lawmen went there with results that were chronicled in the Union City *Times* of October 7, 1882:

> Quite the furor was raised in our usually quiet city last Monday morning at the arrest of Chas. Thorne, partner of Moses Murphy, by two strangers... The arrest was made by Capt. Charles Aull, special officer of Wells Fargo & Co's Express, assisted by Capt. I.W. Lees, Chief of the Detective force of San Francisco. They found Charley eating his breakfast at Branham's restaurant...

The two fugitives were brought back to California in mid-October of 1882, Aull escorting his prisoners to Nevada City. By now a great mass of circumstantial evidence had been gathered by the detectives and local officers were confident of obtaining convictions. The Grass Valley *Union* was impressed by the work:

> The history of this crime, the disappearance of the criminals and their discovery after three years of time, is a strange chapter of criminal history, and the manner in which the case has been worked up by Aull and Lees is one of the most creditable pieces of detective skill of the time...

The two outlaws were tried and convicted the following February, Dorsey managing to escape the murder charge. "One of the jurymen was a soldier with me in the rebel army," he later recalled, "and he held out against the other eleven jurors and thus saved my neck." His partner was not so lucky. Although Dorsey had killed Cummings, Collins was convicted and hanged for the murder at Nevada City on February 1, 1884. Apparently Dorsey's counsel had little feeling for his client as noticed in the *Union:*

> The counsel for the prisoner did not appear to feel much sympathy for their client, as Judge Tyler refused to go into court to hear the verdict of the jury, and is said to have expressed the opinion that he was a scoundrel who deserved to be hanged on general principles...

Dorsey entered San Quentin again on March 15, 1883, to begin serving his life sentence. His record describes him as No. 10760, "...Age, 40; occupation, laborer; height, 5'10½"; complexion, florid; brown eyes and dark hair..." Detective Aull, Dorsey's nemesis, had since been appointed deputy warden of the prison. When Dorsey and several confederates were discovered trying to tunnel out of the hospital building in October of 1885, Aull quickly rounded them up. The San Francisco *Chronicle* reported the aftermath of the plot:

Dorsey spent a good portion of his life in San Quentin prison. Shown here is the front entrance as it appeared in the 1890's. *Courtesy California State Library.*

... Dorsey was taken out afterwards and when questioned took the whole blame upon himself for leading the others into the scheme. He exonerated Sullivan of any participation in the proposed escape and then suddenly sat down on a bench in the room. He bitterly said that he was tired of living, as he had no hope of ever being released, and he preferred being killed while attempting to escape to serving his sentence until death came to his relief. He suddenly sprang from his seat and made a threatening gesture [but] ...the officials saw that the hostile movement was made in the belief that someone would shoot him, and Dorsey was disappointed when he was led off to the cell.

Although he made friends with the noted Black Bart, Dorsey became particulary chummy with a train-wrecker named George Shinn, a trusty. Shinn was allowed to take a cart outside the prison and on the night of December 1, 1887, his tarpulin-covered vehicle passed through the gate with Dorsey hidden in the bed. The two stole a boat and made their way to Sacramento after suffering terribly in the bitter, cold weather. Eventually they made their way to Chicago where they posed as rug cleaners as a means of appraising robbery sites. They also made frequent trips back to California where they committed numerous robberies and stage holdups. Dorsey reportedly shot and wounded a Sacramento saloon owner during one robbery.

By a particularly strange quirk of fate, Roger O'Meara was in Chicago one day when he recognized Dorsey on the street. Not being satisfied with his treatment by the officers after the St. Louis affair, O'Meara wrote a letter to the Nevada County *Transcript* and told of seeing Dorsey. The letter was called to the attention of Jim Hume, chief of the Wells, Fargo detectives, who left as soon as possible for the Windy City. With the aid of William Pinkerton and a half dozen operatives, the two desperadoes were soon captured and behind bars. Returning to California, the officers and their prisoners were interviewed by a Sacramento *Union* reporter who published an interesting description of Dorsey:

His face is one of a thousand. High cheek bones, lantern jaws, stiff and stubby gray mustache and sunken cheeks, all give him a repulsive, yet strangely attractive expression. The eyes, though, are the greatest features. They are almost coal black and very deep set. They appear to be constantly on the alert for some approaching danger and are never at ease. Dorsey is fully six feet in height, broad-shouldered and muscular looking. He is unusually intelligent...

Shinn was remanded to Folsom Prison where he later confessed to all the duo's crimes since their escape. Returned to San Quentin on October 26, 1890, Dorsey was given his old prison number of 10760. He was both philosophical and despondent while talking to a *Chronicle* reporter at the prison:

...I have nothing left on God's green earth but a bad name. I have no money, not even a ten cent piece to rattle on a tombstone...I'm an old man now, and all broke down; I'm buried...There's nothing in stealing. Of all things that is the poorest. I learned this truth only too late in life. By the gods, a man once down in life is down for all time, and nothing can stem the tide of fate that's turned against him.

Settling back into prison life, Dorsey began casting about for another escape opportunity. He had many friends in San Quentin and was delighted to learn of an escape plot from Mickey Delaney, a burglar he had once worked with. There were five other cons in on the plan; Bill Hanlon and Harry Manning, two stage robbers, Abraham Turcott and James Sullivan, both murderers, and another burglar named George Ross. The plan had possibilities. Sullivan had a brother living in Watsonville who was to give some guns to another convict who worked at the prison physician's home just outside the San Quentin grounds. This was done and the five pistols, along with a quantity of ammunition was smuggled into the prison in buckets of milk. The guns were hidden under the floor of the carpenter's shop. Delaney was now to pick his cell lock late at night and release the other conspirators. Warden William Hale learned of the break from convict informants in early September of 1891. The plotters were searched out and all found themselves in solitary on bread and water. Dorsey refused to divulge any details of the plot, but after four weeks in solitary Turcott finally led the officers to the guns. Dorsey resigned himself to his prison life after this.

Fremont Older, editor of the San Francisco *Bulletin,* toured San Quentin in 1911 where he was introduced to Dorsey. "He was the official 'spieler' for the gallows," recalled the editor, "and when the warden and I entered the death room 'Old Charlie,' as he was called, stepped forward to entertain me with the details of how men were hanged. He was an impressive figure—tall, erect, with a military bearing..." To Older's questions as to whether the old convict would be safe outside, the warden responded, "If Old Charlie gave me his word, I'd trust him to go around the world with a million dollars. I'd know he would bring it back, every cent of it."

Older used his influence to obtain Dorsey's parole in December of 1911. The editor liked the old man and put him to work on his ranch. Later the ex-convict worked in a San Francisco park where he finally retired with a small pension. According to Older he had worked hard, saved his money and was able to leave a few thousand dollars to friends who took care of him in his last illness. He is thought to have died in Los Angeles about 1932. Old Charlie had beaten his hard luck beginnings after all.

PRINCIPAL SOURCES ——————————————

Dillon, Richard, *Wells, Fargo Detective,* N.Y., Coward-McCann, Inc., 1969; Older, Fremont, *My Own Story,* San Francisco, Call Pub. Co., 1919; Unidentified clipping of Fremont Older article in author's collection; St. Louis (Missouri) *Republican,* Sept. 23, 1881; Union City (Indiana) *Times,* Oct. 7, 1882; Nevada City *Daily Transcript,* Nov. 1, 1885, Oct. 16, 18, 19, 29, 30, 1890; Grass Valley *Union,* Sept. 2, 3, 4, 7, 18, 1879, Oct. 4, 1882, Feb. 17, 20, 27, Mar. 2, 3, 8, 10, 27, 1883, Feb. 2, 1884; Sacramento *Union,* Oct. 27, Nov. 2, 1890; prison records in California State Archives, Sacramento.

CHRISTOPHER EVANS

A newspaper sketch of Evans from a locket carried by his wife. It shows him as he appeared in 1878, before he grew his beard. *From an undated newspaper clipping in author's collection.*

One of the most unlikely of the far western outlaws, Chris Evans was born in 1847 at Bell's Corners, a small village near Ottawa, Canada. Young Evans ran away from home when he was sixteen years old and headed south. In 1863 he joined the Union army under an assumed name and fought through the war. After Appomattox he reportedly stayed in the army and served with General George A. Custer's Seventh Cavalry. It is thought he deserted and made his way to California sometime between 1869 and 1873.

In the San Joaquin Valley Evans was employed as a farmhand and teamster around Visalia. He married Molly Byrd in November of 1874 and worked both in Inyo and San Luis Obispo counties as a miner. By 1882 he was back in Visalia earning a living by plowing, working for the railroad and doing various odd jobs. There were children now and Evans was a devoted father, educating himself by prodigious reading.

When Evans hired John Sontag to help out on his farm, the two became fast friends. Sontag was a former Southern Pacific railroad brakeman who had been badly injured on the job in 1887. When the company would not rehire him, he became quite bitter towards the corporation and was grateful to Evans for the job. In late 1890 Evans invested in a Modesto livery stable, Sontag contributing his small savings to the down payment. Unfortunately, the stable burned in January of 1891 and both men lost everything.

Meanwhile the second train robbery in California history had occurred at Pixley on February 22, 1889. The bandits dynamited the mail coach and killed a railroad employee before escaping into the night. Another holdup took place on January 20, 1890 at Goshen, some miles nearer to Visalia. Here a tramp was shot and killed. On February 6, 1891, yet another train was stopped at a place called Alila, just south of Pixley. The fireman was killed when the express messenger exchanged shots with the bandits. The two outlaws then disappeared. Bob and

Emmett Dalton were indicted for the robbery, while Bill and Grat Dalton were picked up on suspicion.

When two other trains were stopped at Ceres and Collis, suspicion centered on Evans and his friend, Sontag. Evans had visited Sontag's brother George Contant, in Minnesota during the summer of 1891 and George later admitted they had robbed a train at Kasota. Detectives trailed the two back to California and when the bandit's tracks led from the Collis robbery back to Visalia, the lawmen put two and two together. George Contant (who had kept his original name after his mother remarried) was picked up for questioning while railroad detective Will Smith and Deputy Sheriff George Witty sought to question Evans at home. What happened next was described by detective Smith on August 5, 1892:

> ...[Evans] told me that Sontag had just gone up town. I told him that Sontag had just entered the house. I stepped into the house and pulled aside the portier and there stood Sontag with a double-barrelled shotgun. I stepped to one side and attempted to unbutton my coat to reach my six-shooter, when I saw that Chris Evans had another shotgun down. Witty and I then ran out through the front door...I looked over my shoulder just as Evans, fired at Witty. I stopped and fired two shots at Evans, when Sontag stopped and fired at me. As he pulled the trigger I crouched and the charge went over me, but he fired again, his shot striking me in the back and hands...

Visalia as it appeared in the 1880's. *Courtesy Jeff Edwards Collection.*

Both Smith and Witty were painfully, but not seriously wounded. Evans and Sontag fled in the lawmen's buggy, but returned that night when they had another shootout with officers, this time killing Deputy Oscar Beaver.

Railroad and Wells, Fargo detectives, together with local lawmen and bounty hunters began scouring the mountains for the two fugitives. A Visalia newspaper reporter had heard rumors that Evans had deeded his property to his wife. A search in the Tulare County recorder's office revealed that 13 city lots had been sold by Evans to Sontag in January of 1890 for $1,100. In February of the following year, Evans did deed his wife a piece of property and in April of 1891 John Sontag deeded to Evans' daughter Eva, the same property he had purchased from Evans. Was this shifting of property a means of assuring that Molly Evans and her daugher would have ownership in case something happened to the men?

On September 13, 1892, a posse found Evans and his partner in the mountains, southeast of Visalia. Former Texas Ranger Vic Wilson was in command of two Indian trackers and four lawmen when they rode up to Jim Young's cabin at Sampson's Flat. As the officers were walking towards the door, Evans and Sontag leaped onto the porch and opened fire. Wilson and Andy McGinnis were killed and the balance of the posse ran for their lives after a brief exchange of shots. Sontag was wounded in the arm and in a few minutes the two outlaws had disappeared into the forest.

A $10,000 reward was offered for the killers as the posses continued to scour the mountains. A "wanted" poster of the time describes Evans as follows:

> CHRISTOPHER EVANS (alias Charles Naughton) native of Canada, of Welsh and Irish descent; aged 45; height 5 feet eight or ten inches; weight about 160 pounds; sandy complexion; sandy or light hair, beard and moustache rather dark and sandy; blue eyes; large, bony hands; has a spring in both knees when walking; walks rather fast; when talking grins and smiles...when last seen wore dark grey, square checked suit. Has a wife and family at Visalia, California.

That winter the outlaws kept under cover in the mountains. Rumors were everywhere, much to the annoyance of Molly Evans. "They may say whatever they please now about my husband and Mr. Sontag," she scolded a reporter, "but I and my daughter should not be held responsible for anything they may have done." In April the two outlaws stopped a mountain stage, threatening to kill any bounty hunters they found. On May 26th they ambushed two detectives working for the Harry Morse Agency, badly wounding one of them.

That spring Wells, Fargo detective John Thacker and U.S. Marshal George Gard made plans to capture the outlaws. Two Fresno County deputies and Morse Agency operative Tom Burns met Marshal Gard secretly in the foothills. Patiently waiting their chance, the lawmen ambushed the fugitives at a spot near Stone Corral on June 11, 1893. The fight lasted several hours in the early evening, Evans and Sontag both receiving dangerous wounds. One of the lawmen was crippled in the battle and although Evans escaped during the night, Sontag was captured where he lay the following morning. When Evans was captured the next day at a nearby cabin, both men were brought to Visalia, then to Fresno where they would be tried on a murder charge. Evans lost an eye and an arm due to his wounds, while Sontag died painfully from tetanus and lockjaw on July 3rd.

Evans, a poor farmer who didn't dare spend any stolen money if he was indeed a train robber, now found himself on trial for his life. When a San Francisco dramatist announced he was going to present a stage play based on the outlaw's exploits, the family was delighted. Mrs. Evans and their teen-aged daughter Eva, even signed on to play themselves. "It seems that the Evans family have no money," noted the San Francisco *Examiner,* "and something must be done to raise funds." the play was quite successful, although when it went on the road they were refused a theater in both Visalia and Hanford. The Fresno *Republican* reported:

Photographed shortly after the fight at Stone Corral, Evans is shown here swathed in bandages in the Visalia jail. *Courtesy Fresno City and County Historical Society.*

A deputy poses at the site of Evans' and Morrell's destroyed cabin hideout. It was here that Evans' false arm was found. *Courtesy Annie Mitchell.*

> Notwithstanding the admonition to parents from press and pulpit, boys flocked to the Barton last night in droves to see and hear the Evans and Sontag drama. Men and women were there, too, in great profusion, and the parquet, balcony and gallery were packed. It may be truthfully said that the night was one of unexampled success for outlaws and the management...

Despite top-flight legal repesentation, Evans was convicted of murder and sentenced to life imprisonment on December 14, 1893. But Chris still had a last trick up his sleeve. With the help of an ex-convict named Ed Morrell, Evans escaped from jail after a minor shooting scrape on the streets of Fresno. The fugitives were at large for some two months in the mountains, Evans once writing a letter to the sheriff's office in Visalia:

> Fort Defiance, February 12, 1894
> Will Hall, Under Sheriff.—Well, old boy, I have read an account in the paper which stated that I had threatened to kill you and several others. You will die of old age before you die by my hand or any man's hand that is with me...Of course, we are liable to capture some of those crazy Fresnoites and turn them over to Sheriff Kay for safekeeping. There are four men that I will shoot on sight and their names are: Hi Rapelje, Tom Burns, Elijah Perkins and Perry Byrd. The first two for shooting me for blood money and the last two for betraying me...I feel sorry for Jay Scott and his brothers for they were very kind to me...

124

A posse very nearly caught the two fugitives at the "Fort Defiance" hideout, Evans having to leave his false arm behind in his flight. The outlaws were finally decoyed to Visalia and captured. Returned to Fresno, Evans was shipped immediately to Folsom Prison where he became No. 3055. He was always a model prisoner and was given positions of trust and responsibility.

In early May of 1901 Evans applied for parole as reported in the Fresno *Weekly Democrat:*

> Chris Evans, whose name was on every tongue in the valley a few years ago, has given notice of his intention to apply for a parole...
>
> He was sent to Folsom in 1893, eight years ago, and since that time his conduct has been faultless. He now holds a position of trust in the drug department of the prison... Evans' wife is living in Visalia where she works in the packing houses and takes in washing...

The pardon was refused, but in 1909 daughter Eva again began obtaining signatures for his release. This effort too failed, but when an anti-railroad governor was elected, the palsied old outlaw finally secured his release on the condition that he never return to California. On May 2, 1911 the Fresno Morning *Republican* published this small notice:

CHRIS EVANS IS FREE FROM FOLSOM PRISON

Sacramento—May 1, Chris Evans, the notorious bandit, stepped from Folsom Prison a free man today after seventeen years of imprisonment. He was met at the prison gates by his daughter, Mrs. Guiterrez, in an automobile and the aged bandit had his first joy ride, he being brought to this city in the automobile. He will stay here a few days and then join his wife in Portland, Ore.

Evans died at Portland in 1917, surrounded by the loving family that had always stood by him and which he had nearly destroyed by his criminal actions.

PRINCIPAL SOURCES

Dillon, Richard, *Wells, Fargo Detective,* N.Y., Coward-McCann, Inc., 1969; Maxwell, Hu, *Evans & Sontag,* San Francisco, San Francisco Printing Co., 1893, re-published in 1981 with much added material and illustrations, by Panorama West books, Fresno; Smith, Wallace, *Prodigal Sons,* Boston, Mass., Christopher Pub. House, 1951; Traver *Advocate,* June 15, 1893; San Francisco *Examiner,* July 29, 1893; Fresno *Daily Evening Expositor,* Feb. 23, 1889, May 27, 1893; Fresno *Weekly Expositor,* July 29, 1893; Fresno *Daily Republican,* Aug. 6, 1892, July 30, Oct. 25, 1893; Visalia *Times Delta,* Mar. 3, 1909; Visalia *Daily Times,* Sept. 13, 1892; Large scrapbook of criminal clippings from the 1890s in collections of Fresno City and County Historical Society, Fresno; Prison records in California State Archives, Sacramento.

DICK FELLOWS

This mug shot of Fellows was probably taken after his capture in 1882. *From an old Wells, Fargo mug book courtesy Greg Martin.*

"For daring," once commented Wells, Fargo detective Jim Hume, "he is the equal of any outlaw with whom I have ever had dealings." Hume was speaking of Dick Fellows, California's famed "Lone Highwayman."

Born in Kentucky in 1846, Dick himself once wrote that his real name was George B. Lyttle. He had a brother and sister and his father was David Y. Lyttle, a prominent attorney who once served in the state legislature. When still a boy Dick joined the Confederate army and spent the last months of the war in a northern prison. Returning home he studied for the law, but before he could begin a practice he and his family realized he had a serious drinking problem. He left home in 1866 hoping to gain control of himself and start a new life.

Dick found himself in California the following year, but time and distance didn't alter his problem. "The habit stuck to me," he later wrote, "and of course grew worse and worse. At length I became almost besotted, grew desperate and drifted into the worst company in California." By 1869 Dick was already a fugitive wanted for several stage robberies. He went into hog raising with a friend named Ed Clark, the two men working out of a camp on Castaic Creek in Los Angeles County. One day Clark let a campfire get out of control and they lost their winter food supply. To re-stock their larder, Dick decided to take another sojurn into stage robbery and headed south towards Los Angeles.

Hiding his horse, Dick took up a positon about six miles from the San Fernando stage station. As the Los Angeles stage came along bound for Soledad, the highwayman stopped it only to have an armed passenger jump out the other side just as the coach plunged ahead. Yelling as if he had several companions, Dick got the drop on the passenger and took $350 from him. With the money he shipped the needed supplies to his pal Clark, then set off to stick-up another stage.

126

He stopped another coach in Cahuenga Pass only to have another armed passenger take a pot shot at him as the stage again got away. By fast riding and short cuts, Dick took up an ambush ahead of the coach and succeeded in stopping it. This time the Wells, Fargo box yielded some $435. To avoid any posses, Dick then hid out for several days south of Los Angeles.

On his way back to Castaic Creek the highwayman stopped at a road station to have dinner. Several men recognized him from his wanted poster and after a fight Dick was lucky to get away with a bullet in his foot. He had his wound tended at a friend's home in Los Angeles, but when he noticed officers taking his horse away the outlaw knew his game was up. "I shall have to surrender," he told his host. "There is a reward of several hundreds of dollars for my arrest and you might as well get it." Dick then rode into town in his friend's buggy as the posse followed close behind.

Promptly convicted of robbery and assault, Fellows was sentenced to an eight year term in San Quentin Prison where he was admitted on January 31, 1870. Prison records described him as being 24 years of age, fair complexion with hazel eyes and fair hair. He was pardoned in April of 1874 and drifted south from the bay area.

Perhaps Dick Fellows is among this group of prisoners standing in line at San Quentin in 1871. The stone building was the first cellblock constructed at the prison and was called "The Stones." *Courtesy California State Library.*

In late 1875 Fellows was using the alias Richard Perkins and living in or around the town of Caliente, east of Bakersfield. Caliente was a thriving railroad town with much bullion being shipped there by stage from surrounding mining camps. The Los Angeles stage was held up by Fellows as it was coming into Caliente on November 30th. It was a typical operation as written up in the Kern County Weekly *Courier* of December 4, 1875:

> ... About four miles up the hill, near Crite's house, a man suddenly sprang to the horses heads and cried halt. The driver drew up and was ordered to throw down the express box, which he did, and was then ordered to drive on. It was dark and the driver could only see and hear one man, although it is probable that there were others in the vicinity...

Dick had reportedly secured some $1,800 in the robbery, but when his horse ran away he fell off an embankment in the dark and broke his ankle. He managed to steal another horse, but the animal had recently been shod and was easily followed. Tracked down by a deputy sheriff and the horse's owner, Dick was quickly captured and taken to Bakersfield. He was tried and convicted in early January and again sentenced to eight years in San Quentin. The same night of his conviction there was much singing and celebrating in Bakersfield's makeshift jail. The following morning Fellow's cell was strangely empty. It was surmised that all the noise had been made to cover the racket Dick was making while sawing and removing several floor boards during his escape.

At large for nearly a week, Dick was still crippled by his ankle and found it difficult to avoid posses and eat regularly. He was recaptured while eating breakfast as reported in the *Courier* of January 22, 1876:

> As we intimated last week, the escaped convict, Richard Perkins, came quietly into camp on Saturday morning last. We had a little sympathy for him before, but we are convinced that any man who would permit himself to be captured just after the publication of the *Courier,* thereby depriving us of a most interesting item, is a heartless and depraved creature totally unworthy of the slightest commisseration... The prisoner is a man of fine personal appearance, with an intelligent coutenance, and there is an air of cool and superior audacity about him...

After some $550 worth of rewards were paid to Dick's captors, he was promptly whisked off to San Quentin to begin his second prison term. As No. 6834 he was received in late January, but with time off for good behavior found himself a free man again on May 16, 1881. He drifted south to Santa Cruz where he briefly worked for a local newspaper. He also advertised himself as a Spanish language instructor, but a paucity of pupils turned his thoughts again to other areas of endeavor.

Although not suspected of the crimes at the time, on July 19, 1881, he held up a stage running out of San Luis Obispo, but only obtained a small return. On August 1st he robbed the Duncan's Mills coach and on the 25th of the same

When Fellows languished in its jail, Bakersfield was a typical frontier town of the period. *Courtesy Kern County Historical Society.*

month stopped the San Luis Obispo stage again. The San Luis coach was again robbed on December 27th and on January 2, 1882, a Monterey County stage was held up. The larcenous epidemic caught the attention of Wells, Fargo's Jim Hume and he sent Charles Aull to investigate. It took detective Aull a mere two days to identify Dick Fellows as the principal suspect.

Aull had no sooner launched an investigation with a flood of printed circulars when word was received on January 14th that yet another coach had been stopped by the lone highwayman. Detective Aull quickly narrowed down Dick's whereabouts to the Santa Clara Valley and with the help of local lawmen covered the area with his descriptive circulars. Dick spent one night in a hotel adjoining the rooms where Aull and Monterey Sheriff Franks slept. When the fugitive's landlady told him the streets were lined with lawmen looking for the notorious Dick Fellows, he asked her to fix him an early breakfast so he could "go out and join in the chase." Aull and Franks were reinforced by two San Francisco police detectives and after splitting into four parties, the area between San Jose and San Mateo was thoroughly covered. Alerting everyone they encountered to be on the lookout for the elusive outlaw, the lawmen were rewarded when Dick was recognized at a ranch and captured. He was taken to nearby Mayfield and turned over to Constable Burke of Santa Clara. An astute student of human nature, Dick began flattering Burke that he was to become a celebrity as a result of his capture of the famed desperado. As he had surmised, before long the officer had dropped his guard as reported in the San Francisco *Call* of January 28, 1882, which used Dick's real name:

> ...Burke arrived here [San Jose] on the 6:30 P.M. train today and got...into a streetcar with the prisoner. On First street, opposite the Arguello House, Burke took Lytle into a saloon to get a drink, and coming out Lytle made a break and ran down St. John street, speedily outdistancing Burke...

Aull and a bevy of officers were quickly on the scene, offering a $600 reward for the fugitive. Dick was described at this time as being 36 years old, five foot eight inches tall, large head, brown hair inclined to curl, brown, sandy beard, full face, stout build, weighing 180 pounds, well-educated and speaking fluent Spanish. He was, reported the *Call* article, "the most daring and expert single-handed stage robber this state has ever known." Black Bart, still at large at this time, must have cringed if he read that particular *Call* article!

Aull was furious at what had happened and by morning had circulated 2,000 new circulars alerting the local citizenry. Dick spent the night in a barn, then skedaddled up a nearby canyon. That evening he was found by two local peace officers cooking his supper in a secluded ravine. The following day, Sunday, February 5, 1882, some 700 people visited the San Jose jail to get a look at the noted desperado. On Monday Jim Hume took him to San Francisco, then down to Santa Barbara for trial.

In late March he was tried and sentenced to life imprisonment at Folsom Prison. As the jailer was bringing him his breakfast on April 2nd, Fellows caught him unaware and overpowered him. "It is life or death with me," he snarled, "and I am going to get your revolver!" Running from the jail, he found a horse staked out a few blocks away and attempted to ride off on the animal. Again Dick had horse problems and he was thrown and promptly recaptured by pursuing lawmen.

Late that evening as Dick was waiting for the boat to take him back to prison, he penned a note to the local newspaper:

> Editor Press—Dear Sir: I have just noticed your article of this date in reference to my recent attempt to escape, and also your editorial in regard to my fast career, entitled "It Don't Pay," and after thanking you for your

kindly notices, I have to say that both are in the main correct, and I most heartily concur in what you have to say in the last-named article, and would only add that the same may be said of any unlawful calling, no matter what the provocation. My unfortunate experience has thrown me into the society of thousands of law-breakers from every clime and all walks of life and in every instance the result is the same... "It don't pay."...Good-by.

Dick Fellows.

In 1885 detective Hume wrote that "...it may be said that Dick Fellows is now a promising teacher in the Department of Moral Instruction in the Folsom Prison, and already there are gentle 'twitterings' which will soon reach the throne of executive clemency." In time Hume's sarcasm toward his former adversary mellowed. Both he and Wells, Fargo President John J. Valentine eventually recommended clemency for Dick and on March 8, 1908, he was pardoned and restored to civil life. The old outlaw talked of going to Mexico, but in the end returned home to his sister, Sallie, and other relatives. Nothing is known of his later years, but it has been reported that he visited California in 1915 when he was in charge of the Kentucky state exhibit during the Panama-Pacific Exhibition.

PRINCIPAL SOURCES

Dillon, Richard, *Wells, Fargo Detective,* N.Y., Coward-McCann, 1969; Jackson, Joseph Henry, *Bad Company,* Harcourt, Brace and Co., 1949; Boyd, Harlan W., "The Outlaw Richard Perkins, alias George B. Lytle, alias Dick Fellows in Kern County," *Historic Kern,* Quarterly Bulletin of the Kern County Hist. Soc., June, 1983; Sacramento *Bee,* Jan. 13, 1876; San Francisco *Daily Morning Call,* Jan. 28, 1882; San Francisco *Chronicle,* Sept. 9, 1900; Kern County *Weekly Courier,* Dec. 4, 11, 1875, Jan. 15, 22, 1876; San Francisco *Examiner,* May 20, 1894; San Jose *Mercury,* Jan. 10, 18, 26, 29, Feb. 3, 4, 5, Apr. 2, 22, 1882; Sacramento *Daily Record-Union,* Jan. 1, 1885; Los Angeles *Star,* Dec. 11, 1869, Jan. 22, 1870; Prison records in the California State Archives, Sacramento.

An early posed photo of a stagecoach holdup. *Courtesy Wells Fargo History Room.*

131

JUAN FLORES

Reportedly born in Santa Barbara about 1836, Flores grew up resenting the steadily growing stream of Americans who occupied California during the Mexican War and the later gold rush. Nothing is known of his early life, but he seems to have drifted into a life of crime at a tender age. He was loitering about Los Angeles in March of 1855 when he and two companions stole a team of horses owned by a freighting concern run by the Hardy brothers. The rustlers were picked up on their way to Mexico and young Flores soon found himself on his way to state prison.

At San Quentin Flores was No. 613. He was received on April 27, 1855 to begin serving a three year term for grand larceny. He is described in his prison record as being nineteen years old, a laborer, 5'10" tall, dark complexion, hazel eyes and black hair. He failed in an escape attempt just two months after entering prison. There were many attempts to break out of prison that year, twenty-eight escapes being successful. San Quentin was still in the process of being built at that time and had only one substantial building in which cells were located. There were no walls and the prisoners had to be marched to and from work and feeding locations every day. Making brick and quarrying stone were the main occupations of the prisoners and escape opportunities were many and bloody.

In October of 1856 a ship was taking on a load of prison-made bricks when Flores and another convict named Red Horse led a breakout. Overpowering the brig's captain and crew, the prisoners cast off and headed out into San Francisco Bay. A withering gunfire from guards killed many of the escapees, while cannister shot from a six-pounder killed or wounded many more. The ship made it to Contra Costa County where Flores and some twenty followers headed south, disappearing into the countryside.

Flores and a seasoned convict named Pancho Daniel were leaders of the surviving convicts who quickly formed themselves into a gang calling themselves the "Manillas," Spanish for manacles. Identified members were as follows:

Juan Catabo	Pedro Lopez	Antonio Varelas
Francisco Ardillero	Juan Valenzuela	Encarnacion Berryessa
Jose Santos	Jose Espinoza	Santiago Silvas
Diego Navarra		Leonardo Lopez

By posing as patriots, the convicts obtained aid from various native Californians. At San Luis Obispo, Flores recruited another ex-convict named

Andres Fontes who was harboring a grudge against Los Angeles Sheriff James Barton. Fontes had been sent to prison on a (he claimed) trumped-up charge. He joined the gang on the promise of Flores to help kill Barton.

In early 1857 Flores and his men camped on the outskirts of the small mission village of San Juan Capistrano. Wandering about town on January 18th, Flores was recognized by Garnet Hardy who had a freight team in town. It was the theft of a Hardy team that had originally sent Flores to prison. Well aware that Flores should have been in San Quentin, Hardy sent word to Sheriff Barton at Los Angeles.

Becoming more bold and impudent in the isolated village, the outlaws began stealing items from local stores and terrorizing the inhabitants. They were repulsed when they tried to break into the shop of Miguel Kraszewski who had reprimanded Chino Varelas when his pal Juan Catabo stole a pistol. Later, members of the gang attacked the store of George Pfleugardt, killing him and plundering the premises. By this time a crowd of Indians and half-breeds had assembled and were egging the bandits on, stealing anything the outlaws didn't want. After looting several shops Flores and his men split up into two groups and led their pack animals out of town on January 21st.

Meanwhile Sheriff Barton and a posse of five men had left Los Angeles to investigate Hardy's message. Despite several warnings of the superior numbers of the outlaws, the posse rode on towards San Juan. At a pass in the San Joaquin Hills the lawmen were ambushed by the Manillas and overwhelmed by a superior force as reported in the Los Angeles *Star:*

> The four charged on the robbers, fired their guns and Barton his pistols, and then fought with it clubbed. One of the robbers was heard to say to Barton "G-d d'm you, I have got you now." To which Barton replied, "I reckon I have got you too." Their guns were leveled at each other during the remark, the discharge was simultaneous, but Barton fell, shot through the heart. Our informant states that three of the robbers fell on the first discharge...

Alfred Hardy and Frank Alexander were able to make their escape, but Barton, Bill Little, Charles Daily and Charles Baker were all killed. Reportedly, it was Andres Fontes who had gunned down the sheriff, shooting him three times about the heart, once through the right eye and again through the arm. All the bodies were fired on after death and then robbed.

There was great excitement in Los Angeles when the two surviving possemen returned with the news. All night long preparations were made for the pursuit of the killers. A party of fifty Californians under Andres Pico was joined by various other settler and soldier posses which swarmed after Flores and his men. A large band of Indian scouts was sent into the mountains to guard the passes.

It was exactly a week after the Barton murder that Pico's and other posses trapped Flores and his men in the upper Santiago Canyon of the Santa Ana Mountains. It was hard work following the outlaws through rock and brush-

Above: The old mission of San Juan Capistrano and the adjacent village was the scene of the first outrages of Juan Flores and his followers. *From author's collection.*

Left: Andres Pico was one of the many native Californians who rode with the Americans to capture the Flores gang. *From author's collection.*

choked hillsides, but after numerous skirmishes all but Flores and two of his men were captured. From one of the captives it was learned that Daniel and several others were not with the main bandit party. The Los Angeles *Star* of February 7th noted:

> ...The mountain to which the robbers had fled was almost inaccessible, even on foot, and while the Americans were ascending the hill, Juan Flores, Jesus Espinoza and Leonardo Lopez slid their horses down a precipice to a kind of shelf about fifty feet below, where they abandoned them and escaped down a precipitous ledge.
>
> Dr. Gentry's party discovered the trail of Flores and his associates, pursued it and came in sight of them, when the robbers attempted to evade them by hiding in a cave...From this they fired on their pursuers, wounding one of the party, Francis Goddard. Seeing they were at last caught...they made no further attempt to escape...

While being held at the Yorba ranch that night, Flores and two of his men made their escape. When Andres Pico received this news, he lynched two of his other prisoners named Silvas and Ardillero.

With men stationed at all the passes and water holes, the posses scoured the mountains in search of remnants of the gang. On February 3rd Flores came through Simi Pass in search of water, but was surprised and captured by two soldiers stationed there. Taken to camp the bandit chief was promptly identified and returned to Los Angeles by James Thompson. "He requested Mr. Thompson to bring him to town," noted the *Star,* "so that he might have the benefit of a clergyman, make a confession, and write to his mother..." Most of the bandits had now been either killed or captured.

The Los Angeles citizenry was so overwrought by the events that they were unwilling to let authorities handle the situation. Nine (some accounts say eleven) of the captured desperadoes were hanged by a people's court, while several were sent to the penitentiary. Antonio Verelas, only seventeen years old, was from a good family and was released. Harris Newmark, a member of the vigilance committee, later recalled how the trials were handled:

> ...We met near the veranda of the Montgomery [saloon], and Judge Jonathan R. Scott having been made chairman, a regular order of procedure, extra-legal though it was, was followed; ...naming the criminal, the Judge called upon the crowd to determine the prisoner's fate. Thereupon some one would shout: 'Hang him!' Scott would then put the question... 'Gentlemen, you have heard the motion; all those in favor of hanging So-and-So, will signify by saying, Aye!'

At two o'clock on a Saturday afternoon, February 14, 1857, Flores was taken from his cell by the vigilance committee. He was led to the hill behind the jail where his comrades had been hanged as noted in the *Star* of February 21st:

> ...He expressed a wish to address the people who instantly became silent. His remarks were interpreted, and were merely to the effect—that he was

now ready to die—that he had committed many crimes—that he died without having ill-will against any man... His legs were then bound, and the rope adjusted around his neck, during which he continued in conversation with those in his immediate vicinity. The handkerchief was placed over his head... and immediately after the plank was drawn from under him, the body of Flores swung in the air. The fall was too short, and the unfortunate wretch struggled in agony for a considerable time... The body was kept hanging for about an hour and then was handed over to those who had engaged to take charge of it...

There were some terrible excesses during the Flores excitement, one of the worst taking place at San Gabriel. Billy Rubottom, a prominent rancher at El Monte, sent one of his Mexican vaqueros over to a neighboring farm to see about selling some corn. Later he heard that one of the Flores gang had been captured and killed at San Gabriel and since his vaquero was late in returning he rode over to the old mission village to see what had happened. A drunken mob had acccosted the vaquero, charging him with having the saddle and bridle of Sheriff Barton. He was killed, hacked with knives and shot up, then beheaded before the mob's ferocity was satiated. Luckily Rubottom left home without his weapons. Later he admitted that his first "impulse was to turn on the roomful, find out who had participated in this murder and shoot them down like dogs."

Disposition of Flores' body is not known. Andres Fontes escaped and made his way to old Mexico. The following year Pancho Daniel was captured and when returned to Los Angeles for trial he met the same fate as Juan Flores.

PRINCIPAL SOURCES ─────────────────────

Bell, Major Horace, *On The Old West Coast,* N.Y., Grosset & Dunlap, 1930; Cleland, Robert Glass, *The Cattle on a Thousand Hills,* San Marino, The Huntington Library, 1941; Newmark, Harris, *Sixty Years in Southern California,* N.Y., Houghton Mifflin Co., 1930; Meadows, Don, "Juan Flores and the Manillas," *Westerners Brand Book,* Los Angeles Corral, Book 10, 1963; Kraszewski, Miguel, "Acts of the Manillas," manuscript in the Bancroft Library, Berkeley; San Francisco *Daily Alta California,* Mar. 2, 1857; The *Placer Herald,* Feb. 21, 1857; Los Angeles *Star,* Jan. 31, Feb. 7, 14, 21, 1857; Prison records in the California State Archives, Sacramento.

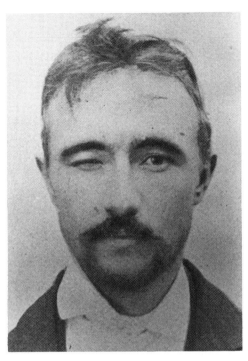

WILLIAM M. FREDERICKS

Mug shot of Fredericks taken by the San
Francisco police immediately after the
bungled bank robbery of March 23,
1894. *From Duke's* Celebrated Criminal
Cases of America.

Although his real name was never known, Fredericks was born in the Alsace
area of Germany about 1872. His family was poor and moved to the United
States about 1878, probably to try and improve their situation. Young William
was sent to sea at an early age to help support the family. He came to California
sometime in 1889 or early 1890 and looked about for opportunities.

Fredericks seems to have worked as a barber in Shasta County, but business
was poor and he drifted south looking for work. He was soon broke and found
himself hitching rides and stealing food. In Mariposa County he burglarized a
cabin, stealing some food and bedding in early May of 1890. Four days later he
stepped out into the road in front of a stagecoach running between Bear Valley
and Mt. Ophir. In its story of the event which appeared on May 17th, the
Mariposa *Gazette* noted that it was the third robbery of the local stage within
the past six months:

> ...The driver, Fernando Davila, was suddenly ordered to stop and throw
> down Wells, Fargo's box. The surprise at the sudden appearance of a
> shotgun, with a desperado back of it, caused an exclamation from the driver
> and prompt obedience to the command. There was only one passenger, Miss
> Millie Farnsworth, who was relieved of between thirty and forty cents...

The robber didn't fare any better with the empty treasure box. After waving
the driver to move on, Fredericks walked to a nearby ranch house where he stole
a horse. Instead of fleeing the area, he loitered around the county and a week

later was picked up as a suspicious character. Lawmen found his shotgun in his hobo bundle, along with the duster he had worn in the robbery. Fredericks realized it was all over. He pled guilty and on May 23rd was sentenced to four years in state prison.

Fredericks could have left Folsom to begin a new life. Instead, he chose to become involved in an escape attempt and to lead the life of a fugitive and desperado. *Courtesy California State Prison at Folsom.*

He entered Folsom on May 26, 1890 as No. 2221. His prison record lists him as being eighteen years old, a barber, 5'8½" tall with a fair complexion, dark gray eyes and light hair. The young convict kept his nose clean and did time as easily as he could. George Contant, or Sontag, arrived at the prison in early November of 1892 to serve a life term for train robbery. When he learned that Fredericks was to be paroled soon, George talked him into assisting in an escape plan being formulated. Fredericks was to go to Visalia upon his release and call on the Evans family, friends of Contant. Eva Evans had been the sweetheart of George's brother and she was to furnish guns for the break. Fredericks was then to return to prison and conceal the weapons in the quarry where the convicts worked. With the guns would be a note explaining where supplies could be obtained after the escape. It seemed like a good plan.

Paroled on May 26, 1893, Fredericks rode the rods to Visalia, but was thrown off trains three times by brakemen who recognized his cheap, convict's clothes. Using the name Johnson, he found Eva Evans who told him where he could steal some guns. In later years Eva recalled that although she liked Fredericks, she "believed he was totally indifferent to the sanctity of human life..." Returning to Folsom, Fredericks hid the guns in the quarry and otherwise completed his part in the escape plan. The break-out itself failed, however, when three convicts were killed and George Contant was badly wounded. Fredericks waited several days at the rendezvous point, but when he learned of the tragedy at the prison he quickly left the area.

With a hobo companion, Fredericks jumped a train heading east. When a brakeman named James Bruce ordered him off the train at Gold Run in Placer County, Fredericks remembered his trip to Visalia. Pulling his pistol he shot and dangerously wounded the trainman. "Run, God Damn you," he was reported as saying, "or I'll give you another." Jumping from the cars, the ex-convict fled into the nearby forest and began walking north, towards Grass Valley. As Bruce was taken to the railroad hospital in Sacramento, posses were formed to look for the murderous hobo.

On the night of June 30th, Fredericks was in the city of Grass Valley. He was standing on a street corner when he was spotted by Nevada County Sheriff William H. Pascoe who was keeping an eye open for the man who had shot Bruce. Pascoe followed Fredericks up the street, but when the ex-convict noticed he was being shadowed he increased his gait. The Sheriff followed him into the yard of a local foundry, but Fredericks waited behind an ore car and killed the lawman with a well directed shot through the heart. "TERRIBLE," screamed the headline of the Grass Valley *Union* the next day. "Sheriff Pascoe Murdered! Assasin unknown, but supposed to be the Tramp who shot brakeman Bruce..." Fredericks was quickly isolated as the chief suspect as reported in the *Union* on July 2, 1893:

> ...A few days ago Warden Aull sent to the Sheriff's office a picture of one Frederickson [*sic*], an escaped convict whom the Warden supposed furnished the pistols and guns to the prisoners, who attempted to escape from the Folsom prison...
> Nightwatchman Shoemaker saw the tramp who shot Pascoe, and gave an accurate description of him which tallies with the picture which he had not seen...

As large rewards were being offered for the killer and posses fanned out over the area, Fredericks scrambled desperately through the mountains trying to get away. All roads and bridges were covered by lawmen, but Fredericks stayed in the woods and was recognized by his broken English near Jones' Bar. Amazingly the fugitive managed to skirt the searching posses and it is thought he fled north into Oregon where he caught a train heading east.

$550.00 REWARD!

WANTED—WILLIAM FREDERICKS.

For the shooting of Brakeman J. T. Bruce, at Gold Run, Placer County, California, on the morning of June 28th, 1893; also, for his supposed killing of Sheriff Pascoe, of Nevada County, at Grass Valley, June 30th, 1893.

No. 2,221. WM. FREDERICKS, committed May 26th, 1890, from Mariposa County, for robbery; four years' sentence. Was discharged from Folsom State Prison May 26th, 1893.

DESCRIPTION.

Is a German; aged 21; a barber by profession; 5 feet, 8½ inches; fair complexion; dark gray eyes and light hair; size of foot, 7; weight, 150 pounds. Short, broad features; medium, round forehead; heavy nose; small mouth; small ears, well out from head; teeth irregular, with small space between two upper front; medium short, thick hands; medium fingers; medium long arms; small scar left of center of head; small scar right side of crown of head; stoop shoulders; slender build. *India Ink Marks:* On right arm—Sailor with arm about ballet girl; also, cottage, and American coat-of-arms, with word "Liberty." On breast—Cowboy, mounted on bronco, holding lariat in right hand. On left wrist—Bracelet; ballet girl, and two Indians. On left arm—Star, two clasped hands, heart, cross and anchor. On upper left arm—Goddess of Liberty and American flag.

Carries hands in pockets when standing; smokes tobacco, and had short-stem corn cob pipe; dressed in dark sack coat and pants (may have overalls over pants); wore low-crown, black slouch hat; wore belt, about 1½ inches wide with common buckle, around waist; probable wore shoes; speaks slightly-broken English; has medium-toned voice; shows teeth when talking; uses liquor to excess.

When last seen he had a large revolver, supposed to be 44 calibre.

He is also suspicioned of being the murderer of Sheriff Pascoe, at Grass Valley, Nevada County, June 30th. Sheriff of Placer County offers Fifty Dollars reward, and the Southern Pacific Company also offer a reward of Five Hundred Dollars for his arrest and conviction.

Send information to W. C. Conroy, Sheriff, Auburn, Placer County; Warden Chas. Aull, Folsom State Prison; or General Superintendent J. A. Fillmore, S. P. Company, San Francisco.

Fredericks was the most wanted fugitive in California at the time this poster was issued. *Courtesy California State Archives.*

Traveling to the larger cities of Arizona, New Mexico, Colorado and Wyoming, Fredericks made a living by burglaries and holdups—most of which he logged in a notebook he carried. In Butte, Montana, he reportedly murdered three Chinese before robbing their cabin. He used the name William Berrigan and frequently boasted to a roommate that he had belonged to the Chris Evans gang of train robbers in California. In January of 1894 he journeyed to Salt Lake City, but by March he was back on the coast, in San Francisco. He lived by petty crimes and most of the time was broke.

On the evening of March 14th Fredericks held up a man in Golden Gate Park and got away with $150. He cased a bank on the corner of Market and Fell streets and concluded it looked like a good prospect for a holdup. On March 23rd he walked in and threatened the teller with a vial of alcohol which he claimed was nitroglycerin. William Herrick, the teller, merely stared at him when he asked for cash. When the bandit pulled his pistol, the cashier grabbed his own weapon and the two began shooting. Herrick was mortally wounded in the exchange. Fredericks received a splinter of glass in his eye, but managed to run from the scene. He was quickly captured and jailed. Although he denied his identity, Detective Captain Isaiah Lees soon had his whole story.

Eva Evans visited the captured outlaw with his lawyer on April 2nd and talked with him for some time. Her role in the aborted Folsom escape attempt

140

was by now well known and when it became known she had visited Fredericks, a search of his cell was quickly ordered. A hole in the cell was found under the prisoner's bunk. It was only an inch in diameter and led to an adjoining cell, but authorities could not find the instrument with which it had been made. Fredericks just laughed at the discovery, claiming the hole had been made by rats.

The outlaw was easily convicted of the Herrick murder and sentenced to hang on July 26, 1895. While he was still lodged in the San Francisco city jail Fredericks made a desperate attempt to escape just two days before his sentencing. He managed to jimmy open his cell door and lay in wait for a guard in a darkened doorway of the jail corridor. The guard managed to fend off a gas pipe wielding Fredericks and the two struggled desperately for several minutes. The prisoner grabbed the guard's key and made a rush for the door, but when the prison desk sergeant appeared Fredericks fled back towards his cell. When he turned and appeared to be drawing a weapon, the officer fired, but missed. At that moment other officers rushed in and the attempted break was over.

The outlaw kept his nerve to the very end. On the gallows at San Quentin he made a brief speech in his broken English, forgiving his enemies and hoping to be forgiven in return. Eleven minutes after the trap was sprung he was pronounced dead by the attending physicians.

A son of the murdered Sheriff Pascoe was present at the execution. "He lived like a brute," he noted, "and died like a brave man. I did not believe he would die game, but he did and he is entitled to that credit."

Charley Michelson, a reporter, wrote a most interesting postscript to Frederick's life which appeared in the San Francisco *Examiner* on July 27, 1895:

> . . . In one of my talks with the condemned man he told me that when he had left the little school in Germany his ambition was to be a soldier, and the career that he had marked out for himself was that of a commander of men . . . Possibly if the boy Fredericks had been given a cadetship instead of being forced by his necessities to go to sea and generally make his way among the hard walks of life, there might have been a Captain Fredericks or a Colonel Fredericks, whose dashing courage would have made him world famous. At all events that is the thought that came to me when they cut his muffled body down.

PRINCIPAL SOURCES

Duke, Thomas S., *Celebrated Criminal Cases of America,* San Francisco, The James H. Barry Co., 1910; Smith, Wallace, *Prodigal Sons,* Boston, The Christopher Pub. House, 1951; Warner, Opie L., *A Pardoned Lifer,* San Bernardino, Index Print, 1909; Secrest, William B., "A Folsom Graduate," *True West,* Sept.-Oct., 1979; San Francisco *Chronicle,* May 16, 26, July 27, 1895; San Francisco *Examiner,* Apr. 3, May 6, 1894; Fresno *Expositor,* July 1, 6, 24, 1893; Mariposa *Gazette,* May 17, 24, 31, 1890; Nevada City *Daily Transcript,* July 3, 5, 6, 7, 1893; Grass Valley *Union,* June 28, 29, July 1, 2, 4, 7, 13, 21, 1893; Prison records in California State Archives, Sacramento.

GEORGE E. GARD

George Gard spent 30 years as a police officer, sheriff, U.S. marshal, railroad detective and private investigator. *From J.M. Guinn's* Historical and Biographical Record of Los Angeles and Vicinity.

Educated in Warren County, Ohio where he was born in 1843, young George Gard came overland to California in 1859 helping an uncle conduct a cattle drive. He worked at various pursuits in San Jose and Mariposa County and served as First Sergeant of a California infantry company during the Civil War.

After the war Gard lived in Los Angeles where he engaged in both public and private occupations. He married Kate Hammell in 1869 and joined the city police force in 1871 when there were only six officers working under the city marshal. The small force of lawmen had their work cut out for them in tough, old Los Angeles.

In late October of 1871 trouble erupted in the Calle de los Negros, part of the tenderloin section of town. A riot between a white mob and a group of local Chinese brought in all the city officers as well as the sheriff and his staff. Gard and fellow officer Emil Harris worked desperately to control the bloodthirsty crowds who lynched and murdered nineteen Chinese—only one of whom was probably connected to the trouble. Gard and Harris tried to save many of the victims and without their efforts others would have died. The Chinese remembered this three months later as reported in the Los Angeles *Star* of January 31, 1872:

> A Present—Officers Gard and Harris were yesterday the recipients of a beautiful gift, consisting of Chinese embroidery, presented by the Wing Chong Company, as a testimonial of their appreciation of services rendered from time to time.

Gard and Harris were quickly recognized also for their detective skills. The *Star* reported that the two lawmen should be appointed to special duty to utilize their investigative talents more fully. " . . . Detectives should be men of stability, good judgement, sobriety, and great discretion. All of these qualifications, we believe, are embraced by the officers mentioned above." The two detective officers did good work in solving the crimes of the frontier town, but when Harris was defeated in running for police chief, Gard left the force—probably because he was not re-appointed by the new chief.

From 1875 to 1879 Gard served as the county's chief deputy recorder and in 1881 was appointed chief of police of the city. He was elected sheriff on the Republican ticket in 1884 and during this period found time to farm and engage in land speculations in the Azusa Valley.

Appointed U.S. marshal for the southern district of California by President Benjamin Harrison, Gard served from February 6, 1890 to May 16, 1894. Never an office lawman, Marshal Gard was quickly in action when counterfeiter Ricardo Gonzales escaped from the Los Angeles County jail. Most of Gonzales' gang had already been sentenced to prison when he made his escape on May 1, 1892. After tracking the fugitive to Albuquerque, the marshal learned Gonzales had gone on to El Paso.

At the Texas border city Gard learned Gonzales had spent several days waiting for funds from some friends. He had adopted the alias of Jose Crespo and shaved off his mustache as a further disguise. The marshal tracked him from Zacatecas to Chihuahua where he checked with the Wells, Fargo agent.

An early view of Los Angeles as it appeared when Gard was a city police officer and detective. *Courtesy California State Library.*

He learned the fugitive was expecting a package and Gard employed a man to call on all the boarding houses in town for Jose Crespo and tell him he had a package marked "Rush Delivery" at the Wells, Fargo office. The ruse worked and when the fugitive called for his package, a police officer was waiting for him.

"I was at once notified," recalled Gard, "and went up to Gonzales and said: 'Hello, Don Gonzales, como esta usted?' A more astonished man never lived."

After consulting with the governor, Gard and his prisoner left that night for Los Angeles. It was an excellent bit of detective work and received wide coverage in the California press.

When two farmers living in Visalia were suspected of several train robberies in late 1892, they killed several lawmen sent to bring them in. Chris Evans and John Sontag spent the winter eluding posses in the mountains. There were literally hundreds of bounty hunters, express company detectives and other lawmen trying to capture them, but the two outlaws remained at large. Gard finally determined to take personal charge of a posse. Meeting Wells, Fargo Special Officer John Thacker in Fresno in May of 1893, plans were formulated to capture the two fugitives. Gard later recalled:

> I was informed by Detective Thacker of the report that Sontag and Evans intended to hold up the express train carrying what is known as the "through safe," in which a good deal of coin and treasure is carried... It was suspected that they proposed this loot as a last cleanup and then intended going either to Yankee Territory in Sonora, Mexico, or to British Columbia... I determined to take a hand in the pursuit of the pair and obtained a warrant from the United States Court in Los Angeles...

Gard and Thacker kept the posse small. They selected Hiram Rapelje and Fred Jackson, two Fresno County deputy sheriffs, and Tom Burns, a private detective from the Harry Morse Agency in San Francisco. The three lawmen were smuggled out of town at night and were soon after joined by Gard who took charge of the operation. Resting by day and moving at night, the posse took up positions in an empty shack along a route known to be used by the outlaws. They were east of Visalia near an old landmark called Stone Corral.

Late on the afternoon of June 11th, the posse ambushed and badly wounded both Evans and Sontag as they were leaving the hills. Sontag was captured where he lay the next morning, but Evans fled to a relative's cabin some miles away where he was quickly picked up by Tulare County officers. Large rewards had been offered for the fugitives and the Fresno and Tulare County lawmen very nearly had a shootout over who was to take charge of the prisoners. "Those retrievers from Visalia," growled Gard, "have no right to any of it. The case is like that of one man shooting a quail and another man getting to it first when it falls and asserting that it belongs to him." Gard himself declined any of the rewards, giving it all to his posse. The marshal was satisfied with a "highly polished" rifle given him by the citizens of southern California in appreciation of his actions at Stone Corral.

When Chris Evans escaped from the Fresno County jail in December of 1893, Gard again formed a posse and was promptly in the field. He was active in the pursuit and was present when Evans was induced to surrender at his Visalia home on February 18, 1894.

Gard headed another posse in April when he brought in two suspects accused of robbing a train and killing two men at Roscoe, near Los Angeles. The two men were later released and the real bandits eventually captured.

After his term as U.S. Marshal was up, Gard was offered the position of Chief of Detectives for the Southern Pacific Railroad. On March 30, 1895, the Oregon Express was robbed near Wheatland and Tehama County Sheriff John Bogard, a passenger, was shot and killed. Bogard had discovered a robbery was

Left: Not an office lawman, Gard is shown here after the gunfight with Evans and Sontag near Visalia. Losing his hat during the fight, he wears a handkerchief on his head. *Courtesy Fresno City and County Historical Society.*

Below: Pasadena looked like this in the 1890's when George Gard lived there and pioneered development of the area. *Courtesy Pasadena Historical Society.*

in progress and had shot one of the robbers just before another bandit opened fire and killed the sheriff. The killer then fled the scene. A massive manhunt was launched with Gard, Wells, Fargo detective Jim Hume and John Thacker spearheading the search. Within days the bandits had been identified as two San Francisco ex-convicts. Jack Brady, the bandit who had escaped after killing Bogard, disappeared for several months, but Gard stayed doggedly on his trail. When the fugitive was finally captured in late July the San Francisco *Chronicle* gave the railroad officer full credit:

> Chief Gard was camped on the trail of Brady for months when detectives Hume and Thacker of Wells, Fargo & Co. laughed at the clew he was following...When the fact became known that a horse had been stolen from the Biggs ranch, only a few days before, Gard was satisfied, from the circumstances, that the man who stole the horse was the man he was after. Brady had worked on the ranch and was one of the few people who could handle the horse...Within a few hours Gard had sent dispatches to every point within a radius of several miles...and the campaign against the elusive man with the sawed-off shotgun proved successful.

When the Southern Pacific cut back its detective force in December of 1895, Gard was retained to look after the company's interests in southern California. At this time he established his own private detective agency and in early April discovered a plot to kidnap financier Cornelius Vanderbilt during a planned visit to California. One of Gard's private jobs sent him on a trip deep into Mexican Yaqui Indian country which at that time was infested with bandits and revolutionaries. He was able to locate and retrieve a stolen bar of gold worth $20,000 and return it to its California owner. For this work he received a $6,000 reward.

It was another private investigation which proved to be his undoing. In late 1903 he was commissioned to investigate the Mexican government's murder claim against a man named Newton Brown. No longer a young man, the exposure incurred by the work brought on an attack of pneumonia and Gard was bedridden for three months. He rallied once, but on March 10, 1904, the Pasadena Daily *News* reported that the "Doctors give up hope for Gard" and his death was expected hourly. He died the following day at his son's home. The old lawman was buried in Los Angeles on March 13 under the auspices of the Grand Army of the Republic.

PRINCIPAL SOURCES ——————————————————————

Guinn, J.M., *Historical and Biographical Record of Los Angeles and Vicinity,* Chicago, Chapman Pub. Co., 1901; Newmark, Harris, *Sixty Years in Southern California,* N.Y., Houghton Mifflin Co., 1930; Traver *Advocate,* June 15, 1893, Feb. 22, 1894; San Francisco *Chronicle,* Apr. 29, July 30, 31, 1895, Apr. 6, 1896, Mar. 11, 1904; Weekly Visalia *Delta,* June 15, 20, 22, 1893; Fresno *Daily Expositor,* July 1, 1893; Fresno *Morning Republican,* Apr. 13, 1894; Fresno *Weekly Republican,* June 16, 1893; The National Archives and Records Service; Wells, Fargo Bank History Room, San Francisco.

Although a prominent Southern California pioneer, Luman Gaskill (left) had a checkered career. Silas (at right) and his brother were a combination that a gang of border bandits found hard to beat. *From J.M. Guinn's* Historical and Biographical Record of Los Angeles and Vicinity.

LUMAN H. and SILAS E. GASKILL

Although neither lawmen, badmen or outlaws, the two Gaskill brothers must be included in any gunsmoke narrative of early California. Silas was born in New York in 1829, while brother Luman began life in Steuben County, Indiana on July 17, 1843. The boys grew up in Michigan, but followed their father to California in 1857. The family worked in the dairy business at Petaluma, but the brothers soon left home to engage in careers as professional bear hunters. Silas claimed to have killed 266 bears during this period and both men hunted from Mendocino to San Bernardino, killing and selling game to the frontier settlements during the 1860s. They farmed at San Bernardino for a time, then took up residence at San Jacinto with their families.

In the spring of 1868 the two brothers moved to a spot called Campo located some fifty miles southeast of San Diego, on the stage road to Yuma. Here they bought up large tracts of land for cattle ranching, while engaging in bee culture. Eventually they became the second largest producers of honey in the country. The Gaskills established a general store which was run by Luman, while Silas operated a blacksmith shop next door. A small village developed which was noted in the San Diego *Union* in April of 1875:

> NOTES FROM CAMPO—This thriving settlement, situated at the southern extremity of Milquitay Valley, will shortly be appreciated as one of the most prosperous little places in San Diego County...

147

Gaskill brothers are carrying on quite a business. They have their mill and dam almost completed, and therefore will soon have in operation their new model of a turbine waterwheel...[The] mill is intended for flouring, sawing and wood turning purposes...There will be enough power to attach machinery for a woolen mill...

Gaskill brothers have a fine herd of goats, mostly wool-bearing, of the fine Angora breed. They have just finished shearing...We had a social gathering here last evening, everybody participating. Dancing was kept up until the small hours. All passed off delightfully.

But there was trouble brewing in the Gaskill paradise. There had been a gold strike and a great deal of political unrest in Mexican Sonora. Badmen and outlaws were as thick as fleas in nearby Tecate Valley. Too, the remnants of Tiburcio Vasquez' gang had been active under the leadership of Clodoveo Chavez, his principal lieutenant. Chavez had recently been killed in Arizona, but rumors of his gang were everywhere. In the last few weeks of November 1875, the village of Campo had gone on alert when it was learned Chavez' gang was in Lower California, planning to attack the town. Guns were placed at strategic locations in town and the Gaskills looked closely at every Mexican stranger. The rumors seemed to be just that, however, and after three weeks of anxiety, the Campo inhabitants relaxed again.

Just after ten o'clock on the morning of December 4th, six Mexican vaqueros rode up and dismounted in front of the Gaskill store. It was Saturday and there was not yet much activity. Later it was discovered that eight to ten compadres lurked in the rocks just outside town, while two wagons waited about a mile away. The six vaqueros stepped inside the store and looked around. Luman Gaskill was puttering away behind his counter and looked up to see three of the visitors turn and walk back outside. The other three Mexicans walked toward the counter and suddenly pulled their six shooters. Gaskill barely had time to yell a warning to his brother next door before ducking under the counter and scrambling toward a shotgun. Two of the bandits vaulted over the counter on top of Luman, Cruz Lopez shooting the merchant through the chest. Blood spattered all over the three men as the bandits left Gaskill for dead and began ransacking the store. Outside, the outlaws were shooting at anything that moved. When the three Mexicans in the store ran outside the battle began in earnest as noted in the report of the San Diego *Union* of December 5, 1875:

...Mr. [Luman] Gaskill, however, ran outside with a double-barrelled shotgun and shot one of the gang twice in the face with buckshot and brought him to the ground.

Another one of the band rushed into the blacksmith shop with the intention of killing Mr. S.E. Gaskill and fired once, shooting through the fleshy part of his shoulder. But that was the last shot he ever fired, for Mr. Gaskill shot him dead in his tracks..."

One of the great gunbattles of the Old West was fought in and around the Gaskill store, shown at right as it appeared sometime after the fight. The creek bed runs behind the store. *Courtesy San Diego Historical Society.*

As another Mexican ran to head off Silas from reaching the store, the blacksmith dropped him also. Meanwhile, a government telegrapher who worked in the store stepped out and exchanged several shots with a bandit, then retreated out of sight under a building.

A Frenchman who had been at the post office was trying to mount his frightened horse when one of the bandits dropped him with a well-aimed shot. Luman, weak from the loss of blood, ducked under the store and stood in the creek which flowed behind the building. He met the telegrapher there also and told him to keep quiet while he would try and reach his home where he could obtain his needle gun. He made it home, but collapsed in a bloody heap, his wife hardly recognizing her bloody mate.

Cruz Lopez, the bandit leader, realized his gang had barely escaped annihilation. He and one of his men scrambled aboard their horses and galloped east on the Yuma road. When he saw his compatriot was wounded, Lopez pushed him from his horse and galloped off leading the extra animal.

The raid was over as suddenly as it had begun. Word of the battle was telegraphed to San Diego and Sheriff William Hunsaker, Dr. Millard and several others immediately left for the scene of action. In Campo the wounded Gaskill brothers were bandaged and put to bed, but it was thought Luman was mortally wounded. The one dead bandit was identified as Fedoro Vasquez from papers found on the body. Another bandit was badly wounded and was cared for under guard. He identified Cruz Lopez, a former member of the Chavez gang, as the leader and the other two outlaws as Pancho Alveto and Roma Cota. A posse of ten local ranchmen immediately rode out after the escaping outlaws, but they had apparently split up and were never caught. Early the following morning another of the bandits crawled up to a house and surrendered. He was desperately wounded and Dr. Millard did not think he could live.

Both the wounded bandits were ironed and put under guard by Sheriff Hunsaker, but late in the evening of December 5th they were taken from the guard and lynched. Several other murders and robberies committed by the gang prior to the Campo raid were later reported. Lopez had also been wounded and reportedly died in Mexico a year later.

Luman Gaskill made a miraculous recovery, but there were rumors of further trouble. Writing to a friend in San Diego, Silas noted their precarious situation:

> We have been told by parties from Tecate that they [the bandits] intend to try us again; that they are determined to rob us before they give it up. They say they will try it next time with force sufficient to go through us.
>
> ...I wish you could see what influence you can use for us and see if we can't get some protection some way. I tell you it is very unpleasant to live where every man you see you think is a robber coming to pull a pistol or a Henry rifle on you and commence shooting without any warning whatever...

A meeting of businessmen of San Diego was held on the evening of December 15th. It was agreed that a posse of local men would be sent to Campo to aid in defense of the town. H.H. Wildy, district attorney elect, volunteered to lead the group and subscriptions were taken to pay the posse which left the next day. Wildy's party was received with cheers in Campo and they stayed on until relieved by an army detachment from Fort Yuma. There were various scares the next few months, large bands of bandits approaching within a few miles of town. Fortunately, they revised their plans when they learned of the reception awaiting them. There were no more bandit raids on Campo.

Luman Gaskill fully recovered from his wounds and lived to enjoy further adventures in the southern border country. When a cattle rancher named Hansen disappeared in 1885, his wagon was found behind Luman's home. Hansen's ranch was located in Mexico, just across the border and several weeks after the disappearance Luman and a friend named Ward were found branding Hansen's cattle. Seized by Mexican authorities, the two suspected rustlers were held in the Ensenada jail for trial. The day of the trial, Ward took sick and died, but Luman was subjected to a lengthy hearing and found guilty of cattle theft. He was sentenced to three years in the Ensenada jail, but when funds ran low the authorities gave him a parole with orders to report to them regularly and not leave the area. Luman moved his family to Ensenada and built a substantial home while engaging in the butcher business.

Luman frequently prospected in the area of his confinement and one day was shown some rich placer diggings by some Mexicans on the Santa Clara ranch. The discovery turned into a minor gold rush, but although it attracted much attention, it soon petered out. Gaskill was reported shot by the disgruntled original discoverers, but either the report was in error or he was merely slightly wounded.

After a rich, full life of high adventure, Luman Gaskill died at the home of a daughter on May 4, 1914. His brother Silas died later that same year.

PRINCIPAL SOURCES ────────────────────

Guinn, J.M., *History of California and an Extended History of Its Southern Coast Counties,* Los Angeles, Historic Record Co., 1907; Lockinwood, Herbert, *Skeleton's Closet,* San Diego, San Diego *Independent,* 1967; San Diego *Union,* Apr. 30, Dec. 3, 5, 7, 8, 15, 18, 19, 28, 1875, Jan. 6, Mar. 15, 1876, Feb. 27, Mar. 3, Mar. 15, 1889, May 14, 1914.

JACK GORDON

The birth of Peter Worthington to a prominent family of old Virginia in the mid-1820s initiated one of the strangest sagas of early California. Indications are that Peter was actually born in Maryland and had two brothers and two sisters. When he was just seventeen, young Worthington killed a man and fled to the far west where he reportedly trapped in the Rocky Mountains. He took the name of John, or Jack, Gordon and to further disguise his identity told his companions that he was an English sailor who had jumped ship. Gordon served with Colonel A.W. Doniphan's command in the Mexican War and while in camp at El Paso del Norte in early 1847 he killed a local citizen in a brawl. Escaping jail, Gordon fled up the Rio Grande where he was captured by Apaches. He lived with the Indians for a time and after winning their trust, was adopted into the tribe. During 1847 and 48 Gordon led raids against Mexican and American settlements and also took an Apache wife.

In September of 1849 Jack Hays, the famous Texas Ranger, arrived in El Paso. He had a commission as Indian agent in the Gila River country, but was also traveling to California with others. In casting about for someone to assist in calling a conference with Indians, Hays heard of the fugitive Gordon and was able to meet him and secure his help. John Nugent, one of Hays' party, described the renegade white man some years later:

> . . . He was about five feet eight or nine inches in height, robust in frame, and wonderfully modeled for strength and muscular activity, while in endurance he excelled any white man or Indian I ever met. Light haired and blue eyed, his face was colorless as to blood, but embrowned by years of exposure to the weather . . .

Gordon was able to arrange a parley with the Indians, but before the meeting could take place, Mexican troops arrived and chased the Apaches off after a sharp fight. When the Indians now refused to meet with the whites for fear of a trap, Gordon rejoined Hays' party and admitted that he had fought with the Apaches against Mexican troops. Traveling on with the Hays party to Tucson, Gordon then left and rejoined the Apaches. When the Mexican authorities slapped a five thousand peso reward on his head, Gordon concluded it was time he left for California.

In the winter of 1850-51 John Nugent was looking out of a window overlooking a rain-swept Montgomery Street in San Francisco. He saw a man riding past wearing a soldier's overcoat with a turned up collar, but Nugent recognized him immediately:

> ..."Muffled as he was, I had no difficulty in recognizing him as John Gordon, whom I had first met at El Paso in September of 1849...As I had afterwards learned, he had broken jail at San Jose the night previous to his appearance on Montgomery street, having been convicted of horse-stealing and sentenced by Judge John H. Watson, District Judge, to two years imprisonment...

Gordon next headed into the gold rush country to lose himself in the mining camps along the foothills. He was reported mining around Coarsegold Gulch, in Mariposa County where a brother, Henry Worthington, lived for a time. One day a bounty hunter showed up in camp hoping to collect the Mexican reward on Gordon's head. At a local miner's meeting, Gordon stood up on a stump, announced who he was and said he was ready for anyone who wanted him. He was not bothered. He was still in the area during the spring of 1853 when a group of state rangers were formed to track down the noted bandit, Joaquin Murrieta. Harry Love, the commander of the group, was only authorized to enlist twenty rangers, but for a time, Gordon and several others went along as unofficial members hoping to share in recovered bandit loot.

In the mid-1850s Gordon is reported in both California and Texas and it is difficult to trace his movements. Prospector Joshua Henshaw mentioned meeting Gordon in the Kern River country in 1855 as a member of a gang of "highway robbers," but his date may be off:

> ...Jack Gordon, from Mexico, was one of this gang, and a splendid shot. He was up to our camp one night and I asked him if I could go shooting with him the next morning. He agreed [and] we went off about two miles to Black Mountain, and the first thing we saw was Mr. Grizzly. Jack took aim with his rifle and it snapped; I fired my rifle, having only balls in it, and they would not take effect. We ran for the trees and Jack got partly up and the bear caught him by the leg. The dog came up and bit the bear, who let go his hold and went for the tree where our Indians had taken refuge and shook one of them down...and killed him. Jack, who was badly wounded, got down and put six shots from a navy pistol into the bear and killed him...

Gordon built a dugout on Tulare Lake where he lived with an Indian woman and engaged in the stock business. This was largely a cover for more insidious work, however. Jeff Mayfield, a longtime resident of the area who knew Gordon well, commented that "It is my belief that Gordon was responsible for the disappearance of several men who left Tailholt and were not heard from afterward. In the mining days there were always men coming and going. When a man left, we often never heard from him again. That made it easy for a man like Gordon to waylay anyone leaving the country." Gordon was a partner of Mayfield's father for a time, mostly in a hog-raising venture. The men drove their stock to the mines where it was sold quite profitably to the pork-hungry miners.

Various sources report Gordon in Texas during 1856, but he was back in Tulare County in April of 1858 when a man named Harris and a "Dutchman" visited Tulare Lake on a cattle-buying expedition. It became known they were carrying some $4,000 in cash and later Harris was found murdered. Two mules had been acquired by Harris at the Orestimba and when one was found loose and the Dutchman seen with the other, foul play was suspected. An account of the following events was published in the *Pacific Sentinel* on June 12, 1858:

> . . . A man named Jack Gordon and some Indians from a rancheria near the lake are in pursuit of the Dutchman and will probably overtake him. Mr. Harris said he lived on the other side of the bay, I think, on Russian River. He said he had four thousand dollars in money with him.

Gordon caught up with the Dutchman, killed him and took his watch and money before disposing of the body. When he returned he told Mayfield that he had killed the robber in self-defense, but that he could find no money. After Mayfield investigated and discovered what really happened, he dissolved his partnership with the killer.

During 1864 Gordon was suspected by Jeff Mayfield and others of being connected with the notorious Mason-Henry gang of so-called Confederate guerillas. Since the gang did not really begin their murderous raids until early in November, Gordon had little time in which to associate with them. During this time he was still mining near Tailholt and hog ranching with a new partner named Samuel "Cap" Groupie. When the partnership was dissolved there were hard feelings. Neighbors, noting that Gordon had butchered several hogs that resembled Groupie's, hid Cap's look-a-like hogs and told him that Gordon had butchered them. Cap swore he would kill Gordon and when the two met on the street at Tailholt the result was noted in the Visalia *Delta* of December 21, 1864:

> More shooting—. . . Tailholt was the scene of a lively little shooting match between a Polander, familiarly known as "old Cap," and the celebrated Jack Gordon, a brave but rather desperate character, and withal a quiet and peacable man when "let alone."
>
> The quarrel . . . commenced about some hogs, which one or the other had charged had been stolen. "Old Cap" took Gordon, unarmed, under cover of a shotgun loaded with buckshot. Gordon asked him to put up his gun until he could get his "six-shooter," . . . and as he did so, "Old Cap" fired and shot him through the abdomen, when he simply remarked, "I'm killed, " and retired to a store near at hand where his arms were, his adversary following, and as he approached, Gordon fired . . . and put a ball plum through his body . . .

Actually, both Jeff Mayfield and an account in a Los Angeles newspaper reported Gordon had been armed at the time of the meeting, but that Groupie got off the first shot. Mortally wounded, Gordon was taken to the store of Levi

Above: Tailholt as it appeared about 1880. Gordon was fatally shot in the street intersection shown just over the roof of the dance hall in left foreground. He's buried on the large hill in the right foreground. *From Schutt Collection, courtesy Special Collections, Library, California State University Fresno.*

Below: Street scene in old Tailholt. Jack Gordon died in Levi Mitchell's store, shown at left. *From Jeff Edwards Collection.*

Levi Mitchell, shown here in 1866, knew Gordon and owned the store were the desperado died. Mitchell was administrator of the Gordon estate and cared for the Indian girl Chescott until her early death. *Courtesy Annie Mitchell.*

Mitchell where he expired in a short time. An autopsy was held on December 15th on the body of "Peter Worthington, alias J.P., Gordon, deceased," and later he was buried in the local boot hill in back of the Mitchell store at Tailholt. Groupie survived his wound and was not prosecuted for the homicide.

Levi Mitchell was made administrator of the Gordon estate and a list of property indicated he was trading with the Indians at the time of his death. Some time prior to his death Gordon had found a young Indian girl wandering alone and had adopted her. As he lay on his deathbed Gordon directed that after his debts and funeral had been taken care of, the remainder of his estate was to go toward support of the child. The girl's name was Chescott and Levi Mitchell and his wife cared for her for a time, but she died at an early age and is buried on the same hill as Gordon.

The man thought to be Gordon's brother, Henry G. Worthington, was a prominent attorney in Mariposa County, but soon left to travel in Central America and Mexico. Later he was a state representative from San Francisco and a congressman from Nevada in 1864-65. He served in various government posts, including U.S. district judge and major general of the militia. He was a warm, personal friend of Abraham Lincoln and when General Worthington died in Washington D.C. in July of 1909 he was the last survivor of those who had served as pallbearers at Lincoln's funeral.

PRINCIPAL SOURCES

Greer, James Kimmins, *Colonel Jack Hays,* Waco, Tex., W.M. Morrison, Pub., 1974: Latta, Frank F., *Tailholt Tales,* Santa Cruz, Bear State Books, 1976; Mitchell, Annie, *Sites to See, Historical Landmarks in Tulare County,* Fresno, Panorama West Books, 1983; Austerman, Wayne R., "The English Apache," *Real West,* Feb. 1986; Nugent, John, "Scraps of Early History," *The Argonaut,* (San Francisco), (undated) 1878; Henshaw, Joshua, "Historical Times in California," manuscript in Bancroft Library, Univ. of California, Berkeley; Visalia *Delta,* Dec. 21, 1864; Los Angeles *Tri-Weekly News,* Jan. 3, 1865; Peter Worthington inquest record and other data from collection of Annie Mitchell, Visalia; Correspondence with Wayne R. Austerman and Annie Mitchell, 1986-87.

WILLIAM HICKS GRAHAM

Little is known of Will Graham's early years, but he was born in Philadelphia on July 21, 1829 and apparently had a good education. He was probably related to the publishing Grahams of that city and reportedly worked on a New York City newpaper when he was a young man. He was living in South America when news of the great California gold discovery thrilled the world. He headed north at the first opportunity, landing at San Francisco from the steamer *Tennessee* in June of 1850.

In the bay city Graham found work as a clerk in the law office of Probate Judge R.N. Morrison. The judge was a cantankerous type and became embroiled in an estate squabble with William Walker, editor of the *Herald* and later a noted filibuster. When the editor accused Morrison of corruption, Walker was challenged to a duel by Graham. No one gave the unknown young law clerk any chance against Walker, who was already a noted duelist. When they met at the old Mission Dolores on January 12, 1851, Graham was no doubt as surprised as anyone at the outcome as noted in the San Francisco *Alta:*

The Plaza of old San Francisco as it looked when Will Graham arrived in June of 1850.
Courtesy California State Library.

Left: Editor William Walker already had a reputation as a fighter when young Graham challenged him to a duel. *Courtesy California State Library*.

Below: Graham's duel with Walker took place at the old Mission Dolores, shown here as it appeared in 1856. *From G. R. Fardon's* San Francisco Album.

...Two shots were exchanged, At the first fire Mr. Walker received his adversary's ball through the leg of his pantaloons and at the second fire was shot through the fleshy part of the thigh...Mr. Graham challenged the editor on behalf of Judge Morrison. We thought the days of Knight errantry had passed away.

Hauled into court on an assault charge, Graham was already involved in another squabble by the time he won his case.

A man named George Frank Lemon introduced Will to a woman named Anne Hughes and the young clerk fell instantly in love. They were married that summer, but when Will discovered his bride was still seeing Lemon, he was furious. Locating his former friend in the bar room of the Oriental Hotel, Graham sloshed a glass of water in Lemon's face. "You know where to find, me," growled the clerk and left to wait for the expected challenge. When it did not come, he published the following notice in two the city's leading newspapers, besides posting it in the public square:

> I hereby post and publish George Frank Lemon as a scoundrel, villain, liar and poltroon and declare him to be out of the pale of gentlemen's society.
>
> William H. Graham

The two men met on the city plaza on July 2nd and after sizing each other up for a time, began shooting as described by an eyewitness:

> ...I heard several shots and saw people running in all directions. I started on a run towards the scene of action when near Kearny Street, opposite the Union Hotel, I saw and heard several shots and saw a man fall by the name of Graham, another man by the name of George Frank Lemon advanced towards him and shot him in the mouth. Graham was also shot in the left arm. As many as nine shots were fired by the parties. Only one other person was injured, he was shot through the wrist...

Graham had been shot in the arm and mouth, a ball taking out a chunk of lip and going through his tongue. Neither wound was very serious, but Will's ego was in a terrible state of disarray. "It is doubtful whether the matter ends here," commented the *Alta* prophetically. Just as soon as his wounds had healed, Graham challenged Lemon again. The next meeting was held outside the city as noted in the *Alta* of September 15, 1851:

> Affair of Honor—An affair of honor came off yesterday morning near the barracks at Benicia, between Mr. W.H. Graham and George Frank Lemon. The parties met and fired seven shots. The last shot wounded Mr. Lemon seriously and the affair was terminated. All the parties returned to this city last evening.

When he heard Lemon would live, Will issued another challenge, but mutual friends interceded and managed to avoid another meeting. The randy Mr. Lemon was reported to be living in New York in 1861 where he was divorced by his long-suffering wife after he was arrested for seducing a widow.

George E. Barnes, who knew Graham in the dueling fifties, described him some years later: "Graham was a thread-paper of a man. You wondered how such a diminutive and slender body could carry such a big heart and stout courage. His face was slightly weazened and his complexion pale, almost colorless."

Will was clerking at the Custom House at this time, but he was also dabbling in politics. Although a Democrat, he belonged to the vigilantes in 1851. He was appointed superintendent of San Quentin Prison in late March of 1856. In April of 1858 he was appointed to the lucrative job of State Sealer of Weights and Measures for several counties, an appointment that outraged some as reported in the *Call:*

> This Will Hicks Graham...is perhaps as bad a man as lives today in California...There has not been a dirty job accomplished in the Democratic convention for six years without the aid of Will Hicks Graham...As an unscruptuous lobby member and hired bill-broker, he has always been conspicuous, even in a crowd of distinguished rogues...His name is another synonym for all that is vile...Two nights before the legislature adjourned, a member of the Assembly, who saw fit...to oppose a bill in which Graham was interested, was abused and insulted by him, within the bar of the chamber, struck with a heavy bludgeon, and his life menaced by a deadly weapon...

Despite this and other "rave" reviews, Graham kept his job and held it until 1861. Meanwhile, he had been studying law all these years and when he left his wife and three children to visit the new silver mines in Nevada, he was a full-fledged attorney. He reportedly shot a man named Jack McBride and one or two others before moving back to California, taking up residence in the mining country of Owens Valley. He was trying a case in the mining camp of Montgomery when he had trouble with a tough named A.J. "Yank" McGuire. The two met in a saloon between court sessions and in the first exchange of gunfire, McGuire took a slug in the chest. Will had only got off the one shot when the cylinder of his pistol fell to the floor. "Cooly stooping down," noted a newspaper account, "Graham picked up the chamber of his revolver, deliberately replaced it and began firing again." Will had his hat shot off and received a minor flesh wound, but McGuire was carried from the room with what was considered a mortal injury. Unfortunately, he survived and in May of 1866 he shot down an unarmed man who had refused to drink with him in a Havilah saloon. McGuire was sentenced to hang for this murder, but he secured a new trial and after spending several years in jail, was released when witnesses could not be obtained for his hearing.

Graham lived to regret his shooting days as noted by an old friend writing in the San Francisco *Call* in 1883:

> Few men ever knew how thoroughly he despised, in his later years, the

reputation of a fighting man. Such a reputation, he would bitterly remark, is a curse to any one. Every reckless fool who wants to get his name up as a desperado, thinks he is duty bound to have a difficulty with you, while you are expected to resent every grievance, real or imaginary, with the knife or pistol. I remember with what earnestness he said, more than once: "If I had my life to live over again, nothing short of absolute dishonor would make me fight anybody!"

Graham moved to the town of Owensville where he captained a volunteer company during the Indian troubles of that region. During this time he was reportedly tutoring law students in his office, one of his pupils being the famed criminal lawyer of later years, Patrick Reddy.

Will's frail physique was symtomatic of health problems and he moved to Los Angeles to seek medical advice. He died there at the Lafayette Hotel on October 16, 1866. A brief notice in the San Francisco press emphasized how few remembered the colorful gunman and politician of the exciting 1850's in the bay city. "He had domestic griefs," penned a friend in later years, "which weighed upon his mind, and, like many another gallant fellow, sought forgetfulness in strong drink. Doubtless this had much to do with his numerous deadly quarrels, for few men were more quiet and inoffensive when sober. Peace to his ashes!"

Disposition of the body is not known.

PRINCIPAL SOURCES

Marryat, Frank, *Mountains and Molehills,* N.Y., Harper & Brothers, 1855; Truman, Major Ben C., *The Field of Honor,* N.Y., Fords, Howard & Hulbert, 1884; Williams, Mary, *History of the San Francisco Committee of Vigilance of 1851,* Berkeley, Univ. of Cal. Press, 1921; *The Argonaut,* May 19, 1877; San Francisco *Daily Alta California,* Dec. 5, 28, 1850, Jan. 13, 14, 15, July 3, 26, Aug. 10, 1851, Oct. 18, 1866; San Francisco *Bulletin,* Mar. 22, Oct. 16, 23, 1856, Nov. 14, 1896; San Francisco *Daily Morning Call,* Apr. 28, 1858; Pioneer Biographical Card in the California State Library, Sacramento; California State Archives, Sacramento.

EMIL HARRIS

Emil Harris wearing his new badge as chief of police of Los Angeles in 1878. *Courtesy Norton B. Stern and the Western States Jewish History Association.*

Born in Prussia on December 29, 1839, young Emil Harris emigrated to the United States with an aunt in 1853. After living in New York for a time, Harris came to California in 1857 where he worked at various jobs as a printer, waiter and bartender. He lived in San Francisco and Visalia, but moved to Los Angeles in early April of 1869 where he again worked as a bartender and became involved in civic life. Sometime in late 1870 Harris was appointed a patrolman on the Los Angeles Police Force. He was possibly a replacement for two recent vacancies in the department. On October 31, 1870 policeman Joe Dye shot and killed City Marshal William C. Warren in a street fight resulting from a squabble over a reward.

Harris was a natural born lawman. The city police force at this time consisted of six officers and the city marshal. There were two watches of three men each —two of the lawmen being mounted. Salary was $100 for the mounted officers and $80 per month for the patrolmen. Other officers of the time were B.F. Hartley, Jesus Bilderain and George E. Gard. The latter was a particular friend of Harris and the two worked well together. Los Angeles was no longer a scattering of sleepy adobes, but contained a large number of substantial buildings. It was still a tough, frontier town, however, and the handful of policemen had their hands full keeping the peace.

On October 25, 1871, a riot erupted in the Calle de los Negros, a sleazy tenderloin district of the town housing a series of saloons and gambling halls. The trouble erupted when a thug named Robert Thompson tried to rob a

162

Chinese merchant. Thompson was shot and killed and policeman Bilderain was wounded as shots were exchanged and some of the Chinese began barricading their doors. A blood and loot-hungry mob quickly formed and saw an opportunity for plunder. They began seizing Chinese and abusing them as matters rapidly got out of control. Harris later testified:

> Between five and six o'clock yesterday evening, while on duty on Commercial Street...I heard some shots fired and ran toward them to Los Angeles Street, and saw an excited crowd in front of Negro Alley...[The sheriff] requested me and all citizens...to stand alongside of him...The excited multitude got the upper hand...one Chinaman came running out [and I] heard a cry of some white persons, "Here is one!" and I succeeded in capturing him...when some parties...about 100 or more took him from me...they cried "Hang him!"...

Sheriff Jim Burns, Harris and other officers were buffeted and overwhelmed by the mob which swirled around them, but they fought desperately to restore order. When it was over, nineteen Chinese had been lynched. Harris later testified that only one had deserved such a fate. Several months later Harris and Officer Gard were presented gifts from one of the Chinese Companies for their bravery that night.

Harris had the usual experiences of frontier lawmen. In April he was escorting several prisoners to jail when he was attacked by two of their friends. A physical fitness enthusiast, Harris promptly subdued all his attackers and heaved the

The notorious Calle de Los Negros, scene of the terrible Chinese Massacre of 1871. *Courtesy California State Library.*

four men into the city jail. When two Frenchmen began shooting up the town, Harris and several others chased them across the river. Harris then secured a hack and ran the fugitives down, depositing both men in the calaboose.

As early as 1872 the Los Angeles *Star* reported:

> ...The large number of arrests made by officers Gard and Harris seem to deserve special mention. They have succeeded in "working up" and ferreting out some very important and difficult cases, and through their energy and vigilance many rough and dangerous customers have been caught...

After breaking up a counterfeiting operation in the city, Harris and Gard were appointed the first detectives on the Los Angeles police force.

Harris ran for city marshal in 1874 and though he was supported by the *Star* and a large portion of the citizenry, he missed election by only twenty-three votes. In May of the same year, Harris was one of the posse selected by Sheriff William Rowland to capture the notorious bandit Tiburcio Vasquez who had been located nearby. Harris and seven other possemen surrounded the cabin of Greek George where the outlaw was hiding. Several men were stationed outside, while Harris led a rush into the house, taking the bandit by surprise. Harris fired and missed as Vasquez scrambled through a window and made a desperate attempt to reach his horse. Officer Frank Hartley and reporter George Beers were waiting for him and gunned down the desperado. Vasquez' wounds were minor, however, and he lived to hang the following year. Harris confiscated the bandit's rifle which he kept as a trophy for many years. Later, when political enemies on the Los Angeles City Council learned Harris had been out of town without their consent, an attempt was made to have him dismissed from the force. It was so obviously a political act that friends had no trouble getting the matter dismissed.

After his defeat for the office of chief, Harris was hired as a deputy sheriff where he again performed good service. Under a dateline of June 20, 1876, at Los Angeles, the San Francisco *Call* noted:

> Deputy Sheriff Harris arrived today on the *Orizaba,* having in charge John McDonald, convicted of wife murder, J.R. Holt, convicted of robbery, and Francisco Gomez and Sylveser Ardaga, convicted of rape, who are all returned here from San Quentin for new trials...

On March 13, 1877, the Los Angeles *Star* reported Harris' capture of several stage robbers:

> Deputy Sheriff Harris has returned from his hunt after the perpetrators of the recent stage robbery near Indian Wells, the result of which has been that three men, who gave their names as Charles Bush, Jack Phillips and Frank Gibson are in custody, charged with being concerned in the affair. Harris arrested Bush and Phillips in San Bernardino...All the arrests were made in the middle of the night, each of the prisoners being taken from his bed...

On the 18th the *Star* commented; "Messrs. Harris and Dunlap deserve great credit for ferreting out this Indian Wells affair and bringing the perpetrators to speedy punishment." The two officers escorted the prisoners to San Francisco for trial on the 20th.

In late December of 1877 Emil Harris was appointed Chief of Police of Los Angeles—one of the first Jewish chiefs in the country. He was presented with a handsome, fine gold watch by his friends and was even congratulated by the San Francisco *Alta* for receiving the appointment. He quickly resolved a bank robbery case in March of 1878 by correctly deducing that it was an inside job. The following month he successfully tracked down a murderer by utilizing several disguises. Despite an active year as chief, Harris found himself voted out of office by an all new city council in late 1878.

Continuing his work as a lawman, Harris was frequently deputized for special assignments such as delivering prisoners to San Quentin. In March of 1879 he established what was undoubtedly the first private detective agency in Los Angeles. In the early 1880s he served as a court constable, but was soon again appointed to the police force. His sleuthing abilities were widely recognized and in late February of 1888 he was appointed chief of the detective force by the Board of Police Commissioners. In April a succession of burglaries in the city ceased when Harris and police detective Metzler arrested a young Englishman. The burglar confessed that he was part of a gang who operated under a local private detective named A.J. Lucas. Obtaining search warrants, Harris and Metzler arrested Lucas after finding a great deal of stolen property in his office safe and home. A letter from Captain Lees of the San Francisco Police established that Lucas had an unsavory record in that city, also.

Harris served briefly as a police captain under Chief James Burns in 1889.

His association with one C.D. Platt, a disreputable jeweler, was nearly Harris' undoing and tainted his impressive record as a peace officer. Platt narrowly missed being convicted of defrauding creditors in 1884 and was noticeably friendly with Harris during his term as police captain. Platt may have been an informer, but both he and Harris were picked up for extortion in March of 1894. Harris was a private detective at the time and he and Platt had been involved in a messy divorce case between wealthy businessman E.E. Crandall and his wife. Police detectives were lying in wait when Harris met Crandall at the latter's office and reportedly demanded $1,000 for the return of some damaging papers and photographs. Harris had obtained the items from Mrs. Crandall. Platt had also received money from Mrs. Crandall and both he and Harris were jailed. Promptly released on a bond secured by friends, Harris received some bad publicity in the Los Angeles *Times* of the 28th:

> As was stated yesterday, up to the present time Harris has managed to keep out of the clutches of the law, although the burglar Bush gave enough information to secure his arrest. Bush's affidavits are in the city and it is

probably that the statements contained in them will have more weight now than when Harris was a police captain. It is possible, however, that another charge of blackmailing may be lodged against Harris by a man named Douglas...

Harris's trial was commenced in Federal court on September 12, 1894. The detective's counsel managed to instill considerable doubt in the prosecution's witnesses. When Harris was put on the stand he bolstered his case further by a credible story of how he merely accepted a retainer from Crandall and not extortion money. Harris sat in the witness chair, commented the *Times*, "as cooly as though every eye in the courtroom was turned in the opposite direction instead of resting upon himself." The implication of the defense was that Harris was a pawn in the bitter fight between Crandall and his wife. A hung jury resulted in the case being dismissed later that month.

During the 1890s Harris continued his private detective work, serving warrants and other official papers for attorneys and conducting a merchant's security patrol. All his life he was active in youth work, physical fitness projects and various Jewish cultural associations. The old lawman finally retired in 1918 and was hospitalized the following year with heart problems. He was eighty-two years old when he passed away at Los Angeles on April 28, 1921.

Downtown Los Angeles in 1885. This bustling view of Spring street is indicative of the boom taking place in southern California during the 1880's. *From author's collection.*

166

Although little-known today, Harris was a famous sleuth in his prime and known throughout the state. He had seen his adopted city grow from a rough frontier town to a burgeoning metropolis of the West Coast. At his death the *Times* stated:

> Finish will be written at the end of another chapter of the city's early history...when funeral services will be held...for Emil Harris, town marshal of the pueblo of Los Angeles fifty years ago...He was one of the best known peace officers in Southern California.

The veteran lawman was buried at the Jewish Home of Peace Cemetery at Los Angeles.

PRINCIPAL SOURCES ─────────────────────────

Guinn, James Miller, *History and Biographical Record of Southern California,* Chicago, Chapman Pub. Co., 1902; Newmark, Harris, *Sixty Years in Southern California,* Boston and N.Y., Houghton Mifflin Co., 1930; Stern, Norton B., and Kramer, William M., "Emil Harris, Los Angeles Jewish Chief of Police," *Southern California Quarterly,* Hist. Soc. of Southern Calif., 1973; San Francisco *Chronicle,* Mar. 27, 1894; San Francisco *Examiner,* Apr. 20, 1894; Los Angeles *Daily Herald,* Feb. 15, 1878; Los Angeles *Herald-Examiner,* Sept. 15, 1974; Los Angeles *Daily Star,* Oct. 24, 25, Dec. 13, 1871, Jan. 29, 31, Sept. 2, 1872, May 15, 22, June 12, Dec. 3, 5, 1874, Mar. 7, 1876; Los Angeles *Times,* Mar. 28, 1894, Apr. 28, 1921.

LEONARD HARRIS

Leonard Harris, although little-known today, was one of the more prominent west coast lawmen of his time. He is shown here when he was a Sacramento police detective in the 1870's. *Courtesy California State Library.*

A native of New York where he was born about 1827, Len Harris came to California during the gold rush of 1849. He probably worked in the mines for a time, then later secured other employment. Little is known of his early years in the state, but he was apparently living in Sacramento in the late 1850s.

Around 1860 Harris was employed as warden of the Sacramento County jail as a member of the sheriff's office. He was as quick with his fists as he was with his pistol as chronicled in the Sacramento *Union* of September 5, 1861:

> ...About noon the fist fight occured at the Fourth District. A carpenter named Whittacker was trying to induce a voter to scratch the name of Len. Harris, Union Democratic candidate for County Warden, declaring that Len. was a Secessionist. Len. happened along at the moment and denied the charge, when Whittacker repeated it, and said he had a right to say what he pleased. A collision ensued, and the carpenter left the spot with his face badly swollen. A bystander said if the crowd had not interfered, Len probably would have killed this man as he was about to draw his pistol...

Harris was employed as a deputy sheriff throughout the 1860s, being appointed undersheriff during the tenure of Sheriff James Lansing. One of Deputy Harris' regular duties was delivering prisoners to San Quentin as reported in the San Francisco *Call* of February 20, 1867:

> STATE PRISONERS EN ROUTE—Deputy Sheriff Len Harris of Sacramento, arrived in town on the Sacramento boat on Monday night, en route to San Quentin where he is going for the purpose of delivering...Mickey alias John Kelly, under sentence...for burglary, Lewis Williams and George Adams, each under sentence...for burglary, and Bill Shattuck, under sentence of one year's imprisonment for grand larceny.

On a stormy day the following March, Len was delivering more prisoners to San Quentin when he hired a sailboat to take his group across the bay. The boatman turned out to be drunk and when his small craft got into the choppy bay it was very nearly swept out to sea. Len had taken the handcuffs off his prisoners when they made a rough landing at the mouth of the bay. After another try, Harris made his delivery.

Harris accepted a position as turnkey and guard at San Quentin, but was not satisfied with the confining nature of the work. He had a dispute with a superior and was suspended from duty, but in July of 1871 Governor Haight visited the prison and reinstated him. Soon afterwards, however, Harris resigned.

After appointment to the Sacramento city police force, Harris served as a regular patrolman, but soon graduated to detective work. In September of 1872 he and another officer arrested the notorious Charles Mortimer as a suspect in the murder of Mary Gibson, a local prostitute. Harris had known Mortimer, whose real name was Flynn, for years having first met him at San Quentin. Len helped prepare the case against the killer and testified extensively at his trial. Mortimer was hanged the following year for the crime.

Sacramento in the 1870's as it appeared in a photograph taken from the capitol dome. *Courtesy California State Library.*

Harris helped Wells, Fargo detectives Jim Hume and Steve Venard capture two stage robbers in January of 1876. The Sacramento *Bee* reported; "The fellows were taken completely by surprise or they would never have surrendered without bloodshed, for both had declared their determination never to be taken alive." One of the outlaws was the notorious Jim Smith, a former member of the old Tom Bell gang who had served three previous terms at San Quentin. The capture was made at Folsom on information provided by local Constable Kimball.

About 1879 Harris joined the detective force of the Central Pacific Railroad. His actual position is not clear and he may have been chief of detectives, although just how many officers the railroad employed at that time is not known. It was an active job as the company combatted train robbers, boxcar pilferers, thieving clerks and other larcenous types throughout the southwest. Harris spent as much time in Arizona as he did in California during the early 1880s and visited Tombstone, Tucson and Phoenix often on business. One day in Tucson he was boarding a train when he observed a drunken cowboy holding a group of passengers at bay. Walking up to the bully, Len took away his weapon and gave him a good tongue lashing before turning him over to a local peace officer.

In late 1883 while Harris was working on a train robbery case with Jim Hume, the two friends had dinner with a noted, former California lawman named Bob Paul who was now sheriff of Pima County, Arizona. Later the three men enjoyed a Mexican vacation together in Hermosillo and Guaymas, Mexico.

During the late summer of 1887 Harris was a member of a U.S. marshal's posse chasing some train robbers into Mexico. Len and another lawman left the posse just before they crossed the line and later heard that Mexican officials had jailed U.S. Marshal Meade and his men, instead of the robbers. The robbers were later killed by Mexican police and Meade and his men were turned loose to make their way home as best they could.

Back in California Harris helped Hume investigate the Clipper Gap train robbery which occurred on Christmas Eve of 1888. A series of train robberies in the San Joaquin Valley took up most of his time, however. A Southern Pacific train had been robbed near Pixley in late February of 1889 and two men shot. Another holdup took place near Goshen a year later. Harris and S.P. detective Bill Hickey had worked hard on these cases, but with no results. When another train was stopped on February 6, 1891, again the robbers escaped leaving few clues. This time the crime was fastened on the Dalton brothers, two of whom were picked up. Despite the efforts of Hume, Harris and herds of local lawmen, the other crimes went unsolved.

On September 3, 1891, Harris and another S.P. detective named A.B. Lawson were riding a southbound train when it was stopped a few miles south of Modesto, near a place called Ceres. When the Wells, Fargo agent refused to open the express car door, a bomb was tossed which blew a hole in the door, but still did not shake the messenger's resolve. As the two bandits were preparing to toss another bomb, Harris and Lawson jumped from the train and opened fire. In the resulting shootout, Harris was badly wounded in the neck, but the outlaws ran to their horses and galloped off into the night. Len was rushed to the hospital at Merced, but he was badly wounded and his recovery was long and painful as noted by the Fresno Evening *Expositor* in June of 1892:

> "...Do you know where the bullet is?" asked the reporter. "I wish to God I did," said Mr. Harris, "I have suffered death many times and it seems to me that unless I have this bullet removed, the pain will kill me. I intend to let the doctors probe again to try and find and then remove it."
>
> Mr. Harris is an heroic sufferer for he preserves his usual disposition, although it is evident he is in great misery...

In mid-May of 1894 Harris was tipped off concerning a plan to rob the railroad station at Boulder Creek, in Santa Cruz County. The informant, one George Sprague, had been in on the robbery plan, but decided to inform on his partner instead. The detective told Sprague to just go along with the plans and that the lawmen would be present at the proper time to nab the robber, a fellow named Alex Azoff.

At 8 o'clock on the evening of May 16th, Harris and two other officers were waiting in a nearby box car when Azoff and Sprague approached and entered the station. The clerk was just gathering the money when Harris stepped into the doorway and called out for Azoff to surrender—that he was surrounded. Quick as lightning, the robber whirled and fired several shots at the lawman and several more out the window. Rushing past the wounded Harris, Azoff then vanished into the night. The old detective had not told his fellow officers that Sprague was working with him and the informer was roughly handled until the weak and bloodied Harris explained the situation.

Prison mug shot of Alexander Azoff, the killer of Len Harris. He was hanged at San Quentin for his crime. *Courtesy Peter Palmquist.*

171

The depot at Boulder Creek where Len Harris interrupted a holdup and was fatally wounded in the resulting shootout. *From California State Library.*

Rushed by special train to his daughter's home in Oakland, Harris was attended by four physicians, but it was soon apparent the old officer had fought his last battle. He died a few minutes before midnight on May 16, 1894. The funeral was held at his Alameda home, then the body was shipped to Sacramento for burial. Azoff was captured a few days later and was convicted and hanged on June 7, 1895.

Under the heading "BRAVE LEN HARRIS IS DEAD," the Sacramento Daily *Record-Union* voiced the opinion of many in its obituary:

> ... Len Harris was one of the bravest and best peace officers that ever wore a badge ... He had been in many very tight places, but no one ever heard of his quailing before a foe.

The veteran lawman was survived by two children, his wife having passed away in 1885. His son, Jack Harris was shot and killed in a pistol duel in Sacramento in 1895.

PRINCIPAL SOURCES

Dillon, Richard, *Wells, Fargo Detective,* N.Y., Coward-McCann, Inc., 1969; Duke, Thomas S., *Celebrated Criminal Cases of America,* San Francisco, James H. Barry Co., 1910; Latta, Frank F., *Dalton Gang Days,* Santa Cruz, Bear State Books, 1976; Wright, George F., (ed.) *History of Sacramento County, California,* Oakland, Thompson & West, 1880; San Francisco *Daily Alta California,* Mar. 19, 1867; Sacramento *Bee,* Jan. 29, Aug. 9, 1876; San Francisco *Evening Bulletin,* July 27, 1871; San Francisco *Daily Morning Call,* Feb. 14, 20, 1867, May 16, 17, 20, June 26, 1894; San Francisco *Chronicle,* May 16, 17, 18, 20, 1894; Sacramento *Union,* Sept. 5, 6, 1861, June 23, 24, 1885, Sept. 5, 1891.

JAMES HENRY
(Thomas McCauley)

Illinois was the birthplace of Thomas McCauley where he was born about 1833. Little is known of his early life, but he and his brother apparently came to California during the early 1850's. Ed McCauley was described by an early chronicler as a "large strong fellow, a rough of pronounced type, whose occupation, if he had any beyond quarreling and fighting, is not set down." The brothers lived near Shaw's Flat, in Tuolumne County where they worked as little as possible and made a living gambling, jumping claims and robbing sluice boxes. Usually accompanied by several other thugs of a like character, they formed a tough, hard-drinking crew.

In October of 1856 Ed McCauley assaulted a man named Fair in a saloon at Whimtown, near Shaw's Flat. Ed and Tom, together with another thug named "Big Dick" were on a drunken spree at the time and after seriously injuring Fair, they were arrested by officers. The trio was tried at Shaw's Flat and compelled to pay a fine of $100 each, primarily on the testimony of a young miner named Bonds. The following day Bonds was sitting in a saloon with a friend when the McCauleys and a crony named Andy Carr walked in. The toughs began badgering young Bonds about his testimony, finally calling him a "damn liar." When Bonds got up to leave, Carr blocked the doorway and shoved him violently away. Bonds then shot and killed Carr as noted in the Columbia *Campaign Gazette:*

> ...immediately on the shot being fired, Edward McCauley stepped up behind Bonds with a fourteen inch bowie knife and plunged it into Bonds' left side...the knife went in the whole length...
>
> Big Dick seized Bonds, and wrested the pistol from him, and Bonds immediately ran out of the house to his cabin...

Tom McCauley scuffled with Big Dick to get the pistol so he could follow Bonds and shoot him, but they later heard he had died from the knife wound. The McCauleys and Big Dick were arrested and held for trial on murder charges. In December it was reported that accomplices attempted to break them out of the Sonora jail. The McCauleys came close to being lynched at one point, but were finally tried, Ed McCauley being sentenced to death and Tom receiving a nine year prison sentence. Ed was hanged with two others on December 11, 1857, while Tom was received at San Quentin on March 18th of the same year.

Tom's prison number was 1120 and he is described in the register as being twenty-four years of age; occupation, miner; height, 5'9"; dark complexion; grey eyes; dark hair and scars on his right thumb and left hand near little finger. There is no record of his leaving prison, but whether he was pardoned or escaped he was free again by 1863 and took up residence in Merced and Fresno counties.

Easily slipping back into his old ways, McCauley changed his name to Jackson and joined a gang of robbers and thugs who specialized in robbing Chinese camps in the foothills, along the Fresno River. When vigilantes lynched Al Dixon, the gang's leader, his followers promptly sought other scenes.

McCauley now began using the name Jim Henry to help cover his tracks. He probably met John Mason in early 1864 after that thug had shot and wounded Joe Anderson, his employer at Tulare Lake. The two met with a large rancher on the Merced River who was a rabid secessionist and wanted to wage guerilla warfare in the valley. Outfitted by the rancher, Mason and Henry tried to put together a gang in the Santa Clara Valley, but a severe drouth coupled with disastrous war news made for little success in the summer of 1864.

Heading back to the San Joaquin Valley, Mason and Henry gave up any ideas of guerilla warfare and took up plunder and murder instead. They killed a sheepherder in the mountains, then looked up Mason's old employer, Joe Anderson, and murdered him. They next gunned down the owner of Hawthorne's stage station near Visalia. Riding north to the next station, the two killers shot down Robinson, the owner, as he was returning home to his wife and children. The murderers then fled the area with several sheriff's posses and a detachment of soldiers on their trail. On November 11th, three days after the murders, a Visalia resident sent the following telegram to Governor Frederick Low:

> Community all excitement over cold blooded triple murder—two (2) desperadoes viz John Mason and John Doe alias Jackson, Miller & etc. killed a German below Firebaugh's Ferry. J. Hawthorne near Fresno City and Robinson at Elkhorn Ranch and are believed to be seeking other victims. People desire you to offer a heavy reward as it may stop much bloodshed if offered. Telegraph here and to Gilroy, we will strike bills with description.
>
> H. W. Briggs

The governor offered a $1000 reward later that month and notices with the promised descriptions of the killers were published in newspapers from Visalia to Santa Cruz. A description of Henry, published in the Visalia *Delta*, was as follows:

> Dark hair and heavy dark beard...except upper lip; chocolate colored pants; old black coat with many holes in it; small black hat, very old and lopped over; dark eyes; wore two shirts;...boots, leggins and spurs' riding large, flea-bitten grey horse, the property of Hawthorne...

A telegram sent to Governor Low asking for prompt action against Mason and Henry. *Courtesy California State Archives.*

By March of 1865 Mason and Henry had recruited some followers and were reported to be stealing horses in Merced County. Various robberies in the Kern River Valley and San Bernardino areas were charged to them, also. Army units in pursuit reported the gang as being twenty men strong at this time, although it is doubtful there were ever that many in the group. Known members of the gang at various times included a man named "Texas," John Rogers, Tom Hawkins, and Joe Dye.

In July Mason and Henry robbed the store of Eugene Calliaud on the upper Kern River. The following evening Mason and Tom Hawkins killed a herder at the Jewett sheep camp in the foothills, the owner barely escaping with his life. The Visalia *Delta* expressed its dismay at the events:

> We are getting disgusted with chronicling the depredations of these two scamps, and begin to think that if they can be secured by neither official nor private effort by military nor civilians, that the honest portion of the community had better sell out and give it [the valley] to Mason and Henry and the Diggers...Probably if the $2500 now offered for their arrest could be made available they might be bought off and induced to transfer their amusements to some other region.

On August 17th they robbed McFarland's store in Lynn's Valley, then headed

175

When Henry was killed his body was brought into San Bernardino where it was put on display. The town is shown here as it appeared in 1865. *Courtesy Steele's Photo Service.*

south where they separated—some said over a woman. Henry and several others were near San Bernardino in September when he sent John Rogers into town for supplies. Rogers proceeded to get drunk and bragged of his outlaw connections to anyone who would listen. He soon found himself accompanying a posse of soldiers and civilians to the outlaw hideout. The camp was surrounded while Henry was still asleep, the resulting fight being described in a dispatch to the Los Angeles *Tri-Weekly News:*

> San Bernardino, September 16, 1865...Day before yesterday morning about daylight, our sheriff, with a posse of three soldiers and two or three citizens, ran across the notorious Henry, of Mason and Henry notoriety, and after making some resistance he was killed by them...
>
> The posse kept as still as possible, but their noise awoke him, when he jumped up, drew a revolver, and resisted to the last, firing three times and wounding one man in the foot. But the shot and balls soon brought him down, covered with wounds, and he died immediately, without saying a word...

Henry's body, reportedly covered with some fifty-seven wounds, was brought to San Bernardino where it was photographed for identification purposes. Many years later it was disclosed that Mason came into town while disguised as a woman and viewed the body. Disposition of the body is not known, but he was undoubtedly buried locally.

PRINCIPAL SOURCES ————————————

Buckbee, Edna Bryan, *The Saga of Old Tuolumne,* N.Y., Press of the Pioneers, 1935; [No Author], *A History of Tuolumne County,* San Francisco, B.F. Alley, 1882; Latta, Frank F., *Tailholt Tales,* Santa Cruz, Bear State Books, 1976; Vandor, Paul E., *History of Fresno County,* Los Angeles, Historic Record Co., 1919; Winchell, Lilbourne Alsip, *History of Fresno County,* Fresno, A.H. Cawston, 1933; The Visalia *Delta,* Nov. 16, 10, Dec. 7, 21, 1864, Feb. 15, Mar. 1, 15, Apr. 12, Aug. 23, 30, 1865, Apr. 18, 25, July 17, Aug. 1, Nov. 7, Dec. 14, 1866; San Francisco *Bulletin,* Oct. 21, Dec. 10, 1856; San Jose *Mercury,* Sept. 28, 1865; Santa Cruz *Sentinel,* Sept. 23, 1865; Los Angeles *Tri-Weekly News,* Apr. 18, Sept. 19, Oct. 10, 1865; Manuscript materials in Fresno City and County Hist. Soc., Fresno; Prison records in California State Archives, Sacramento.

DR. ALEXANDER W. HOPE

Born in Virginia about 1826, Dr. Hope served in the Mexican War and apparently arrived in California during the gold rush in 1848. Although obviously younger, he is listed as being 30 years of age and a physician in the 1850 Los Angeles census. He was a member of the first California state senate and established one of the first local drug stores besides being one of the earliest physicians in southern California. A brave man, Dr. Hope was in the forefront of the fight for law and order in his adopted state.

Indian raiders from the Utah Territory constantly harrassed the California ranchos and Dr. Hope organized patrols to augment the local forces commanded by state militia general Joshua Bean. One such expedition was reported in the Los Angeles *Star* of June 4, 1851:

> A scouting party commanded by Dr. Hope left Gen. Bean's camp about three weeks ago, intending to be absent five days. They returned yesterday and reported having had an engagement with the Pah-utahs in which thirteen Indians were killed. Dr. Hope and his men, only five in number, were in a natural fort when they were attacked by the Indians who gathered in great numbers.

Because of the isolated locale, native resentment against Americans, and a floating population, crime was rampant in southern California during the 1850's. When the city marshal and his few deputies could no longer control the criminal element in Los Angeles, Dr. Hope volunteered his services and was appointed Chief of Police in July of 1851 by Mayor Benjamin D. Wilson. Ninety of the best citizens of Los Angeles volunteered to serve under Hope, including the mayor, Abel Stearns, W.T.B. Sanford, Juan Sepulveda, Ygnacio del Valle, Jose Antonio Carrillo, Judge Benjamin Hayes, J.W. Rains, Tomas Sanchez, Stephen Foster and John G. Downey. The badges of the lawmen consisted of white ribbons Dr. Hope had printed which read in both English and Spanish: "City Police—organized by the Common Council of Los Angeles, July 12, 1851."

Although order was maintained in the city for a time, it soon became evident that a more mobile striking force was needed to protect the area. The *Star* stated the problem quite succinctly in the summer of 1853:

> The people of this county have long felt the necessity of having among them an efficient military force, which could be brought out promptly in aid of

177

Los Angeles was just a rough and sprawling adobe village in the 1850's when Dr. Hope was fighting to protect it from Indians and outlaws. *Courtesy California State Library.*

the laws and for the protection of life and property. We are not only exposed to predatory visits from Indians from the neighboring mountains...but recently we have seen an organized band of robbers, well mounted and well armed, traveling the country unmolested...

Although Mayor Ben Wilson captained a mounted police force formed in July 1853, this group was superceded by the establishment of the Los Angeles Rangers on August 1st. The first meeting was held at Getman's Montgomery Saloon where a hundred members were enlisted, only twenty-five of which would be active members. The men were to furnish their own weapons, but otherwise would be supplied by the county and private donations. The following year the group was authorized by the state government. Dr. Hope was elected captain of the Rangers, his officers and men being listed in the *Star* as follows:

E. Bevoort, 1st. Lieutenant, John G. Phillips, 2nd Lieutenant, W.T.B. Sanford, 3rd Lieutenant—William Little, J.B. Winston, Thomas Rand, Gabriel Allen, Green Marshall, G.W. Hart, E.A. Morehouse, W.W. Perkins, O. Morgan, John Jones, G.L. McManus, J.Q.A. Stanley, W.C. Getman, Ely Smith, H. Bell, H.I. Allison, E.C. Hare, Edward Hunter, T.S. Hereford, W.O. Ardinger and Pat Halpin. David W. Alexander was elected treasurer and clerk.

178

On August 6, 1853, the *Star* published the following item:

> Our kind friend Dr. A.W. Hope, of the Drug Store, will please accept our thanks for that delicious peach he presented us with on yesterday evening, It was the first we have seen this season.

A Ranger barracks was established in town and ranchers such as Phineas Banning, Don Ignacio del Valle and Isaac Williams supplied the best horse flesh in the area, often at no charge. Other ranchers furnished supplies. No Ranger equipment or mounts were allowed to be used for private purposes and horses were stabled in town ready for use at a moments notice.

The Rangers captured or killed many outlaws and were present at the first legal execution in Los Angeles County in February of 1854. The preceding month Captain Hope had personally arrested the bandit leader Atanacio Moreno when he had tried to pawn some stolen property. A typical fast-acting Ranger expedition was reported in the *Star* on February 11, 1854:

> Convict Arrested. Last Saturday the Rangers received intelligence that a party of horse thieves were encamped at the Puente on their way to Sonora. A party started in pursuit...and arrested three men, bringing them before the justice who told them it was their duty to deliver the prisoners to the nearest justice in Shasta County...

The Rangers often responded so promptly to trouble that the local press had trouble keeping up with them as reported in the *Southern Californian* the following November:

> Los Angeles Rangers—In our last week's issue we regret to say that we neglected to notice the active and prompt assistance rendered by the Los Angeles Rangers in assisting in the arrest of some of the most dangerous desperadoes in this country, and who are, no doubt, in some way connected with the brutal murder of Mr. Ellington, of the Monte...Our only excuse to offer to the Rangers is that the actions of this company are so prompt, active and secret, that in almost all cases the company is out on scout, returned, and the prisoner arraigned, before our citizens are aware of an outrage being committed...

Few people of today can appreciate the long, wearying hours in the saddle put in by these rugged Rangers. Although they received fresh horses and supplies from most of the outlying ranches, there were a few who either charged for their services or refused to shelter the volunteers as noted in the following *Star* article:

> The Rangers, on several recent occasions, have made long and toilsome exucursions in search of suspicious characters and stolen property. Upon some of these excursions they have made important discoveries, upon others they have returned weary and unsuccessful. Generally they have received most cheerful hospitality from rancheros. On one occasion, however, they were repulsed during a rain storm, after having been in the mountains for a week...

179

On August 6, 1854, a big celebration was staged for the Rangers on their first anniversary of service. After a parade through town, the festivities were resumed at a dinner party at the Bella Union Hotel. Toasts were offered to the president and various army generals, concluding with a tribute to Captain Hope, "The peaceful citizen, the fearless and energetic soldier and firm friend — may his shadow never be less!" The *Star* reported the party was a great success.

The Rangers operated sporadically over the next few years, as they were needed. They were still in existence in January of 1857 when they participated in the pursuit of the killers of Sheriff Barton. At this time, however, they were commanded by John Stanley, the original captain having passed away after a brief illness. Dr. Hope had died on January 17, 1856 and was mourned sincerely by all who had known him. The *Star* of January 19th paid its respects:

> ...Dr. Hope was a useful and respected citizen — energetic, prompt and always willing to render a service to his fellow citizens at a moments notice. As a private man, he was hospitable, generous and kind. He leaves many warm friends to regret his unexpected death.

The cause of death was not given. Horace Bell, one of Dr. Hope's Rangers, later recalled that his old commander was buried in an unmarked grave in the Fort Hill cemetery at Los Angeles. The location has been lost over the years and the brave frontiersman who occupied it all but forgotten.

PRINCIPAL SOURCES ───────────────────────

Bell, Major Horace, *Reminiscences of a Ranger,* Santa Barbara, Wallace Hebberd, 1927; Bell, Major Horace, *On the Old West Coast,* N.Y., Grosset & Dunlap, 1930; Guinn, J.M., *Historical and Biographical Record of Southern California,* Chicago, Chapman Pub. Co., 1907; Newmark, Harris, *Sixty Years in Southern California,* N.Y., Houghton Mifflin Co., 1930; Krythe, Maymie R., "First Hotel of Old Los Angeles—The Romantic Bella Union," *Hist. Soc. of Southern California Quaterly,* Mar., 1951; Los Angeles *Star,* May 26, 1851, Aug. 6, Sep. 17, 1853, Jan. 21, Feb. 11, 18, 1854, Jan. 19, 1856, Jan. 31, 1877; Census for the City and County of Los Angeles for the year 1850; California State Archives, Sacramento.

JAMES BUNYAN HUME

James B. Hume was one of the best and
most respected lawmen of the Old West.
Courtesy California State Library.

Although born in Delaware County, New York, on January 23, 1827, young
Jim Hume moved with his family to Lagrange County, Indiana, ten years later.
He worked on his father's farm while a young man, but in 1849 he felt the tug of
gold fever. Jim and his brother, John, left with a small party in March and
traveled overland, arriving in California in mid-August of 1850. Jim mined
steadily for the next ten years, but was only moderately successful and wearied
of the hard work.

In March of 1860 Hume was appointed a deputy tax collector and in 1862 he
was selected as the city marshal of Placerville. He was a good officer and was
re-elected by a healthy margin when he ran for office in April of 1863. The
following year Sheriff William H. Rogers appointed Jim his undersheriff, just in
time for him to participate in one of the most noted stagecoach holdup dramas
in the history of the West.

A group of men identifying themselves as Confederate soldiers robbed two
stages on the Placerville-Nevada road on July 1, 1864. Some $30,000 was
obtained, the robbers leaving a receipt for their loot. Hume was out of town at
the time and returned to find a fellow deputy had been killed when he caught up
with the outlaws at the Somerset House, a local inn. The leader, Captain
Ingram, and his gang had been surprised at the rapid appearance of two
deputies and in the resulting shootout at the inn had killed one lawman and
wounded the other before riding away. One of the outlaws had been badly shot
up also, and was later captured. Hume was promptly on the trail as noted in the
San Francisco *Alta:*

... After the excitement and smoke of the battle is over, the victors naturally look after the spoils. Deputy Sheriff Hume, assisted by officer Hanford, returned Saturday evening from a visit to the spot... where the gang so ingloriously fled from their friends, bringing back the plunder left in their haste, consisting of five horses and saddles, six pair of blankets, and eight hundred dollars in gold bullion found in their mountain camp. To the indomitable perseverance of Sheriff Rogers and his deputies, the public owe a debt of gratitude...

Hume recovered a portion of the plunder left behind when the bandits had been surprised at the Somerset House. Most of the Confederate outlaws were captured or killed and Hume received much credit for his work in running them down.

In late summer of 1867 Hume was wounded in a gun battle with a gang of bandits who had been pillaging travelers on the Placerville road. The *Alta* made note of the incident in its issue of September 25th:

[Deputy] Sheriff Hume struck the course they were taking, came up and last night, together with three or four men, laid for them at a point on the road... At about eleven o'clock the robbers came up, all armed with rifles. Hume ordered them to stop, whereupon one of them fired a shot, taking effect in the fleshy part of Hume's arm... Hume then ordered his men to fire, and when the smoke cleared away they found two lying, one dead and the other not hurt. The third one they saw fall off the bridge (but)... Hume is on his track and no doubt he will have to "throw up the sponge."

Charles Treher, alias Dutch Jake, had been killed while Hume took David Grammond and Ormstead Thurman, Alias Billy Harris, into custody. All had prison records.

In 1868 Hume ran for sheriff of El Dorado County and was elected. Despite his excellent record as a lawman, however, he was no politician and when he ran for re-election in September of 1871, he was defeated. Wells, Fargo Express Company asked Hume to head up its new detective bureau, but he first took a leave of absence to serve as deputy warden of the Nevada State Prison. He accomplished much in straightening out prison affairs, but was caught up in another political cross-fire and was delighted to take over his duties as Wells, Fargo's new Special Officer in March of 1873.

Prior to Hume's hiring, the express company had employed private detectives such as Steve Venard and Henry Johnson to investigate robberies. Hume continued this practice when needed, but generally he either worked alone or in conjunction with local peace officers. His first important case was the holdup of the Grass Valley stage in late July of 1873. Four men had taken over $7,000 in gold coin, but Hume had a suspect in custody the next day who admitted complicity. A second suspect was picked up when Hume heard he had deposited a gold bar with his landlady. The suspect turned out to be Louis Drebellis, another of the robbers, and when he squealed his partners were quickly rounded up.

Above: Sheriff Jim Hume of El Dorado County, poses with his good friend and deputy, John Cartheche in 1868. *Courtesy John Boessenecker.*

Below: [Left] The Parrott Building, on Montgomery street in San Francisco, was the headquarters of Wells, Fargo & Company when Jim Hume assumed his duties as special officer in 1873. *Courtesy California State Library.* [Right] Ormistead Thurman, alias Bill Early, had a thirty year crime career and was arrested several times by Hume. *Courtesy Greg Martin Collection.*

Hume's caseload was tremendous. Out of 31 robberies in 1875 he was only able to secure 6 convictions, but he was making it tough for the outlaws. He was instrumental in putting Kern County stage robber Dick Fellows away for eight years in 1876, but many of his cases were years in solving.

When Eph White and George Rugg held up the Marysville stage on July 31, 1877, Hume literally tracked them down by identifying their boot marks—this and other evidence resulting in court convictions. Hume had to cover other states as well as California and he frequently utilized Wells, Fargo guards as detectives so as to cover more ground. George Hackett, Bob Paul and later John Thacker aided him immensely.

A persistent thorn in Hume's side was a clever highwayman calling himself Black Bart. Beginning in the summer of 1875, Bart held up some twenty-nine coaches until he left behind an important clue during an 1883 robbery. A laundrymark on a handkerchief was traced to a San Francisco resident named Charles E. Boles. The suspect was over fifty years old, but was quickly identified as the bandit and sentenced to a long term at San Quentin. One of Bart's friends in prison was another stage robber and killer named Charles Dorsey. He had been convicted of robbing a coach in Nevada County where a passenger had been killed, Dorsey's partner being hanged for the murder. Dorsey escaped from prison in 1887, but Hume was able to recapture him and a partner in Chicago in 1890 and put him away for good.

The Wells, Fargo lawman was embarrassed in early 1882 while engaged on a case in Arizona. A dispatch from Tombstone dated January 8th was published in the San Francisco Morning *Call:*

> The Benson stage was stopped last night about one o'clock, half way between Contention and Tombstone, by two masked men, J.B. Hume, detective of Wells, Fargo & Company, and eight other passengers were on board...Hume had two fine revolvers which the robbers took from him...Wells, Fargo & Co. offer a reward of $300 for the capture of the robbers.

Hume was married in 1884 and late that year submitted a fourteen year summary of all his company's robberies which had taken place since 1870. Listed were 313 stage holdups, 23 burglaries and eight attempts at train robbery. Hume had aided in the impressive total of 240 convictions for these crimes. But there had been a price. Ten bandits had been killed and seven lynched, while two Wells, Fargo guards were dead and six had been wounded. Four passengers had been killed also, and several injured. Over $400,000 had been stolen from the company during this period and it had cost nearly a million dollars to chase, capture and convict the outlaws.

In early March of 1885 Hume aided in the capture and conviction of one of the trio who had wounded him in 1867. The San Francisco *Chronicle* reported:

Hume married late in life and is shown here with his young son.
Courtesy California State Library.

William Harris was brought to the central police station Sunday evening by Detective J.B. Hume of Wells, Fargo & Co., and the Sheriff of Amador County, en route to San Quentin to serve a term of seven years for stage robbery... Harris, whose real name is Ormstead Thurman, has escaped several times and is considered a very desperate man. Detective Hume recaptured him in El Dorado County in November, 1867...

Although stagecoach robberies were to plague the West into the twentieth century, by the late 1880s train robberies were becoming increasingly tempting to outlaws. In late August of 1881, the first train was wrecked for the purpose of robbery in California, but it was to be another seven years before that particular type crime became serious in the far West. In February of 1888 a Southern Pacific train was held up near Pixley in the San Joaquin Valley. In December another train was stopped in the valley, near Goshen. The Dalton brothers were prime suspects after another train was stopped the following year, but although Grat Dalton was arrested, his brothers Bob and Emmett fled the state. Bill Dalton was held for a time, also, but was released for lack of evidence. Grat was tried and convicted, but escaped and joined his brothers in Oklahoma. When a train was held up at Ceres in September of 1891, Hume was a member of the posse. Another train robbery fastened suspicion on two Visalia farmers named Chris Evans and John Sontag. The pair turned out to be dangerous gunmen and killed several lawmen before John Thacker devised a plan that resulted in their ambush and capture.

On June 15, 1893, Hume's friend and longtime shotgun messenger, Mike Tovey, was killed as he rode as a stage guard on the Ione-Jackson road. Hume and Thacker worked long and hard to find the killer, but with no luck. Sheriff Ben Thorn arrested William Evans as the killer, but even after a supposed confession Hume refused to believe he was guilty. Evans was convicted and sentenced to a long prison term, but Hume was vindicated when new evidence suggested Evans was innocent and he was parolled in 1909.

Over sixty-years-old in the 1890s, Hume still worked at a relentless pace, traveling up and down California and across the country. The grind inevitably told on the old manhunter and he began suffering ill health. Little by little he relinquished his work load to Thacker and others. Hume died at his Berkeley home on May 18, 1904, at the age of seventy-seven. The San Francisco *Chronicle* paid tribute to one of the longest careers and most successful officers on the west coast:

> This country has produced few men who have made such a remarkable record in the persistent and successful pursuit of that class of robbers who prey specially on the express and transportation companies...

PRINCIPAL SOURCES ─────────────────────

Dillon, Richard, *Wells, Fargo Detective,* N.Y., Coward-McCann, Inc., 1969; San Francisco *Daily Alta California,* July 2, 3, 27, 1864, Sept. 10, 25, 1867; San Francisco *Chronicle,* May 19, 1909; San Francisco *Daily Morning Call,* Jan. 9, 1882; Sierra *Sun-Bonanza,* Dec. 27, 1874; Grass Valley *Union,* Mar. 11, 1885; James B. Hume scrapbooks, Wells, Fargo Bank History Room, San Francisco.

Fred Jackson's rugged face mirrored the life he had lived as a frontier peace officer for thirty years. *Courtesy Marilyn Allen.*

FREDERICK EUGENE JACKSON

A descendant of Andrew Jackson, "Old Hickory" himself, Fred Jackson was born in Wyalusing, Wisconsin, on November 4, 1861. His early years are obscure, but the family moved to California sometime in the 1870s and Fred spent his teenage years in the hills of Shasta County. "Fred was a crack shot," recalled a niece. "We used to live in the hills above Red Bluff. I was a little girl then and he was about 17. He would let me carry his shotgun when he went hunting...He was such a good shot they finally barred him from the rifle matches they used to have."

Apparently Jackson worked as a lawman in Nevada in the 1880s. It was during this period that he met Eugene Thacker, son of the noted Wells, Fargo detective, and the two became lifelong friends. He may have worked for Wells, Fargo for a brief time, also. In the early 1890s he was a deputy sheriff under Fresno County Sheriff Jay Scott and lived with a sister in Fresno in the central San Joaquin Valley.

When a series of train robberies took place in the San Joaquin Valley in the early 1890s, suspicion was directed at two Visalia farmers named Chris Evans and John Sontag. The two suspects fled rather than submit to arrest, and killed three officers in several shooting scrapes. When no progress was being made in

187

locating the fugitives in the mountains east of Visalia, two prominent lawmen met in Fresno to discuss the situation. Wells, Fargo's John Thacker conferred with United States Marshal George Gard in May of 1893 to map strategy to capture the outlaws. There were rumors of other planned holdups and a posse assembled to go into the hills and watch the trails Evans and Sontag were known to frequent. The possemen chosen were Fred Jackson and Hi Rapelje, both Fresno County deputy sheriffs, and Tom Burns, a private detective working for a San Francisco agency. Marshal Gard was to obtain a federal warrant in Los Angeles, then join his three men in the field. The Fresno *Republican* later noted that Jackson had been selected because he was a "keen, vigilant and brave officer" who had considerable experience with desperadoes in Nevada.

Smuggled out of town at night in a wagon so as to keep the expedition a secret, the posse scouted the mountains and finally took up a position in an old cabin on a trail the outlaws had been known to use. On June 11, 1893, Evans and Sontag walked right into the posse's ambush and a desperate gun battle took place. Many accounts state that Jackson fired the initial—and premature —shot of the fight. Jackson always denied this and most evidence supports his version. After an hour or so of exchanging shots, both outlaws were badly wounded and Jackson was seriously hit in the leg. During a lull in the firing, Rapelje drove his wounded partner into Visalia some eighteen miles away. He was put up in a hotel and physicians summoned as recorded in the Weekly Visalia *Delta* of June 15th:

> Drs. Bernhard and Patterson were called in to attend Deputy United States Marshal Jackson. His left leg was badly shattered and the chances of saving it were slim indeed. During the afternoon it was finally decided to amputate the limb, and the patient was placed under the effects of chloroform and the operation was successfully accomplished this afternoon...
>
> The patient rallied from the shock well, and it is thought that the operation will not be followed by any direful results. His attending surgeons say...he will make a good recovery...

The badly wounded Evans had escaped from the battlefield, but was quickly captured at the home of a relative. Sontag was also terribly shot up and later died in the Fresno jail. Evans lost an eye and an arm as a result of his wounds and later was visited by Jackson in his jail cell. The two men talked amicably about the battle in which both had been maimed for life.

There were more than $11,000 in rewards offered for the two desperadoes, but disposition of the funds were never made quite clear. Gard himself refused any of the money stating that Jackson "who lost his leg in the encounter should receive the largest share of the reward" and also "life employment by Wells, Fargo or the Southern Pacific..." There was a great deal of trouble over the rewards, many Tulare County lawmen and others trying to get in on the act. Wells, Fargo became disgusted with the squabbling as reported in the San Francisco *Examiner* of July 28, 1893:

Wells, Fargo & Co. have made up their minds that they will not be bothered by the claims of the different Sheriffs, Marshals, etc. who claim to be entitled to the reward of $5,000 offered by them for the capture of the train robbers, Evans and Sontag. Today they filed a complaint in the United States Court in which they name as respondents George E. Gard, H.L. Rapelje, F. Jackson, T. Burns, G. Witty, W.E. Hall, E.H. Perkins, W. English, John Doe, Richard Roe, Henry Black, John Prime, Henry the Second, George the Third, Charles the Fourth and Henry the Fifth...

Although the paper was being facetious, two of the reward claimants took their squabbling more serious than most. As they left the Los Angeles court where a hearing was held and boarded a train, Tom Burns and George Witty exchanged ugly words. When the train reached Glendale, Witty stepped out on the platform to get some air and was followed by Burns. The two lawmen argued and Burns shot Witty through the hand. The two then grappled and fell from the train, Witty being seriously injured in the fall. Witty didn't press charges over the incident.

Jackson was indeed offered a job by Wells, Fargo and after a suitable convalescence period, went to work for the company. A shotgun guard with a wooden leg was a novelty as well as good public relations, but apparently Jackson got along just fine. There is no record of much excitement while doing

For many years Jackson served as a Wells, Fargo shotgun messenger, probably the only one-legged guard in the company's history. *Courtesy California State Library.*

His wooden leg seldom interfered with Jackson's life and he is shown here at left on a friend's Nevada ranch around the turn of the century. *Courtesy Wells, Fargo History Room.*

guard duty—until one rainy night in March of 1899. Fred and another guard, the noted Reason McConnell, were riding inside a coach traveling between Angels Camp and Valley Springs. It was pitch black outside when suddenly two highwaymen stopped the coach and demanded the treasure box. Thrusting their Winchesters through the coach windows, Jackson and McConnell interrupted the proceedings as recounted by Jackson later:

> Mr. McConnell tried to shoot, but the cartridge in his gun would not explode. I took three shots at one of the robbers who might have been thirty yards away...Only one shot came from the robbers...There was only $136 on the stage at the time.

One of the bandits was severely wounded and both were promptly captured and easily convicted. Although the two were quite young and inexperienced, Jackson was the hero of the hour.

This same year Fred was married and when a child was born he decided to quit Wells, Fargo and settle down. In 1900 he was appointed an Amador County deputy sheriff under Tom Norman. He had many exciting experiences, not the least of which was a rugged Sierra manhunt for a group of escaped convicts in 1903. He held various peace officer posts for the next ten years or so, but was never so happy as when he was prospecting for gold—"desert-ratting," he called it. He last worked as an officer in 1935.

Jackson spent his final years living in a small cottage in Glendale, California. He died there on January 27, 1949, survived by his wife, Annie Petter Jackson and a step-daughter, Olive Becker. Fred was eighty-seven years old at his death and was buried in North Hollywood. "Here forever lies a part of the Old West" commented the minister at his funeral and it was a fitting tribute to a brave lawman who refused to let a severe handicap hamper his career as a peace officer in old California.

PRINCIPAL SOURCES

Glasscock, C.B., *Bandits and the Southern Pacific*, N.Y., Grosset & Dunlap, 1929; Maxwell, Hu, *Evans and Sontag*, San Francisco, San Francisco Printing Co., 1893 (reprinted in 1981); Traver *Advocate*, Apr. 27, 1893; San Francisco *Chronicle*, Aug. 7, 14, 17, 28, 1903; The Visalia *Delta*, June 22, 18, July 6, 15, 20, 29, 1893; Amador *Dispatch*, Mar. 31, 1899; San Francisco *Examiner*, Mar. 25, 26, 1899; The Glendale *News Press*, Jan. 28, 1949; The Fresno Weekly *Republican*, June 16, July 19, 1893; Mrs. Marilyn B. Allen to the author, Sept. 1969-June, 1971; Wells Fargo Bank History Room, San Francisco.

HENRY J. JOHNSON

One of the more noted, but least known lawmen of the west coast was born in Glasgow, Scotland, about 1818. Henry Johnson joined his local police force at an early age and quickly displayed his aptitude to be one of the new detective police, an officer who investigates crimes. He moved to Australia where he again served as a detective before emigrating to San Francisco in 1855. Establishing a home in the city for his wife and child, Johnson applied to the local police force the following year and was appointed to the Special Police—a member of the regular force, but paid by the residents of the beat he patrolled. His detective background soon became apparent and in the years that followed he was frequently paired with Isaiah W. Lees, also a noted sleuth and head of the San Francisco Police detective department.

In mid-March of 1857 Johnson and Lees arrested a mugger—called a "garroter" in those days—named John Corbett. When he tried to establish his innocence in court, the officers promptly demolished his claims, as noted in the *Alta:*

> ...The prosecution called officers Nugent, Lees and Johnson, all of whom testified that they had frequently seen the defendent in company with known thieves...and officer Johnson said he had seen him in company with the notorious Brace, who was hung by the Vigilance Committee...

The sprawling port city of the gold rush was the greatest training ground in the world for detectives and Johnson and his fellow lawmen obtained wide experience in every type of crime. In early April, Johnson, Lees and several other police officers arrested an absconding sheriff from Klamath County whom they recognized from descriptions. Late that same month when a ship's passenger was missing, the officers canvassed the city and finally located him, drugged and robbed, in a local brothel. In November Lees and Johnson were on the carpet for roughing up a tough saloon owner who ran a fencing operation for young thieves. The officers received a mild reprimand and were reminded by the police court judge to keep an eye on the saloon owner who was suspected of murder.

The detectives were constantly on watch for fugitives and criminals in the city as reported in the *Alta* on December 15, 1858:

> An Armed Vagrant—Officers Lees, Johnson and Chappel arrested, night before last, a villainous Mexican named Manuel Claveras, at a dance house

Lewis Mahoney was a burglar and rustler with a long criminal record. *From the California Police Gazette, March 20, 1859.*

When Henry Johnson arrived in San Francisco, Portsmouth Square was the heart of the city. *Courtesy California State Library.*

on Pacific Street. Johnson testified before the Police court yesterday that he drew out of either leg of his trousers a knife and pistol, which were exhibited in court... The fellow was arrested on 'general principles' as he was well known to the officers as a desperado.

In February and March of 1859 Johnson participated in working up the Billman murder case and the prosecution of the notorious bandit, Lewis Mahoney. In August he helped Lees ferret out the perpetrators of the Freeman & Company Express robbery. The case was a classic of detective work, the officers quickly and carefully following up clues and interviewing suspects, then putting the data together. It was determined that a company employee was the culprit and he was successfully prosecuted for the crime.

One of Johnson's earliest cases with Wells, Fargo occurred in July of 1860 as recorded in the San Francisco Daily *Herald and Mirror:*

Our readers will recollect that the express of Wells, Fargo & Co. was robbed of $20,000 in Butte County on the 9th of June and that since that time no clue has been obtained to the robbers. Last Saturday night two of our experienced detectives, Capt. Lees and Johnson arrested a man named Owen Castle, alias Martin, on board the Oakland ferry boat, on the charge of being a participator in the robbery. Castle was well armed and undertook to resist at first, but was soon overcome and compelled to enter the station house...

In early January of 1861 Johnson and Lees received a reward of $250 from the British consul at Panama for their help in capturing a gang of burglars. When a woman discovered that both her lover and some $2,500 of her money were missing, she contacted Johnson and Lees. From her description they traced the man to a ship bound for New York and promptly sent a letter by Pony Express warning officers of that city to be on the lookout. By this means the man was apprehended and the money returned. Johson had an excellent detective record by this time and besides his regular police work, he was appointed Special Officer for the Pacific Mail Steamship Company in 1863. The following year he was also appointed Government Detective by General Irvin McDowell, commander of the Department of the Pacific.

Sometime during 1867 Johnson also began working on a free-lance basis as a Wells, Fargo detective in addition to his other duties. He was probably not a regular employee of the company, but was utilized whenever needed on a time basis. One of his cases was chronicled by the Sacramento Daily *Union* on December 9, 1867:

> Detective Henry Johnson and Wm. R. Warnock, of Wells, Fargo & Co., who worked up the matter of the robbery of WF&Co.'s treasure box on the Ione and Jackson stage, on Monday last, and arrested the robbers with the aid of the local officers, returned to the city last night bringing receipts for all but $40 of the treasure.

The traffic in prostitutes, both Chinese and white, into San Francisco was a monstrous problem. One day in early 1868 while on duty at the PMSS wharf, Johnson was advised that a notorious flesh peddler was bringing ashore two young girls who had no idea they had been brought West for anything other than chambermaid jobs. The detective had the pleasure of collaring the white slaver and his madam boss and kicking them off the wharf. As the two screamed for the girls' passage money which they were forced to forfeit, Johnson smiled and motioned them to move on. "The girls were taken where kind friends...will see that they are properly cared for," observed the *Alta*.

Detective Johnson was the recipient of another reward according to the *Alta* of June 17, 1868:

> REWARD OF MERIT-Detective Henry Johnson of this city has just received $1,000 from Governor Blasdel, of Nevada, for the detection and arrest of Eugene Le. Fevre, the escaped murderer from that state. It will be remembered that Le Fevre was discovered in San Quentin where he had been sent under an alias for a crime committed in the northern part of the state...

Later that month Johnson and Lees arrested two express company thieves from New York after the company had telegraphed Johnson for assistance. Utilizing only poor descriptions and what other clues they could muster, the two detectives located the men even though they were using assumed names and

San Francisco in the 1870's had grown considerably from the fledgling city Johnson had known in the early days. *Courtesy California State Library.*

had lost themselves in the city upon arrival. In August Johnson was dismissed from the police force for political reasons, but was reinstated the following day. Weary, no doubt, of the insecurity and politics of his police job, Johnson went into private detective work as indicated in the city directory of 1871:

> ANSBRO & CO. . . . (Thomas Ansbro, P.S. Allis and Henry Johnson private detective and inquiry office, 411½ California, rooms 17 and 18.

Ansbro was also a former Special Police Officer, but the partnership seems to have only lasted a few years. Johnson, still a Wells, Fargo detective in 1870 and '71, was deputized with Captain Lees as a deputy U.S. marshal to bring three stage robbers to the city from Monterey in late July of 1870.

In early February of 1874 Johnson was again appointed to the regular police force, but since little notice of him has been found in the press, perhaps he was assigned to office or court duty. After a brief illness the following year, he died on July 30, 1875, mourned by his wife and four children. He was 57 years old.

Although overshadowed by the impressive career of James B. Hume, Johnson was one of the earliest of the Wells, Fargo detectives who operated for the company in a private capacity. "During his long career in public business in this city," eulogized the *Alta*, "he was engaged in ferreting out and bringing to justice many intricate cases which came in his line of business."

Henry Johnson was in the forefront of the fight against crime in early California.

PRINCIPAL SOURCES ──────────────────────────

San Francisco City Directories, 1856-1875; U.S. Census, 1860, San Francisco; San Francisco *Daily Alta California,* Feb. 11, Mar. 16, 17, Apr. 6, Sept. 28, 1857, Jan 31, Mar. 1, June 18, Oct. 6, Nov. 5, Dec. 15, 27, 1858, Feb. 5, 23, Mar. 14, 19, Aug. 3, Oct. 6, Dec. 8, 1859, Jan. 5, Mar. 30, Nov. 29, 1860, Jan. 6, Mar. 1, 1861, Jan 3, 1862, Jan. 19, 1864, July 9, 1867, Feb. 14, June 17, 1868, Aug. 1, 1875, *California Police Gazette,* Feb. 27, 1859, Wells, Fargo Bank History Room, San Francisco.

ISAIAH WRIGLEY LEES

Captain Isaiah W. Lees was a famous San Francisco police detective for nearly fifty years. *Courtesy the Bancroft Library.*

Perhaps the most famous of the early California police detectives, Isaiah Lees was born in Oldham, Lancashire, England, on Christmas day, 1830. His family emigrated to the United States the following year where his father worked in a locomotive shop in Paterson, New Jersey. When the father died, eight-year-old Isaiah was apprenticed to work in a machine shop to learn the metal working trade. Later he worked in the Colt gun factory as a teenager. He came to California in 1849 and mined briefly, but found that the hard work did not pay well enough. Returning to San Francisco, Lees worked at the Donahue Iron Foundry for several years, then operated a tug on the bay. He apparently took an interest in police work after helping investigate a murder in late 1852. On October 26th of the following year he joined the city's police force as a patrolman.

Lee's abilities at following up clues were promptly recognized and he was soon detailed to a comparatively new facet of police work—detective duty. There were only fifty-six officers on the force at this time, but old San Francisco was the greatest training ground for lawmen in the West. It was a tough town, filled with thugs, thieves, conmen, gamblers and outlaws of every description. Lees was quickly promoted to assistant captain, but still had to spend much time on the streets. Election-riggers and crooked politicians ruled the town and Lees and other officers were badly mauled at a local hotel when they tried to

197

restore order at a political meeting. A few days later when three of the same thugs tried to provoke him in a coffee house, Lees fought them off and managed to haul their leader, a vicious prize fighter named "Wooley" Kearney, off to jail as reported in the *Alta* of February 20, 1854:

> ...Officer Lees succeeded in getting Carney [*sic*] to the station house. Carney appeared very ready to go...and after his arrival assured the officers that he didn't care about being arrested as he would send to Judge Wells and get his discharge...

Judge Alexander Wells, a state supreme court justice who had obtained the release of all the rioters, was later seen drinking with them at a local saloon.

This same year Lees discovered and captured a gang of Chinese burglars who were trying to burrow under a street and into a bank vault. When he went into the tunnel Isaiah was injured in the resulting fight, but managed to bring out all the burglars.

One night in an alley Lees caught a thug breaking windows. Told he was under arrest, the man pressed a pistol against the officer and fired six times. Lees supposed he was mortally wounded, but hauled his prisoner to the station house before proceeding to the hospital. Peeling off his shirt, the lawman discovered the bullets had all coursed around his silk undershirt, merely leaving welts. "Some years later I met the man again," Lees once recalled. "He was—no, I'll not tell his name for my memory for faces is the only proof that he was the one, but I'll tell you that when I saw him again he was worth his millions and was a United States Senator."

In 1856 crime and political corruption seemed so rampant in the bay city that a force of several thousand vigilantes took over the city. When Lees raided Wooley Kearney's shack and confiscated a trick ballot box, it was taken from him by the vigilantes. In March Lees had a brawl with his boss, City Marshal Hampton North. During an argument, Isaiah drew a knife on his superior and was promptly jailed and suspended from the force. "The board gives you all the credit for being a good officer," commented the mayor during Lees' hearing, "one of the best in the department, but it is necessary that insubordination should be discountenanced." The trouble had little influence on Lees' career since he was appointed to a full captaincy the following July.

When a vicious saloon owner threw acid in the face of a discarded mistress, Lees carefully pieced together a variety of clues leading to a conviction. His work on the case was widely heralded in the press, the *Bulletin* notice of October 26, 1856, being a fair example:

> ...The judges and attorneys all remarked that it was by far the most remarkable case that they had ever witnessed. On an examination of the investigations and discoveries of Capt. Lees, of the police, the reader will be reminded of the famous "Officer Bucket of the Detectives," characterized

by Dickens in "Bleak House." Captain Lees has certainly displayed a great deal of ingenuity and has approved himself very good as a detective and deserves credit...

In 1858 Isaiah acquired further fame when he and other officers rescued an ex-slave named Archy Lee. The black man's former owner was attempting to kidnap him and return him to the South when Lees and his men intercepted them as they attempted to board a steamer in the bay. The officers were "heroes of the hour" when they returned Archy to a pier lined with cheering black people. The case was a famous one and after much litigation, Archy was freed by the courts after being heavily supported by black residents of the state.

In the early 1860s Lees successfully investigated the noted Bonney case, the Visitacion Valley murders and the La Meet killing, but it was the Chapman case which caught the fancy of the state and a nation gripped by civil war. When a group of Southerners tried to outfit the schooner *J. M. Chapman* as a privateer to prey on coastal shipping in support of the Confederacy, Lees led a boarding party that seized the ship as it was cruising illegally out of port. And, it was Lees who carefully located and pieced together minute wads of chewed-up documents that were used in evidence for the prosecution. Most of the "pirates" received prison terms and large fines. During the war Lees also served as a deputy U.S. marshal.

Lees' success as a detective was achieved by assembling all his clues and fitting them together. If the pieces didn't fit, he had merely put them together incorrectly and he would begin again. He seldom failed. "The forte of Lees and Ellis," penned Mark Twain while working as a local newspaper reporter in 1864, "is the unearthing of embezzlers and forgers. Each of these men are the best in one particular line, but at the same time they are good in all."

Lees' capture of the notorious William Gray, alias "Jersey" Gregg, in January of 1868 was typical of the many bruising encounters he had with badmen. The officer had seen Gray a few days previous to the encounter and been told that he would never again submit to an arrest. When a robbery victim described his assailants, Lees identified Gray and an accomplice named Jackson as the culprits. Assisted by another officer, Isaiah soon traced them to a local railroad depot. As his partner cornered Jackson, Lees faced Gray who immediately went for his pistol. Lees' own weapon hung up in his pocket and he leaped on the bandit, seizing his pistol hand. The fight was described in the *Bulletin* in its issue of January 2nd:

> ...As they clinched Gregg attempted to bite Lees in the face, but could not reach it. He then seized his left hand and bit it badly in several places. At last the officer lifted his antagonist clear off his feet and hurled him with terrific force into a window, smashing it into atoms...Although disarmed, Gregg still fought until Lees told him if he did not surrender he would finish him on the spot. He then gave up...

A newspaper sketch of Lees' noted fight with Bill Gregg in 1868. During the desperate struggle most of the windows of the railroad depot were broken. *From the San Francisco* Examiner *of February 16, 1890.*

Left: Bill Gregg as he appeared in the 1868 San Francisco police mug book. *Courtesy Christian de Guignè Collection.*

In the 1870s Lees frequently chased criminals across the country and engaged in international investigations. When a Spanish soldier named Pereda absconded from Cuba with some $60,000 in stolen army funds, he fled to New York and then to San Francisco. Lees located the fugitive and after making the arrest, gave the money to the Spanish Consul. The case caused considerable stir when Pereda sued Lees, the consul and the police chief, but Lees' action was sustained when the thief was convicted after several trials. In evaluating the police force in December of 1873, the *Bulletin* noted:

> Captain Lees is the most experienced detective on the force and has a national reputation. His success has been astonishing and he never turns back on the trail of a rascal until he collars him.

The theft of the painting *Elaine* from a San Francisco art gallery in 1875 initiated the great detective's swiftest investigation. He snagged the kidnappers and retrieved the painting the day following the crime and when *Elaine* was again put on display, a portrait of Captain Lees was hanging beside it.

That same year Isaiah threw his hat in the ring to run for chief, but he found the political entanglements to be overly restrictive, and withdrew. In 1882 he helped track down and arrest two stage robbers who had killed a passenger during a holdup in 1879. One of the robbers was hanged and the other sent to prison for life.

In 1895 Lees investigated and helped prosecute the bizarre Theodore Durrant murder case. Durrant, a medical student and pervert, murdered two girls in a local church and so brazenly maintained his innocence that he nearly escaped the noose. There was a lack of hard evidence in the case, but Lees wove such a tight and complete net of circumstantial evidence that the killer was convicted and finally hanged. When a gang of international forgers raised the amount of a local bank check from $12.00 to $22,000, Lees tracked them down. They had all worn disguises during the operation, but the detective was able to piece together true descriptions and locate and convict them all. The head man of the gang, Charles Becker, was recognized as one of the most notorious forgers in the world and Lees sent him up for a long term.

In 1897 San Francisco Police Chief Patrick Crowley retired and Lees was named in his place. It was a long-held ambition, but sadly the old detective's wife had died just a few months earlier and could not share his triumph. He prosecuted many more successful cases before his retirement in 1900. He had served forty-seven years on the force, one of the longest on record.

Above: San Francisco in the 1890's was no longer a frontier town and crime had become much more sophisticated. *From author's collection.*

Left: By the time he was appointed chief in 1897, Lees was a legendary figure. He is shown here leading a parade during his final years in office. *Courtesy the Bancroft Library.*

An 1875 San Francisco police mug book. Prior to 1860 Lees kept a collection of daguerreotype criminal portraits, but later kept his "Rogues Gallery" in leather books as pictured here. *In author's collection, courtesy Special Collections, Library, California State University Fresno.*

Although the owner of a large criminal history library, Lees himself always refused to write up his own fascinating life story. "Too many people would be hurt by a book telling the complete story of my life in San Francisco," he said. Few could disagree when William Pinkerton called him "the greatest criminal catcher the West ever knew."

Although Lees is often credited as being the founder of the police mug book system, or the Rogues Gallery, he was not. In his old age he claimed to have originated the taking of criminal portraits, but it had begun much earlier in Europe, almost as soon as photography itself was developed. Certainly, he was one of the earliest users of the system in the West. Quite wealthy at the time of his retirement, the old lawman had been accused of blackmail and other crimes for money several times during his career. Actually, he seems to have made some good property investments in the early days and no charges were ever filed against him.

When the veteran officer died on December 21, 1902, the funeral was one of the largest in the city's history. Adjourning the Superior Court in respect for Lees' memory, Judge Lawlor reflected the feelings of most when he said:

> The state of California, and it may be said in some measure the entire nation, owes a debt of magnitude to the deceased. Isaiah W. Lees, above all men who have ever been connected with the administration of justice in California, has done more to vindicate the law and discourage crime...

Chief Lees was buried next to his wife in their vault at Laurel Hill Cemetery. He was survived by a daughter and son, and remains the most noted police officer in California history, although he is little known today.

PRINCIPAL SOURCES ——————————————————

Duke, Thomas S., *Celebrated Criminal Cases of America,* San Francisco, James H. Barry Co., 1910; Sullivan, G.W., *Pioneer Biographies,* San Francisco, Enterprise Pub. Co., 1888; *The Exempt Firemen of San Francisco,* San Francisco, privately published, 1900; Secrest, William, B., *Dark and Tangled Threads of Crime,* biographical ms. on the life of I.W. Lees, in progress; San Francisco *Daily Alta California,* Feb. 19, 1854, Mar. 6, 1858, Oct. 24, 1860, Jan. 25, 1861; San Francisco *Bulletin,* May 30, Oct. 26, 1856, March 16, 1863, Sept. 29, 1871; San Francisco *Chronicle,* Apr. 5, 1875; San Francisco *Daily Morning Call,* Nov. 5, 1895; The *Examiner,* Dec. 22, 24, 1902; Lees Collection, The Bancroft Library, Univ. of Cal., Berkeley.

HENRY LOVE (Harry)

Although characterized by some as a bully and coward, Love was nothing of the kind despite his tragic and senseless death. *Courtesy California State Library.*

According to his 1860 California voter registration, Harry Love was born in Vermont in 1810. He went to sea at an early age, fleeing home and a stepmother with whom he could not get along. As a mariner he reportedly visited California as early as 1839, but by the mid-1840s life at sea had palled on him. He was working as a stevedore in Mobile, Alabama, when General Zachary Taylor called for emergency reinforcements in the opening scenes of the Mexican War. A group of volunteers was mustered in at Mobile and Harry Love was appointed a sergeant in the group on July 2, 1846. By the time the unit made its way to Texas the emergency was over and Love was mustered out in early August at New Orleans. It is clear from later applications for bounty land that this is the only war service Love saw. Later, however, he returned to Texas and served with the army in a civilian capacity.

After the war Love continued to work with the army as both a scout and dispatch rider. In January of 1849 he carried news of the election of President Zachary Taylor from Camargo to Santa Fe—a thirty-eight day trip through extremely dangerous country. "Love is a gallant fellow," wrote an officer at Santa Fe, "and I hope he will reach you safely." Twice during the trip he was chased by hostile Indians. He returned to Fort Brown, Texas, and in mid-August the Corpus Christi *Star* noted that he was still carrying dispatches:

> To Capt. Harry Love, who arrived here today from the Rio Grande, we are indebted for late Brownsville papers.

It seems likely Love's title of "captain" stemmed from his sea-going days when he reportedly commanded his own ship. He was anxious to go to California in these early days of the great gold rush, but he held off when offered command of an army flatboat expedition which was to explore the upper Rio Grande. His employer, Major W. W. Chapman, considered the results of Love's expedition to be very important when he returned in September of 1850. Harry had been promised another boating command on the river, but when this failed to materialize he booked passage for California.

Arriving in San Francisco in December of 1850, Love mined for a time and later supervised construction of a dam. He was already a noted personage and when his mining aspirations did not pan out he looked about for other opportunities as reported in the Sacramento *Union* on February 28, 1852:

> EXPLORING PARTY—We learn that Capt. H.H. Clark and other gentlemen of Tuolumne County are engaged in organizing a company, the object of which is to seek adventure and gold in the wild region of . . . the Rio Gila. Harry Love, the celebrated express rider of the Rio Grande, will accompany the party . . .

The Gila River project apparently fell through and Love was living in Mariposa County in late April when Allen Ruddle was killed and robbed by several Mexican bandits. A posse with Love in command was promptly on the trail of the killers. It was later determined that Joaquin Murrieta and one of his men had murdered and robbed Ruddle, then fled to the San Luis Gonzaga ranch where they rendezvoused with others of the band. The bandits were surprised in their camp, but managed to elude the posse in the darkness and fled south. Most of the posse gave up the chase, but Love and another man headed for San Buenaventura where they captured one of the gang. Near Los Angeles the prisoner tried to escape and Love shot him through the head, reporting the incident to Justice Joseph Mallard at Los Angeles. The Los Angeles *Star* noted the killing in its issue of June 26th:

> Mr. Harry Love . . . was the name of the man who shot the Sonorenian prisoner while conveying him to this place. Mr. Love was one of the most fearless of Gen. Taylor's express riders at the time of the Mexican War, in which capacity he rendered great and arduous services.

In the spring of 1853 Love was apparently living in Mariposa County where he was recognized as having captured one of the Ruddle killers. In late April a petition to the state legislature was being circulated suggesting that a state ranger force be organized to track down the bandit gangs headed by "Joaquin" who were terrorizing the gold rush country. On May 17th the formation of a 20-man unit of California Rangers was authorized by the legislature, Harry Love being selected as the leader because of the Ruddle affair and his Texas record. The official act noted that the purpose of the rangers was to track down the FIVE Joaquins who commanded the bandit gangs; "Joaquin Muriati, Joaquin Carrillo, Joaquin Ocomorenia, Joaquin Valenzuela and Joaquin Bottellier."

From the start the Rangers hardly knew who they were looking for. William Howard, one of the Rangers, later wrote that the Murrieta they were looking for was "a stout, broad-shouldered [man]...about 40 years old, was the description given by Bill Burns [*sic*] who had played cards with Murrieta. We also wanted Manuel Garcia—three fingered Jack—; Capt. Claudio . . . Pedro Gonzales, [and] Valenzuela."

The Rangers themselves were a strange mixture of professional men and tough adventurers. Pat Connor, later a general in the army, was elected first lieutenant, with noted gunman Bill Byrnes as acting first lieutenant. George Evans and Charley Bludworth were elected second lieutenants, the rest of the company consisting of privates. Philemon T. Herbert and Judge Walter Harvey, two hot-headed southern politicians, both quit the command early in the campaign and were replaced by others.

By early June Love and his men had captured several outlaws and were pressing Joaquin and his band closely. After much hard riding the Rangers came upon a group of Mexican mustang runners on the morning of July 25, 1853. The men were sullen and uncooperative and when Ranger Bill Byrnes recognized Murrieta, a fight commencd in which at least four of the gang were killed and two captured. One of the dead men was identified as Joaquin Murrieta and another as Three-Fingered Jack, his lieutenant. Both were beheaded, Jack's deformed hand also being lopped off as evidence. The Sacramento *Union* reported:

> HEAD OF JOAQUIN—Capt. Harry Love arrived in town yesterday from Mariposa, bringing with him the trunkless head of the bandit chief, Joaquin. The trophy will be ready for exhibition, we believe, today, as it is now in process of preparation.

A $1,000 reward was paid the Rangers, bolstered the following year by an additional $5,000. In November of 1853 another $1,000 was given the Rangers by Chinese residents of San Francisco, but the real object of the campaign, recovered bandit loot, was not realized. After exhibiting the head and hand throughout the gold rush country, Love sold his trophies sometime in late 1853.

Perhaps wishing to settle down after a strenuous life, Love bought a sawmill in the mountains near Santa Cruz with his reward money. The mill had been owned by Mrs. Mary Bennett and operated by her sons. A huge, strong-willed divorcee, Mrs. Bennett was attracted to Love and the two were married in May of 1854.

The following month Love sailed on the *Yankee Blade,* perhaps for a brief visit to Texas. On the Isthmus of Panama there was trouble among the passengers when an actress named Susan Denim deserted her husband and took up with actor C.E. Bingham. When Bingham was shot and dangerously wounded it was reported a delegation of passengers, including Love, had done the shooting. It was later discovered, however, that Love was not only a friend of Bingham, but had prevented earlier violence to him when the passengers objected to his liason with a married woman. Harry returned to San Francisco in late August and was reported surveying a road from San Jose to the Stanislaus mines in November.

Settling down at his sawmill, Love discovered his wife was a tough, single-minded harridan and the two quarreled continually. Love farmed and tried to lease his unprofitable mill as early as 1860, but it was swept away in the floods of 1862. Other bad luck seemed to plague the old ranger. His house burned down in May of 1864 and there were other troubles as reported in the Santa Cruz *Sentinel* a few years later:

> FIRE BY AN INCENDIARY—Harry Love informs us that on last Sunday about 12 o'clock he was apprised of the fact that his entire crop of newly cut and partly cocked hay, some hundred tons, valued at six hundred dollars, was on fire. Harry is having touble about his land and it is supposed this has something to do with the burning of his hay...

When he ran for justice of the peace in late 1867 he was defeated. His marriage too was in a shambles and his wife finally left him and moved to Santa Clara where she owned considerable property. Harry was drinking more now, his world seeming to be crumbling around him. He tried for a reconciliation with Mary as noted in the *Sentinel* in late December:

> GONE FROM OUR GAZE—Harry Love, of Joaquin notoriety, and who for many years has been a resident of the San Lorenzo Valley, has emigrated to Santa Clara... Harry has got a heart as large as that of a bulluck, and no man ever entered his dwelling without sharing its hospitality.

Tall and regal in bearing, Harry had been known locally as the "Black Knight of the Zayante," referring to the creek on which he had lived. But he was no longer the man he once was. Between Mary's overbearing ways and Harry's drinking the reconciliation hardly got off the ground. When the two quarreled over a handyman named Chris Eiverson who had been hired by Mary, matters took a serious turn. Love ordered Eiverson away, but was told that only Mrs. Love could fire him. On June 29, 1868, Love determined on a showdown. When Eiverson and Mary returned from a buggy ride to town, Harry was waiting for them at the house gate with a pistol and shot gun. As the couple drove into view the fight erupted as reported in the San Jose *Patriot* of June 30th:

> ... Eiverson immediately sprang from the wagon, and looking towards the gate, saw Harry Love behind the fence, with the barrel of the shotgun protruding through it and pointed at him. He immediately drew his revolver, and both parties fired simultaneously. Eiverson was shot in the face and arm with some small bird shot, inflicting no serious injury. His pistol shot did not hit Love... Advancing, and firing as he advanced, cool and undismayed by Love's rapid firing, Eiverson reached the fence, and bending over, fired again, the ball striking Love in the right arm... Both parties came together at the house, when Eiverson struck Love a heavy blow on the back of the head...

206

This photograph of Love was reportedly taken in Santa Cruz by E.P. Butler in late 1865. *Courtesy the Bancroft Library.*

When the fight was broken up physicians were summoned and it was decided to amputate Love's shattered arm. The old ranger died a short time later from shock and an overdose of chloroform. A coroner's jury concluded, "We find he (Love) came to his death by a pistol shot in the hand of Christian Eiverson, a German, the same being in self defense."

Although his wife was quite wealthy, Love's estate at his death consisted of an express wagon, a wolf skin, some old clothes and $1.50 in cash. The $150 funeral costs were eventually paid the following year by step-son Winston Bennett. Love was buried in the Santa Clara Mission Cemetery and lies today in a virtually unmarked grave. An attempt to erect an historical marker over the grave in 1979 was abandoned when several Mexican-American citizens protested the project. Ironically, the grave of the brutal and bloody bandit Tiburcio Vasquez, located in a nearby cemetery, is marked by a large and attractive monument.

PRINCIPAL SOURCES

Latta, Frank F., *Joaquin Murrieta and His Horse Gangs,* Santa Cruz, Bear State Books, 1980; Viele, Mrs. Teresa, *Following the Drum,* Austin, Tex., Steck-Vaughn Co., 1979; Romero, Michael, *Joaquin Murrieta: The Life of a Legend,* San Jose, 1979; Corpus Christi *Star,* June 2, Aug. 11, 1849; New Orleans *Bee,* June 19, 1849; Brownsville *Sentinel,* Aug. 21, 1849; Los Angeles *Star,* June 19, 26, 1852; San Francisco *Daily Alta California,* June 20, 1853, July 30, 1854; San Joaquin *Republican,* June 8, 1853; Sacramento *Union,* July 30, 1853; Santa Cruz *Sentinel,* Dec. 21, 1867; State of Alabama, Dept. of Archives and Hist., Montgomery, Ala.; Santa Clara County Clerk's Office, San Jose; Cal. State Archives, Sacramento; Soc. of Cal. Pioneers, San Francisco; National Archives, Washington, D.C.

JAMES O. McKINNEY

Jim McKinney was sociable and law-abiding when he wasn't hanging out in saloons with thugs and gamblers. Trouble was, Jim spent most of his time in saloons. *Courtesy Jeff Edwards Collection.*

Illinois had the somewhat dubious distinction of being the birthplace of Jim McKinney in 1860. The family moved to Missouri during the 1870's, then moved again in 1878, this time taking up residence in the booming silver mining camp of Leadville, Colorado. The father, Andrew McKinney, worked as both a miner and teamster while his four sons engaged in odd jobs. Jim, the eldest of the boys, apparently had some trouble in Leadville and skipped town late in 1879 or 1880. He headed west and stayed for a time with relatives in Tulare County, California. Later his parents and brothers joined him there, the elder McKinney taking up farming.

Jim always packed his pistol, even when plowing on one of the large farms in the area. A friend, noticing his constant carrying and practicing with his weapon, asked him why he was always armed. "Some fellers are looking for me," replied the gunman.

McKinney was in a succession of brawls and shooting scrapes in the saloons of Visalia and Farmersville. One time he shot a saloon floosie through the cheek when she got in the way of one of his shenanigans. When things got too hot, Jim skedaddled north to one of the railroad towns. In Merced he hung out with Bob McFarlane and Al Hulse, two thugs after his own heart. Both were killers, McFarlane having recently been barely acquitted after a Merced saloon killing in June of 1884. Jim was soon up to his old tricks. He and McFarlane pulled their pistols on a Snelling bartender who had no sense of humor and brought charges against them. McFarlane went to San Quentin for two years, while McKinney was also convicted as noted in the *San Joaquin Valley Argus* of March 28, 1885:

Convictions—James McKinney was convicted of assault last week and sentenced to pay a fine of five hundred dollars or be confined to jail for 250 days.

Since troublemaking and loafing did not pay too well, Jim had to serve his time, the same paper reporting his release the following April. Merced people obviously took their shooting much too seriously and Jim headed back for his old stamping grounds in the south, resuming his career by making himself obnoxious in Porterville where his family now lived. A reform-minded editor named Aubrey Lumley found himself drinking in the same saloon with Jim one evening and was startled when the badman began shouting threats at him. When the newsman began walking towards him McKinney pulled his pistol, only to have it misfire. Lumley proceeded to soundly thrash the bully.

In November of 1889 Jim was drinking in the Reception saloon when he again became embroiled in a ruckus as reported in the Visalia Weekly *Delta:*

> ...Carter [the bartender] testified that on the evening of the difficulty McKinney and others came into his saloon and after taking a drink concluded to try their luck at wrestling. Later in the evening they desired to wrestle again, but Carter interfered, requesting them not to do so as it made too much noise which might drive the customers away. At this McKinney flared up, declared that he was a privileged character and approached Carter with his hand ominously placed upon his hip pocket. As Jim drew near, Carter, behind his bar, raised a pistol and called upon constable Rady to take Jim in charge. Rady stepped up, made Carter lay his pistol down and then taking hold of Jim started with him toward the door. When yet beside the bar with the grasp of the officer upon him, McKinney leveled his revolver on Carter and snapped it three times in rapid succession. Before he could draw the trigger the fourth time the constable had his prisoner outside and the row ended...

Bartender Tap Carter had had trouble with McKinney several nights earlier and was fed up with the gunman's highjinks. He preferred charges and Jim found himself again behind bars, this time in the county jail at Visalia. His cellmate was his old pal Bob McFarlane and both men decided they had urgent business elsewhere—anywhere! The prisoners were able to affect a hole in the roof of their cell which admitted them to the floor above. It was 10 o'clock at night and with no other prisoners in the jail they simply walked out and disappeared into the night.

Heading north, the fugitives obtained help in Merced County and managed to elude pursuing lawmen. They caught a train at Sacramento and were soon out of the state. Jim was in Utah and later Cheyenne, Wyoming, where he wrote a letter to a friend in Porterville. When the letter was published in the local press, Sheriff Dan Overall wired Cheyenne to have the authorities pick up the outlaw and hold him. Jim was taken into custody at Rawlins on January 15th and the sheriff and his prisoner were soon on their way back to California.

McKinney now found himself in very serious trouble. Facing three criminal charges, his trial in superior court at Visalia began on February 12, 1890. He was convicted of simple assault and was immediately put on trial for an assault made on officer Lee Wren a few months previously. Again he was convicted. The third trial concerned the jail-breaking rap and damage to a county structure and again he was easliy convicted. On March 9th McKinney was sentenced to five years for the escape and two years for assaulting officer Wren. For trying to shoot Tap Carter he was fined $500 and sentenced to three months in the county jail. "All lovers of law and order," preached the *Delta,* "of right and justice, uphold the court in inflicting upon James McKinney the fullest extent of the law in the three cases mentioned above." Realizing he had gotten off quite easy, Jim reportedly just smiled.

Admitted to San Quentin on March 11, Jim found himself as No. 14030 and is reported to have been assigned work in the bakery. In September of the following year Governor Markham received a petition urging McKinney be given a pardon. Surprisingly, various Tulare County lawmen, merchants and officials signed the document, including Tap Carter. But the governor had some sense even if these people did not. Jim stayed behind bars. Without liquor he seems to have been a model prisoner, however, and elicited consistently good reports from both Warden Hale and his employer in the bakery. With his good behavior and the resulting time off, Jim was released on December 11, 1894.

Spending several months in San Francisco gambling, Jim soon drifted back to the southern San Joaquin Valley. He gambled in Dave Mosher's Mint Saloon in Porterville, pimped for a girl friend and took on a few gun jobs guarding water ditches. After running a saloon near Maricopa for a time, Jim showed up in Bakersfield where he began drinking and gambling. Bakersfield was an oil boom town, and Jim was soon in trouble again. On the morning of September 13, 1900, McKinney shot and killed a gambler friend named Tom Sears. Both men were drunk at the time, but it was little more than a vicious murder. McKinney was acquitted by a jury, probably glad to be rid of another badman. Jim was happy to get out with a whole skin and promptly skipped back to Porterville.

Back home Jim felt, rather than saw, the changing moods and morals of the twentieth century. He gambled again in Mosher's saloon, but he was brooding about the town's recent incorporation which signalled another outcry against vice—Jim's business. When he began drinking heavily a blow-up was not long in coming, as recorded in the Fresno Morning *Republican* of July 29, 1902:

> Porterville, July 28—At an early hour yesterday morning Jim McKinney, gambler and "bad man," ran amuck, killing one man and wounding four others, two possibly fatally. His victims are:
>
> Will Lynn, gambler—dead
> George Barron, printer—wounded
> John Willis, night watchman— wounded...
>
> William B. West, rancher— wounded
> William Tompkins, night watch- man—wounded.

Top: Porterville was a peaceful enough farming community, unless Jim McKinney was in town. *Courtesy Schutt Collection, Special Collections, California State University Fresno.* Bottom: Two lawmen pose on the street of Porterville just prior to leaving on the search for McKinney in 1902. *Courtesy Jeff Edwards Collection.*

Jim and his friend Scotty Calderwood had been pretty well boiled when they started taking pot shots at saloon furniture, electric fans and even a poker game in a dive called Scotty's Chop House. After several lawmen tried to arrest him on the street, McKinney gunned them down and fled to his girl friend's house where he obtained a rifle and shotgun. Rushing out into the street again, Jim mortally wounded his friend Billy Lynn, then seized a buggy and tore around the streets shooting at anything that moved. The killer was nursing a minor leg wound when he obtained some money from Dave Mosher and fled the area.

A fugitive desperado of the first magnitude now, Jim was chased across the deserts of California and Arizona, deep into old Mexico. He was able to successfully elude his pursuers for a time, but when he ran low on money he decided to return to California. More desperate than ever now, he murdered and robbed two travelers south of Kingman, Arizona, then headed west towards Bakersfield. A posse with Indian trackers chased him relentlessly across the desert, even as California posses were forming to try and cut him off. Two deputies exchanged shots with him on April 12, 1903, a rifle bullet plowing a painful furrow across the desperado's chest. Once again, however, he managed to escape capture.

Jim's description at this time noted that he was "well built, with light brown hair, gray eyes and a sandy moustache. He weighs about 160 pounds. The forefinger of his right hand is gone to the first knuckle." The fugitive was a ragged and dirty shell of his former self when he reached Bakersfield about April 16th. His old friend Al Hulse concealed him in his room at a Chinese Joss House where he was staying with a prostitute. But Jim's time was running out. Sheriff Henry Lovin from Arizona was in town, as were the Tulare and Kern County sheriffs and deputies—all fresh from the McKinney chase. When it was reported that Al Hulse had been heard to say that McKinney was in town, City Marshal Jeff Packard promptly gathered his deputies to close in on the Joss House where Hulse lived.

About ten o'clock Sunday morning, April 19, 1903, Packard and some eight other lawmen converged on the Joss House. The marshal and deputy Will Tibbet went in to search the place while others guarded the exits. As Packard and his deputy opened a locked door with a pass key, they were met by a volley of rifle and shotgun fire, mortally wounding them both. Hulse and McKinney burst from the room, but Jim was shot and killed by Bert Tibbet, the wounded deputy's brother. Other officers joined in the shooting, some thirty-two shots being fired in the battle. Jim McKinney was dead, but at a terrible price. The Bakersfield Daily *Californian* screamed its headlines the next day:

McKINNEY'S HEAD SHATTERED WITH A LOAD OF BUCK-SHOT...BERT TIBBETT FIRED THE CHARGE THAT ENDS OUT-LAW'S CAREER...JEFF PACKARD HAS ANSWERED LAST CALL...

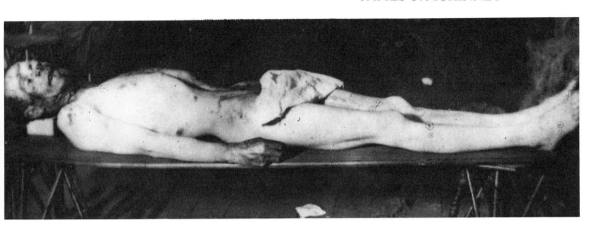

Above: The ugly end of an outlaw. McKinney's corpse as it appeared on the Bakersfield mortician's slab. *Courtesy Jeff Edwards Collection.*

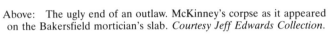

At right: Bert Tibbet, shown here, killed McKinney just moments after the outlaw had killed his brother Will Tibbet, father of the famed opera singer Lawrence Tibbet. *Courtesy Kern County Historical Society.*

Below: The crowd at the Chinese joss house on the day of the shooting where McKinney, Tibbet and Marshal Packard died. *Courtesy Richard Tibbet and Chris Brewer.*

Hulse had disappeared after the fight, but was picked up later. McKinney's body was escorted home by his brothers and delivered to his weary mother. "For her there is only pity," consoled the *Californian*, "felt in her grief over her boy's wrong-doing and tragic death." He was buried in the Porterville cemetery, next to his father, where he lies today in an unmarked grave.

Al Hulse underwent several trials after being named by the dying Will Tibbet as the one who shot him. Rebecca Tibbet, the dead deputy's mother, was a good Christian woman and visited Hulse in his cell to pray with him. Bert Tibbet, Jr., recalled that after a series of such visits Hulse screamed to his jailor, "Get that angel out of here. I can't stand it any longer. I killed her boy!" A short time later Hulse committed suicide in his cell by nearly severing his head with his razor.

Lawrence Tibbet, the famed Metropolitan Opera baritone, was a son of Will Tibbet who had died so gallantly in McKinney's last shootout.

PRINCIPAL SOURCES ───────────────────

Doctor, Joseph E., *Shotguns on Sunday*, Los Angeles, Westernlore Press, 1958; Edwards, Harold L., *The Killing of Jim McKinney*, Porterville, Edwards Book Pub., 1988; Hughes, Guy, *Battle of the Joss House*, N.Y., Carlton Press, Inc., 1968; Mitchell, Annie R., *The Way it Was.*, Fresno, Valley Pub., 1976; Miller, Thelma, *History of Kern County, California*, Chicago, Clarke, 1929; Merced, *San Joaquin Valley Argus*, Aug. 9, 1884, Mar. 28, Aug. 15, 1885; Bakersfield *Californian*, Dec. 23, 1900, Apr. 20, 21, 22, 23, 1903, May 21, 1966; Visalia *Weekly Delta*, Dec. 5, 1889, Feb. 6, 20, Mar. 13, 1890; Porterville *Enterprise*, Aug. 1, 1902; Fresno *Morning Republican*, July 29, 30, 1902, Apr. 7, 8, 15, 16, 18, May 7, 1903; Prison records and pardon files in California State Archives, Sacramento.

JOHN MASON

Born about 1835, nothing is known of Mason's early life or even when he first came to California. He appeared as a hostler working at Fort Tejon in 1860 where he reportedly went by the name of John J. Malone, which may have been his real name. After some sort of trouble, he headed north where he found work in the Tulare Lake area. For a time he herded sheep, an isolated and favorite occupation of men on the dodge. When he had a dispute with his employer, one Joseph Anderson, Mason shot and wounded him, then fled into the surrounding plains.

In the spring of 1864 Mason teamed up with a man named Tom McCauley who sometimes used the alias Jackson, who was now calling himself Jim Henry and had a long criminal career, including a record at San Quentin. Both men were on the run, Henry having barely escaped a lynch-minded posse that had hanged the leader of a robber band to which he belonged. The two outlaws probably met on a valley ranch where they were working to keep a low profile.

George G. Belt, a former alcalde at Stockton and an Indian trader, was a wealthy rancher on the Merced River. Although a native of Maryland, Belt was characterized by one early writer as a "fiery Southerner." He reportedly became interested in forming a Confederate guerilla unit, or perhaps even a Pacific Republic should the south lose the Civil War now raging. There was much southern sympathy in California and such schemes were a source of constant rumors at the time. The Chapman privateer incident at San Francisco and the Bullion Bend robbery by admitted Confederate raiders, lent credence to such rumors.

In some way Mason and Henry became acquainted with Judge Belt. The rancher probably had no idea he was dealing with thugs and criminals and when they showed an interest in his Southern sympathy, Belt offered to help support a Confederate guerilla force if they could form one. Although Henry was reportedly a native of Illinois, Mason was probably a Southerner and was eager to take up Belt's cause. The two were criminals first and Southern sympathizers second, however. Their interests centered more around plunder than politics.

Eighteen sixty-four was a year of terrible drouth in California and after failing to organize a gang in either the San Joaquin or Santa Clara valleys due to the hardpressed farmers and bad war news, the two psuedo-Confederates gave up any ideas of being rebel raiders. As they rode back into the San Joaquin Valley late that year, they sought out Mason's old employer, Joe Anderson, and killed him.

About midnight on the night of November 8, 1864, Mason and Henry rode up to Hawthorne's stage station, west of Visalia. After calling the owner to the door, they savagely shot and killed him without warning. "You'll be questioned about this," Mason snarled to several stagehands. "Tell them I killed him. I, John Mason, and tell them what I did it for... He was a damned Black Republican, had voted for Lincoln and must die." The following morning the two killers appeared at the Elkhorn station just down the road where they shot and killed E.G. Robinson as he was returning from voting. A telegram to Governor Frederick Low from Millerton lawyer E.C. Winchell was typical of numerous petitions asking for aid and rewards:

Millerton, Fresno Co.
Nov. 18, 1864

Dear Sir:

The absence of the Sheriff of this County in pursuit of the murderers of Anderson, Hawthorne and Robinson has prevented my obtaining a correct description of their persons, clothing and animals until now...

On Wednesday night last Mason and Jackson (Henry), with two Mexicans, made a raid upon the Chowchilla River, 25 miles north of here, and on the confines of Mariposa Co. and robbed a number of China mining camps, of all the gold dust...

Sheriff's posses from both Millerton and Visalia were promptly in the field, but even with the help of army troops from nearby Camp Babbitt, the killers escaped. Governor Low issued a proclamation on November 14th offering $500 each for the capture of any of the gang and on the 30th the Visalia *Delta* published a description of Mason as follows:

Mason and Henry were frequent visitors to Visalia, shown here as it looked in 1863. *Courtesy Jeff Edwards Collection.*

Thick set man; about 5 feet 7 inches in height; weight, 165... age, 30 or 32 years; limps in one leg, and has a rocking walk; scar on one cheek; hair light color and very long... small whiskers on the chin, reddish color... light complexion; front teeth are black and decayed; wearing new boots; blue overalls; check shirt, hat made of coyote skin... one six shooter and butcher knife.

In February of 1865 a detachment of army troops mistook a pair of travelers for Mason and Henry and in a shoot-out near San Bernardino, killed one of the men and wounded the other. The following month the outlaws were reported stealing horses in Merced County. From there they fled to the Kern River area where they robbed Eugene Calliaud's store on Greenhorn Mountain. The next evening Mason and a recent recruit named Tom Hawkins appeared at the Jewett brother's sheep camp on the lower Kern River. Here a herder was killed and Philo Jewett barely escaped with his life. A brief item in the Los Angeles *Tri-Weekly News* on April 18, 1865, gave some idea of just how hard-pressed the outlaws were:

> A dispatch says that a detachment of soldiers surprised the murderer Mason, at the head of the Great Panoche Valley, and wounded him badly in the hips, but he escaped. Another detachment was to be sent out to hunt him up.

In August Mason and Henry robbed McFarland's store in Lynn's Valley, then apparently split up for a time—some say over a woman. But time and the odds were running out for the desperadoes. In September Henry was ambushed and killed by a San Bernardino posse. When he heard of his erstwhile partner's death, Mason reportedly viewed the body while dressed as a woman.

The following year Mason attempted to form a new gang and approached a miner by the name of Ben Mayfield. He told him of his former operations, but young Mayfield was not interested and turned him down. Afraid he had talked too much, Mason now vowed to kill Mayfield. The two met at a mutual friend's cabin in Tejon Canyon in early April of 1866. Both men stayed up most of the night, each trying to get the drop on the other. Early in the morning Mason tried to pull his pistol as he was laying in bed, but Mayfield was faster and killed him. The *Delta* commented:

> The Killing of Mason—We suppose there was not a man in the country who did not rejoice at the killing of this murderous desperado which was brought about by Benjamin Mayfield...It appears that Mayfield was arrested in Los Angeles County for this act and tried for murder and has actually been convicted and is to be hung... If the man is guilty of any crime... let him be punished, but do not hang him for ridding the world of a devil incarnate!

Mayfield had made the mistake of trying to hide Mason's body instead of admitting the killing and turning himself in. He was undoubtedly well aware of the large number of secessionists in the state and was afraid that a Southern jury would convict him of killing a confederate guerilla. And he was right! He was taken into custody and tried in Los Angeles, a hotbed of Southern sympathizers during the late war. Fortunately, a flood of petitions from Tulare, Kern and Inyo counties secured a new trial with results noted in the San Francisco *Call* of January 4, 1867:

> JUSTLY ACQUITTED—It will be recalled that some months ago a man named Mayfield was convicted in Los Angeles and sentenced to be hanged for slaying the outlaw Mason. We . . . urged the injustice of allowing a man to be hanged for having performed a praisworthy act. The result was steps which led to a new trial, which led to Mayfield's acquittal. We have been informed by gentlemen for whom he has worked that Mayfield is an honest and hard-working man, and that there is no grounds for the insinuation . . . he was a member of either Mason's or any other outlaw gang.

Disposition of Mason's body after it was retrieved from where Mayfield had buried it is not known, although it was probably interred somewhere in Tejon Canyon.

George Belt didn't long survive his proteges. He was in Stockton on business on June 3, 1869, when he was shot down on the street by William Dennis, a former associate. The men had been quarreling over property for several years. Belt died instantly and Dennis was easily convicted of murder. Being 70 years of age at the time, the killer died in prison and brought to an end the bloody saga of Mason and Henry.

PRINCIPAL SOURCES ───────────────

Barker, Captain John, *San Joaquin Vignettes, The Reminiscences of Captain John Barker,* Bakersfield, Kern Co. Hist. Soc. 1955; Latta, Frank F. *Tailholt Tales,* Santa Cruz, Bear State Books, 1976; Winchell, L.A., *History of Fresno County and the San Joaquin Valley,* Fresno, Cawston, 1933; San Francisco *Daily Morning Call,* Jan. 4, 17, 1867; Visalia *Delta,* Nov. 12, 23, 30, Dec. 7, 21, 1864, Feb. 15, Mar. 1, 15, May 17, July 19, 1865, Apr. 25, 1866, Jan. 16, 1867; Santa Cruz *Sentinel,* Jan. 7, Sept. 23, 1865; Documents in Governor's Reward File, California State Archives, Sacramento.

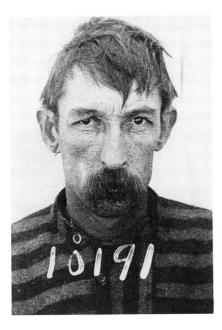

EZRA A. MINER (Bill)

Bill Miner spent almost as much time in prison as he did on the outside. His career as a bandit and desperado is second to none in Western history. *Courtesy California State Archives.*

The most colorful of all the Old West's highwaymen was born in Ingham County, Michigan, on December 27, 1846. Young Bill Miner came to California about 1860 after his father died. Bill and two sisters lived with their mother, Harriet J. Miner, at Yankee Jims in Placer County. In May of 1864 Bill joined the 2nd California Cavalry at Sacramento. He was given $25 of his bounty, but military life quickly palled on him and he deserted in late July. Returning home he became involved with a woman of doubtful morals and in early 1866 was picked up for horse theft and robbery. Sentenced to three years in state prison he was processed at San Quentin on April 15, 1866 as convict No. 3248. His record describes him as being 5 feet, 9¼ inches tall, weighing 145 pounds, wearing a mustache under a long, thin nose. He was only 19 years old and beginning a lifetime of crime and incarceration.

Released on July 12, 1870, Miner lost no time getting mixed up with bad company. In January of 1871 Miner, Charles Cooper and "Alkali Jim" Harrington stopped a stagecoach just ouside San Andreas and got away with the Wells, Fargo box. After a shootout in San Jose, Harrington was later captured in Mayfield, while Miner and Cooper were picked up in San Francisco. Police Chief Patrick Crowley and one of his detectives took the three captives back to the gold rush country to verify their movements. An account of the trip in the San Francisco *Bulletin* of February 11, 1871, concludes with:

> ...At the last place where the officers and their prisoners stopped for food, Miner stole a steel table knife which he concealed in his coat sleeve for the evident purpose of sawing off his irons. The instrument was found when he was searched...

Left: A San Quentin guard tower as it appeared during Bill Miner's lengthy stretches there. *Courtesy California State Library*.

Right: James Harrington, alias "Alkali Jim," was one of Miner's early partners in stage robbing. Harrington had a long record and served prison terms in both California and Missouri. He died in Colusa County in 1884. *From San Francisco Police mug book, courtesy San Francisco Police Department Credit Union*.

Below: An old ball and chain from the Calaveras County jail is the type worn by Miner when he was tried at San Andreas. *From author's collection*.

Alkali Jim and Miner were ironed to the floor with manacles and chains weighing 45 pounds to each man. They could not succeed in obtaining bail. No more of the stolen treasure has been recovered.

At their trial in Calaveras County, Miner and Alkali Jim were made to wear their irons while in court. When their attorney demanded the shackles be removed, the court refused. The matter was appealed to the Supreme Court and when the prisoners obtained a favorable ruling sometime after receiving a ten year sentence apiece, they were accorded a new trial. They should have quit while they were ahead, however. This time the judge gave them 13 years.

Miner was a thoroughly hardened convict by this time. In 1879 he was associating with a San Francisco burglar named "Scotty" Gibson and the two mercilessly beat up a fellow convict named Smith. Gibson and Miner were flogged for their actions, but in September of this same year Gibson murdered Smith in prison.

Discharged in 1880, Miner headed east. In Colorado he became known as "California Billy" after teaming up with Arthur Pond, alias Billy LeRoy. The two reportedly held up two stages in October of 1880, then stopped several more aided by Pond's brother. After a desperate gun battle with a posse, the Pond brothers were captured. Miner managed to escape, but was reportedly in the crowd when a Del Norte mob took the Pond boys from jail and lynched them.

In March of 1881 Miner and a new partner named Stanton Jones held up the Del Norte stage. The two bandits were cornered by a posse at Villa Grove and were captured when they quietly surrendered . Sheriff William Bronough, of Saguache County, was taking the captured bandits back to Del Norte when Miner snatched a pistol and managed to shoot and wound both Bronough and a deputy. Free again, Miner knew Colorado was too hot for him now. He and Jones headed west, their presence in California being chronicled by a notice in the Sacramento *Union* of November 8, 1881:

> Stockton, November 7th—At 5:30 this morning the stage from Sonora to Milton was robbed near the Garibaldi Mine...by four masked men who stopped in front and called a halt...The chief of the gang then with military precision, stationed his men with waves of his hand, without a word being spoken...The Wells, Fargo boxes were sledged open and the contents appropriated...The robbers then turned their attention to the passengers...

Wells, Fargo promptly offered a reward of $1,800 for the robbers whom they identified as Bill Miner, William Miller, Jim Brown, alias Stanton Jones, and the notorious Jim Crumm. The loss was given as $2,435 in coin and $800 in dust, while a passenger lost some $550. A reward poster described how Miner had bought a fine suit of clothes in Oakland on October 26th. Wells, Fargo detective Charles Aull tracked the bandits to Miller's ranch near Sacramento where Crumm was captured. Although Miner and Miller made their escape, Aull kept doggedly on their trail and after a brief exchange of gunfire they too were soon in custody. All were easily convicted, Miner receiving a 25 year

221

sentence. He entered San Quentin on December 21, 1881 and was given No. 10191.

Bill recognized the severity of this latest sentence and made an attempt to escape in 1884. All he accomplished, however, was the loss of four years of good behavior credits. He was seriously slashed and wounded by another convict in May of 1889, but was deemed not critical by the time his two sisters arrived from Sacramento to visit him.

In late November of 1892 Miner again attempted an escape, but again failed. A convict named Joe Marshall worked in the machine shop and had made a grappling hook with which to scale the wall. Miner and Marshall were cellmates and managed to smuggle a drill into their cell, piece by piece. Early on the morning of November 29th the two men finished drilling their way out of their cell. They were sneaking toward the stairs on an outside walkway when a guard opened fire with a shotgun. Marshall was instantly killed with a head full of buckshot. Miner received several shots also and he dropped with a bad wound in the neck. "I did not have any pain when the bullet broke my jaw," he later reported, "but it hurts now. The guard did not call out or make any noise to let us know he was there. If he had we should have gotten back to [cell] 47 because it is no use to go up against buckshot." An investigation disclosed that authorities knew of the impending break and the guard had been hidden in ambush.

Sometime in 1897 Governor James H. Budd visited the prison and Bill managed to obtain an interview in the jute mill where he worked. Miner could always be charming and the governor left saying he would do what he could about restoring Bill's lost credits. When no word was forthcoming, the old outlaw wrote a series of letters to Budd pleading that he intercede in his case:

> ...Governor, I believe four of the Board are your appointees, and if you would write them a letter personally signed by you, certainly your wishes would be at once complied with. I have been here for 16 years, and am now serving on my 17th year of solid confinement...If such action as I suggest is not satisfactory to you—will you not send a commutation to the Board that will release me...

The outlaw's credits were restored in 1900 and he was finally released on June 17, 1901, some five years short of his full term. He was 57 years old when he stepped through the prison gates into a new world, but he was still a frontier outlaw at heart.

He went to live with a married sister at Bellingham, Washington, where he obtained work in an oyster packing plant. Perhaps he even planned to go straight, but on September 23, 1903, he and three companions held up train No. 6 just east of Portland. The express messenger showed fight after the car door was dynamited, and one of the bandits was killed. Miner and the two other outlaws fled in the dark. A wounded companion was abandoned and Miner and the remaining bandit split up.

Miner fled to Michigan, but turned up in British Columbia in the summer of 1904. He was quickly back in action and held up a Canadian Pacific train near Mission Junction on September 10th. The take was some $7,000 in currency and much more in bonds. Posing as a prospector in the area gave Miner an alibi while away casing future holdups. He was using the name "Edwards" and was quite popular locally. A Great Northern train was stopped in October of 1905 and some $36,000 was reported stolen. Later the railroad scaled down this amount to only $1,000.

On May 9, 1906, Miner, "Shorty" Dunn and Louis Colquhoun stopped another Canadian Pacific train east of Kamloops, British Columbia. Little cash was obtained, however, and less than a week later the trio was captured by a detachment of the Northwest Mounted Police.

Both Miner and Dunn were sentenced to life imprisonment, while Colquhoun received a 25-year sentence. Bill entered New Westminister Penitentiary as No. 980 on June 2, 1906. The following year Miner and three other convicts made plans to break out. They escaped on August 7, 1907, but all were promptly recaptured. All, that is, but Bill Miner who had disappeared over the border.

Although suspected of several other robberies in the Northwest, Miner surfaced some time later in Pennsylvania using the name "George Anderson." He paired up with a man named Charlie Hunter and the two worked in a Georgia sawmill while planning a robbery. On February 18, 1911, Bill and Hunter held up a Southern Express train at White Sulphur, Georgia. Unable to blow the safe, the two bandits rode off with a small strongbox containing some $1,500. The local Gainsville *News* was outraged at the crime:

Left: When he was captured shortly after the Kamloops robbery, Miner sat for this mug shot for the Canadian authorities. *Courtesy Provincial Archives of British Columbia.*

Below: Miner and his partners in a wagon after being captured in 1906 in British Columbia. The old outlaw is in the rear seat. *Courtesy Provincial Archives of British Columbia.*

Hardly anyone would believe the story at first, but the truth dawned at last and they were confronted with the fact that here, in a free, civilized, God-fearing and law-abiding community, a train robbery was committed that would abash the most god-forsaken Wild West country to be found. That such a daring hold-up could take place at their door was inconceivable... The robbers made a successful getaway...

Miner was quickly identified and lawmen were alerted by telephone throughout a wide area. When he was captured some 20 miles away from the robbery site, Miner gave his name as William A. Morgan, but photographs soon positively identified him. He was easily convicted and sentenced to 20 years in the Georgia State Prison at Milledgeville.

The veteran outlaw was not about to sit back and resign himself to his fate, however. He made several attempts to escape, but each time was recaptured. After his third try in 1913 he was returned to prison tired and sick from his ordeal. "I'm getting too old for this sort of thing," he reportedly told the guards. And he was right. Under the headline "OLD BILL MINER NOW A FREE MAN," the Milledgeville *News* reported the bandit's death on September 2, 1913:

> Bill Miner, Georgia's most noted prisoner, escaped from the Georgia state penitentiary for the third time Tuesday night at 9:30 o'clock, but he went out through the gates that lead to the Great Eternity in company with the angel of death. A notorious character has been ushered into the great Unknown and with him went all the secrets of an indescribable life...

The old outlaw was buried in the Milledgeville City Cemetery on September 12, 1913, after authorities had given up trying to find a relative. Miner's long criminal record made him one of the most noted of the western outlaws, but despite the romantic aura which envelopes his name today he was little more than an incorrigible, lifelong criminal. He found it impossible to be anything else and forfeited many opportunities to go straight. He will be remembered as a colorful desperado who outlived the frontier conditions that had spawned him.

PRINCIPAL SOURCES ─────────────

Anderson, Frank W., *Bill Miner,* Surrey, B.C., Heritage House Publishing Co., Ltd., 1968; Horan, James D., *The Pinkertons: The Detective Dynasty That Made History,* N.Y., Crown Pub., Inc., 1968; Rickards, Colin, "Bill Miner - 50 Years a Holdup Man," The English Westerners *Brand Book,* London, Jan., 1966; San Francisco *Bulletin,* Feb. 4, 5, 11, Nov. 11, 1871; San Francisco *Daily Morning Call,* Apr. 11, 1882; San Francisco *Chronicle,* Nov. 8, 1881; San Francisco *Examiner,* Nov. 30, 1892; Sacramento *Daily Union,* Nov. 8, 1881; Correspondence with Mark Dugan and John Boessenecker whose biography of Bill Miner is in progress; Prison records in California State Archives, Sacramento; Wells, Fargo Bank History Room, San Francisco; Military records in National Archives, Washington, DC.

ATANACIO MORENO

Born in old Mexico about 1830, Atanacio Moreno was described by one early Los Angeles resident as being "tall, straight, fine appearing... he belonged to the best blood of Sonora." His early life is virtually unknown, but he apparently came to California during the gold rush in 1850. He established a business in the southern California community, and early resident Horace Bell recalled that he stood well in society and was highly respected. When his business failed, about August of 1853, Moreno disappeared from town and was not heard from for some months.

On the evening of December 7, 1853, Los Angeles Constable Jack Whalen proceeded to serve a murder warrant on a desperado named Jesus Senate in the Mexican section of town. He found Senate playing cards and grabbed him by the arm, but was shaken off. Whalen had foolishly not drawn his weapon and when he seized the outlaw again, Senate plunged a long knife into the lawman's heart. Whalen lived but a few minutes, while Senate fled across the Los Angeles River and disappeared. The murdered man was buried the next day, court being adjourned in his honor.

Senate belonged to a local outlaw band comprised of some half dozen desperadoes who had recently arrived in California after escaping jail in Tucson. In Arizona they had made a living killing and robbing small, unsuspecting emigrant parties, but had finally been captured and jailed. Once in southern California they commenced the same operations, but with a little more imagination.

When the first contingent of prostitutes arrived in the angelic city during November of 1853, they opened their bagnio in a large house on upper Main Street. On January 20, 1854, the house held a grand party for the gamblers and other steady customers of the village. While the ball was in full swing, a group of Mexican bandits burst into the room and quickly made everyone prisoner. The masked leader announced that the house was surrounded by others of the gang and if any resistance was offered, everyone would be murdered. All the girls and patrons were systematically robbed, the prostitutes even losing their jewelry and clothes. Afterwards, the bandits disappeared into the night.

Riding out of town the outlaws stopped at the home of Martin DeLong and pounded on the door. After gaining admittance, they proceeded to plunder the premises as noted in the columns of the Los Angeles *Star* the following day:

225

. . . After collecting all the property they deemed valuable enough to take away, they each proceeded to inflict the last injury upon him by committing a diabolical outrage upon his defenseless wife. Mr. DeLong was sick with ague at the time, though scarcely able to walk he came over to the city in the day and made affidavit of the facts before the District Judge, who immediately issued a warrant . . .

Captain A.W. Hope promptly mustered his Rangers and patrolled the town that night. The next day information on the whereabouts of the outlaws was received and the Rangers galloped out of town on a long, but unsuccessful, search. Several days later the bandits returned and after plundering several houses in the Mexican part of town, rode off carrying several girls. Again the Rangers were in the saddle and scouring the surrounding country, but again they returned grim and empty-handed.

Left: When Moreno brought in his cartload of dead bandits, he was hailed as a hero by all the residents of old Los Angeles. *From the 1927 edition of Horace Bell's* Reminiscences of a Ranger.

Below: A rough adobe frontier settlement surrounded by desert, Los Angeles in the 1850's was terribly exposed to depredations by Indians and outlaws alike. *Courtesy California State Library.*

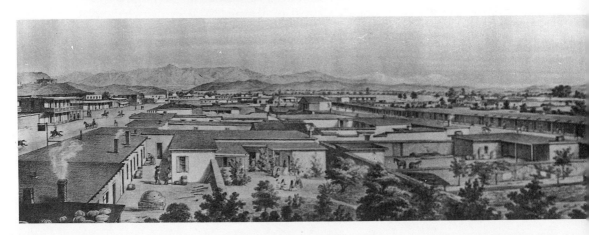

It was pouring rain on January 25th when a cart was wheeled into the yard of the old adobe which served as the office of Sheriff James Barton. Atanacio Moreno was the driver and the contents were noted in the *Star* on January 28th:

CAPTURE AND DEATH OF TWO MURDERERS—We gave an account last week of the outrage at Mr. DeLong's house. We are able to give the particulars of the capture and death of two of the biggest villains that have troubled our community. Senate, the murderer of Jack Whalen, and Luis Burgos, the masked man who often declared himself to be the veritable Joaquin, are killed. Their bodies were brought into town on Wednesday morning, delivered to the sheriff and buried...

Moreno claimed to have been captured by the outlaw gang and held for ransom. He had waited for his opportunity, then killed the two outlaws and brought them to town. He lost no time claiming the $1,500 reward for Senate. He was pointed out all over town as the hero of the hour who had single-handedly killed two of the desperadoes who had been terrorizing the city.

On February 8, 1854, Charlie Ducommun, who ran a shop on Commercial Street, ran into Captain Hope's nearby drug store. Ducommun had recognized the gold watch of Mr. DeLong that had been taken by the bandits—a watch he had sold to DeLong! Atanacio Moreno was in the store at that moment trying to pawn the watch. Hope and several others rushed over and seized Moreno and summoned DeLong as a witness before a justice of the peace. DeLong not only identified his watch, but made further revelations as reported in the *Star:*

...Mr. DeLong identified the watch, and also the shirt which the prisoner had on as the property taken by the robbers in the recent attack upon his house. He also testified that Atanacio was a leader in that affair—that he threatened him with a drawn sword...and took the watch with his own hands.

Moreno finally confessed his guilt. Far from being a captive of the outlaws, he had actually been their leader and had killed Senate for the price on his head. The other bandit had returned to camp at an awkward moment and was also killed. Moreno was tried for grand larceny, found guilty and sentenced to 15 years at San Quentin.

Received at the prison on April 10, 1854, Moreno is described in the records as a 24 year old merchant. Horace Bell notes that he made an escape attempt for which he was severely punished. If this is true it did not seem to damage his record since he was pardoned and discharged on May 11, 1858.

Little is known of the balance of Moreno's life. Bell wrote that he went home to Mexico for a time, but was soon back in California and involved in crime again. He was convicted in Los Angeles of grand larceny in late 1863 and was received at San Quentin again on December 3rd to begin serving a ten year term. This time he was No. 2651 and was described as "age 39, laborer 5'7¼", dark complexion, hazel eyes, black hair..."

Atanacio Moreno was discharged on February 22, 1872, and Bell reports he was not heard from again. Perhaps he returned for good to his old home in Mexico.

PRINCIPAL SOURCES ————————————

Bell, Major Horace, *Reminiscences of a Ranger,* Santa Barbara, Wallace Hebberd, 1927; Newmark, Harris, *Sixty Years in Southern California,* Boston, Riverside Press, 1930; [No author], *An Illustrated History of Los Angeles County, California,* Chicago, Lewis, 1887; San Francisco *Daily Alta California,* Feb. 5, 1854; Los Angeles *Star,* Jan. 12, Feb. 11, 21, 28, 1854; Prison records in California State Archives, Sacramento.

HENRY NICHOLSON MORSE

One of the most prominent and effective of the West Coast lawmen, Harry Morse matched wits and traded bullets with outlaws for more than forty years. *Courtesy California State Library.*

New York City was the birthplace of Harry Morse on February 22, 1835. Always large for his age, he went to sea when only about ten years old, shipping as a seaman and not as a cabin boy. He sailed between Liverpool and New York, but in 1849 joined a venture for California. He landed at San Francisco in August of that year.

Young Morse worked for a time in the mines, then in an Oakland butcher shop. Later he was employed at various odd jobs. Between 1857 and 1862 he operated an express service between San Francisco and Oakland, then sold out to go into the grocery business. In 1863, during the Civil War, he was appointed deputy provost marshal for Alameda County and helped break up a Confederate conspiracy that had planned the overthrow of the state government. This same year he was elected sheriff of Alameda County while only twenty-seven years old.

The young merchant promptly developed into a superb, natural-born lawman. He familiarized himself with all outstanding warrants of his office, then spent many months traveling alone through the surrounding counties acquainting himself with his territory. "In a short time," he later wrote, "the whole country became as familiar to me as my own hand." When he went after an outlaw he generally chased him from the county, killed or captured him. Narcisco Bojorques, for example, was accused of participating in the killing of a settler and his family. Morse tracked the desperado to the Mission San Jose and shot him off his horse near Sunol in a running gunfight. Although Bojorques escaped, he was chased from the area and was later killed in the gold rush country during a shootout with another hardcase.

The young sheriff had an exciting night duel with killer Naratto Ponce in 1867, both men firing at each other's gun flashes. Ponce was badly wounded, but escaped, although Morse stayed on his trail. When the fugitive was again located, Morse took two other lawmen along for the capture. They surprised the killer in a house in Pinole Valley and the battle was on as noted in Morse's official report:

> ...I was on the opposite side of the creek from him, and turned back and ran down the hill as fast as possible, dismounting and got over the fence and ordered Naratto to stop and lay down his pistol....He continued running and I fired at him. I fired four times without effect. I then ordered him to stop again, he kept on and I fired the fifth shot and he pitched forward and fell to the ground....He died in about five minutes. I knew him from the marks on his body that he is the same man that Conway and myself shot some six weeks ago in Livermore Valley.

Morse's tracking of the vicious murderer Joe Newell is a classic of determination and detective work as best told by the Los Angeles *Star* in November of 1868:

> On Wednesday Sheriff Morse, of Alameda County, arrested Joseph Newell, charged with the crime of killing an old man named Morgan Leighton... Since that time Sheriff Morse has been on the track of the accused, tracing him through all his devious wanderings, sometimes without the slighest trace of his man, and at other times coming on parties who had seen such a one far ahead. At last he heard of him at the Lievre station, Mud Springs, Willow Springs, Soledad; traced him to the outskirts of Los Angeles, where he turned off west, and finally came upon him at a tent of railway laborers. He brought him to town, lodged him in jail, and took him... on the steamer *Orizaba,* which left Thursday.

Morse captured badman Joe Newell after a long chase that took him from Alameda to Los Angeles following the slimmest of clues. *From an old police mug book courtesy John Boessenecker.*

230

When five men were killed during the robbery of a store near Stockton in December of 1869, the killers managed to elude pursuers and disappear. Six months later Morse learned purely by chance of the hideout of the bandit gang's leader, Jesus Tejada. After several false starts and much undercover work, Morse captured Tejada and brought him back for trial. "Unfortunately," Morse later noted, "for the ends of justice the outlaw never suffered the penalty of the law, but died a natural death in jail soon after the trial and conviction."

In January of 1871 another small country store was robbed in the Sunol Valley. The three Mexican bandits had wantonly killed the clerk and Sheriff Morse was soon on their trail. In mid-May he finally located the gang leader, Juan Soto, in the mountains southeast of Gilroy. Taking several other lawmen with him, Morse made the hard ride to the area and stopped at an old adobe rancho for information. Inside he suddenly saw Soto sitting at a table, glaring at him. Quickly pulling his pistol, the lawman told him to put up his hands and when Soto refused, a Mexican woman grabbed the sheriff's arm. In a flash Soto had seized his own pistol and Morse retreated outside. The outlaw rushed from the house and they exchanged four shots each, Morse dropping to the ground and actually dodging Soto's shots. As Soto retreated to the house to obtain another pistol, Morse ran for his horse and grabbed his Henry rifle. When Soto again appeared, the resulting fight was recounted in the *Oakland News:*

> ...In the meantime Morse having got possession of his rifle, fired at the fugitive about 150 yards off, and shot him through the right shoulder. Soto staggered with the wound, and at once returned toward Morse with a pistol in each hand. At this point Sheriff Harris, having heard the firing, came up at full speed and seeing the situation of things, fired at Soto with his Spencer rifle, but missed his aim; Soto rushed on toward Morse who, getting another chance, fired again, shot the desperado through the forehead and tore the top of his head off. This ended one of the most exciting and terrific combats we have ever heard of...

Morse's vendetta against the outlaws had gained wide publicity and his latest exploit was recognized in the legislature as reported in the San Francisco *Chronicle:*

> Sheriff H.N. Morse of Alameda County received an unprecendented compliment at the hands of the Senate upon the consideration of a bill for his relief for the capture of Jesus Tejada and the killing of Soto, another desperado. Mr. Tompkins read Morse's modest recital of his encounters with these villains, and then paid Morse a glowing eulogy. Senators Pendergast, Fowler and Evans all followed in the same strain, and on the passage of the bill the ayes and noes were called and every Senator present voted aye. Morse is a brick...

Morse captured Tomas Bustamente—the noted Procopio, nephew of Joaquin Murrieta—in early February of 1872. Both Procopio and Soto had been confederates of Tiburcio Vasquez and when that bandit chief led a raid on the small village of Tres Pinos where three men were killed, Morse was ultimately drawn into the manhunt. After a raid on Jones' store on the San Joaquin, and a Christmas foray into the village of Kingston, Vasquez was being sought by dozens of posses who rarely even caught sight of their quarry. In January of 1874 Governor Newton Booth obtained $5,000 from the legislature and commissioned Morse to put together a team of lawmen to kill or capture Vasquez. Sheriff Tom Cunningham, of San Joaquin County, was selected as Morse's lieutenant and with seven other possemen the pursuit was commenced. The gang had been considerably shot up during the Kingston raid and had split up, making their trail all the more difficult to follow. Morse's dispatch to the governor in late March gives some idea of the rigors of the campaign:

> I rode some 40 miles through the mountains today to get to the outside world and a post office. . . . I have been 4 days hunting the hiding place of Chavez, he must be somewhere in these canyons as he was not able to ride since his wound. We are camped at the head of Sapato Chino Creek in Fresno County, a terrible rough country. We are in the saddle from early dawn until dark. We were quite sore . . . the first few days out, but we have got over that. . .

Morse had finally tracked Vasquez to southern California by the following month, but when he told Los Angeles Sheriff Billy Rowland of the bandit's location, that wiley official took the information and captured Vasquez himself.

Despite his success, Morse had by this time acquired enough mining and ranch properties to allow him to give up his law enforcement work. Too, he had undoubtedly become disenchanted with the red tape and penny-pinching of his county bosses. Morse was famous throughout the state for his work, yet when he presented a bill to the Alameda County Supervisors in April of 1876, it was rejected. The reimbursement, a livery bill for $2,555, was disallowed even though the sheriff was required to return all mileage fees to the county. Livery and traveling expenses amounted to nearly half his salary and he paid it all himself!

Retiring in 1878, Morse visited the east and returned home to take life easy. He had not realized the intrigue his work held for him, however. It wasn't long before he became involved in private detective work. Projects for San Francisco merchants soon evolved into statewide investigations. Eventually he employed some 60 operatives, including an agent in Japan.

Morse participated in the investigation leading to the capture of the noted Black Bart in 1883. His work in various San Francisco fraud and smuggling cases brought him even more renown and he no longer spent endless hours in the saddle chasing badmen. When two Visalia farmers were accused of train robbery and killed several lawmen, Morse quickly had men in the field as noted in the Fresno Morning *Republican* of June 7, 1893:

Harry N. Morse, the manager of the Morse agency, yesterday admitted that he wants the reward offered for the capture of Evans and Sontag, and wants it very much. He stated that he had sent Black into the mountains for the purpose of gathering information concerning the habits and resorts of the outlaws...

Black, up to the time he was shot, had furnished reports almost daily to Morse showing just what Evans and Sontag were doing...At the time of the recent stage robbery, Black was hot upon their trail and arrived at the scene of the hold-up about thirty minutes after its occurrence...

Black had been wounded by the outlaws, but his partner, another Morse operative named Tom Burns, now took up the chase. Burns was in the posse that shot it out with the two desperadoes just a few days after the above article appeared. Just how much of the reward Morse obtained is not known, but he presented Burns with a new 45-90 Winchester rifle in recognition of his work.

Morse posed with Ben Thorn, (center) John Thacker (top right) and Appleton Stone (top left) of the San Francisco police, all of whom played a part in the capture of Black Bart. Seated left is Sheriff Tom Cunningham. *Courtesy John Boessenecker.*

233

Morse's detective agency as it appeared in a San
Francisco directory of 1895. *From* San Francisco
Illustrated Directory, 1895.

Morse did investigative work for the defense of Theodore Durrant, the
accused perpetrator of the 1895 "Crime of the Century" murders. In this he was
pitted against the noted San Francisco police detective, Captain Isaiah Lees.
The press made much of the antagonism between the two great detectives, but
Durrant was convicted on strong circumstantial evidence and executed in 1898.

During his years as sheriff, Morse had maintained his weight at 155 pounds,
but he was described in 1888 as being 5 feet 10½ inches tall and weighing exactly
200 pounds. The old lawman lost his wife in 1907, but at the time of his own last
illness had the satisfaction of knowing that a grandson was assistant
superintendent of his widely known detective agency. Morse was nearly eighty
years old when he passed away at his Oakland home on January 11, 1912. His
name is carved high on the list of great lawmen and brilliant detectives of old
California.

PRINCIPAL SOURCES ————————————————————————

Greenwood, Robert, *The California Outlaw, Tiburcio Vasquez,* Los Gatos, Talisman Press, 1960; Guinn,
J.M., *History of the State of California and Historical and Biographical Record of Oakland and Environs,*
Los Angeles, The Historic Record Co., 1907; Shinn, Charles Howard, *Graphic Description of Pacific Coast
Outlaws,* San Francisco, R.R. Patterson, ca. 1890-1895, republished in 1958 by Westernlore Press with an
intro. and notes by J.E. Reynolds; San Francisco *Bulletin,* Jan. 20, May 13, 14, Oct. 30, 1871; San Francisco
Daily Morning Call, Apr. 7, 1876, Jan. 8, Mar. 12, May 14, 21, 28, Dec. 31, 1882; San Francisco *Chronicle,*
Mar. 16, 1872; Alameda County *Gazette,* Nov. 9, Dec. 17, 1867; Los Angeles *Star,* Nov. 7, 1868; California
State Archives, Governor's Reward Files, Sacramento.

CHARLES MORTIMER
(Charles J. Flinn)

Characterized by detective Len Harris as "the worst man in the state," Charley Mortimer had few equals as a versatile thug, thief and killer. *From the San Francisco Police mug book, courtesy Christian De Guigne.*

Born in Vermont in 1834, Charles Mortimer, whose real name was Charles J. Flinn, grew up with three brothers and two sisters. He engaged in crime at an early age after the family moved to Boston, Massachusetts. A term in the state reform school failed to impress him and upon release young Charley was promptly involved in a series of robberies. He was soon apprehended and this time served a term in the state prison. After doing his time he joined the navy, but jumped ship in Panama where he resumed his criminal activities. Always on the move, he soon left for California, landing at San Francisco on May 5, 1858.

For the next few years Mortimer committed many crimes and worked intermittently in Sacramento and the gold rush country. When he assaulted and robbed Conrad Phister in early 1862 he was caught and sentenced to one year in San Quentin. His photograph, No. 54 in the San Francisco Police Rogues Gallery, was accompanied by the following description:

> Native of Maine; occupation, farmer; age 23 years and 6 months; height 5 feet 6 inches; weight 160 pounds; hair, light; eyes, blue; complexion, light; full face, red cheeks, good looking; has a crucifix with lighted candles, three pierced arrows on his right forearm, printed in red and black ink, and on his left arm the letters C.J.M.; also on one arm, the name of Flinn.

Upon his release from prison Mortimer engaged in various petty crimes in Sacramento and San Francisco. He was arrested as a pickpocket in April of 1864. In August of that same year he executed one of his more daring and imaginative robberies. Early one morning he rang the bell at the residence of Charles Wiggin, a well-to-do clerk of the mayor. Telling the maid he had an appointment, Mortimer went upstairs and into Wiggin's bedroom. After chloroforming Wiggin, the thief took everything of value he could carry, then calmly waved to the maid and walked out the door. Shortly after this he robbed a pawn shop, viciously beating and nearly killing the clerk on duty. He then promptly left San Francisco and headed south.

Mortimer was quickly identified as the Wiggin robber and police detective George Rose was detailed to find him. Receiving word the fugitive had been seen at Belmont, south of the city, Rose arrested his man and prepared to return to San Francisco. When Mortimer hinted at some loot buried nearby, the officer took him to the site. As the two men approached the location, Mortimer suddenly seized a rock and knocked the lawman down. In a desperate struggle, the thief took Rose's knife and stabbed him in the throat. "He grabbed for his pistol," Mortimer later wrote, ". . .and I took it from him after a short struggle and then beat him about the head with it." When Mortimer disappeared into the night, the lawman managed to crawl to a nearby farmhouse and secure aid. A massive manhunt for the fugitive was launched from San Francisco, but was unsuccessful.

Rose miraculously survived the brutal attack as chronicled by a young reporter named Sam Clemens in the *Call* of September 16, 1864:

> Detective Officer Rose, who a few days ago was beaten and stabbed near Santa Clara by a prisoner named Mortimer. . . is now entirely out of danger, and will be about the streets again shortly. We are glad it is so, for while rascality is so plenty hereabouts, the city could ill afford to lose so accomplished a detective. . .

Mortimer foolishly hid out in San Francisco for a brief period, then headed north with two thugs named Shanks and Black Jack. He committed numerous highway robberies as well as plundering many houses and stores. While working with a new partner named Bob Ferry, the two thieves were captured on the Klamath River by a heavily armed posse. Now using the name of George Foster, Mortimer and Ferry pled guilty to grand larceny at their Yreka trial in February of 1865. One evening, just a few days later, Mortimer was able to pick several locked cell doors to admit himself, Ferry and several others into a corridor where they pounced on the jailor. Fleeing into the bitter cold night, the shackled prisoners put as much space between themselves and Yreka as their condition would permit. Ferry and murderer Tom King were quickly picked up, but Mortimer and George Maguire, another prisoner, kept moving and were out for several days.

As they approached the roadhouse of one Cherokee Mary, the two fugitives were surprised as several lawmen appeared with leveled weapons. The Yreka Weekly *Union* recounted what happened next:

> Foster [Mortimer]. . .had hardly cleared the porch before Sherman was close on him singing out for him to "stop" or he would shoot, but Foster had no time to stop, what he wanted was to get away. Instantly Sherman. . . gave

him a charge of buckshot, one shot taking effect in the back of Foster's neck, who threw up his hands...

All the erstwhile fugitives were soon back in jail where their heads were shaven, "penitentiary style." Mortimer was given a bottle of brandy to pull on while the buckshot was being carved from his cheek. "Foster is quite jolly over the affair," reported the *Union,* "takes it as a matter of course, and has no fault to find with any one. "As soon as he was able to travel, Mortimer and the others were taken downriver on the Sacramento boat by Sheriff A.D. Crooks on their way to San Quentin. They stopped over in the San Francisco jail where a startling incident took place as reported in a local newspaper on March 15, 1865:

> ...As the procession entered the calaboose through the outer office, Rose was standing by the doorway conversing with Captain Baker, and chanced to look up as the prisoners with clanking chains filed past him. Foster had his head completely muffled up on account of his wound and hid his face as he passed to avoid recognition, but the quick eye of the detective recognized him at a glance by the outline of his figure, and with the exclamation, "That's Mortimer, by _____!" Rose was by his side in an instant. The officers... restrained Rose from some act of violence...and hurried him away...

Mortimer spent the next seven years in San Quentin and was released in January of 1871. Rose had been dismissed as a Special Policeman in May of 1868 and had left the city. Mortimer quickly became involved in crime again and took part in the robbery of the Santa Cruz treasury soon after his release. He also began living with a prostitute named Carrie Spencer who aided him in various crimes.

Mortimer served several terms in San Quentin, shown here as it appeared during his residency. *Courtesy California State Library.*

Sacramento as it appeared during the Mortimer trial and hanging. *Courtesy California State Library.*

When a Sacramento saloon keeper named Mary Gibson was found murdered on the morning of September 20, 1872, Mortimer was picked up as a suspect. The previous night two police officers on the street had noticed that he was scratched up and disheveled. Mortimer was drunk and told the officers he had been in a fight. He also had displayed some money to the lawmen who knew he had previously been broke. Sacramento policeman Len Harris arrested him the following day and took charge of some property identified as belonging to the dead woman. Carrie was also arrested as an accessory. The San Francisco *Bulletin* of November 18th noted their appearance in the Sacramento courthouse:

> ...In the County Courthouse this morning, as the prisoners who had been present at the empanelling of the Grand Jury were about to be sent below, Charles Mortimer, the murderer, made an assault upon his woman, Carrie, who was also one of the prisoners, and endeavored to catch her by the throat, having the impression that she had turned against him...

Mortimer himself later stated that he had only spoken to Carrie and that a group of officers, anxious to separate them, had shoved him into her.

In February of 1873 Mortimer was taken to Santa Cruz to testify in the treasury robbery case. On his return trip he talked to a San Jose *Mercury* reporter who noted that "Mortimer possesses a glib and oily tongue... is regarded as the very prince of liars." He bragged to the newsman that Policeman Rose had been his accomplice for several years and had planned the Wiggin robbery. Rose was gone by this time and could not defend himself, but a few years later he was charged with a crime in Salt Lake City.

On March 13, 1873, Mortimer's trial began for the murder of Mary Gibson. A great mass of evidence was produced against him, but he insisted that witnesses could provide an alibi for him. When he gave Carrie a long list of instructions she was to follow in her testimony, she weakened and turned them in to the police.

While Mortimer was in the Sacramento jail a man in San Francisco was indicted for the murder of a prostitute named Caroline Prenel. The man's trial was postponed and he was later released when some of Prenel's stolen jewelry was traced from a pawnshop to Mortimer. Several stones had been remounted and were found in Carrie Spencer's cell. The trial lasted three days and Mortimer was easily convicted of the Gibson murder. He was sentenced to hang on May 15th.

In early April a brother of Mortimer's arrived in town. William Flinn operated a tailoring business in Lynn, Massachusetts with his brothers, Edward and Frank. He visited his brother in jail, but they did not speak when Mortimer failed to recognize him. Just after midnight on April 16, 1873, William Flinn climbed the jail yard wall and made his way to a back door. He rang the bell, then hid, but the jailor was on his guard. When the deputy saw the visitor was armed, he shot him in the chest and mouth. Flinn turned and ran into the jail, dropping his pistol before falling in front of his brother's cell. He raised his head, but then died without speaking. "During his stay in town," commented the *Bulletin,* "he has made attempts to bribe witnesses in the Mortimer case to swear falsely."

On being told Flinn was dead, Mortimer turned deathly pale and demanded to be shown the body to see whether it was really his brother. He suddenly seemed to appreciate the immensity of the tragedy that had occurred and later wrote; "On the first intimation that he got that I was in trouble he left his business and all that he held dear in this life—mother, brothers and all—and came three thousand miles to learn the nature of my troubles..."

The attempted rescue caused a sensation. The sight of his dead brother, however, seemed to snap the condemned man's mind, and he spent most of his time until the execution staring at a pile of his dead brother's clothes topped with a lock of his hair. Another brother, Frank Flinn, arrived in Sacramento on May 10th, but Mortimer gave no sign that he recognized him.

239

Mortimer had only a brief time to live when this woodcut was made to illustrate his autobiography. The differences between his first mug shot and this portrait are startling. *From his autobiography.*

Charley Mortimer was hanged on schedule, the authorities and attending physicians having diagnosed him as merely feigning insanity after his brother's death. Frank Flinn took the bodies of his two brothers home to their aged mother and both were buried in the family plot in Lynn, Massachusetts.

In an uncharacteristic gesture, Mortimer penned his memoirs while in the Sacramento jail. It was an effort to somehow repay his attorney, Samuel Denson. The manuscript was published first in the Sacramento *Daily Record,* then later as a book. It is one of the most revealing and fascinating documents in California criminal history. "Oh Carrie," he wrote in a foreword, "you have brought all this trouble on me..." It was Carrie, Mortimer maintained, who had murdered a drunken Mary Gibson in a fit of jealously.

PRINCIPAL SOURCES ─────────────────────

Branch Edgar M., *Clemens of the Call,* Los Angeles, Univ. of Cal. Press, 1969; Mortimer, Charles (Charles J. Flinn), *Life and Career of the Most Skillful and Noted Criminal of His Day, Charles Mortimer...,* Sacramento, William H. Mills & Co., 1873; Wells, Harry L., *History of Siskiyou County, California,* Oakland, D.J. Stewart & Co., 1881; Wright, George F., *History of Sacramento County, California,* Oakland, Thompson & West, 1880; San Francisco *Daily Alta California,* Mar. 15, 1865; San Francisco *Bulletin,* May 16, 1870, Nov. 18, 1872, Jan. 28, Feb. 4, 13, Mar. 13, 14, 15, 16, 17, Apr. 16, 18, May 7 12, 15, 1873; San Francisco *Daily Morning Call,* Sept. 11, 16, 1864, Yreka *Journal,* Feb. 17, 1865.

WILLIAM MULLIGAN

There are no known photographs of Mulligan, but this woodcut from a Thomas Nast sketch shows him at the Sayers—Heenan fight in England. *Courtesy New York Public Library.*

Described by a contemporary as "low of stature, slight of frame, active as a cat, the expression of a bull terrier, and as quick in an encounter," Billy Mulligan was reportedly born in Ireland in the later 1820s. He came to New York at an early age and was apprenticed to a cooper, but hard work didn't fit in with the boy's career plans. Young Billy was strong and tough and he easily became a fighter and saloon bully who mixed into politics and election fixing. In "slow" times he drifted into a life of crime. A lawyer once summarized Mulligan's early years in a courtroom statement:

> Mulligan commenced life by a burglary in this [New York] city, and, having broke jail, found his way to the Mexican War where he figured largely among that captured people as an assassin. He is reported on one occasion to have shot a superb looking officer, whose horse he was leading by the bridle, merely for the fun of seeing the "greaser" jump; and on another with having coldly blown out the brains of a dying soldier at Humantia while the ear of the confessor was bending to the poor creature's lips.

Although one early source credits Billy with serving in Jack Hays' Texas Rangers during the war, Mulligan's own story was that he went to New Orleans in 1847 and saw service in Mexico with the Louisiana Mounted Volunteers. He returned to New Orleans the following year and came to California during the gold rush of 1849.

Mulligan, Yankee Sullivan, Chris Lillie and E. Hopkins, all New York thugs and prize fighters, turned up in the gold rush town of Sonora in 1850. Headquartering at Holden's Hotel, the gang gambled, jumped claims and promoted fights in the surrounding area. On March 6, 1851, Mulligan shot and wounded William Anderson in a fandango hall brawl. Anderson died some three weeks later, but since he was considered the aggressor, Billy was not held.

Late that year Mulligan moved back to San Francisco. When the Garra Indian uprising panicked southern California, San Francisco Sheriff Jack Hays was authorized by the governor to raise several companies of volunteers. Mulligan was elected lieutenant of gambler Dan Aldrich's company, but the Indian scare had been greatly exaggerated. Only a small portion of the group actually went south and Billy wasn't with them.

Mulligan had a pistol duel in a gambling hall in November of 1851. He had argued with a man named Rhodes in a Washington street bordello and when the two met in the Bella Union they renewed their scrap as noted in the San Francisco *Alta California:*

> . . . Some words arose when parties . . . addressed Mulligan and begged him not to create a disturbance in the house. Mulligan was about acquiescing by moving off when some one said, "he's got a pistol!" Mulligan then turned . . . and commanded Rhodes to draw, whereupon both drew their pistols . . .

The two men emptied their weapons at each other, Mulligan taking two shots, in the arm and a scalp wound. In the process he managed to drill a bystander through the leg and Rhodes in the finger. The brawl carried over into another room as the two wrestled and pounded each other with their empty revolvers. Both combatants were arrested, but before Billy could be arraigned he was shot in the leg during a fight on the plaza between two other men.

He was defeated when he ran for city marshal, but served two years with the County Treasurer's Office as a political payoff.

San Francisco in the 1850's, with its gambling, political corruption and rampant crime, was just the right place for Billy Mulligan. *Courtesy California State Library.*

Reported in Tuolumne County again in September of 1853, Billy refereed a prize fight between his old cronies Yankee Sullivan and Hopkins who performed before a crowd of many thousands. Such fights were usually fixed and when things got too hot in the gold fields, Billy would head back for San Francisco.

In June of 1855 Mulligan and Yankee Sullivan had a disagreement after viewing a cock fight on Commercial Street. Name-calling quickly evolved into a scuffle which friends interrupted. The two went at it again in a saloon, but police separated them this time. The two thugs then went to a room where a vicious fight resulted in Sullivan being badly beaten up by Mulligan's fists and pistol.

Billy was appointed a deputy by Sheriff David Scannell as another political payoff for keeping his precincts in line. He was good at keeping voters away from the polls or herding them there, depending on what his political bosses wanted to accomplish, and it paid him nicely in both cash and official appointments.

He was acting as turnkey at the county jail at the time of the great vigilante excitement of 1856 and could only stand glowering when an army of vigilantes took Jim Casey and Charles Cora from the jail. After Casey and Cora were hanged, Mulligan, Yankee Sullivan and others were also picked up and jailed at vigilante headquarters. A sweep of known criminals and political thugs was made and after being photographed, Mulligan and others were shipped out of the city. Sullivan, reportedly afraid of being shipped back to Australia as an escaped criminal, committed suicide in his cell.

After arriving back in New York City, Billy told anyone who would listen of his ill-treatment and what he would do if any vigilantes dared visit the east. And he was as good as his word. He delighted in scanning the papers and any visiting vigilante was attacked by Mulligan and his friends and badly beaten. After a dozen such incidents the San Francisco *Alta* was moved to comment:

> The continued outrages perpetrated upon Californians by the man Mulligan and his confreres, ought to be sufficient warning to all those called to the East...to take proper care...
> We do not propose to waste any words upon this brutal piece of living and breathing humanity, but...urge upon those who may have occasion hereafter to visit New York from California...to provide themselves with... weapons of defense...to use them stoutly,...as they would...upon a rabid dog...

San Franciscans were cheered in May of 1858 when word was received that Mulligan himself had been badly beaten in a saloon brawl the previous month. Both his eyes were badly gouged and his nose partially bitten off. After recovering he again resumed his life as a gambler and promoter. He was frequently in court, was a second to John Morrisey in his noted prize fight with Heenan and traveled to England for the Heenan-Sayers fight. During a dispute with Morrisey in the latter's New York saloon, Billy pulled a pistol and took a shot at a police officer. He was promptly arrested, but instead of the usual light fine he was accustomed to because of his political connections, he found himself tried, convicted and sentenced to four years in Sing Sing. On December 18, 1860, the *Alta* reported:

> ...The New York papers are lauding Judge Gould to the skies for his indifference to political influences—an unusual thing in New York. What must they think, if Mulligan is such a bully and terror in New York, of his career in San Francisco—a place one tenth as large? And what an admission this is of the justice of the banishment...

Just before being shipped off to prison Billy married Mary Lewis, the madam of the brothel on Houston Street. "...As the locality where Mrs. Mulligan resided," snickered the *Alta,* "is not a very respectable or virtuous part of New York... it is a fair inference to suppose that our quandom San Francisco rowdy has married a woman of doubtful reputation." Although he spent some time in prison, Billy was able to obtain his release and helped raise a local regiment during the Civil War. Because of his record, Mulligan was not allowed to join his unit and it was a disappointed ex-con who deserted his wife and headed west. He landed in San Francisco on February 1, 1863, prompting the *Call* to comment:

> Billy Mulligan—This individual, who years ago when taking his departure from San Francisco was accompanied to the streamer by a large number of our most respectable citizens, returned on Sunday, and strange to say has created no excitement amongst his former admirers.

Apparently not wanting to push his luck too far, Billy went over to have a look at Virginia City, Nevada. While there he had a duel with Tom Coleman at Austin, the latter being wounded in the finger and leg before the affair was called off.

Returning to San Francisco, Mulligan was drinking more than ever and was repeatedly hauled before the police court. After a protracted binge in early July of 1865, he was suffering from more than his usual quota of delerium tremens and imagined the vigilantes were again after him. He sought shelter in the police jail one night, but the following day barricaded himself in his room at the St. Francis Hotel and fired several shots from his window. When Captain Lees and several police officers arrived, Mulligan screamed that he would kill the first man who tried to enter his door. Jack McNabb, a desperado and friend of Mulligan, tried to talk the badman into surrendering and was shot and killed for his trouble. A bystander on the street was also gunned down when Mulligan opened fire on police officers.

Captain Lees knew what he must do. After consulting with the district attorney, he stationed a sharpshooter across the street who patiently waited for an opening. "Only two or three shots were fired," noted the *Examiner,* "when Mulligan fell, a ball having struck him in the head." Breaking down his door the police found Billy stretched out full length in the hallway, his brains scattered over the walls and floor. The *Alta* noted on July 19th:

> FULLY JUSTIFIED—To save any chance for doubt on the subject, we will say that the act of Officer Hopkins in shooting Mulligan yesterday, is fully endorsed by Chief Burke and Captain Lees and by every man in the community conversant with the facts... The utter pity is that the shot was not fired an hour sooner and a valuable life thereby saved.

There was no funeral, the body merely lying in state at the Broderick fire engine house for a day. The remains were shipped to Sacramento where a brother, Barney Mulligan, lived. There is no record of the grave site today.

PRINCIPAL SOURCES ⎯⎯⎯⎯⎯⎯⎯⎯

Bancroft, Hubert Howe, *Popular Tribunals,* San Francisco, The History Pub. Co., 1887; Buckbee, Edna Bryan, *Saga of Old Tuolumne,* N.Y., Press of the Pioneers 1935; Coblentz, Stanton A., *Villains and Vigilantes,* N.Y., Thomas Yoseloff, Inc., 1936; Johnson, Kenneth M., *San Francisco As It Is,* Georgetown, Talisman Press, 1964; San Francisco *Daily Alta California,* Nov. 19, 1851, Aug. 20, 1858, May 2, 1859, Dec. 2, 8, 1860, July 8, 9, 1865; San Francisco *Bulletin,* Jan. 16, 1863; San Francisco *Daily Morning Call,* Feb. 2, 1863; *California Police Gazette,* Sept. 2, 1865; San Francisco *Examiner,* July 8, 1865; Austin, Nev., *Daily Reese River Reveille,* Aug. 2, 4, 5, 1864; N.Y. *Times,* Aug. 10, 11, 1865; Wells, Fargo Bank History Room, San Francisco.

JOAQUIN MURRIETA

This drawing, made about 1895, is still the only reasonably authentic representation of what Murrieta looked like and matches contemporary descriptions of the captured head. *From* Overland Monthly, November, 1895.

Located some fifty miles south of the border in the Sonora Province of Old Mexico, the Pueblo de Murrieta was the birthplace of the most noted of the early California bandits. Born in 1832, Joaquin grew up in this area of Mexico and acquired some education. He was still a teenager when word of the great California gold discovery filtered down from the north. His family had long been miners and stock-raisers in Sonora and in the spring of 1849 the youthful Joaquin, with several brothers and other relatives, left for California. With him also was a young neighbor girl named Rosa Feliz whom he reportedly had married.

Almost nothing is known of Murrieta's early movements in California. He probably gravitated first to Tuolumne County where there was a large Mexican camp at Sonora. The 1850 census of the area lists an "M. Murrieta," who may have been a relative. Joaquin reportedly mined at various locations. When his claim was jumped and he was beaten and Rosa raped, the young miner became quite bitter towards the Americans. He moved to Murphys, in Calaveras County, and ran a monte game there in late 1850 when he was not mining. When his brother was lynched after being falsely accused as a thief, Joaquin was whipped as an accessory. Infuriated at the cruel treatment, Joaquin is reported to have killed some of his tormentors. The newspapers of the time frequently reported such incidents and the intolerance of many Anglos towards Mexicans made it quite likely these events did occur. In the San Francisco *Herald* of April 18, 1853, Joaquin himself is quoted after an interview at a rancher's home on the Salinas plains:

> ... He had been oppressed, robbed and persecuted by the Americans in the placers—had lost $40,000—been driven from a piece of land he was working with an American companion—had been insulted and grossly maltreated without justice—had been flogged—and he was determined to be revenged for his wrongs...

A man named William Lang was identified by early settlers as a leader in the crowd that had brutalized Joaquin. Lang's existence was amply documented when he was shot and killed by Sam Green at Murphys on June 26, 1852. Joaquin apparently had to leave the mining country after he had killed several of his tormentors and he established a small ranch in Niles Canyon, in Alameda County. This ranch is mentioned in the *Herald* interview and was Rosa's home while Joaquin engaged in running mustangs down into Mexico. There was undoubtedly a good deal of stolen stock mixed in with his mustang herds, but in any case mustang running in those early days was quite profitable as noted in the San Francisco *Alta* in July of 1852:

> MUSTANGS—Judge Marvin informs us that on his way down from the Fresno he saw several gangs of Spaniards on the plains, between the Merced and the San Joaquin, engaged in catching wild horses, which they drove into corrals. One and two thousand mustangs are sometimes seen in bands on these plains...

When not running captured and stolen horses, Joaquin and some of his men would rob miners, travelers and teamsters in the mining country. The bandits kept always on the move to avoid capture. Traditionally Murrieta has always been blamed for the murder of Allen Ruddle which occurred in late April of 1852. The incident was recorded in the Sacramento *Union* of May 6th:

> ...A correspondent of [the *San Joaquin Republican*] writing from Mariposa under date of the 28th ult. says that Mr. Ruddle, a citizen of that place was murdered near the Merced River. He started for Stockton on Monday last to purchase goods; had on his person some five hundred dollars and was attacked...near Forbes' Ranch, on Dry Creek, by two Mexicans. The poor fellow was both lassoed and shot. Shortly afterwards a posse was raised who followed the scoundrels to the mouth of the Merced...

The posse was apparently headed by Harry Love, who was working in the area at the time. Love tracked the killers to the San Luis Gonzaga Ranch where Murrieta and some dozen men were surprised in camp. The outlaws panicked, but were able to make their escape in the darkness as the posse searched the area. Some of the outlaws were riding double, so Joaquin stole some horses from an Orestimba Creek rancher, then fled south towards Los Angeles. At Tejon Pass the gang was surprised by a group of Indians who captured, stripped and robbed them. Fortunately they were freed before the Orestimba rancher arrived to claim his stolen stock. The incident was noted in the Los Angeles *Star* of June 12, 1852:

> Jose Zapatero, another chief, has since taken a number of horses from some Sonoreans, which were pursued to the Tejon, and delivered them over to the authorities...

After leaving the Indians, the bandits made their way to San Gabriel, near Los Angeles. Here Joaquin apparently took up with a woman named Ana

Benitez. On the night of November 7th General Joshua Bean, a state militia general and saloon owner, was murdered. Although a local cobbler was blamed for the crime, Reyes Feliz, Rosa Murrieta's brother, was picked up on suspicion and admitted to other offenses. Before he was hanged he confessed that:

> . . . I belonged to the company of Joaquin Murrieta . . . We robbed, Joaquin Murrieta, the late Pedro and myself. In Avisimba . . . we robbed 20 horses, which we brought to the "Tejon." There the Indians took some of them from us; others, the owner took who went in pursuit of us . . .

Disturbed at the recent loss of several men, Joaquin fled north. According to Ana Benitez, "Joaquin had gone to the Tulares to sell about 30 horses he had stolen . . ." The *Star* reported that "On the night of Tuesday, the 25th ult., the entire stock of horses belonging to Messrs. White and Courtney . . . were stolen from San Gabriel . . ."

Joaquin again assembled his men in the north, probably at a place called Yaqui Camp, in Calaveras County. An early notice of his activity is an article in the Stockton *San Joaquin Republican* of January 26, 1853:

> From Calaveras—(per Brown's Express)—It is well known that during the winter months a band of Mexican marauders have infested Calaveras County and weekly we receive details of dreadful murders and outrages committed in the lonely gulches and solitary outposts of that region. The farmers lost their cattle and horses, the traders tents were pillaged and the life of every traveler was insecure. Success had recently emboldoned the band of villains to commence a system of outrages more daring still . . . From the neighborhood of San Andreas, in one night, they stole 70 horses; every evening the news arrived in camp of some fresh robbery or murder.
>
> The band was led by a robber named Joaquin, a very desperate man, who was concerned in the murder of 4 Americans some time ago, at Turnerville.
>
> . . . On Friday night another man was murdered at Yaqui Camp and about the same time a Chinaman was found dead at Bay State Ranche and an American at Foreman's Ranche,
>
> This was beyond human endurance and 5 men left on Saturday from Yaqui Camp to find the villains . . .

The posse found twelve of the gang near San Andreas with a large number of horses in their possession. Afraid to attack such a large party, the lawmen retreated while the bandits attacked the Phoenix Mills, killing two Americans there. One of the outlaws was badly wounded in an exchange of gunfire and he was tracked down and killed the next day. Two others of the gang were captured and immediately lynched. Large meetings were held at various towns and all Mexicans were warned to leave the area. Several other posses fought skirmishes with the superbly mounted bandits who always managed to escape. Another of the gang, Antonio Valencia, was captured and hanged at Jackson on February 15th.

Perhaps a dozen Chinese and half that many Americans had been killed in a few weeks time. Many others had been wounded. Several times the posses had shot and wounded an outlaw and captured horses and supplies, but always the desperadoes managed to escape. "This town is under the greatest excitement," noted a dispatch from Jackson. "A large meeting . . . was held this evening and severe measures taken . . . Nearly the whole population has volunteered to turn out in the pursuit tomorrow. $1,000 are [*sic*] offered for the head of Joaquin . . ." Although they hadn't managed to capture him, the posses did drive Murrieta from their county.

The *San Joaquin Republican* announced Joaquin's new field of operations:

> Joaquin in Mariposa County—Mariposa, Mar. 6th—Two weeks ago Joaquin made his appearance with 12 of his gang in the town of Hornitos, a large Mexican camp on Burns Creek, about 20 miles from Mariposa.
>
> Last Thursday he repeated his visit alone and when two Americans recognized him and tried to arrest him he shot one in the arm and the other in the belly. Joaquin escaped, unharmed . . .

After a number of murders and robberies in the Mariposa area, a flood of petititons from the ravaged counties finally resulted in legislative action. The governor had already offered an inadequate $1,000 reward, but an added $10,000 was quickly whittled back to $1,000. Many of the legislators were concerned about offering a reward for someone who had not been duly convicted of a crime. Still, something had to be done. On May 17, 1853, a bill was signed into law authorizing the formation of a twenty man force of California Rangers to be led by a noted Texas frontiersman named Harry Love. Curiously, the act specified that the rangers were to kill or capture the gang of robbers led by the *five* Joaquins-"Joaquin Muriati, Joaquin Ocomorena, Joaquin Valenzuela, Joaquin Botellier and Joaquin Carillo . . ." By early June, Love and his rangers were in the field.

Sending out small scouting parties, Love managed to recover some thirty stolen animals and capture several bandit suspects. By the end of the month the rangers headed southwest towards the coast range, a known hideout of outlaws. They arrived at San Juan Bautista on July 12th and prowled a wide area to the south and east, traveling mostly at night. By a stroke of luck Captain Love apprehended a brother-in-law of Joaquin's named Jesus Feliz. Thinking the outlaws had already left the area, Feliz agreed to guide them to where a mustang roundup had been in progress. Love found a large group of vaqueros at the rendezvous—too many for him to arrest, so he merely recorded everyone's name and appropriated several obviosly stolen animals. Then the rangers left.

Returning on the morning of July 24, 1853, Love and his men discovered a smaller band of vaqueros and caught them unaware. When one of the rangers recognized a "Joaquin," there was an exchange of pistol fire and some four of the Mexicans were killed and two captured. Others made their escape. One of the bodies was identified as "Joaquin" and the head was removed as proof of his death. Three-Fingered Jack, Joaquin's lieutenant, was also decapitated and his hand removed. Returning to the gold rush country, Love secured a number of affidavits identifying Joaquin and the $1,000 reward was paid and divided among the rangers. Later the legislature voted another $5,000 for Love and his men whose three months tour of duty was now completed.

Over the years various accounts have identified the head of the famed bandit as that of someone else—usually an Indian. At this late date it is probably not possible to prove it definitely was Joaquin Murrieta who was killed, but it is certain that the head belonged to a young, good looking Mexican who fit the bandit's general description. The San Francisco *Herald* described the head when it was first brought to town as follows:

> ...It is that of a man about the middle size, apparently between twenty and twenty-five years old. The forehead is high and well developed, the cheekbones elevated and prominent and the mouth indicative at once of sensuality, cruelty and firmness. The hair, of a beautiful light brown...

A ferryman who was the first to see the head after the battle, later described it as being "very light in complexion for a Mexican and I recognized it as the head of a dashing and handsome young man whom I had often seen riding around the vicinity of the reservation. I never suspected that he was the famous desperado..." Descriptions and other data leave little doubt that it was a young Mexican who had been killed, and not an Indian.

The head was exhibited for years, mostly in the San Francisco museum of a quack doctor named Louis Jordan. The trophy was reportedly destroyed during the great earthquake and fire of 1906. Despite all this, a recent biography of Murrieta asserts that he was not killed by the rangers, but was shot later by pursuing officers and subsequently died at his Niles Canyon home. Not wanting the hated "Gringos" to know they had killed him, Joaquin had his wife and sister bury him in a room of his home, rather than outside. Excavations at the site of the Murrieta residence during the summer of 1986 failed to turn up any skeletons within the confines of the foundation, however.

Whatever the bandit's actual fate, he is celebrated today as the most noted, and tragic, of California's early outlaws.

PRINCIPAL SOURCES

Latta, Frank F., *Joaquin Murrieta and His Horse Gangs,* Santa Cruz, Bear State Books, 1980; Secrest, William B., *Joaquin, Bloody Bandit of the Mother Lode,* Fresno, Saga West, 1967; Callison, Charles M., "Searching for Murrieta's Home and Grave in Canada Molino Vallejo," *Calif. Hist. Courier,* Apr./May, 1987; San Francisco *Daily Alta California,* July 3, 12, Aug. 3, Dec. 15, 1852, June 20, July 15, Aug. 5, 1853; San Francisco *Bulletin,* Dec. 3, 1899; Mariposa *Gazette,* Mar. 3, 10, 1883; Placerville *Herald,* Aug. 3, 1853; Stockton *San Joaquin Republican,* Jan. 26, Feb. 2, 17, 19, 23, Mar. 12, June 8, 1853; Los Angeles *Star,* Dec. 4, 1852; Sacramento *Union,* Feb. 15, 24, Mar. 22, 1853; Legislative Documents and Governor's Papers in California State Archives, Sacramento.

WILL BE EXHIBITED
FOR ONE DAY ONLY!

AT THE STOCKTON HOUSE!
THIS DAY, AUG. 12, FROM 9 A. M., UNTIL 6, P. M.

THE HEAD
Of the renowned Bandit!

JOAQUIN!
AND THE

HAND OF THREE FINGERED JACK!
THE NOTORIOUS ROBBER AND MURDERER.

"JOAQUIN" and "THREE-FINGERED JACK" were captured by the *State Rangers*, under the command of Capt. Harry Love, at the Arroyo Cantina, July 24th. No reasonable doubt can be entertained in regard to the identification of the head now on exhibition, as being that of the notorious robber, *Joaquin Murietta*, as it has been recognised by hundreds of persons who have formerly seen him.

From author's collection.

Below: The old Niles Canyon adobe where Joaquin Murrieta and his wife lived. By 1919 the old structure had disappeared. *Author's collection.*

Neagle was always good copy and San Francisco newspaper artists had a field day sketching the feisty little gunman in the 1890's. *From San Francisco* Examiner *of August 13, 1896.*

DAVID BUTLER NEAGLE

Born in Boston, Massachusetts, on October 10, 1847, Dave Neagle moved with his parents to San Francisco in 1852. Mrs. Neagle died shortly after their arrival and young Dave was raised by his father in the Mission District. The boy received some education, but by the time he was fifteen he was already mining at the gold camp of Florence, Idaho. Returning to the coast, Neagle attended school until his father's death in 1863 when he again left to work in the mines—this time at Virginia City, Nevada. In 1868 he joined the rush to the White Pine District in eastern Nevada. Dave was mining at Pioche in 1870 when he visited Salt Lake City. There he met and married Bertha Boesque. Their daughter Emma was born in November of that year.

Dave's first shooting scrape of record was with Jim Levy in late May of 1871 at Pioche. The men quarrelled over the gunfight of some friends and Neagle had shot and painfully wounded Levy in a street fight. The following September Neagle is mentioned as one of the casualties in the great fire that destroyed Pioche, but he was apparently not seriously injured.

In 1874 he joined the rush to the California gold camp of Panamint where he opened his popular Oriental Saloon. Neagle was elected the local mining recorder, invested in real estate and wrote letters promoting the new mining camp. Panamint, however, never prospered. Dave met the prominent Senator William Stewart, one of the town's principal developers, and the two became lifelong friends. A disastrous flood hastened the town's demise and in March of 1876 Dave sold out and moved to Virginia City where a sister lived. The following year he was mining near Prescott, Arizona, and for a time operated a saloon and mine in Bodie, California.

Neagle apparently arrived in Tombstone, Arizona, about 1879 where he served as foreman of the Sunset Mine for eight or ten months. When the mine shut down he was appointed a deputy sheriff for the new county of Cochise in early 1881 and participated in the Earp trouble of those stirring times. Although accused by some of being friendly with the Earps, an article in the Tombstone Daily *Nugget* on January 31, 1882, shows at least that he did not let friendship interfere with duty:

> ...Deputy Sheriff Neagle started out in search of his man [Sherman McMasters], whom he found encamped with the entire Earp posse in the vicinity of Pickmeup. Contrary to the expectations of some, no resistance was offered to the arrest, and the plucky deputy returned to town with his prisoner...

This same month Neagle was elected chief of police in Tombstone. In the spring he was forced to kill a gunman who opened fire on himself and a deputy. Neagle seems to have been a good officer. "He was honest and courageous," recalled Wyatt Earp, "[and] did all of [Sheriff] Behan's work that needed a fighting man." When he ran for sheriff on the Independent ticket that fall, however, he was defeated in a bitter campaign. The Weekly *Epitaph* of October 21, 1882 stated:

> ...His hasty, ungovernable temper; his inclination to harsh measures; his habit of drawing and using firearms to intimidate when unwarranted by facts, all prove him to be an unfit person to trust with... the office of sheriff...

Always looking for new mining country, Dave moved to Butte, Montana where he staked out some property and contracted with a mine to supply wood. He had trouble with a partner who skipped out with a payroll in August of 1884. After a hard horseback pursuit of his erring associate, Neagle winged him in a shooting contest and brought back the purloined payroll none the worse for wear.

Returning to San Francisco, Dave was appointed a deputy sheriff and license collector by the local Democratic Party bosses. He apparently had a good enough reputation as an officer to be appointed a special deputy U.S. marshal during two congressional elections. "Both times," wrote United States Marshal J.C. Franks, "I assigned him to a precinct notorious for the rough character of its voters, where he acquitted himself with great credit: and it was mostly due to his great coolness and firmness that for about the first time in its history no disturbance occurred at this polling precinct at either election."

Taking a break from license collecting one day in September of 1888, Neagle attended the Sharon-Hill divorce trial in which Sarah Hill was trying to prove she had been married to, and not just shacked-up with, the wealthy United States Senator William Sharon. During the course of the trial Sarah had married her attorney, the noted duelist and ex-state supreme court justice, David S. Terry. On this particular day Sarah became such a nuisance she was ordered removed from the court. As the U.S. marshal attempted to take her from the room he was asaulted by Terry who was subdued after a wild melee. During the fight Neagle took a knife from Terry and helped to restore order. Neagle was a small man, weighing about 145 pounds and about five feet, eight inches tall. Terry, although 65 years of age, was a vigorous man, over six feet tall and weighing nearly 250 pounds.

Duelist and state supreme court justice, David Terry was a legendary figure whose giant frame overawed most men, but not pint-sized Dave Neagle. *Courtesy California State Library.*

When Terry later threatened the life of Supreme Court Justice Stephen Field who had sentenced him to a jail term, Marshal Franks remembered Neagle. Dave was appointed a special deputy U.S. marshal to accompany Justice Field any time he was in California on court business.

In mid-August of 1889 Field and Neagle were traveling between Los Angeles and San Francisco when the train stopped at Lathrop for breakfast. Terry and his wife were on the same train and saw Field in the restaurant. While Sarah returned to the train for some reason, Terry walked up behind Field and struck him on the head. As he raised his hand to strike again, Neagle jumped to his feet and told him to stop. Terry then turned toward the bodyguard. "I never before saw such a demoniacal expression in a man's face in my life," Neagle later recalled. "It meant murder and I knew it in a moment." Whatever the expression meant, Dave swiftly drew his pistol and shot Terry dead. Although criticised in some quarters for the killing, most justified Neagle's action—one editor commenting that "someone ought to have killed Terry a quarter century ago!" Perhaps the best witness was Santa Barbara County Sheriff Robert Broughton who was sitting opposite Field and witnessed the whole incident. "It was Terry's fault," he later wrote to his wife, "no matter what they say."

When censured for the killing, Neagle was philosophical. . . and practical:

> . . . I got there first, that's all . . . What chance would I have had against him, a man who weighed 240 pounds while I weigh only about 145? . . . Suppose Justice Field had been killed or seriously injured, what would have become of me? I would have been compelled to go to Africa or some other country; but I believe that I would have turned the pistol to my own head and blown my brains out . . .

Although Dave was discharged after a circuit court hearing, the killing involved federal versus state's rights and became quite celebrated. *In re Neagle* evolved into a landmark case and has been cited hundreds of times in legal literature. Field himself was quite mindful of the tragedy he had survived. On the day of Dave's exoneration, Field presented him with a handsome watch and chain which read as follows:

Stephen J. Field
to
David Neagle
As a token of appreciation of his courage and fidelity to duty
under circumstances of great peril at Lathrop, Cal., on the
14th day of August, 1889

Neagle was employed as a bodyguard and gunman by the Southern Pacific railroad for several years, but other than a few nasty confrontations with newspaper editors and others, he had no serious trouble. In 1899 he served as bodyguard for his old friend Senator Stewart who was running for re-election in Nevada. Dave still engaged in mining, and as late as 1912 was working as a mine superintendent in Tuolumne County, California.

The railroad station and restaurant at Lathrop as it looked at the time Neagle gunned down Judge Terry. *Courtesy Holt-Atherton Center for Western Studies, University of the Pacific.*

About 1920 Neagle retired and moved to Oakland. Few were aware of the colorful history of the little man who died there on November 28, 1925. Although pushed into the background by others, the feisty and controversial Neagle carved his own niche in frontier history. He was survived by his wife and two children, but his burial place in unknown.

PRINCIPAL SOURCES ————————————————

Kroninger, Robert H., *Sarah & the Senator*, Berkeley, Howell-North, 1964; Swisher, Carl Brent, *Stephen J. Field, Craftsman of the Law*, Wash. DC, Brookings Institution, 1930; Osgood, Stacey, "The Life and Times of David Neagle," *The Westerners Brand Book*, Chicago, Apr., 1962; San Francisco *Daily Morning Call*, Aug. 5, 1896; San Francisco *Chronicle*, Aug. 5-31, Sept. 7, 1889; Tombstone *Epitaph*, Oct. 21, 28, 1882; Reno *Evening Gazette*, Feb. 21, 1891; Tombstone *Daily Nugget*, Jan. 31, 1882; Pioche *Daily Record*, Dec. 24, 1874, Aug. 15, 1875, Dec. 20, 1876; Oakland *Tribune*, Nov. 30, 1925; 1860 Federal Census of San Francisco; San Francisco city directories, 1860-1865; Ms. material in Ariz. Hist. Soc., Tucson; Nev. Hist. Soc., Reno; National Archives, Washington, D.C.

ROBERT HAVLIN PAUL

Although widely heralded as an Arizona
lawman in the days of the Earp brothers,
Bob Paul had an equally impressive
career as an early California officer.
Courtesy Arizona Historical Society.

Born in Lowell, Massachusetts on June 12, 1830, Robert Paul moved with his
family to New Bedford where he attended the public schools. In the summer of
1842 he shipped out as a cabin boy on the whaling ship *Majestic*. After a series
of voyages and adventures, he was discharged at Honolulu in late 1848. News of
the great gold discovery in California was the topic of the day and young Bob
traveled to San Francisco where he arrived in late February of 1849.

After working his way around the mining country for several years, Paul
finally settled in Calaveras County, taking up residence at Campo Seco. He
engaged in mining until September of 1854 when he was elected constable. Just
one month later he was appointed a deputy under Sheriff Charles A. Clark,
beginning a long and illustrious career as a frontier lawman.

Both Paul and fellow deputy Ben Thorn engaged in the pursuit of the
Rancheria killers in August of 1855. When Tom Bell's gang of highwaymen
became quite active in the summer of 1856, lawmen throughout the mining
country were put on the alert. After Bell's abortive attempt to rob the

257

Camptonville stage in August, the outlaws split up, but were pressed relentlessly by the officers. Paul made some important discoveries when he interviewed captured gang member Juan Fernandez, alias Spanish John. The prisoner talked to try and save his own neck and gave the deputy a marked bullet used by the outlaws as a secret sign of identification among themselves. Using the bullet, Paul stopped at the hotel operated by Jack Phillips late one night and extracted much important information leading to the arrest of several gang members, including Phillips. The *Calaveras Chronicle* reported the closing days of the Bell gang:

> ARREST OF SEVERAL OF TOM BELLS'S GANG... By some means reliable information has been obtained of the different rendezvous of the gang, and two different parties started hence, several days since to capture them—Sheriff Clark, with deputies Shuler, Paul and McCormick, went to Yuba County, and under Sheriff Mulford, Deputy Sheriff McNish, with Messrs Sands, Palmer and Adams to Tulare County. So far six of the gang have been arrested...

Mulford and his men arrested several of the outlaws at Bell's ranch, which was located on the San Joaquin River. Paul's group picked up two more suspects. Bell himself was captured by a vigilante posse on October 4, 1856, and lynched.

Paul's prominence in the running down of Bell's gang was noted by Wells, Fargo expressman B.F. Moore some years later: "About the most vigilant officer cooperating with us was R.H. Paul, or "Bob" Paul, as most of us endearingly called him."

When D.L. Mulford was elected sheriff of Calaveras County he appointed Bob Paul as his undersheriff in October of 1857. In early January of 1859 Paul located the murderous desperado Jose Luis Cortez. At Forest Hill the lawman was told Cortez had surrounded himself with a crowd of his countrymen and would refuse to be arrested. Brushing aside warnings, Paul invaded the bandit hideout alone and took both Cortez and another fugitive into custody without incident. On the way to Sacramento, both prisoners tried to escape from Paul and Constable John Boggs. Although the other prisoner got away, Paul managed to hang onto Cortez who was safely jailed until he could be removed for trial. The San Andreas *Independent* reported:

> ...It is nothing but just to note that the Shriefalty [sheriff's office] of Calaveras has been remarkable by perseverence in the pursuit of criminals...
> If all officers in the state should discharge their duty as faithfully as has Under Sheriff Paul in this particular, the state would soon be rid of the legion of rascals that infest it.

Bob was elected sheriff in his own right in September of 1859, receiving 2,651 votes, some 600 more than George C. Tyron. He appointed old friend Ben Thorn his undersheriff and the two lawmen made a good team. Chasing an escaped convict named Green who was wanted for various crimes in Calaveras, Sheriff Paul and Thorn tracked him to the village of Princeton, in Mariposa County. The fugitive was chopping wood when the officers approached him and, drawing a knife, fled toward some thick nearby chapparal. Thorn had the best horse and knowing Green would escape if he made the thicket, galloped forward and dropped the running outlaw with a well placed shot. Although Green was only wounded, some were disturbed by the incident. "We are inclined to think Thorn fired rather too quick," noted the Mariposa *News* of December 11, 1860. In a spirited defense of his deputy, Paul replied to the charge in a letter to the San Francisco *Bulletin* later that month:

Mokelumne Hill as it appeared in 1856 when Bob Paul lived there. *Courtesy Calaveras County Museum.*

Editor Bulletin—... Without detailing the circumstances and dilating upon the notoriously desperate character of the felon, I appeal to your known impartiality and love of justice to inform the public... that not only do all persons acquainted with the facts of this particular case... clear our efficient undersheriff of all blame for acting without deliberation; but they and all others who know Mr. Thorn well are convinced that he... would disdain to use the full power placed by the law into his hands. Save in a case of extreme emergency.

Re-elected in the fall of 1861, Paul served until defeated by George Tyron in late 1863. After leaving office he engaged in various enterprises, principally mining. The sheriff's office was a lucrative one and Bob tried for the Republican nomination again in 1869, but lost. He had been warmly endorsed by the

Calaveras Chronicle, the editor commenting that "Calaveras never had a better official than Mr. Paul, nor who attained a greater degree of personal popularity."

Although he secured his party's nomination in 1871, Paul lost the sheriff's race, this time to his old friend and deputy, Ben Thorn. He went to work for Wells, Fargo in October of 1874 as a shotgun messenger. In early February of 1878 he was on the stage run between Visalia and Lone Pine when he reported the details of the killing of Sheriff Thomas Passmore of Inyo County to the Visalia *Delta.* Passmore had attempted to arrest a murderer in Frank Dabeen's Lone Pine saloon, but was shot and killed as he tried to leave. Palacio, the killer, was also gunned down and mortally wounded, but was still alive when Paul left. Later two others who had been in the saloon were found dead on the road after being ordered to leave town.

Bob turned up in his old stamping grounds the following May as reported in the Calaveras *Chronicle:*

> Ex-sheriff R.H. Paul of this country, now residing at Visalia, Tulare County, paid us a short visit this week. "Bob" is in the employment of excellent health, looks as natural as life and is the same jovial, genial, free-hearted gentleman as ever. He has a host of friends here who are glad to see him and who hope he may never weigh less. Mr. Paul is in the employment of Wells, Fargo & Co.

Paul worked for many years as a Wells Fargo stage driver and guard. Here a coach is shown on the street in Old San Andreas. *Courtesy Calaveras County Museum.*

Later this same year Paul, his wife and three children moved to Arizona. He continued his work with Wells, Fargo both as a guard and as a detective. He was elected sheriff of Pima County in late 1880, taking office in April of the following year. After serving several terms as sheriff, Paul worked as a Southern Pacific railroad detective and in 1891 received the appointment as United States marshal for Arizona Territory.

In March of 1901 word was received in Calaveras that Paul was dying at this home in Tucson. The prominent lawman passed away on March 26th as reported in the Calaveras *Chronicle;*

> DEATH OF A NOTED EX—SHERIFF. Robert H. Paul who was formerly a resident of Mokelumne Hill and for the past thirty years has been an officer in California and Arizona, died at his home . . . last Tuesday morning. Death was due to Bright's Disease.
>
> Mr. Paul, during the early days of Calaveras, first came into prominence as a fearless officer while he was living at Camp Seco . . . In 1858 [*sic*] he was appointed deputy sheriff of this county and chief among his daring deeds . . . was the breaking up the notorious Tom Bell gang of desperadoes . . .
>
> The deceased leaves a widow and five children, of whom two, Walter and Edith, live in San Francisco.

Overshadowed in California by Ben Thorn and others, Paul's long record as an outstanding lawman can be favorably compared to that of any of the more noted officers of his time. He is remembered chiefly today as a prominent character of Arizona's Tombstone days and few historians realize he was chasing desperadoes in California when Wyatt Earp and the Clantons were still in their swaddling clothes. Not the stuff of legend, Paul still had a long and distinguished career as a brave and highly capable officer.

PRINCIPAL SOURCES ──────────────

Angel, Myron (editor), *History of Placer County,* Oakland, Thompson & West, 1882; Boggs, Mae Helene Bacon, *My Playhouse Was a Concord Coach,* Oakland, Howell-North, 1942; The *Express Gazette* (Wells Fargo), Apr. 15, 1901; San Francisco *Daily Alta California,* Dec. 16, 1860, Apr. 9, 1861; San Francisco *Bulletin,* Dec. 17, 1860; Calaveras *Chronicle,* May 4, 1878, May 15, 1869, Mar. 30, 1901; Fresno *Expositor,* Feb. 20, 1878; San Andreas *Independent,* Oct. 10, 1857, Jan. 15, Apr. 16, May 7, Sept. 24, 1859; Ms. material in Ariz. Hist. Soc. and Calaveras Co. Museum and Archives; Wells Fargo Bank History Room, San Francisco.

A disputed portrait of Henry Plummer, the prototype of the crooked sheriff of innumerable Western novels. *Courtesy Montana Historical Society.*

WILLIAM HENRY HANDY PLUMER

Recent research indicates that the noted outlaw-sheriff of old Montana was born in Maine in 1832. He was the seventh child of Jeremiah and Elisabeth Plumer and undoubtedly received a fairly good education for the time. He was once described by a man who knew him in later years as a gentleman of "intellect, polished, genial and affable." He seemed certain to make his mark in the world.

Although his name is spelled "Plummer" in nearly all published references, recent genealogical research and the only two known signatures of the man have established the family name to be correctly spelled PLUMER as in this brief biography.

Arriving in California in 1852 during the gold rush, Plumer settled in the mining town of Nevada City, some fifty miles northeast of Sacramento, in the Sierra Nevada. He mined briefly but quickly lost interest in such drudgery and found work in a local bakery. In April of 1854 he bought an interest in the business and by soliciting trade in the local saloons and bordellos, created a brisk trade. He also established a political base. He felt comfortable with the saloon element and made friends with such thugs and criminals as Cyrus Skinner, Jack Cleveland and Bill Mayfield.

Selling out his bakery interest, Plumer ran for city marshal in a special election in early December of 1855. He was easily defeated by young David Johnson who, to pacify Plumer's pals in the saloon element, appointed Henry a deputy. Joining the local Democratic political organization, Plumer promptly wrangled a membership on the executive committee and began campaigning for the marshal's job. At the regular election the following May he was elected by a nice plurality. The election was generally characterized as a farce, Plumer forces terrorizing the polls and bringing in men from all over to vote the party ticket. David Johnson became a deputy under Sheriff W.W. Wright.

In October of 1856 the notorious outlaw Jim Webster and a fellow inmate escaped from the Nevada City jail. Webster was quickly recaptured, but the following month made another break with two members of the Tom Bell gang, the Farnsworth brothers. The fugitives were soon spotted outside town and Marshal Plumer notified. It was dark several hours later when Plumer, Sheriff Wright, David Johnson and another deputy reached the scene. Plumer had neglected to tell his posse that several citizens were watching the escapees' hiding place. As they approached the site, Plumer's group was fired on by these citizens, Sheriff Wright being killed instantly, while David Johnson was mortally wounded. Plumer was widely criticized over the incident, both for forgetting the others were on guard and for starting late after haggling over a reward. "This sad affair," noted the Nevada *Journal* of November 7th, "has thrown a gloom over the entire community. The feelings of those who have innocently taken the lives of their friends cannot be described."

Nevada City in 1856 was a typical, sprawling California mining town and Henry Plummer was in his element. *Courtesy California State Library.*

Plumer helped formulate a plan to obtain a confession from one John Myers who was accused of trying to incinerate Nevada City. Released on bail, Myers fled to the town of Folsom accompanied by an undercover lawman named Whitehead. Pretending to be a member of a bandit gang, Whitehead led Myers into confessing to a number of crimes, including the arson attempt at Nevada, in order to obtain membership in the gang. When Whitehead had Myers repeat his confession to another of his "gang" members, the arsonist's doom was sealed as reported in the Marysville *Herald* of April 21, 1857:

> ...Marshal Plumer and O'Brien arrived at Folsom that night and arrested Myers in bed. He was brought to Nevada, and is now lying in jail. Some fears were entertained that he would receive summary justice from the crowd, but they proved groundless.

Plumer received the Democratic nomination for a state assembly seat on the ticket, but was defeated in the general election of September 9, 1857. A writer to the Sacramento *Union* characterized the marshal as "...the leader of the reckless, rowdy gang of gamblers and loafers [who] has succeeded by trickery and trading with a few leading politicians... in forcing himself on the Democratic party as one of their nominees for the legislature." Other matters soon took the marshal's mind off this disappointment, however.

A young woman named Lucinda Vedder had complained to Marshal Plumer about being mistreated by her husband. In remonstrating with the man, there had been harsh words exchanged and Plumer warned Vedder not to further abuse his wife. When the marshal began socializing with Mrs. Vedder, the situation became more aggravated. By the time the woman moved into a hotel room across the hall from Plumer, the two men were exchanging threats. The Nevada *Journal* noted the culmination of the situation on the night of September 25, 1857:

> Tragedy on Spring Street—Our city was thrown into a high state of excitement last Friday night with the announcement that John Vedder had been shot and killed by Marshal Plumer. For some time great indignation was manifested but has greatly subsided...

Vedder had caught his wife and Plumer at the former Vedder home shortly after midnight and during a confrontation, the marshal had shot him down. Mrs. Vedder claimed that her husband had drawn a weapon and fired before Plumer had shot, but others claimed there was no pistol found anywhere near the body. "What he [Plumer] was doing there," noted the Marysville *Herald,* "no one but the Being who knoweth all things can tell." Despite testimony that Vedder had armed himself earlier and threatened the marshal, the situation and evidence smacked strongly of murder. Plumer received a second-degree murder conviction and was sent to San Quentin for ten years.

Plumer was received at the state prison on February 22, 1859, as prisoner No.

San Quentin state prison as it appeared during Plummer's sojurn
there. *Courtesy California State Library.*

1573. His old friend Cyrus Skinner was there and no doubt showed him the
ropes. Other convicts were men he had brought to San Quentin as a lawman.
Plumer obtained work in the infirmary and kept his nose clean while devising a
plan of escape. By late summer he had convinced a prison physician that he had
tuberculosis. A letter-writing campaign by his Nevada County friends, combined
with early predictions of his death by the prison doctors, finally achieved the
desired results as reported in the San Francisco *Alta* of August 18, 1859:

> Two prisoners were pardoned by the Governor yesterday, and leave today,
> viz; Henry Plumer, convicted in Yuba County...has during his stay in the
> state prison acquired the respect and regard of all the officers here and is a
> young man in every way worthy of the governor's clemency.

Back in Nevada City the ex-convict made a remarkable "recovery" from his
affliction. His friend E.O. Tompkins, who had assumed the marshal's office
upon Plumer's arrest, now appointed Henry a city constable. The new lawman's
first arrest, however, involved an escaped convict named "Ten Year" Smith.
Plumer, whose imminent death was predicted by the prison doctors, was not
eager to return with Smith to San Quentin and advertise his sudden good

265

health. He was greatly relieved when Smith solved the dilemma by escaping from jail and disappearing.

Plumer had lost his constable's job by the time he had a fight in Irish Maggy's whorehouse on February 13, 1861. When it was thought J. W. Muldoon would die from a crack on the head delivered by Plumer's pistol during the scrap, the ex-lawman lit out for Carson City, Nevada, where he visited with his friend Bill Mayfield. He returned to Nevada City when word was received that Muldoon had recovered, but late that year he was in yet another brawl. On October 29, 1861 the *Democrat* noted:

> Homicide—About two o'clock last Sunday morning a difficulty occurred at a house of ill-fame on Commercial Street between Henry Plumer and William Riley resulting in the death of the latter. It appears that they had both been drinking pretty freely and had got to quarreling in the entry when Riley struck Plumer on the head with a knife, cutting through his hat and inflicting a deep wound in the scalp. Plumer at the same time drew a revolver and fired at Riley...and must have killed him instantly...

An eye witness sketch of Henry Plummer's death. Ned Ray, dressed in buckskins, hangs from the left. In the middle is Buck Stinson with Plummer at the right. *Courtesy Montana Historical Society.*

Badly wounded, Plumer had been arrested and placed in jail where he was attended by a physician. When he had sobered up enough to realize the situation he was in, he began casting about for a solution to this latest problem. It was not thought he was strong enough to try and get away, but when a cell door was left open during visiting hours, Henry leaped to his feet and disappeared into the night. The *Democrat,* long the local party organ, was philosophical in its article the next day:

> There is no prospect of his being caught. The circumstances connected with the killing of Riley as generally understood, would hardly justify Plumer's conviction for murder, but this being the second man he has killed in Nevada, and knowing that there was a strong prejudice against him in the county, doubtless thought it prudent not to risk a trial.

Again Plumer fled to Carson City where he was given refuge by Bill Mayfield. Washoe County Sheriff John Blackburn was determined to capture Plumer and was convinced Mayfield was hiding him. Drunk and belligerent, Blackburn accosted Mayfield and demanded to know where he was hiding Plumer. Mayfield's insistence that he knew nothing of his friend's whereabouts infuriated the sheriff. In a brief scuffle, Mayfield stabbed the lawman to death and later skipped town. Plumer meanwhile took advantage of the excitement and struck out for the northwest where new gold strikes were being reported.

In January of 1862 Plumer appeared in Lewiston, Idaho, where he registered at the Luna House. He was reportedly with a woman, although he failed to log her name on the hotel register. Here he found Cyrus Skinner and other thugs he had known in California. Plumer's career as sheriff at Bannack and his duel role as lawman and outlaw chief in Montana is well known. He was hanged by vigilantes on January 10, 1864, along with other members of his gang who were accused of various crimes. By any standards he was among the most colorful of the old west's badmen and his name will forever epitomize the crooked sheriff of western novels and films. He was buried at Bannack.

PRINCIPAL SOURCES

Dimsdale, Thomas Josiah, *The Vigilantes of Montana,* Viginia City, Mont., D.W. Tilton and Co., 1866 (and many subsequent editions); Langford, Nathaniel Pitt, *Vigilante Days and Ways,* Chicago, A.C. McClurg & Co., 1927; Mather, R.E. and Boswell, F.E., *Hanging the Sheriff,* Salt Lake City, Utah, Univ. of Utah Press, 1987; Pauley, Art, *Henry Plummer, Lawman and Outlaw,* White Sulphur Springs, Mont., The Meagher County News, 1980; San Francisco *Daily Alta California,* Aug. 18, 1859; Nevada *Democrat,* Oct. 29, 31, 1861; Marysville, *Herald,* Apr. 21, Sept. 30, 1857; Nevada *Journal,* Nov. 7, 14, 1856, Oct. 2, 9, 16, 1857, Feb. 14, Aug. 26, Oct. 29, 1861; Prison records in California State Archives, Sacramento.

JOHN A. POWER(S)

This old woodcut that appeared in Judge Edward McGowan's 1857 book, is the only known likeness of Jack Powers, standing at right. *From the 1857 book,* Narrative of Edward McGowan.

Reportedly born in Ireland about 1827, John A. "Jack " Power came to the United States at an early age and grew up in New York City. In 1846 he enlisted in Stephenson's California Regiment during the Mexican War. Although his name is given as Power on regimental records , he seems to have always been referred to as Powers, with an "s", since that time. Powers and his comrades spent some fifteen months in garrison duty at Santa Barbara, California and were mustered out in September of 1848. The great gold rush was on and most of the ex-soldiers headed for the mines, Jack joining in the expedition. Most of the men decided that with winter coming on it would be more practical to put their plans on hold until spring, however.

Powers and many of his friends spent the winter in San Francisco, the fast-growing port city of the gold rush. The ex-soldiers formed an association which they called the "Hounds" and spent most of their time gambling and in saloons. Many of the New York regiment were Bowery thugs and other toughs

Santa Barbara was a beautiful Spanish coastal village that was frequently in turmoil due to Jack Powers and his men. *Courtesy Karl Obert.*

and they quickly gained a reputation for being trouble-makers and rowdies. On July 15, 1849, on the pretext of collecting a judgement for the local sheriff, the Hounds raided a Chileno settlement where they tore down tents, stole property and assaulted whoever resisted them. At least two persons were killed and several badly injured before the thugs retired. A hastily assembled vigilance committee rounded up many of the perpetrators. Although judged not guilty during a hearing, Powers and a number of his cronies were kicked out of town.

Jack went to the mines where he made a good stake, probably by gambling rather than work. He ran this up even more in the Stockton gambling halls, but lost nearly everything while gambling on a riverboat traveling back to San Francisco. In the bay city again, he sought to regain his fortune at the gambling tables and horse track. A contemporary described him as he appeared at the Mission Dolores at that time:

> . . . Jack Powers, always well mounted and dashing along to show the merits of his nag. Jack Powers! with black beard and flowing hair—his glittering, restless, omnivagant eye—the worst we ever looked upon in any living creature—a fascinating terror—sure index of the devil time eventually proved him to be.

After assembling another stake, Jack traveled up and down the coast looking for opportunities. He made many friends among the native Californians while gambling and attending their fandangos and fiestas. When he returned to Santa Barbara in 1851, however, he was badly wounded at one of these events, being

269

stabbed seven times during a brawl. Most of the wounds were minor and he recovered quickly.

In May of 1852 Powers took part in some local Indian troubles as chronicled in the Los Angeles *Star* and datelined at Santa Barbara:

> On the 10th instant Mr. John Powers, of this city, having lost some horses, again went down to the mission, but the Indians had robbed two travelers on the road of their horses, saddles and bridles, leaving them to proceed on foot. Powers, with twenty-five men, pursued and overtook them a few miles this side of Don Carlos Carillo's rancho, and by representing to them that he had an armed force of one hundred and fifty Americans, succeeded in getting three of his horses...

Although some of his associates were thugs and Californio vaqueros of more than questionable character, Powers attained a certain prominence in the southern portion of the state. Horace Bell, who knew him, wrote that Jack was "the most noted character, probably, in all California at the time referred to..." Continued Bell:

> When I arrived in Los Angeles [1853] Jack was here although he properly resided in Santa Barbara. Jack was a great gambler and when he walked through a crowd of gamblers it was with the air of a lion walking among rats. Gifted with mental qualities of the highest order, with the manners of a true gentlemen, with a form and face physically perfect, with a boldness and dash that made him a leader among men, Jack Powers, under favorable circumstances, might have attained to the most honorable distinction...

A brief look at Jack's gambling activities was provided by the Los Angeles *Star* of April 2, 1853:

> On Saturday the ceremonies at the church ended. On the same day, in the afternoon, a grand cock fight came off on the Plaza... between Don Pio Pico and Mr. John Powers, which was continued at intervals for several days...
>
> On Monday a race came off between Moore and Brady's horse, John Smith, and Mr. J. Powers mare, Sarah Jane, for $2,400 a side which the horse won by about a length. This was decidely the prettiest race we have seen in the city...

Using his land bounty awarded for army service, Powers settled on the Arroyo Burro Ranch near Santa Barbara, although it had already been claimed by Dr. Nicholas Den. When the property was awarded to Den, Sheriff William Twist gathered a posse in town with which to evict Powers. A fight erupted on the town plaza during which a Powers' man was killed and two others wounded. During the melee the sheriff was stabbed in the back, but managed to shoot and kill his assailant before collapsing. Jack had been at the ranch when this had happened. "In the afternoon," noted an account in the Los Angeles *Star* of May 7, 1853, "Powers, having heard of what had taken place, drove into town with his party and paraded the streets for a short time, but no further bloodshed followed." Jack managed to hang onto the ranch until a settlement could be made with Dr. Den, but later that year he sold his property and livestock to take up gambling and other pursuits on a full time basis.

El Camino Real, the old Spanish coastal highway linking San Francisco with the south, gained a reputation for murder and robbery during the 1850s. Because of his association with native Californio vaqueros known to be badmen and robbers, Powers was soon suspected of being a bandit chief who headquartered at the rancho of Jose Antonio Noriega. He was always able to provide an alibi, however, whenever a robbery or murder took place.

When the disreputable Judge Edward McGowan was chased out of San Francisco by the vigilantes in 1856, Powers hid him from his pursuers in Santa Barbara. During the Flores bandit gang excitement in the south the following year, Jack was indicted for burglary in Los Angeles, but skipped town and fled to San Francisco. He had no intention of going to trial in a town currently hanging captured bandits. When he was finally tried in April of 1857, he was easily acquitted and returned to his old haunts on the coast.

Two Basque cattle buyers were found brutally murdered near San Luis Obispo in December of 1857. When known associates of Powers were the last men seen in their company, rumors flew thick and fast. Powers arranged for the defense of his friend, Nieves Robles, and he was promptly acquitted by what some called a "packed California jury." Jack, meanwhile, had been gambling in San Francisco and had a comfortable alibi.

In May of 1858 Powers had his great race against time. He had made a saloon wager that he could ride twenty-four California mustangs 150 miles in eight consecutive hours at the local Pioneer Race Course. The race, which attracted much attention among sporting characters, was easily won by Jack at $2,500 a side. Jack's hostelers for the race were two notorious Californios named Huero Rafael and Pio Linares. The San Francisco *Herald* noted:

> ...It was indeed a Herculean undertaking which few men, however experienced as riders, would be willing to assume, least of all with the expectation of going such a distance in a few hours on horseback; but it only goes to prove the great powers of physical endurance which some men can bring themselves to by a severe course of training...

Powers' constant association with desperadoes, however, had made him an increasingly suspicious character and ultimately led to his downfall. When two Frenchmen were reported murdered at their ranch east of San Luis Obispo, the country was quickly up in arms. A servant who had been spared by the murderers identified Santos Peralta as one of the killers and Peralta was lynched that same night. A near-by rancher had also been killed by the robbers and the finding of his body added to the excitement. After a posse had a run-in with the killers, they were able to identify them as Huero Rafael, Miguel Blanco,

This is said to be a photo of Pio Linares, Powers' right-hand man, although the pistol in his right hand appears to be a model manufactured after his death. Linares was a dangerous outlaw who attended Powers during the great race against time in San Francisco in 1858. *Courtesy San Luis Obispo Museum.*

Froilan Servan and Desidera Grijalva. Others were suspected and when Joaquin Valenzuela was picked up he was promptly lynched also, for other crimes. A search was made of Pio Linares' house for any of the fugitives and when Linares fled he implicated himself as a suspect. Since all the wanted men were known associates of Powers, his name headed the wanted list published in the Santa Cruz *Sentinel* on June 5, 1858:

> Rewards for the Banditti . . . Jack Powers, an Irishman and generally known as a gambler, $500; Pio Linares, a native of this country, dark complexion, slender, with large sleepy eyes and no beard, $500; Rafael Morrey [sic] alias El Huero . . . Rafael is tall, slender, and quite handsome, with light mustache, $500; Miguel Blanco, also of this country, of low stature, about 20 years of age, handsome, with a bold face and no beard, $200 . . .

Grijalva, Jesus Valenzuela, Nieves Robles and several others were also listed with $200 rewards on their heads. Linares was cornered and killed in a nearby forest, while several others of the gang were captured and lynched. Powers and Rafael were still at large and had by this time been fully implicated in the crime. A deputation of vigilantes went to San Francisco to pick up Powers, but he was warned by friends and sailed for Mexico aboard the steamer *Elisabeth Owens* on June 3, 1858. Rafael and Valenzuela had probably already headed south, also.

Jack stayed in Hermosillo for a time, then took up a ranch in Arizona, near the border. On November 15, 1860, the San Francisco *Bulletin* printed the following notice:

> Tucson, Arizona, November 3, 1860...Intelligence was received here about a week since that Jack Powers was found murdered at a ranch upon which he had recently located, near the boundary line. His body was so much mutilated by hogs as to be scarcely recognizable; and from appearances it is supposed he was killed with a blow from behind with an ax...

Powers' peons and vaqueros had apparently quarrelled with him and after his murder had thrown him into a hog pen and fled, taking any valuables and stock. An enigma in his own time, as well as today, Powers had many friends who refused to believe he was a murderer and leader of outlaws. Yet, his associates were of the worst sort and right or wrong, in those days as now, men were judged by the company they keep. Major Horace Bell wrote what perhaps can stand as Powers' epitaph:

> Alas, poor Jack! He was full of a noble generosity, and deserving of a better fate.

PRINCIPAL SOURCES ————————————————————

Angel, Myron, *History of San Luis Obispo County, California,* Oakland, Thompson & West, 1883; Bell, Major Horace, *Reminiscences of a Ranger,* Santa Barbara, Wallace Hebberd, 1927; Mason, Jesse D., *History of Santa Barbara County, California,* Oakland, Thompson & West, 1883; Ross, Dudly T., *Devil on Horseback,* Fresno, Valley Pub., 1975; Woodward, Art, "A Few Notes on Jack Powers," *Westerners Brand Book,* Los Angeles Posse, Dec., 1954; San Francisco *Daily Alta California,* Aug. 2, 1849; San Francisco *Bulletin,* July 16, 1858; San Francisco *Evening Post,* June 27, 1896; Santa Cruz *Pacific Sentinel,* May 29, June 5, 25, July 17, Oct. 2, 1858; Los Angeles *Star,* Apr. 2, May 7, 1853; Governor's Correspondence, California State Archives.

HIRAM LEE RAPELJE

A prominent Fresno County lawman for over 30 years, Hi Rapelje was always first in line when a posse was being formed or a good scrap was imminent. *From the Fresno* Morning Republican *of July 6, 1919.*

Born in Ontario, Canada, on March 20, 1851, Hi Rapelje ran away from home at an early age and went to live with a sister in Port Huron, Michigan. He came to California with his parents about 1867 and when still a teenager was driving stagecoaches in the coast range of mountains. Later he moved to Merced County and it was while chauffering early stagecoach tourists into Yosemite Valley that he accepted an appointment as deputy sheriff in the early 1880s. While later serving under Sheriff J.L. Crittenden he aided in the pursuit and capture of two horse thieves as noted in the Merced *Argus* of January 24, 1885:

> ...Sheriff Crittenden [sent] Hi Rapelje and Al Dowst to scour the valley east and south to Madera, from whence Deputy Rapelje reported that no trace had been discovered of the parties, when he was ordered to the Coast Range where they proceeded as rapidly as possible, frequently obtaining fresh horses in the settlements through which their way led them, arriving at the village of Tres Pinos on Monday morning, and at once came upon and arrested the two men and recovered the stolen property...

Rapelje was instrumental in the capture of two suspected robbers of the Yosemite stage in late May of 1885. While in Fresno for a court appearance at the trial of the accused bandits the following September, Hi volunteered to assist a local Fresno County officer in the arrest of a notorious horse thief named Romero Gerterio. The two lawmen found the badman working at a sheep-shearing ranch and began reading their arrest warrant to him as described in the local press:

> ...Gerterio commenced to back away from the officer and when about eight feet distant he threw his revolver in view and discharged it at Mr. White, the ball passing near his left side. Almost immediately the Mexican turned and shot at Deputy Sheriff Rapelje, the ball whizzing in close proximity to the officer's left ear. The officers then drew their revolvers and fired two shots at the Mexican's legs, but failed to bring him to bay. Gerterio again raised his pistol and shot at Mr. White, when both officers fired at his breast and the Mexican fell dead...

Rapelje went back to stage driving into Yosemite and in April of 1887 told a Fresno *Expositor* reporter that an average of two stage loads of tourists a day were visiting the famous valley. Hi stayed active in politics and was elected the first city marshal of the city of Merced in March of 1889. In 1892 he is reported as being in business at Toll House, in the mountains in the eastern part of Fresno County. When Jay Scott was elected Fresno County sheriff late that year, he appointed Rapelje as one of his deputies.

A series of train robberies were being investigated at this time and two of the alleged robbers, Chris Evans and John Sontag, were at large. The outlaws had killed several lawmen and a large contingent of bounty hunters, railroad and Wells, Fargo detectives were on their trail. When U.S. Marshal George Gard and Wells, Fargo detective John Thacker put together a posse, Hi Rapelje was one of the officers selected. Gard, Rapelje, Tom Burns and Fred Jackson ambushed the two fugitives on June 11, 1893, badly wounding and capturing both men. Rapelje played a prominent part in the desperate gun battle and was later quoted as saying "there was no intention of trying to capture Sontag and Evans alive... It was our intention to kill them without giving them any show whatever!" Rapelje is known to have received a large share of the reward offered for the desperadoes.

In September of 1893 Siskiyou County Deputy Sheriff John Harman arrived in Fresno looking for murderer Donati Probasco. Rapelje helped locate the fugitive and the two officers lay in wait for the killer in his cabin near Coarsegold. The capture was reported in the Fresno Morning *Republican* of September 22:

> When he came in the officers covered him with their pistols and ordered him to surrender, when a desperate fight began. Probasco attempted to get his shotgun, but Harman managed to get hold of it and snatched it out of his hands... He made a desperate hand to hand fight of it. In the tussel he got a clasp knife out and tried to open it with his teeth. Rapelje, who did not want to shoot him, managed to...clip him on the side of the head with his revolver and laid him out...

275

Rapelje stands at far left after the gunfight at Stone Corral. Sontag lies wounded in the foreground. Hatless U.S. Marshal George Gard stands third from the right with Tom Burns at his right. The other men were not in the fight. *Courtesy Fresno City and County Historical Society.*

About March of 1894 Rapelje went on duty in Fresno's Chinatown section, across the tracks from the rest of the city. He was still a deputy sheriff, but when not assigned other duties he worked as a watchman in Chinatown where he was paid for his service by the Chinese companies.

In March of the following year Rapelje assisted in the arrest of Louis Pares, a notorious rustler whose gang had been stealing cattle for some time. "The prompt manner in which the gang was rounded up is due to the efficient work of Hi Rapelje and John Ashurst," reported the *Republican.*

When Indian outlaw Jim Haslip was captured in August of 1896, he complained that when Hi and several other officers surprised him in camp several months before, they had opened fire on him as he made his escape. "The officers did not 'yell' before they shot at him, which he did not think was right," penned a reporter.

Aside from his deputy position under Jay Scott, Rapelje became more and more involved in his job as a nightwatchman in Chinatown. It was the typical problem of special officers everywhere who were paid directly by the property owners whose interest they must look out for. Although saloon owners and

276

merchants paid his salary, Rapelje found himself seriously entangled with payoffs from gamblers, lottery operators and other illicit operations. But he was a big man in Chinatown and delighted in the title of "Mayor of West Fresno." When he interceded for a Chinese gambler in court in February of 1897, the *Expositor* grumbled "Surely Hi Rapelje's reputation as an officer must suffer by such work as this..." This same month during a drinking bout, Hi and saloon owner Tom Maloney drew their pistols on each other, but were separated before a shooting occurred.

The gambling and prostitution in West Fresno brought in a steady stream of gamblers, tong members and hatchet men from San Francisco. Chinese killing became more and more frequent as rival tongs battled for control of the area's vice. A long-awaited climax to the situation took place on the evening of April 19, 1899. Rapelje was enjoying a drink in Brown's saloon when the firing commenced and he ran into a nearby alley where two Chinese were shooting at a third Chinese on the ground. Hi ran up and knocked one of the highbinders down with his pistol, then turned and did the same to the other. There was more shooting going on further up the alley and as one of the Chinese fled, Rapelje yelled for him to stop, then shot him in the head. Three Chinese were killed that night and several badly wounded in what was a power struggle between several tongs. At first Hi did not admit to the killing of Leong Tung, a notorious

Rapelje's boss, Fresno County Sheriff Jay Scott (left), poses on the scaffold that hanged a wife murderer in 1893—one of the last men hanged locally in California. *Courtesy Fresno City and County Historical Society.*

hatchet man. He was afraid of Chinese vengeance. At the inquest, however, he admitted what had happened and was exonerated.

At the time of the Chinese war Rapelje was no longer a deputy sheriff, but was still a Chinatown watchman, operating a hack service as well. Later he served as a Kern County deputy and worked for a time as an officer for the Huntington Lake Power Company.

Always feisty and ready for a scrap, even in old age, the Fresno Morning *Republican* reported on December 6, 1914 when Hi was hauled in on an assault charge:

> . . . The trial brought out that Alveso reached as if for a pistol, when he and Rapelje began their argument and that the latter at once drew his revolver and covered him. After Rapelje had searched Alveso and failed to find a gun, he pocketed his own weapon and fought it out with his hands. At this juncture the police interfered.

During World War I the old lawman served as a guard on the Santa Fe Railroad.

Rapelje died at his Fresno home on July 14, 1919, survived by his wife, Zella, and son Harry. "With the death of Hiram L. Rapelje," noted the *Republican,* "passes one of the old pioneers who grew up in the strenuous days of the stage coach . . ." When the body was cremated the door was closed on one of the most noted of the early San Joaquin Valley lawmen.

PRINCIPAL SOURCES ————————————————————

Maxwell, Hu, *Evans and Sontag,* San Francisco, The San Francisco Printing Co., 1893 (re-published in 1981); *A Memorial and Biographical History of the Counties of Merced, Stanislaus, Calaveras, Tuolumne and Mariposa, California,* Chicago, Lewis Pub. Co., 1892; San Francisco *Chronicle,* June 22, 1893; Visalia *Delta,* June 15, 1893; Fresno *Weekly Expositor, May 27,* June 17, Sept. 9, 1885, Oct. 27, 1886; *Daily Evening Expositor,* Feb. 16, 18, 1897; Fresno Morning *Republican,* July 28, Sep. 22, 1893, Jan. 21, Oct. 6, 1894, Apr. 20, 21, 22, 28, 1899, July 5, 6, 1919; Fresno City Directories, 1913-1919.

JOHN SONTAG

John Sontag was described by
contemporaries as strikingly
handsome, an opinion
substantiated by his various
photographs. *Courtesy Tulare
County Historical Society.*

Born on May 27, 1860, John Contant and a younger brother, George, were
raised in Mankato Minnesota. When he was about four John lost his father in
an accident and following his mother's re-marriage he adopted his step-father's
name of Sontag. The mother, Mary Sontag, was a strong Roman Catholic and
she pressured her oldest boy to accept the priesthood. John wasn't interested in
religion, however. To avoid trouble in the family he left home in 1878 and headed
west for California. He eventually settled in the San Joaquin Valley.

By the mid-1880s young Sontag was working for the Southern Pacific
Railroad as a brakeman. One summer evening as he was uncoupling cars in the
Fresno yards, a load of iron slipped and struck him in the back. The local press
ran this notice on August 31, 1887:

> John Sontag, the brakeman on the railroad who was so severely injured
> while coupling cars the other night, is resting quite comfortably. Dr. Rowell
> expresses his opinion that only one rib has been broken, and the backbone
> severely wrenched. Good nursing and Father Time will pull him through.

Sontag's injuries may have been more serious than was at first supposed since
he spent some time in the Sacramento railroad hospital. Later he claimed to have
still been quite ill when he was dismissed from the hospital and his feelings
toward his erstwhile employer became progressively bitter.

Sontag was still ill and out of work when he met Visalia farmer Christopher
Evans late that same year. Evans hired him to help at his farm and later the two
discussed their mutual disgust with the railroad. The Southern Pacific had been
a mixed blessing for years, charging exhorbitant rates and dispossessing settlers

who could not afford their payments on the railroad land. The Mussel Slough Tragedy, in which seven men died in a fight with railroad agents, was still fresh in people's minds.

In September of 1881 the first attempt to rob a train in California was made at Cape Horn Mills, although Tiburcio Vasquez had made a half-hearted effort also in 1873. In February of 1889 a train was successfully robbed near Pixley, in the San Joaquin Valley. George Contant was later to state that his brother admitted to him that he and Chris Evans had robbed this train and obtained some $600. Two passengers were killed during the incident, however. Lawmen were quickly on the scene in and around the small town of Pixley and the Tulare *Register* noted:

> This city was thrown into a state of considerable excitement last night by the report that train No. 17... had been held up by masked men at Pixley and robbed.
> ...Just as the train was pulling out of Pixley, two men wearing long masks reaching below the waist climbed upon the engine and covered the engineer, Pete Bolger, and the fireman, C.G. Elker, with revolvers...

Evans and Sontag are thought to have repeated their train robbing performance at Goshen in late January of 1890, using their loot to finance a livery stable purchase in Modesto. When the stable was destroyed by fire, they reportedly held up yet another train at Ceres on September 3, 1891. No money was obtained in this latter venture, but detective Len Harris was badly wounded by the robbers. Sontag felt this was a good time to visit his family in Minnesota. When he reported his larcenous far western adventures to his brother, George became anxious for some of the same excitement. The brothers held up a train near Racine, Wisconsin in November of 1891, obtaining nearly $10,000 from the express car. Soon after this John returned to California. George, who had a prison record, followed him before long.

Back in California, Chris Evans' daughter Eva became engaged to John Sontag, although she was still a teenager. In January of 1890 Evans deeded Sontag a series of city lots for $1,100. In April of the following year Sontag deeded this same group of lots to Eva. Just where these poor farmers acquired the money for such real estate transactions probably aroused some local speculation.

Another train was robbed at Collis, just west of Fresno, on August 3, 1892. George Sontag later confessed that he, his brother and Chris Evans were the robbers. The bandits' buggy was traced to Visalia and suspicious statements made by George resulted in railroad detective Will Smith and local deputy sheriff George Witty calling at the Evans home. They asked to see John Sontag and after an exchange of words, suddenly guns were drawn. The lawmen were chased from the house, Witty being wounded as he ran. Evans and Sontag fled in the lawmen's buggy and when they returned that night for supplies, more shooting resulted in the death of Deputy Sheriff Oscar Beaver. The two fugitives disappeared into the nearby mountains.

On September 6, 1892, Wells, Fargo and the Southern Pacific Railroad issued a joint reward of $10,000 for the two outlaws. A description of John Sontag on the poster reads as follows:

> John Sontag, alias John Contant, is a native of Mankato, Minnesota, 33 years of age; height 5 feet 11 inches; weight, 165 pounds; even cut features; fair complexion; prominent cheek bones; rather good looking; hair dark and mustache medium and slightly lame in right ankle. When last seen on September 4th at Supervisor Ellis' house with Chris Evans he wore dark felt hat, dark pants and vest, coat lighter colored, gold watch and chain. They were armed with shotguns, Winchester rifles and revolvers...

The fugitives took refuge in the mountains where Evans was right at home. Railroad detectives, local posses and bounty hunters now flooded into the hills, but the two outlaws always managed to elude them until the morning of September 13, 1892. They were making breakfast in a mountain cabin owned by a friend named Young when a six-man posse with two Indian trailers approached the small frame dwelling. Spotting the posse, Evans and Sontag neatly ambushed them, killing Vic Wilson, the leader, and Andy McGinnes. The rest of the lawmen were routed after a brief exchange of gunfire, with Sontag receiving a bullet through the arm. One of the lawmen, Sanger Constable Warren Hill, later commented on the fight:

> I want to tell those people who think Evans is doing it all and that Sontag is keeping in the background are mistaken. He is as game as Evans and stood right by his side pumping lead into us. The first shot or two were fired from the house, then Evans and Sontag came out and sent a perfect fusilade into us. I never saw bullets so thick in my life and the dust was flying all around us...

The two outlaws continued to hide out in the mountains that winter of 1892-93, although they made several trips into Visalia to see Evans' family and secure supplies. George Sontag had meanwhile been convicted and sent to Folsom prison for the Collis robbery. Probably the most hunted outlaws in the country, Evans and Sontag were pursued by reporters as much as by lawmen and bounty hunters. Even Joaquin Miller, the celebrated poet, claimed to have interviewed the pair in May of 1893. This same month they stopped the Sequoia stage looking for detectives and reportedly shot up a bounty hunter named Black at Camp Badger.

But time was running out. U.S. Marshal George Gard and a three man posse were in the hills waiting for the outlaws to come down to the valley again. On June 11, 1893, Evans and Sontag were themselves ambushed near a landmark east of Visalia called Stone Corral. Both men were badly wounded after a desperate gunfight which put one of the posse out of action. They were captured the following morning, Sontag being propped up and photographed in one of the most dramatic scenes in western frontier history.

By the time Mary Sontag had arrived from Minnesota, both outlaws had

Courtesy Paul Caulkins and Juanita Browne.

Ten Thousand Dollars
REWARD !
For the Arrest of Chris Evans and John Sontag, Train Robbers.

WHEREAS, On the 22d day of February, 1889, Wells, Fargo & Co's Express car, on the Southern Pacific Co's train, was robbed near Pixley Station, Tulare County, California; and

WHEREAS, On the 21st day of January, 1890, said Express car, on the Southern Pacific Co's train was robbed near Goshen, Tulare County, in said State; and

WHEREAS, On the 3d day of September, 1891, an attempt was made to rob said Express car, on said Southern Pacific Co's train, near Ceres Station, Stanislaus County, in said State; and

WHEREAS, On the 3d day of August, 1892, said Express car, on said Southern Pacific Co's train, was robbed near Collis Station, in Fresno County, in said State; and

WHEREAS, GEORGE C. CONTANT, alias SONTAG, JOHN SONTAG and CHRIS EVANS have been duly indicted by the Grand Jury of Fresno County for the commission of said last named robbery; and

WHEREAS, Said Wells, Fargo & Co and said Southern Pacific Co. have heretofore offered large rewards for the arrest and conviction of any of the parties engaged in the above named robberies;

NOW, THEREFORE, The said rewards are hereby withdrawn, and in lieu thereof the two said Companies do hereby jointly offer a reward of TEN THOUSAND (10,000) DOLLARS for the arrest and delivery to the Sheriff of Fresno or Tulare Counties of said JOHN SONTAG and CHRIS EVANS, or FIVE THOUSAND (5,000) DOLLARS for the arrest and delivery to either of the said Sheriffs of either JOHN SONTAG or CHRIS EVANS, the said reward to be payable on said delivery

CHRIS EVANS when last seen, was at Supervisor Ellis' house, 20 miles north of Visalia, on Sunday, September 4th, at 7 P. M., when in company with Sontag he left in a cart drawn by a sorrel horse, four white feet, white face, and lame in fore foot. ... Evans wore gray and brown coat and vest with stripes, blue overalls, light colored woolen shirt, with ... check stripe, pointed shoes, broken across the ball of the foot. He is about 45 years of age, native of Calaveras, Canada, sandy complexion, sandy or gray hair; beard and moustache rather dark and sandy, blue eyes, height 5 feet 6 inches, weight 160 pounds; when talking stoops and pulls ... moves his head sideways from shoulder to shoulder; has a ... in both knees when walking, rather fast ... bony hands; has slouching appearance, when talking ... length of time, has slight ... and droops or shuts his left eye; has shrill, squeaking voice.

JOHN SONTAG, alias JOHN CONTANT, is a native of Mankato, Minnesota, 35 years of age; height, 5 feet 11 inches; weight, 165 pounds, even features, fair complexion, ... cheek bones; rather good looking; hair dark, and moustache medium and dark; lame in right ankle. When last seen on September 4th, at Supervisor Ellis' house, in company with Evans ... he wore dark felt hat, dark pants and vest, coat lighter colored, gold watch and chain. They were armed with ... Winchester rifle, and revolvers.

A. N. TOWNE,
Genl Manager S. P. Co.

E. M. COOPER,
Agent Wells, Fargo & Co.

Dated September 6th, 1892.

Below: A re-enactment of the fight at Young's cabin, photographed around the turn of the century. *Courtesy Annie Mitchell.*

The morning of his capture at Stone Corral, the wounded Sontag was photographed where he lay by a Visalia photographer. *Courtesy California State Library.*

been removed from the Visalia to the Fresno County jail. They had adjoining cells and although Evans lost an eye and an arm as a result of his wounds, he rallied quickly. Sontag, his arm and shoulder terribly smashed by bullets, never fully recovered. Eva Evans, sitting by his side, remarked that she could feel his fever with her hand three inches from his head. When peritonitus and tetanus set in it was just a matter of time. His jaws locked and he had to be fed soup through a broken tooth. He bit his tongue in half and was being shaken by convulsions when he died on July 3rd. A team of physicians performed an autopsy as noted in the Fresno Morning *Republican* the following day:

> It was found that the bone of the upper arm was shattered to pieces close to the socket, and that with the exception of a small fragment the bullet had passed on across the body, just missing the spinal column... [and] out of the body on the left shoulder blade.
>
> At no point had the bullet penetrated the cavity of the body and it was the opinion of the physicians present that he would have recovered had his arm been amputated promptly at the time of the injury.

Ironically, Chris Evans' wife claimed her husband's arm had been unnecessarily removed to make him a cripple.

283

At Sontag's funeral Hi Rapelje, one of the posse at Stone Corral, gazed down at the body and commented, "A braver man never lived!" Jim Hume, the Wells, Fargo Special Officer, held similar feelings toward his former enemy:

> ...I have never known a man to be wounded so badly and in the physical condition that he was at Stone Corral, and never utter a word or sound in regard to his pains. It struck me that he was a most heroic sort of man—one of extraordinary nerve.

He was buried on the Fourth of July in Fresno's Catholic Calvary Cemetery. Only his mother, Mrs. Evans and several others were in the small funeral cortege that wound its way out to the cemetery. Firecrackers could be heard all over town. Later in the month word was received that Sontag's step-father contemplated suing the parties responsible for John's death, but no such action was ever reported.

PRINCIPAL SOURCES ————————————————

Dillon, Richard, *Wells, Fargo Detective*, N.Y., Coward-McCann, Inc., 1969; Maxwell, Hu, *Evans & Sontag*, San Francisco, San Francisco Printing Co., 1893 (re-published in 1981); Smith, Wallace, *Prodigal Sons*, Boston, The Christopher Pub. House, 1951; Visalia *Weekly Delta*, Mar 14, 1889; Visalia *Daily Times*, Sep. 13, 1892; Fresno *Daily Evening Expositor*, Feb. 23, 1889, May 27, 29, June 12, 1893; Fresno *Weekly Expositor*, Aug. 31, 1887; Fresno *Daily Republican*, Aug. 6, 12, 1892; Fresno *Morning Republican*, July 4, 1893; Fresno *Weekly Republican*, June 16, 1893; 1890's criminal scrapbook in possession of Fresno City and Co. Hist. Soc., Fresno.

John Sontag's grave headboard in the Fresno cemetery. The year of death is mistakenly given as 1892. *Courtesy the Fresno Bee.*

HENRY J. TALBOT
(Cherokee Bob)

Bret Harte grew up in 1850s California and gathered the raw material for his renowned short stories while working at various odd jobs during gold rush days and after. He did newspaper work in San Francisco in the 1860s and in the offices of the *Golden Era,* in the rooms of the Bohemian Club, and later as editor of the old *Overland Monthly* he listened to the tales of gold rush pioneers that he would mold into such classics as "The Heathen Chinee," "Tennessee's Partner" and many others. Harte's most remembered character was the tragic John Oakhurst in "The Outcasts of Poker Flat," but his personal favorite seemed to be the gambler Jack Hamlin in "Brown of Calaveras" which appeared in 1870. At least Hamlin reappeared several times in later Harte stories.

An acquaintance of Harte's recalled that the Hamlin character was based on a gold rush gambler named Bob Talbot. The two names do have the same number of syllables, while the descriptions make the comparison even more obvious. The men's nicknames, also with the same number of syllables, leave no doubt as to Harte's inspiration. Talbot was known from Los Angeles to Walla Walla as Cherokee Bob, while Jack Hamlin's sobriquet was Comanche Jack. Both characters are hardly remembered today, however.

Henry Talbot once stated in court that he was from Barbour County, Alabama, but this was apparently a ruse to disguise his identity. He appears to have been born about 1834 in Wilkes County, Georgia. This was originally Cherokee Indian territory and the Talbot family was prominent and wealthy. Henry's father had taken a Cherokee wife, resulting in their children's swarthy complexion and Henry's later colorful nickname. He was still a boy when he headed West in 1849. It isn't known just when he arrived on the West Coast, but a brief item in the San Francisco Daily *Alta California* in late January of 1850 probably refers to him:

> Police Court—Five men were arrested early yesterday morning for riotous and disorderly conduct at a house in Kearny Street. Their names were Robt. Benson, Alex. Speck, A. McGurley, Saml. Atkins and Henry Talbot. They were taken before the Alcalde who imposed a fine of $10 each on Talbot and McGurley...

Talbot apparently came to California with an older brother and after touring the gold rush country looking for opportunities, the boys became gamblers.

285

Major Horace Bell once noted that in Los Angeles Cherokee Bob was pointed out to him as one "who had killed six Chilenos in one fight, and although he had been riddled with bullets and ripped and sliced by knives, yet he had never failed to get his man when he went for him." Since Bob did spend some time in Tuolumne County, Bell is probably referring to a fight that took place at Melones Diggins on June 12, 1851. Melones, located a few miles from Sonora, was the scene of a desperate fight between Mexicans and Americans as noted in the Sonora *Herald:*

> A terrible affray took place at Meloney's Diggings on Thursday evening last in which one or two Americans and three or four Mexicans were killed and a number mortally wounded. The fight commenced about two women in a gambling saloon. The Mexicans drove the Americans from the house, and the latter in turn... regained possession...

Bob and his brother apparently shilled for each other in their gambling, his brother using the name Dr. William Ewing. They lived in Jamestown in 1854 and early in the morning of February 15 were gambling, drinking and making enough noise to disturb various neighbors who were trying to sleep. When a hotel keeper named Thomas Brown asked them to quiet down, an argument erupted. Brown was shot in the stomach and died some nine days later. Bob and a man named Rucker were arrested, but his brother, Ewing, who was identified as the slayer, escaped. Later the fugitive was arrested at Big Oak Flat, but he escaped again after being wounded by an officer. Although it was determined that Bob's 36 calibre Navy Colt had done the shooting, he was apparently released and lost no time in leaving the area and heading south.

Turning up in Mariposa County, Bob and a pal named Sam White were picked up in early March for horse stealing. Talbot refused to give his name and his trial records list him only as "Cherokee Bob." Both men were convicted and sentenced to ten years in state prison. The San Quentin prison register also only lists Talbot's nickname:

> No. 354, Cherokee Bob: Georgia; crime—grand larceny; rec'd March 21, 1854; sentence—10 years; county rec'd from—Mariposa; age—21, gambler, 5'9", dark complexion, black hair and eyes...

Before the year was out Bob was engaged in a desperate escape attempt. On December 28 a large number of prisoners seized a prison boat after grabbing a captain of the guard as a hostage. There was a bloody battle and several other guards were overpowered and their weapons taken. Under a withering gunfire from the other guards, the prisoners tried desperately to get their sloop under way. Cherokee Bob held Captain B.F. Pullam up as a shield, telling him to "stand up and be shot like a man for we all have to die together." The guards continued to fire, however, and both Bob and Pullam were wounded before the sloop moved out into the bay. The convicts, most of them wounded, managed to land in Contra Costa County, just north of present Oakland. Posses were

Bob and a pal were tried for horse stealing in Mariposa, shown here as it appeared in the late 1850's. *Courtesy the late Roy Radonovich.*

quickly in pursuit and most of the fugitives were soon in custody. James Estell, the prison director, listed 20 convicts as having escaped, but several were killed and many wounded. Estell's report of the bloody outbreak notes:

> In addition to the above, Valentine, two Mexicans, Moses with two others, were severely wounded in the fight in the attempt to take the sloop. Moses will probably die tonight. Cherokee Bob was found whilst the pursuit was being carried on so lively in the hills in Contra Costa. He says Watkins was shot in the arm and another ball had passed through his lungs. He was spitting blood when they separated and was thought to be dangerously wounded...
>
> Cherokee Bob was sinking rapidly this evening and could give but little addtional information. He was at times slightly delirious...

By January 5 only three of the escaped convicts were still at large. Although thought to be mortally wounded, Cherokee Bob recovered and was soon making plans for a new escape. On May 12, 1855 rumors of another mass escape spread like wild fire, but quickly proved to be highly exaggerated. The rumors were initiated when Cherokee Bob, Bill White, Thomas Hodges and several

287

others who were out chopping wood, escaped into some nearby thickets. Later it was charged that a guard named Gray had been in on the plot and this seems to have been the case. Cherokee Bob, meanwhile, promptly put some distance between himself and the dreaded prison.

Heading south, Bob worked two weeks at the Monterey mission where he cut hay. From there he went to San Jose, then to the Pulgas Rancho at the southern tip of San Francisco Bay where he worked at making shingles. He gambled constantly, an acquaintance noting that he led "a public life." He was frequently seen shooting at targets with ex-governor John McDougall who was also staying at Schell's Hotel.

About the middle of November Bob decided it would be safer if he visited Mexico for a time and he started south for Los Angeles. On November 10 two prominent Monterey men were murdered on the road and lawmen up and down the coast were on the lookout for the killers. Bob, riding south with several acquaintances, aroused suspicion and was followed by a man named Parkinson. In the south, Talbot stopped at San Gabriel where he gambled and met some friends of his Sonora days. He asked that he not be called by name and was using the alias of "Wilbur Flemming." He played poker and monte and won five horses and a little cash. He sent a man to Los Angeles to buy supplies for his Mexico trip, but before he returned Bob was arrested as reported in the Los Angeles *Star* of December 22, 1855:

> Important Arrest—Yesterday morning Mr. Petersen and Captain Henlinger upon information received of Mr. Parkinson, of Santa Barbara, arrested at the mission of San Gabriel, a man known as "Cherokee Bob" who is believed to be the murderer of Messrs. Wall and Williamson, of Monterey...
>
> At the time of his arrest he attempted to draw his pistol, but his captors, knowing their man, were prepared... and he surrendered and was disarmed...

The evidence against Talbot was slim. It was known he was an escaped convict by now and he was identified as being in the area of the murder shortly after it had occurred. A ring he had lost at gambling was suspected of being the former property of Isaac Wall, one of the murdered men.

At a hearing before Judge Benjamin Hayes in Los Angeles, witnesses established that Bob was indeed a former convict and gambler, but there was no creditable evidence produced to connect him with the murders. The questionable ring was easily identified and explained by Bob himself:

> The ring... I took off the finger of a brother of F. M. Schell... three or four days before I left, and I am sure that Mr. Wall would never own such a ring as that, and if he did, that he would never put it to the use that I had it for—for it was a trick ring... used in gambling...

Judge Hayes could find no reason to hold Bob and remanded him to the

Bob was captured and had a hearing at the small settlement of San Gabriel where Roy Bean had his headquarters saloon. *Courtesy California State Library.*

Monterey authorities. In custody of officers he was brought to Monterey on the *Sea Bird,* landing on January 9, 1856. Two days later he was back in San Quentin to resume his interrupted term.

Bob applied to Governor John B. Weller for clemency in early March of 1858. Ignoring his escape, Bob claimed to have served four years of his sentence. "Four years in this place of infamy," he wrote, " have been more than sufficient to expiate the crime I was convicted for." He claimed to have been too ashamed to write to his aged father and even concealed his name to keep the old man from discovering his whereabouts. Although something of a humanitarian, Weller apparently saw through Bob's pleading and ignored his request.

When he was ultimately pardoned, Talbot was discharged from prison on May 15, 1860. He had seen enough of California and followed his brother to the Northwest country. He headquartered for a time at The Dalles, Oregon, on the Columbia River. According to M.W. Shinn, he fleeced the teamsters who frequented the Mt. Hood saloon and worked the riverboats plying the river. When there was talk of the new Territory of Idaho being established, Bob headed for Walla Walla in Washington Territory, the jumping off point for the Colville mines and the Salmon and Snake River country. Walla Walla was booming and Bob found the local gambling element right up his alley.

These were Civil War times and as an outspoken secessionist, Bob was soon in trouble again. On the night of April 12, 1862, a group of soldiers from nearby Fort Walla Walla created a disturbance in a local theater. When several local lawmen tried to quiet them, other soldiers rushed to their aid and a general brawl resulted. Bob needed little encouragement to join the lawmen against the hated Union soldiers, and in the resulting shootout one soldier was killed and another wounded. The two lawmen were wounded also, along with a bystander.

The next morning a squad of soldiers searched the town for Bob who wisely kept under cover. Mayor Elias B. Whitman was outraged at the soldiers' conduct and wrote a steaming letter to Colonel Henry Lee, the post commander. Lee, while not condoning his men's behavior, deplored the "wanton, and . . . premeditated murder" of a trooper "by one of the most noted offenders who has for the past few years figured in the criminal annals of California under the sobriquet of Cherokee Bob."

Although sustained by the local press, Bob fled to Lewiston, Idaho, where he visited his brother and met up with Henry Plumer whom he had known in San Quentin. In June of 1862 he left for the booming mining town of Florence in company with a pal named Bill Mayfield and a woman known only as Cynthia. In Florence Bob acquired a saloon that did a flourishing business. Trouble, however, soon followed.

Tradition has it that Bob was infuriated when Cynthia wasn't accepted at a New Year's dance held in town. He had a dispute over the incident with a man named Jakey Williams and Cynthia became concerned there would be a fight. And there was. In a general gunbattle with Williams and others, Bob and a pal named Willoughby were gunned down in the street. Bob's pistol had reportedly mis-fired and he fell with a mortal wound. Barney Owsley, who claimed to have been there, later stated that Cynthia had hoped to prevent the murder of Williams by removing the caps from Bob's pistol. The fight was reported in the Walla Walla *Washington Statesman* on January 17, 1863:

> SHOOTING AT FLORENCE—Henry Talbotte, better known as "Cherokee Bob," and a man named William Willoby were shot in Florence on the 2nd instant by two men named John D. Williams and O. Robbins, on whom they had made an assault with intent to kill. Williams and Robbins had an examination before Justice Rand and were acquitted. Willoby received fourteen balls in his body and was killed in the affray. Talbotte received five balls and died two days afterward.

Bob's death occurred on January 5, 1863 and he was buried in the Florence cemetery. Although one of the more colorful of the West Coast gunmen, the California career of Cherokee Bob has been largely unknown and today he is merely a footnote in far west frontier history.

PRINCIPAL SOURCES ──────────────────────────

Bell, Horace, *Reminiscences of a Ranger,* Santa Barbara, Wallace Hebberd, 1927; Langford, Nathaniel Pitt, *Vigilante Days and Ways,* Missoula, Mt., Univ. of Mont. Press, 1957; Lyman, William D., *Lyman's History of Old Walla Walla County, Embracing Walla Walla, Columbia, Garfield and Asotin Counties,* Chicago, S.J. Clarke Pub., 1918; Mather, R.E. and Boswell, F.E., *Gold Camp Desperadoes,* San Jose, History West Pub., 1990; Shinn, M.W., "Cherokee Bob, the Original Jack Hamlin," *Overland Monthly,* July 1890; Timmen, Fritz, "Deadly Belle of the Ball," *True Frontier,* May, 1970; San Francisco *Daily Alta California,* Jan. 26, 1850, Dec. 29, 1854, Jan. 6, May 14, 1855; San Francisco *Daily Herald,* Dec. 29, 1854, May 13, 1855; Monterey *Sentinel,* Jan. 12, 1856; Los Angeles *Star,* Dec. 22, 29, 1855; Walla Walla *Washington Statesman,* Apr. 19, 1862; Walla Walla *Union Bulletin,* 1936, (undated clipping); Inquest records in Tuolumne Co. Hist. Soc.; Court records in Mariposa Co. courthouse; Fort Walla Walla correspondence in the National Archives, Wash., DC; Prison records and pardon files in California State Archives, Sacramento.

JOHN NELSON THACKER

Ex-sheriff John Thacker was foreman for the large San Joaquin Valley ranch of John Sutherland when this photo was made in the early 1870's.
Courtesy Fresno City and County Historical Society.

A native of Meller County, Missouri where he was born in 1837, John Thacker migrated to Nevada in the early 1860s. He settled in Star City, later establishing a ranch on the Humboldt River. In 1868 he was elected sheriff of Humboldt County and although serving only one term, he proved himself a capable officer. His later boss, Jim Hume, once recalled an incident from this period:

> ...On one occasion two murderers escaped from his deputies and went into Arizona. Thacker followed them and single-handed brought them out. That was a feat requiring an abundance of courage. It cost him $1,500 besides his time and trouble...

When Thacker left office a local newspaper referred to him as "big-souled, warmhearted, steadfast friend, a faithful officer and a chivalrous gentleman."

Just what prompted Thacker's move from Nevada is not known, but by about 1870 he was working as a foreman for John Sutherland, a large stockman in the San Joaquin Valley of California. Thacker moved to Marysville in 1873 where he was married that year. In 1875 he was employed by Wells, Fargo as a shotgun messenger, but apparently left the company for a short period of time. When he later returned to work for the express company, he made it his life's work.

For most of his years with Wells, Fargo, Thacker was the lieutenant of James B. Hume, the company's chief special officer and detective. Thacker traveled all over the west investigating crimes against the company and chasing bandits.

When a railway express car was attacked at Montello, Nevada, in February of 1883, it was successfully defended by Wells, Fargo guard Aaron Y. Ross. Hume sent Thacker to investigate and within five days he reported the gang captured in the wilds of Utah. In this and most other criminal cases, whenever possible the Wells, Fargo detectives worked with local officers in making arrests.

Thacker helped Hume compile their noted "Robbers Record" report which was published in 1885. This was a list of all Wells, Fargo robberies for the period 1870 to 1884 and contained full data on all the criminals listed—whether they were captured or killed, how much was stolen and returned, conviction data and other pertinent information. It was a remarkable document and although the company had lost $415,312 to thieves and outlaws and had spent nearly one million dollars waging "war" against the criminals, Hume's and Thacker's record of capture and conviction was, on the surface, impressive. Most of the actual captures and convictions, however, had been obtained by local peace officers.

Thacker played a part in the investigation and eventual capture of Black Bart (Charles E. Boles), the most successful of the early stage robbers. When two bandits robbed an express car at Clipper Gap east of Sacramento in December of 1888, Thacker worked long and hard on the case. Investigating with other officers, he pinned the crime on two brothers named Gordon. One of the Gordons was captured and confessed to the crime the following July.

In late October of 1891 Thacker looked into a series of stage robberies in northern California. In conjunction with local lawmen he arrested Bill Howard and Abe Jones for the crimes, also picking up an accomplice named Rice. Accompanied by several other officers, Thacker was taking his prisoners to Redding in a stagecoach on a stormy evening when Howard and Jones suddenly leaped from the vehicle and disappeared in the night. Howard was later ambushed and killed by lawmen at his father's house, while Jones remained at large for some time. Thacker, as the frequently successful representative of a large corporation, was often played up in the press which rankled some of the lawmen who worked with him. The Redding *Free Press* of November 21, 1891, made this terse comment:

> ...And while we are speaking of stage robbers and Wells Fargo detectives, we take this occasion to remark that Detective Thacker is a decided success in blowing his own horn and appropriating all the credit in making these arrests. The San Francisco papers all contained glowing descriptions of the arrest of the stage robbers made by Detective Thacker, "assisted by local officers," while, as a matter of fact, the robbers, Abe Jones and Bill Howard were discovered and tracked by Lakeview officials...Thacker himself shackled the men in such a manner that they managed to slip the shackles off their boots and Jones and Howard succeeded in jumping out of the stage...

While investigating another series of stage robberies in Shasta County in May of 1892, Thacker was again assailed for his methods. When a coach was robbed and a popular shotgun messenger killed, Thacker was promptly on the scene. One of the bandits was captured after being badly wounded during the holdup. Thacker was able to identify him as Charley Ruggles who had been working in the area. The other bandit was thought to be John Ruggles, brother of the captured outlaw. The detective asked the local press to refrain from publishing any information. "We wish to offer an apology to our readers," grumbled the Redding paper, "for suppressing the news last Saturday which was done by us under protest at the request of Detective Thacker; and after giving our promise, the whole matter . . . was given to the San Francisco *Examiner* . . ."

John Ruggles was soon apprehended and jailed with his wounded brother. Before Thacker could recover the stolen loot, however, the brothers were lynched early one morning in Redding. The double hanging took place when it was discovered that the Ruggles boys' defense strategy included accusing the popular, murdered shotgun messenger of being a party to the holdup.

In late May of 1893 Thacker met U.S. Marshal George Gard in Fresno. Two Tulare County farmers named Evans and Sontag were accused of several valley train holdups and had killed three lawmen while avoiding arrest. Wells, Fargo and the Southern Pacific Railroad were both offering large rewards and despite a local swarming of lawmen and bounty hunters, the two desperadoes remained at large. In a secret meeting with Fresno County Sheriff Jay Scott, a plan was devised to track down the fugitives. It was Thacker's plan to put a small posse into the field, keep them out of sight, but constantly survey the trails known to be frequented by Evans and his partner. Two Fresno County lawmen and a private detective were to be led by Marshal Gard. The party left Fresno in a wagon at night and slipped quietly into the hills of the Sierra. On June 11, 1893, the posse ambushed and badly wounded both outlaws. They were promptly deposited in jail and Thacker was widely praised for his strategy.

When the Scott Valley stage was held up some nine miles from Yreka on September 25, 1897, Thacker was again quickly on the scene. Working with other officers and Wells, Fargo agents, Thacker traced a stolen $20 note to a man named William Harrall. When other evidence further indicated the suspect's guilt, a deputy named Radford procured a warrant and met with Thacker and another lawman near Harrall's home at Delta, in Shasta County. Afraid he would be recognized, Thacker waited at a nearby depot as Radford and Deputy George Stewart knocked on the suspect's door. When he opened the door, Harrall also opened fire, killing Radford and wounding Stewart before being shot to death himself, his screaming wife and child clinging to him. "Detective Thacker," stated the San Francisco *Chronicle*, "thinks that Harrall is an old offender. A holdup between Shovel Creek and Ager and another between Yreka and Fort Jones, he says, have been traced to Harrall. He was following in the footsteps of Black Bart."

When James B. Hume passed away in 1903, Thacker had already assumed most of his duties and was immediately appointed to his post. But the old

Above: Thacker was well along in years when this newspaper sketch was published in the 1890's. *From San Francisco* Chronicle *of October 15, 1897.*

Right: Thacker was instrumental in tracking down the Ruggles brothers, but before the stolen loot could be recovered, the two bandits were lynched by Redding citizens. *From author's collection.*

detective was also in the twilight of his life. He was sixty-six years old and just a few years later, on November 1, 1907, he retired. He died at his Oakland home in January of 1913, survived by his wife, Sarah, and two sons. Eugene Thacker, one of his boys had already been working for Wells, Fargo for many years as a detective.

An unidentified newspaper article at the time of his death paid John Thacker perhaps his most fitting tribute:

> Some of the newspapers in eulogizing John N. Thacker, the veteran Wells, Fargo detective, for his grit and bravery, use the term that he had "notches on his guns." Thacker has been officer and detective in this state and Nevada for over thirty years and it is to his credit that there is not a notch on his gun. In his career of hunting and capturing criminals he has exercised intelligence, courage and suasion and has not resorted to killing his fellow-being for either glory or...reward.

PRINCIPAL SOURCES ─────────────────────────────────

Dillon, Richard, *Wells Fargo Detective,* N.Y., Coward-McCann, 1969; Larson, Pansilee, "Our County Sheriff," *The Humboldt Historian,* Winter, 1979; Fresno *Weekly Expositor,* June 16, 1893; Fresno *Daily Republican,* Aug. 12, 1892; Redding *Free Press,* Oct. 31, Nov. 7, 21, 1891; San Francisco *Chronicle,* Oct. 15, 16, 1897; San Francisco *Examiner,* Oct. 15, 16, 1897; Fresno City and Co. Hist. Soc. Archives, Fresno; Wells Fargo Bank History Room, San Francisco.

BENJAMIN KENT THORN

A Calaveras County lawman for nearly 45 years, Ben Thorn was one of the most noted of the early California officers. *Courtesy Calaveras County Museum.*

Of Danish and English ancestry, Ben Thorn was born at Plattsburg, New York on December 22, 1829. He moved to Chicago with his parents when he was four-years-old and obtained a good, basic education. Later he did farm work, clerked in a store and for a time taught school. He crossed the plains to California during the gold rush of 1849 and mined for a brief period on the Yuba River.

In the early 1850s he mined in Amador and Calaveras counties, working several claims at San Antonio in the latter area. He was active in politics and was appointed a deputy sheriff under Charles A. Clark in April of 1855. That fall he was also elected constable. This was the beginning of his long and dramatic career as a frontier lawman of old Calaveras County.

Action came quickly enough for the young deputy. In June of 1855 he captured the notorious Sam Brown and a friend named Bunty Owens. The pair had killed several Chilenos in a gambling dispute. When Brown saw Thorn and a companion approaching, he took a bead on the young deputy with his rifle. "Thorn had proceeded but a short distance toward the place," reported one account, "when Brown lowered his rifle off of him, and Thorn said he never felt so happy as he did about that time." The lawman took the prisoners to a justice court for a hearing, staying up all night to guard them from a lynch mob of Chilenos. Brown received a two year term at San Quentin.

An old timer remembered meeting Thorn when he was collecting miner's tax licenses in 1856:

With his badge on his vest, Thorn stands at the rear of this group of Calaveras County officials. *Courtesy Calaveras County Museum.*

> I was alone at our cabin in Yaqui Camp when Ben Thorn brought in a big Yaqui Indian that weighed 200 pounds. The Indian's head was bleeding and a white handkerchief was tied around it. Ben Thorn said to me, "Here's a man that owes me two licenses. I asked him for it and he asked me if I wanted to fight, so he showed fight and I hit him over the head two or three times with the six-shooter."

John Phipps had killed a man named Morales with an ax in 1854, then disappeared. Thorn located Phipps and arrested him near San Antonio in March of 1857. He also captured the brutal killer, Howard Maupin, at a Marysville dance house in October of 1857 and with fellow deputy Bob Paul arrested Pedro Ybarra late the following year. Ybarra had shot down his mistress and her new lover in the summer of 1854. Despite hunting up a variety of witnesses against the killer, Thorn was unable to obtain a conviction. Years later, however, he was able to send Ybarra up on a stage robbing charge. Another personal encounter of Thorn's was reported in the San Andreas *Independent* of February 27, 1858:

> Resistence to an Officer—On Sunday night last, Deputy Sheriff Thorn was called upon to arrest a pugilist offender against the peace and dignity of San Andreas, when, resistance being made a la Hyer, a blow was laid upon the

bellicose individual's head with a "Colt" that placed him hors de combat for about half the time that silence reigned in heaven on a memorable occasion...

Deputy Thorn spent considerable time tracking a brutal killer named Santiago Molino who was accused of some five murders in various parts of the state. Locating the killer at a small mining camp in Mariposa County, Thorn and a fellow deputy named Wesson stopped at his cabin and informed Molino of their business. The Mariposa *Gazette* of January 7, 1859, chronicled what happened next:

> ...Molino made an attempt to reach his bed, but the officers knowing him to be a desperate character, drew their revolvers and intercepted him, when a scuffle ensued. After a short struggle he concluded to give himself up; on going out the door...Molino jerked loose from the officers and made for the brush. They then gave chase, but finding it difficult to overtake him, fired three shots...and killed him instantly...

When Robert H. Paul was elected sheriff in September of 1859, he made Thorn his undersheriff. Both were dedicated lawmen and made life difficult for the criminal class. The two officers found ex-convict and bandit Charles Williams chopping wood in Mariposa County on December 6, 1860. When the fugitive sought escape in a thicket, Thorn shot and wounded him. Another time, as horse thief and murderer Jesus Bealova was being escorted back to his cell after having his photograph taken, the outlaw jumped Thorn and seized his pistol. The lawman fought back desperately. He managed to throw Bealova to the ground and, turning aside the pistol, jammed a finger up his nose and held him until help arrived. The San Francisco *Alta* reported the badman's trip to San Quentin on April 9, 1861:

> DESPERATE CRIMINAL—Jesus Bealova arrived in town last night from Calaveras County, in charge of Deputy Sheriff B.K. Thorn. Bealova, who is a stout, savage looking Mexican, murdered a man in Calaveras County and was sentenced to death. His sentence was afterwards commuted to life imprisonment...

When Sheriff Paul was defeated for re-election in 1863, Thorn was not reappointed a deputy. He again pinned on his deputy's star when James Oliphant assumed office in 1865 and two years later Thorn himself successfully ran for sheriff. A popular politician and highly respected lawman, Thorn was to retain his office for most of the next thirty years.

On September 30, 1868, local mine superintendent Elkanah Said was on his way to Mokelumne Hill with a carriage full of bullion. In a bandit ambush, Said was killed, but a passenger whipped the horses and saved the treasure. Sheriff Thorn and his deputies found a hat and sack of provisions near the site and were able to trace the goods to a storekeeper who identified several Mexicans and two Frenchmen as the buyers. Thorn was promptly on the trail as related in the Calaveras *Chronicle* of October 31, 1868:

> Arrests—Two Mexicans were arrested in Columbia on Monday last, by Sheriff Thorn and Constables Mathews and McLennan, on suspicion of having been implicated in the murder of Mr. Said, near Railroad Flat a short time since. We have received but little information in regards to the arrests, excepting that the men made a desperate resistance, firing a number of shots at the officers...

Thorn lost the trail of the remaining suspect at Mariposa, but he picked up one Jose Coyado in April of 1869. Tried for the murder, Coyado was hanged in June of 1872 while Andres Molino, another of the killers was sentenced to life imprisonment. It was said that the sheriff had spent some $1,500 of his own money in tracking down the murderers.

The *Chronicle* was unstinting in its admiration of the lawman's tracking and prosecution of the murderers. "Too much praise cannot be awarded Sheriff Thorn for the activity, perseverance and ingenuity he has evinced in ferreting out the murderers." Yet a few months later the paper's admiring prose had turned into bitter, partisan carping when Thorn was running for re-election:

> B.K. Thorn, Democratic nominee for Sheriff, is the "spinal column" of that party in this county. Defeat him and you paralyze the organization. He is the electrician who for the past four years has galvanized the Democratic corpse into a semblance of life. If he is beaten at the coming election, the Democracy are making their last fight in this county; should he be successful, two years hence the Confederates will gain control of affairs...Republicans...stand by your nominee...

Thorn was re-elected September 1, 1869 by a solid majority and went on to win the next three elections. In 1871 he ran against his old friend and former boss, Bob Paul, but Thorn's popularity was too much to overcome. When the Democratic party seemed out of favor, Thorn simply ran as an Independent.

While out of office in 1875, Thorn was embarrased by a serious accident. He had been losing chickens to a nocturnal prowler and determined to sit up one night and catch the thief. Judge A.H. Coulter cut through Thorn's back yard that evening on his way home. He stopped at a tree to light a cigar, unaware it was the very tree where the ex-sheriff's chickens were roosting. "Thorn says he was sure the match was being used to stupify the fowls," noted the *Chronicle,* "and fired. The first shot passed through Coulter's clothes and before he could recover enough to cry out, a second was fired. The judge suffered a painful wrist wound and Thorn lost no more of his chickens.

Thorn had long waged war on the stage robbers and bandits of his area, chasing Bill Miner and other noted outlaws of the time. Even when out of office during 1875 - 79, his services were always available as reported in a San Francisco *Call* item of March 20, 1876:

Thorn locked up many hardcases in this San Andreas jail cell. Here Black Bart was held when he plead guilty to stage robbery and was sentenced to a term in San Quentin in 1883. *From author's collection.*

Jackson, March 19—Ben Thorn, ex-sheriff of Calaveras, and F.N. Ross, ex-deputy sheriff of Amador, assisted by John Vogan and others, made an important arrest near town this morning in the person of the noted stage robber, Joaquin, alias Antone. The party surrounded the house where Joaquin was said to be concealed. Thorn, followed by Vogan, went to the door of his room and commanded him to open it. After a little parley he opened it, suddenly presenting himself with a knife in one hand and a pistol in the other, but finding himself covered by Thorn's pistol and the back window guarded by Ross, he surrendered.

Ben was again returned to office in 1879. In November of 1883 he was still sheriff when Black Bart held up his last stagecoach. Thorn and a posse were quickly on the scene and in nosing about for clues it was Ben who came up with some personal effects of the bandit. A handkerchief showed a faint laundrymark and it was this simple bit of evidence that resulted in Bart's San Francisco

299

capture. Thorn met Bart and a contingent of detectives at Oakland and accompanied them back to Calaveras County. Here, Bart finally broke down, gave up the stolen loot and pleaded guilty in the San Andreas courtroom. He was sentenced to six years at state prison. Thorn's expense claims for the investigation and hearing are interesting:

> To arrest C.E. Bolton, alias Black Bart, $2.00; 729 miles actually traveled from November 3rd to November 14th inclusive in searching for prisoner, $218.70; R.R. fare from San Francisco to Milton for prisoner, $4.10; Tools, $.50; 46 miles travel with C.E. Bolton, $13.80; Taking C.E. Bolton into court and return, $.60; Amount paid barber for shaving Bolton, $.50...

Term after term Thorn ran for office and was re-elected, but by the late 1890s the old lawdog was getting weary. He was elected for the last time in 1898, achieving a remarkable record for success and longevity in office. He was visiting a daughter in San Francisco when the end came as reported in the Calaveras *Prospect* of November 18, 1905:

> Last Wednesday morning there passed away in San Francisco a man who for more than thirty years was a central figure in Calaveras County. On that day at the home of his daughter, Mrs. Adolph Soher, Ben K. Thorn crossed the divide after a lingering illness of many months...

Thorn has long been recognized as one of the most efficient and active officers in the state and the passage of time has not tampered with his fame. The beautiful brick home he built for his wife in 1859 may still be seen in San Andreas.

PRINCIPAL SOURCES ────────────────

Buckbee, Edna Bryan, *The Saga of Old Tuolumne,* N.Y., Press of the Pioneers, 1935; Dillon, Richard, *Wells, Fargo Detective,* N.Y. Coward-McCann, Inc., 1969; Wood, Richard Coke, *Calaveras, The Land of Skulls,* Sonora, The Mother Lode Press, 1955; *Representative Citizens of Northern California,* Chicago Standard, Genealogical Pub. Co., 1901; *Las Calaveras,* The Calaveras Co. Hist. Soc., Oct. 1969; Sacramento *Bee,* Feb. 16, 1876; San Francisco *Daily Morning Call,* Mar. 20, 1876; Calaveras *Chronicle,* Oct. 31, Nov. 7, 1868, Jan. 23, Apr. 24, Aug. 21, 1869, June 22, 1872; San Andreas *Independent,* Feb. 27, 1858; Calaveras *Prospect,* Nov. 18, 1905; Documents and research materials in the Calaveras Co. Museum and Archives, San Andreas, California.

TIBURCIO VASQUEZ

Rogue, robber and roué, Tiburcio Vasquez
was a thorn in the side of California
lawmen for nearly 20 years. *Courtesy Wells,
Fargo Bank History Room.*

Born in Monterey, California on August 11, 1835, Tiburcio Vasquez came from a respectable family and grew up with three brothers and two sisters. He had some education, could read and write and speak English, but at an early age he began associating with local toughs and criminals. At a fandango one night in 1854 Tiburcio and two friends became involved in a brawl. When Constable William Hardmount interfered, he was killed. Vasquez and Anastacio Garcia fled the scene, but their friend, Jose Higuerra, was caught and lynched. At the tender age of nineteen Vasquez found himself an outlaw. His pal Garcia was later referred to as one of the worst criminals in the state. Young Tiburcio could could hardly have picked a more sinister Fagan, and the boy learned his lessons well.

In July of 1857 Vasquez surfaced again when he ran off a herd of horses at Los Angeles. He was caught as he tried to sell the animals and was sentenced to five years in the state prison. He was received at San Quentin on August 26th and according to his own statement "was pretty roughly handled. The treatment was very rigorous. The discipline at that time was undergoing reform." While working in the prison brick yard, Vasquez participated in the mass escape of June 25, 1859, in which a number of guards and prisoners were killed and wounded. Free for a time, Vasquez was returned to the prison the following August on a larceny conviction from Amador County. After serving one year

The Rear Wall and Gate of the State Prison showing the scene of the recent escape.

A contemporary illustration in the *California Police Gazette* depicts the 1859 escape from San Quentin when Vasquez gained his freedom. *From the* California Police Gazette.

for this crime, plus the balance of his first term, he was released on August 13, 1863 and returned home to Monterey.

Although he claimed to have tried to lead an honest life, Vasquez promptly became associated with Juan Soto, Faustino Lorenzano and other outlaws. When he was linked to the murder of a butcher at Enriquita, he fled north, but was returned again to San Quentin on a larceny conviction from Sonoma County. He served out his new term and was released on June 4, 1870. He sought out his old companions once more and was possibly with Juan Soto at the time a store clerk was robbed and murdered at Sunol in Alameda County. Sheriff Harry Morse killed Soto in a furious gunfight in May of 1871 at about the same time Vasquez was assembling his own gang.

Procopio Bustamente, a nephew of Joaquin Murrieta, had been released from San Quentin in March of 1871 and was looking around for opportunities. He needed little coaxing to take up with Vasquez. Other reported members of the new gang were Sancho Barcenas and Francisco Galindo. On August 17, 1871 Vasquez and his men stopped the Visalia stage near Soap Lake in Monterey County. In what was to become a trademark, the passengers were robbed and tied up after being told to be still or they would be killed. Posses were quickly on the trail and Barcenas was shot to death near Santa Cruz as reported in the San Francisco *Bulletin* of September 15, 1871:

> Santa Cruz, September 14th—The name of the Spaniard killed by the sheriff's posse at Pike's Pole last night was Sancho Barcumes [*sic*] and not Procopio as was at first supposed. He was one of the gang implicated in the Visalia stage robbery...

Vasquez himself was recognized on the street at Santa Cruz, and in a shootout was badly wounded by Marshal L.T. Roberts. After recuperating in the coast range, Vasquez and Procopio left for old Mexico where they kept out of sight. Their stay in the south was brief, however, and they soon returned to San Francisco.

Procopio was captured in the bay city, but Vasquez had already headed for the coast range where he began assembling a new gang. Recruiting an acquaintance named Clodoveo Chavez, Tiburcio committed a number of petty crimes while scouting for larcenous opportunities. Early in 1873 Vasquez and Chavez stopped at the house of Abdon Leiva, a blacksmith and laborer. Vasquez had heard that a large payroll was to be deposited by a rancher at Firebaugh's Ferry store. Taking Leiva, Chavez, an army deserter named Charles Weeks, August deBert and one Romulo Gonzales, Vasquez rode up to Hoffman's store at the ferry on the evening of February 26, 1873. The Fresno *Expositor* related what happened in its issue of March 19th:

> ...They made their appearance in the store about dark, all masked save one, and commanded those in the store to lie down on the floor and keep quiet. Enforcing their demand by presenting cocked revolvers, they proceeded to tie the captors hands...The robbers then began to make a general search for coin and valuables. About this time the stage drove up which startled the outlaws somewhat, but a deputation went out and took charge of what money the driver had and also Wells, Fargo & Co.'s box... Mrs. Hoffman's watch was also returned upon her entreating them so to do, the robber having it saying that they didn't come there to rob women...

The watch incident, scoffed at by historians as a romantic fable ever since, actually happened and was corroborated by local Constable Harry Thomas.

The following July Vasquez planned to rob a Southern Pacific payroll train. When the attempt failed, the outlaws plundered the Twenty-one Mile House, a restaurant and hotel near Gilroy. Returning to Leiva's house, Vasquez laid low for a few weeks and it was probably at this time that one of his men went on a drunk at the New Idria mines settlement. When the outlaw insulted J.W. Maxwell, the mine superintendent, Maxwell ran the fellow out of town, sending a shot across his poop deck for emphasis. Vasquez called on Maxwell the next day and warned him to report such conduct to him as his men had orders not to bother the settlement. If his man had been shot, warned the bandit leader, he would have killed every American in the place!

On August 26, 1873, Vasquez, Teodoro Moreno, Abdon Leiva, Chavez and Romulo Gonzales rode up to the isolated village of Tres Pinos, in the coast range near San Juan Bautista. The outlaws drifted into town in pairs, tying up and robbing the inhabitants of Snyder's Store and Davidson's Hotel. Suddenly there was shooting—a sheepherder who did not understand a command was killed by Moreno. A teamster running for cover was also killed, while Vasquez gunned down and killed Leander Davidson as he tried to close a door. Gathering together their loot, the bandits galloped off, the Salinas *Index* reporting:

> ...If the citizens of that locality had acted with sufficient energy and promptness, and had followed the band at once, forcing every man they came across to arm and join...the band would have been killed or taken, together with the stock and plunder; but the inhabitants were terror-stricken

and entertained fears of a subsequent visit and revenge by the terrible Vasquez...

Fleeing south to the rugged mountains south of old Fort Tejon, Vasquez tried to keep out of sight. Moreno and Gonzales had already scattered and only Chavez, Leiva and his wife, Rosario, were with him. The group's ranks were thinned futher when Leiva caught Vasquez and Rosario together. The betrayed outlaw left camp and headed straight for the nearest authorities to whom he sang loud and clear. Abandoning Rosario, Vasquez and Chavez headed north to Cantua Canyon after some brushes with the searching posses. Instead of laying low for awhile, Vasquez promptly planned a new series of raids.

Recruiting a new gang consisting of Blas Bicuna, Isadore Padillo, Manuel Gomez and Monteras, Vasquez and Chavez headed east across the San Joaquin Valley. They raided Jones' Store, near Millerton on November 10, 1873, then gathering more recruits at the California Ranch settlement, the bandits rode south toward the village of Kingston on the Kings River.

It was the day after Christmas when the bandits took over Kingston, robbing and tieing up the inhabitants of several stores and the hotel. Rancher John Sutherland received word of what was happening and taking several of his cowboys along, they opened fire on the outlaws, driving them from town. Several bandits were wounded and two horses were crippled. "They manifested no desire to take life," noted the Kern County *Courier,* "their leader exercising restraint over them in that respect. He was heard to remark that they had already done quite enough in that way."

Again posses were everywhere scouring the Mexican settlements in the valley. They were extremely hard on any suspicious Mexican, the rough handling bringing a protest from the Mexican consul and censure from the governor. On January 19, 1874 three Mexicans arrived in Millerton bringing in a thug named Ignacio Ronquel from the California Ranch. Ronquel, an ex-convict, admitted to being with Vasquez during the Kingston raid and was quickly tried and shipped off to prison. "A cursory glance at our citizens," noted the Millerton *Expositor,*"...would have convinced Vasquez himself that Millerton was no place for him as almost every person we saw would pass for a walking arsenal." There were several reported lynchings as the posses continued their sweep of the San Joaquin Valley.

Chavez, wounded in the leg at Kingston, had rejoined his boss by mid-February. Together with one other gang member, they stopped the Bakersfield stage at Coyote Holes in the Mojave Desert, robbing some sixteen other travelers who happened along. A teamster who did not move fast enough was shot in the leg by the bandit chief, "as a gentle reminder," said Vasquez, "that such conduct was dangerous." The outlaws then fled south.

With a $3,000 state reward now on his head, time was fast running out for Vasquez. In mid-January of 1874 Sheriff Harry Morse of Alameda County was commissioned by Governor Newton Booth to stop the bandit's reign of terror. Selecting eight good men to make up his posse, Morse began combing the bandit hangouts for word of their whereabouts. They traveled over 2,720 miles and were out over sixty days when Vasquez was finally located near Los Angeles. Morse informed Sheriff William Rowland, then returned to his posse as reported in the Kern County *Courier* of April 18th:

> ...It is interesting to know that sheriff Morse, of Alameda, with a party of well-armed men, is scouting among the haunts of Vasquez. Sunday evening last they bivouacked at the Tejon and created no little alarm at first until their character was known.

Although he had discounted Morse's information at first, Sheriff Rowland soon learned the Alameda lawman was correct. An eight-man posse was quietly assembled after it had been confirmed that Vasquez was staying at the house of one Greek George, some ten miles from the city. Stationing several lawmen around the house on May 14, 1874, a rush was made on the premises. Policeman Emil Harris jumped through the door and fired at Vasquez just as the outlaw vaulted through a window. Newspaper reporter George Beers was outside the window and later wrote:

> At the sound of Harris' shot I stepped into the path leading along the west side of the house, and the next instant the agile form of Vasquez came flying around the corner towards me, and I fired. He threw up both hands, at the same instant crying out, "No shoot! No shoot!" and Hartley gave him a charge of buckshot...

The outlaw suffered minor wounds and was brought into Los Angeles just before five o'clock that afternoon. He was taken to San Francisco by steamer where he arrived on the 27th. Before being transferred to San Jose for trial, Vasquez spent some time in the Salinas jail. He was visited there by the prominent rancher Henry Miller who gave him $20 for his legal fund. It was Miller's payroll at Firebaugh's Ferry that Vasquez had tried to steal, but it had arrived late and was saved.

Los Angeles as it looked when Vasquez was captured and brought into town. *Courtesy California State Library.*

Tried and convicted for the Tres Pinos murders, Vasquez was sentenced to hang on March 19, 1875. He met death bravely, his last word being, "Pronto!" He is remembered today as much for his many betrayed women as for his long list of crimes.

He was buried by his family on the fringes of the Santa Clara Mission Cemetery. A simple wooden cross marked the site for many years, but in 1930 the cemetery management marked the grave with an impressive monument—a monument the bandit chief hardly deserves.

PRINCIPAL SOURCES ──────────────────────────

Greenwood, Robert, *The California Outlaw, Tiburcio Vasquez,* Los Gatos, Talisman Press, 1960; Hoyle, M.F., *California's Age of Terror: Murieta and Vasquez,* Hollister, Evening Free Lance, 1927; Latta, Frank F. *Saga of Rancho El Tejon,* Santa Cruz, Bear State Books, 1976; San Francisco *Daily Alta California,* June 27, 1859; San Francisco *Bulletin,* Sept. 18, Nov. 25, 1873, May 15, June 3, 1874; Kern Co. *Weekly Courier,* Jan. 3, Feb. 28, Apr. 18, 1874; The Fresno *Expositor,* Mar. 5, Nov. 25, Dec. 31, 1873, Jan. 28, Mar. 17, 1874; The King City *Rustler,* May 6, 1971; Los Angeles *Star,* May 15, 16, 1874; 1850 Monterey Co. Census; Prison records and other documents in California State Archives, Sacramento.

SHERIFF'S OFFICE,
County of Santa Clara.

San Jose, March 18 1875.

To *A. C. Bassett* Esq

SIR.— Pursuant to the Statute in such cases you are hereby invited to be present at the execution of Tiburcio Vasquez, at the Jail of said County, in San Jose, on the 19th day of March, A. D. 1875, at 1:30 o'clock P. M.

J. H. ADAMS, Sheriff.

PRESENT AT JAIL ENTRANCE.   NOT TRANSFERABLE

The invitation to the hanging of Vasquez. *Courtesy Santa Clara County Museum.*

STEPHEN VENARD

Steve Venard, although little known,
was one of the nervier of
California's frontier lawmen.
Courtesy John Boessenecker.

Born in Lebanon, Ohio, about 1824, Steve Venard obtained a good education at a Waynesville academy. He came to California during the gold rush, arriving in September of 1850 after a trip across the plains. He was mining in Nevada City in October of 1851 when he wrote home describing his travels over the northern part of the state while searching for gold. "...And if you hear any young housekeeper inquiring for employment," he noted, "just send her here to me and I will pay her better wages to superintend my little house...than she can get in the state of Ohio where she would have to perform five times the labor." When mining did not pay enough to suit him, Steve worked at odd jobs and in 1853 was in partnership with Sam Connell in keeping a grocery store on Broad street.

After serving as a deputy sheriff under W.W. Wright in the mid-1850's, Venard ran for city marshal in 1857, but was defeated. He was later elected marshal and served two terms in the 1860's. He also was defeated when he ran for sheriff and in the spring of 1866 was engaged in private business.

At this time there had been a great many robberies in the area prompting the Nevada (County) *Daily Transcript* to suggest that a private reward be offered:

> Something must be done—This county is infested by a gang of highwaymen
> who are constantly committing robberies. At first they confined operations
> to teamsters, footmen and private conveyances...

Several stages had been robbed previously when the North San Juan coach was stopped on May 16, 1866. Sheriff Robert Gentry promptly put together a

Nevada City as it appeared in the 1850's. *Courtesy Pat Jones.*

Sketch of Venard that appeared in *Harper's Weekly* after his battle with the robbers. *From* Harpers Weekly.

posse composed of his brother Al, A.W. Potter, J.H. Lee, Frank McKee and Steve Venard. Six passengers had been robbed and nearly $8,000 taken from the stage's strong box. Gentry's posse was on the trail an hour after the report was received. Striking the trail of the bandits in some particularly rough country, Venard was sent to follow them on foot while the balance of the posse kept to the road hoping to cut them off when the bandits attempted to cross the river on a bridge. What happened next is concisely reported in the Nevada *Daily Gazette* of May 16, 1866:

> Venard was armed with a Henry repeating rifle containing 16 loads. He followed the tracks to within about a mile of Hoyt's, when he suddenly came upon the robbers, who were only about 20 feet from him. Venard immediately fired and shot one of the robbers dead. One of the others jumped behind a rock and raising his head, snapped his revolver at Venard, but the cap exploded, and the next instant a bullet from Venard's rifle had penetrated his brain. Venard then turned his attention to the third robber...and fired upon him twice, the second shot killing him...

The beautifully engraved Henry rifle given to Venard by Wells, Fargo. *Courtesy Wells, Fargo Bank History Room.*

When Steve rejoined the posse he told the astounded lawmen that he had shot and killed all three bandits. By two o'clock in the afternoon of the day of the robbery, the robbers were dead and the money recovered. The bodies were retrieved from the scene of the fight with great difficulty and were identified as Jack Williams, alias George Shanks, Robert Finn and George Moore. Both Finn and Moore had prison records. "It took nearly four hours to get the bodies to the nearest point on the road," noted the *Transcript*, "and in some places the bodies had to be dragged. Had Venard been killed it is hardly probable that his body would ever have been found."

Steve was offered the $3,000 Wells, Fargo reward, but refused anything more than half. He was quickly appointed a local deputy sheriff and was commissioned a lieutenant colonel in the state militia by the governor. Wells, Fargo later presented him with a handsome, gold-mounted Henry rifle. The weapon was beautifully engraved with a depiction of the incident and the date. Newspapers all over the state applauded the brave deputy's action. A typical comment was included in an editorial in the San Francisco newspaper, *Spirit of the Times:*

This gentleman is entitled to the thanks of the people in the entire state and not alone of Nevada County, for the daring and bravery in disposing of the robbers of the San Juan stage...

Another newspaper tersely commented that "A few such lessons as Venard has given will put an end to that sort of amusement in California. Venard has done more good than all the criminal trials which have taken place in that section of the country for years." Hundreds of people visited the site of the battle and Steve and several others recreated the scene for a local photographer.

After his stint as a deputy, Venard worked as a shotgun guard and also as a detective for Wells, Fargo. The company sent him over to Mendocino County when a series of stagecoach robberies took place in the summer and fall of 1871. The stage between Healdsburg and Cloverdale was held up four times, a passenger being killed and another wounded. Venard posed as a hog rancher and worked undercover with several local lawmen in ferreting out the bandits. The *Mendocino Democrat* of November 17, 1871, noted the capture of the five gang members and Venard's arrest of the leader, John Houx:

> ...Houx was arrested in a saloon at Cloverdale, into which he had been invited to take a drink...He seemed reluctant to enter, but finally did so. While at the bar Venard, the detective, suddenly seized him in front and ordered him to throw up his hands, at the same time saying he was arrested...

The capture of two others of the gang was detailed by a correspondent of the San Francisco *Bulletin* that same month:

> ...For the capture of "Lody" Brown, a plan was arranged by Steve Venard, the noted detective in the service of Wells, Fargo & Co., which was highly successful. He and Sheriff Reynolds lay in ambush beside a spring to which "Lody" came to water his horses, whereupon they issued forth and laid hands upon him. One of them then discharged a gun and cried out, "Come down! Come down! We've killed a deer!" which enticed Bigfoot to the spot and he also was nabbed...

Venard may or may not have been on the company payroll at this time. He may have only been utilized when needed, or he may have been a shotgun messenger when not engaged in detective duties. He was working for the company after James B. Hume took over as chief special officer for Wells, Fargo in 1873. A notice in the Sacramento *Bee* in January of 1876 chronicled an exploit of the detectives:

> STAGE ROBBERS CAPTURED—In Folsom yesterday morning, aided by Len Harris, Steve Venard and Constable Kimball, detective Hume captured two desperadoes who are wanted for various stage robberies... One of these men, Geo. Wilkins, alias Geo. Wilson, alias Texas, has served twenty years in the state prison already...

When Venard died in 1891 he was penniless and his funeral costs were borne by friends. *Courtesy Wells, Fargo Bank History Room.*

These two desperadoes, and their leader, Charlie Pratt, had robbed two stagecoaches earlier that month. All three men had long prison records and when Venard and Hume rounded up Pratt a short time later, they were soon doing time again in San Quentin.

By 1883 Steve was back in Nevada City working as a constable and night watchman. He had a run-in with local tough Joe Lawrence and had to beat him severely with his revolver one night when he would not submit to arrest. Sometime later Lawrence, while in a drunken rage, tried to rape a step-daughter and when his wife interfered, he drove them both from the house. When he came to town searching for the two women later, he was arrested. Venard was taking him around to locate bondsmen, when Lawrence suddenly drew a knife and cut the constable several times. The two fought furiously, but Lawrence broke away from the wounded officer and made his escape. After several days of being a fugitive, Lawrence wrote a letter apologizing for his conduct and stating that he would never touch liquor again if his wife would take him back. His wife knew better and later when he was captured he jumped bail and disappeared.

After ranching for several years in the state of Nevada, Venard returned to California and died at the Nevada County hospital on May 20, 1891. "He was a man of strictly temperate habits, honest and brave," commented the Nevada Daily *Transcript* in its obituary. He was also penniless and when he died a collection was taken up among his friends to pay for his burial.

PRINCIPAL SOURCES ————————————

Wells, Harry L., *History of Nevada County, California,* Oakland, Thompson & West, 1880; Wilson, Neill C., *Treasure Express,* N.Y., The Macmillan Co., 1938; "Stephen Venard, Nevada County Pioneer," *Nevada Co. Hist. Soc. Bulletin,* Dec., 1967; "Steve Venard," *The Grizzly Bear,* Nov., 1907; Nevada *Daily Transcript,* May 9, 22, 25, June 3, 7, 1866; Nevada *Daily Gazette,* May 16, 17, 18, 22, 1866; Grass Valley *Union,* Mar. 23, 25, 1883, May 24, 1891; San Francisco *Bulletin,* Nov. 15, 1871; Wells Fargo Bank History Room, San Francisco.

JOHN DAVID WATHEN
"Wylackie John"

Killer, rustler, perjurer. . . Wylackie John
Wathen was as deadly as a rattlesnake
to anyone who got in his way. *Courtesy
Robert Lee.*

Vincennes, Indiana was the birthplace of one of the most ruthless characters of California's early days. Born in 1833, John D. Wathen came to California in the 1850s and settled in the northern portion of the state. When he was involved in some trouble in the Sacramento Valley, he fled to the Mendocino mountains to avoid arrest. He lived with the Wylacki Indians for several years, acquiring a wife and several children. By 1855 he was working on the Nome Lackee reservation as an interpreter and later was transferred to the new Indian reservation in Round Valley in Mendocino County.

Wathen probably went to work for George E. White sometime in the 1860s. One of the earliest settlers in Round Valley, White eventually acquired over 35,000 acres of the best rangeland in Mendocino, Trinity and southern Humboldt Counties. As foreman and henchman for the powerful rancher, Wathen displayed a penchant for murder, theft and intrigue which made him a feared and legendary figure in the Yolla Bolly country. The San Francisco *Call,* in October of 1895, reported:

> Wylackie John was a remarkable man. . . He had no small vices; he did not dissipate, he did not smoke or chew tobacco, he dressed well. . . kept himself neat and was always suave and polite. . . With these graces he was wholly without honor, entirely unscrupuous, a robber, a murderer, a poisoner, a perjeror, having an absolute genius for planning evil.

A contemporary described him well a few years earlier; "He did not wear a cowboy rig, and he was not adorned with knives and six-shooters. He was a man of medium size, mild mannered and extremely suave, and had the appearance of a prosperous stockman. He would touch his hat politely, inquire solicitously about a man's health, talk pleasantly with him and shoot him in the back on his way home along a lonely trail..."

Wylackie John's story reads like a movie script. White wanted all the rich rangeland for himself and it was Wathen's job to acquire land and run off any new settlers. His men would dress up like Indians and burn homesteader's cabins and kill their cattle. He would hire his own cowboys or others to either kill newcomers or make life so miserable for them they would be forced to leave. Others would be framed and sent to prison. A typical case was an unlucky settler whose property White wanted. The man had a colt that looked almost exactly like one of White's animals. Wathen stole the colt and put it in White's pasture and when the settler had him charged with stealing the animal, the case was taken to court in Covelo. During the trial the stolen horse was tied in front of the court room, but Wathen switched the animal for White's colt while the trial was in progress. When the colt was examined and found to be actually White's animal instead of the stolen one, the case was thrown out of court.

Wathen and his gang of tough cowboys would steal a band of sheep and drive them to Round Valley. Along the way he would have other bands of sheep driven across his trail so as to confuse the tracks. By the time the stolen mutton was in the valley, mixed with other bands of sheep and the earmarks changed, the crime was almost completely undiscernable.

When Wylackie directed the killing of a man named Packwood in 1873, he and one of his men took credit for the killing, but perjured "self-defense" testimony easily freed them. When a settler named Grieves testified for the prosecution, Wathen had him killed also. A principal witness in the case was paid to leave the county, but when he did so Wylackie was close behind and reportedly ambushed him on the trail.

George White, a large land owner and stock-raiser, was the king of Round Valley (below) and a vast surrounding area. This newspaper sketch shows him as he appeared in the 1890's. *Sketch from an undated newspaper clipping in the author's collection. Photo courtesy Rena Lynn.*

On October 13, 1879 Constable William Host found evidence of a rustled steer in the woods near Mendocino City. Securing aid, the investigating posse was ambushed by four outlaws who had planned to rob the sheriff after a tax-collecting trip. Two of the posse were killed and others wounded, but other posses were quickly formed on the trail. The manhunt, one of the longest in California history, resulted in the capture or killing of all the outlaws after a chase lasting some eight weeks. In a curious exhibition of civic virtue, Wathen was a member of the posse, as was a young man named Clarence White, a relative of Wylackie's employer.

Clarence White, the killer of Wylackie John. *Courtesy John Keller.*

Wathen soon discarded his Indian family and had affairs with several settler's wives. He sought to make his liason with Mrs. Thomas McPherson more convenient and talked her husband into moving closer to Wathen's home ranch in which he and George White were partners. When he began courting Ellen Anthony he discarded Mrs. McPherson, but he had already destroyed her marriage. The couple separated and their two children were sent off to live with McPherson's brother. Later when he tried to talk to his wife, she pulled a pistol on him and in the resulting struggle McPherson shot and killed her. The rancher fled, threatening to kill Wathen and several others whom he blamed for ruining his home. He was later killed by some of Wylackie's henchmen.

In 1880 Wathen married Ellen Anthony and began raising another family. By 1885 the couple had four children, all of whom were mentioned in George White's will.

In 1881 the two Van brothers took up sheep ranching in George White's section of Trinity County. One night Wylackie John gathered together a group of his men and surrounded the newcomer's cabin. Whooping and yelling like Indians, they opened fire and drove the frightened sheepmen from the area. A nearby rancher named Nowlin had refused to come along on the expedition and had talked so vehemently against the raid that Wylackie decided he must be done away with. When Nowlin still wouldn't leave after his home was burned and his property stolen or scattered, a gunman was sent to kill him. Nowlin killed the gunman instead, but Wylackie's men made the killing look like murder and Nowlin was sent to prison. He was later released when new evidence was brought out.

Sheepman George Ericson also got in White's way. When Ericson began acquiring more land in 1882 and '83, Wathen was directed to run him out of the area. Ericson's stock was rustled and chased away, his fences were torn down and various false charges were filed against him. The financial strain of all this nearly ruined the rancher, but he stayed and defied the brutal White. When a killer was sent to murder him, Ericson ran him off in a hail of bullets only to find himself charged with assault. In September of 1886 Ericson was finally ambushed and killed. His murderer actually sold his family the lumber with which to construct his casket!

When George White decided to get rid of his third wife, a second cousin named Frankie White, she countersued and the case dragged on for five years. Wylackie John trumped up a variety of adultery charges and perjured testimony to bolster his boss's case and incurred the enmity of his wife's family. Clarence White, a local rancher who had ridden with Wathen's posse in 1879, was a brother of Frankie's and was outraged at the charges being leveled at his sister. Threats were exchanged between Clarence and Wathen and on the afternoon of January 2, 1888, the trouble reached a boiling point.

Frankie White's divorce proceedings set in motion events leading to the death of Wylackie John. *Courtesy the late Estle Beard.*

Wylackie was escorting a woman of questionable reputation into the courtroom as a witness when he met Clarence White in a hallway. The two men exchanged angry words and reached for their pistols. Wathen's hung up in his heavy overcoat and White swiftly drilled him with one well-placed shot in the head. The coroner's report was published in the Ukiah *Dispatch Democrat* of January 27, 1888:

> The ball that killed John D. Wathen entered about an inch posterior and one and a half inches above the outer point of the left eye, and lodged in the skull on the opposite side, whence it was then taken. He lived about an hour...

Clarence White was easily acquitted of any blame in the killing, while the settlers of the area were delighted that one of the worst of the local gunmen was gone. Even the judge celebrated the verdict in one of the local saloons and was nearly arrested for his intemperance. George White later stated that a doctor had testified that Wylackie's head wound indicated he could not have seen his slayer when he was shot. Clarence White responded angrily to the charge:

> George White knows that to be a lie. There was no such testimony adduced, as any one can see who takes the trouble to examine it. If there had been do you suppose the jury would have returned within eight minutes with a verdict of not guilty?

Wylackie John was gunned down in the hallway of this Covelo saloon when he tried to pull his pistol on Clarence White. *Courtesy Robert Lee.*

...I might call to mind a certain time when he (George White) offered great inducements to me to kill D.T. Woodman so that he could take his stock. Also another time when he offered me $1,000 to kill Ben Arthur. Another time he proposed to me to kill George Geary...and...Tom Hayden...I asked him why he did not do it himself, and he said that if he killed a man it would cost him $100,000 to get out of it, but that if he got some one else to do it he could get the person cleared for a trifle...

Wylackie John Wathen was buried in the Covelo cemetery. It was the beginning of the end of George White's ranching empire as his many divorce cases and other trials brought out so much testimony against him that he never regained the hold he once held on his vast ranching domain. He died in 1902, bringing an end to one of the most murderous episodes of California history.

PRINCIPAL SOURCES ─────────────────

Carranco, Lynwood and Beard, Estle, *Genocide and Vendetta,* Norman, Okla., Univ. of Okla. Press, 1981; Keller, John, *The Saga of Round Valley, Last of the West,* Ukiah, Mendocino Co. Hist. Soc., 1976; Keller, John, *The Mendocino Outlaws,* Fort Bragg, Mendocino Co. Hist. Soc., 1974; Lynn, Rena, *The Stolen Valley,* Willits, L & S Pub., 1977; Palmer, Lyman, *History of Mendocino County, California,* San Francisco, Alley, Bowen & Co., 1880; San Francisco *Daily Morning Call,* Oct. 21, Nov. 4, 1895; Ukiah *Dispatch Democrat,* Jan. 27, June 3, 1888; San Francisco *Examiner,* Feb. 5, 19, Mar. 22, 1888; Correspondence and research materials from the late Estle Beard, Covelo, California.

GEORGE WORK

Born in New York state about 1805, George Work came to California in 1848 in the vanguard of the great gold rush. He was mining in Tuolumne County when he married a young Mexican woman named Gregoria Garcia. The couple made their home in Sonora where their son was born in September of 1849.

Work was elected the first sheriff of Tuolumne County in April of 1850. The Foreign Miners Tax Law had recently been enacted requiring all foreign miners to pay an assessment and there was widespread opposition to the law's enforcement. The tax collector, Lorenzo A. Besancon, fixed May 13th as the deadline for payment or the claim owner would be forced to cease operations. By May 12th, a Sunday, Sonora was filled with angry, armed foreign miners and the new sheriff was first put to the test as noted by a visiting newspaper correspondent:

> . . . In the evening the sheriff, Mr. Work, was accosted by a Mexican who asked him if he was . . . the officer who intended to enforce the payment of the license. On replying that he was, the Mexican made an attempt to stab him, when a person standing by, named Clark, with a single stroke of a bowie knife, nearly severed his head from his body. Thirty armed Americans soon arrived from Mormon Gulch and the whole American population were on the alert all night.

Feeling was running so high that Work assembled a large posse to accompany the tax collector on his rounds. An account in the Stockton *Times* on June 1st noted that Work's posse consisted of some 500 men and it was only by forceful and overbearing means that serious conflicts were avoided. At the end of his collecting journey, Besancon refused to turn over some $13,000 worth of collections, claiming expenses in maintaining the sheriff and his posse. During this period Work attempted to disarm a drunken foreigner in the street of Sonora and was almost stabbed from behind. Once again the sheriff was saved when his assailant was stabbed by an American.

Tuolumne County scarcely had time to settle down when four Mexicans were brought into town by a group of Americans who charged them with murdering two miners. They had been interrupted while trying to burn the bodies. Immediately a large crowd assembled and as details of the crime were circulated, cries of "String 'em up," were heard. When a rope was passed around the situation became increasingly ugly as recorded in the Sonora *Herald* of July 13, 1850:

George Work helped bring law and order to old Sonora. *From a lithograph in California State Library.*

> ... Our active and worthy sheriff, George Work, declared that the first man
> who interfered with the prisoners, while they were in his charge, should do
> so only at the peril of his life. Judge Marvin... begged the multitude to
> allow the law to take its regular course...

Despite the sheriff's determination, the crowd was so noisy and unruly that
Justice of the Peace Richard C. Barry found it impossible to function and
retired for a consultation. While the court was in recess, the mob seized the four
prisoners and took them off to be tried by "Judge Lynch." They were found
guilty and were actually under the tree where they were to be hanged when
Sheriff Work, deputy Bill Ford and two judges rode into the crowd and seized
the ropes. The officers made pleas for the men's lives and for allowing the law to
take its course, then galloped off for jail with the prisoners. It was later proven
that the men were innocent and had merely discovered the bodies and were
burning them as a sanitation measure.

Judge Barry, a former Texas Ranger, was a curious character who ruled as
much from his own sense of right and wrong as from any law book in his
possession. When Sheriff Work brought Jesus Ramirez before him for stealing

319

Work's mule, Barry found the prisoner guilty. He was sentenced to pay court costs plus one hundred dollars, but it was quickly discovered that he had no money. "I rooled," wrote Judge Barrry in his court docket, "that George Work should pay the costs of coort as well as the fine, and in default of payment that the said mare mule be sold...to meet the expenses of the...coort."

When Sheriff Work arrested John Wilson for the murder of George Palmer in April of 1851, crowds again assembled for a lynching party. Work managed to foil the crowd's intentions, but Wilson later managed to escape and fled the area. He was recaptured in Los Angeles in early August while using the name of Thornley and was soon back again in Sheriff Work's "hotel."

On June 15, 1851, the sheriff rushed into a saloon where a fight was taking place among the crowd of some fifty Chilenos. Work tried to separate the combatants only to have them turn on him as reported in the diary of a Sonora merchant:

> ...With some difficulty Mr. Work parried the thrusts of the knives and extricated himself from the infuriated crowd. Once outside he stopped, and turned around, and seeing a man advancing upon him with a knife, drew his pistol and shot him dead. The police coming to the assistance of the [sheriff] a fight took place, in which as one party had revolvers and the other only knives, the Chilenos, although more numerous, got worsted, three of them being killed outright, two mortally wounded, and several slightly wounded...

When a notorious thief and killer named Jim Hill robbed a store at Campo Seco, he was quickly captured by Work and several deputies at a Sonora brothel. Fearing trouble because of Hill's bad reputation, the sheriff took him to Campo Seco for trial, but upon arrival the prisoner was seized by a mob that immediately tried him as noted in the Sonora *Herald* of July 5, 1851:

> It was voted to hang the prisoner in an hour and a half, and a committee of five were appointed to confer with him and endeavor to obtain disclosures in reference to others and their whereabouts. In this they were successful.

Work and several deputies stood by as a scaffold and grave were prepared, but when they saw the ardor of the mob had subsided somewhat, they rushed in, seized Hill and raced back towards Sonora with the prisoner in a cart. Alerted to the sheriff's intentions, a crowd was waiting for him in Sonora. When the mob shouted and ran after the cart, Work smashed into a lampost and had to make a run for the jail. Although a hundred pistols were drawn, no one wanted to shoot the brave sheriff. "I was standing in front of the store when they passed," wrote merchant William Perkins. "The form of the prisoner I shall never forget. His body was bent, probably to escape a bullet, and his head pushed forward as he strained every nerve in the fearful race."

Pistol in hand the sheriff dragged his prisoner to the very door of the jail only to find his way blocked by a Colonel Cheatham. With the mob closing in and

Cheatham blocking the jail entrance with a cocked pistol in his hand, Work looked about desperately for help. "It's no use George," panted Deputy Bill Ford. "We have done all we can." The prisoner was surrendered and immediately lynched.

When the sheriff had to hang a horse thief named Jose Corrales in early January of 1852, a witness reported the lawman broke down and covered his face with his hands. The prisoner was hanged from a tree with a platform contructed beneath it.

Work was no longer sheriff when he visited Adamsville in early August of 1854. The new County of Stanislaus had been created just a month earlier and the rough village of Adamsville was the county seat. Work was in town to attend the trial of his friend Thomas Leggett who was contesting the election of Judge H.W. Wallis. The two men had run for the office of county judge and bitter wrangling had resulted from a very close contest. When the case decided for Wallis, partisans continued drinking and arguing the case in the local saloons. One account states that Work had been drinking freely on August 7th and after an argument with a man named Early Lyons the two men agreed to step into the street in front of the local hotel and fight a duel. A letter published in the Stockton *San Joaquin Republican* gave a more detailed account:

> ...It appears that Lyons had been very quarrelsome for the last three or four days and at the time was in a difficulty with some person residing at the county seat, and Mr. Work endeavored to pacify him, upon which Lyons raised his pistol and fired two shots at Work, each of which entered his breast near the heart. Work fired four shots before he fell to the ground. Lyons immediately walked away to the blacksmith shop, about fifty yards from where Work fell, took the double barrelled shot gun and fled...

Work died the following day. No one attempted to stop Lyons who disappeared later along the river. No trace of him was ever found. Lyons had killed a man named Dr. Fredonia in Stockton the previous year and had bragged about other killings. He had been one of the first residents of Tulare County in 1852.

Work was not returned home to Sonora for burial. He was a brave and concientious lawman who brought the law to early Tuolumne County only to die in a trivial and senseless brawl.

PRINCIPAL SOURCES

Brotherton, I.N., *Annals of Stanislaus County,* Santa Cruz, Western Tanager Press, 1982; Buckbee, Edna Bryan, *The Saga of Old Tuolumne,* N.Y., Press of the Pioneers, Inc., 1935; Elias, Sol P., *Stories of Stanislaus,* Modesto, priv. pub., 1924; Lang, Margaret Hanna, *Early Justice in Sonora,* Sonora, Mother Lode Press, 1963; Perkins, William, *William Perkins' Journal,* Berkeley and Los Angeles, Univ. of Cal. Press, 1964; Stoddart, Thomas Robertson, (ed. and annotated by Carlo M. De Ferrrari) *Annals of Tuolumne,* Sonora, Tuolumne Co. Hist. Soc., 1963; San Francisco *Daily Alta California,* May 28, July 19, 1850, Aug. 11, 1854; Sonora *Herald,* July 13, 1850, Apr. 26, May 31, 1851; Stockton *San Joaquin Republican,* July 2, 1851; Stockton *Times,* May 25, 1850; 1850 Tuolumne County Census.

BIBLIOGRAPHY

Although book-length studies of early California lawmen, badmen or outlaws are few in number, the general topic has been touched on in express company literature, many local histories and various biographical works. What little published material there is on the subject runs the gamut from such entertaining and well-researched books as Richard Dillion's *Wells, Fargo Detective,* to the scatterbrained autobiography of convict Ed Morrell titled, *The 25th Man.* In between is sandwiched the sum of our published knowledge on this little-chronicled early California theme.

Probably one of the more intriguing works in the genre is the autobiogaphy of Charles Mortimer, published in Sacramento in 1873. Although an obscure item today, it is a haunting study of a life-long criminal written as he waited to be hanged. The insights into the law-breaker's mind, as well as the chilling recounting of numerous acts of larceny and murder make it a classic of its kind. Mortimer's personality would have been a delight to a modern psychologist and the horrifying climax to his story, when his brother tries to rescue him and is killed, proves once again that truth is often stranger than fiction.

Much of this field of literature must be read with caution, however. Although long held up as the epitome of scholarship on the California outlaw, Joseph Henry Jackson's *Bad Company* turns out, under close scrutiny, to be seriously flawed in certain areas with poor research and misinformation. Not content with garbling history by a lack of dates and muddled research, Jackson seemed obsessed with creating his own version of history by promoting a personal theory that Joaquin Murrieta was a myth. His tenet was eagerly accepted by other writers and historians as fact, discouraging research on the subject for many years. Jackson must be given credit, however, for the first serious attempt at research on some of his subjects.

Fortunately, the quality of work on the subject is improving. Roger McGrath's recent *Gunfighters, Highwaymen and Vigilantes* is a thorough and enlightening treatise of the badmen of Aurora, Nevada, and Bodie. Likewise, John Boessenecker's *Badge and Buckshot* is the most authorative work yet done on a select group of early California lawmen and outlaws.

The following bibliography of early California lawman—outlaw literature, although by no means complete, represents the main body of work on the subject to date. Many of these volumes were used in the preparation of this work, while others were not. Various county histories and other works with only minor reference to the subject are not included. What is listed here can be rated from excellent to poor, although most have contributed in some fashion to the authentic history, or the legend, of the lawmen and desperadoes of California's frontier days.

Anderson, Frank W., *Bill Miner, Stagecoach and Train Robber,* Surrey, B.C. Heritage House Pub. Co., Ltd., 1968.

Angel, Myron, *History of Placer County, California,* Oakland: Thompson and West, 1882

Asbill, Frank, and Argle Shawley, *The Last of the West,* New York, Carlton Press, 1975.

Asbury, Herbert, *The Barbary Coast,* N.Y.: Alfred A., Knopf, Inc., 1933

Bancroft, Hubert Howe, *California Pastoral,* San Francisco: History Co., Pub., 1888

————, *Popular Tribunals,* (two volumes), San Francisco: History Co., Pub., 1887

Bell, Horace, *On the Old West Coast,* N.Y.: Grosset & Dunlap, 1930

————, *Reminiscences of a Ranger,* Santa Barbara: Wallace Hebberd, 1927

Block, Eugene B., *Great Stagecoach Robbers of the West,* N.Y.: Doubleday & Co., 1962

Boessenecker, John, *Badge and Buckshot: Lawlessness in Old California,* Norman: Univ. of Okla. Press, 1988

Boggs, Mae Helene, *My Playhouse Was a Concord Coach,* Oakland: Howell-North, 1942

Buckbee, Edna Bryan, *The Saga of Old Tuolumne,* N.Y.: Press of the Pioneers, 1935

Buchanan, A. Russell, *David S. Terry of California, Dueling Judge,* San Marino, Calif.: Huntington Library, 1956

Burns, Walter Noble, *The Robin Hood of El Dorado,* N.Y.: Coward McCann, Inc., 1932

Cain, Ella M., *The Story of Bodie,* San Francisco: Fearon Pub., 1956

Carranco, Lynwood, and Estle Beard, *Genocide and Vendetta,* Norman: Univ. of Okla. Press, 1981

California's Age of Terror, Murieta and Vasquez, Hollister: Evening Free Lance, 1927

Chalfant, W.A., *Gold, Guns and Ghost Towns,* Stanford: Stanford Univ. Press, 1947

————, *The Story of Inyo,* Los Angeles: Citizens Print Shop, 1933

Coblentz, Stanton A., *Villains and Vigilantes,* N.Y.: Thomas Yoseloff, 1957

Cossly-Batt, Jill L., *The Last of the California Rangers,* N.Y. and London: Funk & Wagnalls Co., 1928

Cunningham, J.C., *The Truth About Murietta,* Los Angeles: Wetzel Pub. Co., 1938

The Death Penalty, the Men Who have suffered it at San Quentin Prison, no author or publisher given, 1903.

Dillon, Richard, *Wells, Fargo Detective,* N.Y.: Coward-McCann, 1969

Doctor, Joseph, *Shotguns on Sunday,* Los Angeles: Westernlore Press, 1958

Duke, Thomas S., *Celebrated Criminal Cases of America,* San Francisco: James H. Barry Co., 1910

Edwards, Harold L., *The Killing of Jim McKinney,* Porterville: Edwards Book Pub., 1988

Ellis, Henry Hiram, *From the Kennebec to California,* Los Angeles: Warren F. Lewis, Pub., 1959

Fanning, Pete, *Great Crimes of the West,* San Francisco: pub. by the author, 1929

Fargo, Frank F., *A Full and Authentic Account of the Murder of James King, of Wm., Editor of the San Francisco Evening Bulletin, by James P. Casey, . . . ,* San Francisco: J.W. Sullivan, 1856

Ford, Tirey L., *California State Prisons, Their History, Development and Management,* San Francisco: James H. Barry Co., 1910

Friedman, Lawrence M., and Robert V. Percival, *The Roots of Justice: Crime and Punishment in Alameda County, California, 1870 - 1910,* Chapel Hill: Univ. of N. C. Press, 1981

Glasscock, C.B., *Bandits and the Southern Pacific,* N.Y.: Grosset and Dunlap, 1929

Gray, Henry M., *Judges and Criminals, Shadows of the Past,* San Francisco: printed for the author, 1858

Greenwood, Robert, (compiler), *The California Outlaw, Tiburcio Vasquez,* Los Gatos: Talisman Press, 1960

Greer, James Kimmins, *Colonel Jack Hays, Texas Frontier Leader and California Builder,* Waco, Texas: W.M. Morrison, Pub., 1973

Hansen, Gladys, and Frank R. Quinn, *Behind the Silver Star, An Account of the San Francisco Police Department,* San Francisco: San Francisco Archives, 1981

Harlow, Alvin F., *Old Waybills,* N.Y., London: D. Appleton-Century Co., 1934

Hoffer, Dominga L. Cervantes, *Tiburcio Vasquez—Bandit,* Puyallup, Wash.: Historic Memories Press, 1964

Hughes, Guy, *Battle of the Joss House,* N.Y.: Carlton Press, 1968

Hume, James B., and John N. Thacker, *Report of Jas. B. Hume and Jno. N. Thacker, Special Officers, Wells, Fargo & Co.'s Express, Covering a Period of Fourteen Years, Giving Losses by Train Robbers, Stage Robbers and Burglaries, and a Full Description and Record of All Noted Criminals Convicted of Offenses Against Wells, Fargo & Company Since November 5th, 1870,* San Francisco: H.S. Crocker & Co., 1885

Jackson, Joseph Henry, *Bad Company,* N.Y.: Harcourt, Brace and Co., 1949

Keller, John, *The Mendocino Outlaws,* Fort Bragg: Mendocino Co. Hist. Soc., 1974

————, *The Saga of Round Valley, Last of the West,* Ukiah: Mendocino Co. Hist. Soc., 1976

Lamott, Kenneth, *Chronicles of San Quentin,* N.Y.: David McKay Co., Inc., 1961

Lang, Margaret Hanna, *Early Justice in Sonora,* Sonora: Mother Lode Press, 1963

Latta, Frank F., *Dalton Gang Days,* Santa Cruz: Bear State Books, 1976

————, *Joaquin Murrieta and His Horse Gangs,* Santa Cruz: Bear State Books, 1980

————, *Tailholt Tales,* Santa Cruz: Bear State Books, 1976

List of Convicts on Register of State Prison at San Quentin, Sacramento: State Printing Office, 1889

Mather, R.E., and F.E. Boswell, *Hanging the Sheriff, A Biography of Henry Plummer,* Salt Lake City: Univ. of Utah Press, 1987

————, *Gold Camp Desperadoes,* San Jose: History West Pub., 1990

Maxwell, Hu, *Evans & Sontag,* San Francisco: San Francisco Printing Co., 1893 (re-published in 1981 with much added material and new illustrations, by Panorama West Books, Fresno)

McGowan, Edward, *The Narrative of Edward McGown, Including a Full Account of the Author's Adventures and Perils While Persecuted by the San Francisco Vigilance Committee in 1856,* San Francisco: pub. by the author, 1857

McGrath, Roger D., *Gunfighters, Highwaymen & Vigilantes,* Berkeley, Los Angeles, London: Univ. of Calif. Press, 1984

MacLean, Angus, *Legends of the California Bandidos,* Fresno: Pioneer Pub. Co., 1977

Morrell, Ed., *The Twenty-Fifth Man,* Montclair, N.J., New Era Publishing Co., 1924.

Mortimer, Charles (Charles J. Flinn), *Life and Career of the Most Skillful and Noted Criminal of His Day, Charles Mortimer,* Sacramento: William H. Mills & Co., 1873

Mullen, Kevin J., *Let Justice be Done,* Reno & Las Vegas, University of Nevada Press, 1989.

Myers, John Myers, *San Francisco's Reign of Terror,* Garden City, N.Y.: Doubleday & Co., Inc., 1966

Nadeau, Remi, *City Makers,* N.Y.: Doubleday & Co., 1948

————, *The Real Joaquin Murieta,* Corona del Mar: Trans-Anglo Books, 1974

Newmark, Harris, *Sixty Years in Southern California,* N.Y.: Houghton Mifflin Co., 1930

Pauley, Art, *Henry Plummer, Lawman and Outlaw,* White Sulphur Springs, Mont.: Meagher County News, 1980

Pitt, Leonard, *The Decline of the Californios,* Berkeley: Univ. of Calif. Press, 1970

Ridge, John Rollin (Yellow Bird), *The Life and Adventures of Joaquin Murieta,* Norman: Univ. of Okla. Press, 1955

Rivors, C., *A Full and Authentic Account of the Murders of James King, of Wm., Dr. Randall, Dr. Baldwin, West and Marion, etc.,* Rochester, N.Y.: E. Darrow & Brother, 1857

Romero, Michael, *Joaquin Murrieta: The Life of a Legend,* San Jose: Priv. pub., 1979

Ross, Dudley, T., *Devil on Horseback,* Fresno: Valley Pub., 1975

Sawyer, Eugene T., *Life and Career of Tiburcio Vasquez, The California Bandit and Murderer,* San Jose: priv. pub., 1875

Sargent, A.A., *Narrative of the Life and Adventures of Major C. Bolin, Alias David Butler, etc.,* Nevada City: priv. printed, 1858

Secrest, William B., *Dangerous Men,* Fresno: Saga West Pub. Co., 1967

————, *The Great Yosemite Holdups,* Fresno: Saga West Pub. Co., 1968

————, *Joaquin, Bloody Bandit of the Mother Lode,* Fresno: Saga West Pub. Co., 1967

Senkewicz, S.J., Robert M., *Vigilantes in Gold Rush San Francisco,* Stanford: Stanford Univ. Press, 1985

Shinn, Charles Howard, *Graphic Description of Pacific Coast Outlaws,* Los Angeles: Westernlore Press, 1958

Smith, Wallace, *Prodigal Sons,* Boston, Mass.: Christopher Pub. House, 1951

Stewart, George R. *Committee of Vigilance: Revolution in San Francisco, 1851,* Boston: Houghton Mifflin, 1964

Truman, Major Benjamin C., *Life, Adventures, and Capture of Tiburcio Vasquez; The Great California Bandit and Murderer,* Los Angeles: Los Angeles Star, 1874

Walter, William W., *The Great Understander,* Aurora, Ill.: priv. pub., 1931

Warner, Opie L., *A Pardoned Lifer,* San Bernardino: Index Print, 1909

Williams, Mary Floyd, *History of the San Francisco Committee of Vigilance of 1851,* Berkeley: Univ. of Calif. Press, 1921

Wilson, Neil C., *Silver Stampede,* N.Y.: MacMillan Co. 1937

_____, *Treasure Express,* N.Y.: The MacMillan Co., 1936

Wood, R.E., ed., *Life and Confessions of James Gilbert Jenkins; The Murderer of Eighteen Men, Etc.,* Napa: pub. by C.H. Allen and R.E. Wood, 1864

Wood, Raymund F., *Mariana La Loca, Prophetess of the Cantua & Alleged Spouse of Joaquin Murrieta,* Fresno: Fresno Co. Hist. Soc., 1970

Wood, Richard Coke, *Calaveras, The Land of Skulls,* Sonora: Mother Lode Press, 1955

INDEX

[Cities, towns and a few other geographical locations, not otherwise identified, are all in California.]

Adams, ————: 258
Adams, George: 168
Adamsville: 321
Ager: 293
Ahern, William: 57
Ahwahnee: 47
Alameda: 172
Alameda County: 13, 64, 66, 67, 102, 229, 230, 231, 247, 302, 304
Alameda County Supervisors: 232
Albuquerque, N. M: 143
Aldrich, Dan: 242
Alexander, David: 178
Alila train robbery: 108, 109, 120, 178
Allison, H.I: 178
Alsace area of Germany: 137
Alveso, ————: 278
Alveto, Pancho: 150
Alvitre, Felipe: 61, 62
Amador County: 53, 185, 191, 295, 299, 301
American River: 31, 32
Anderson, George: 223
Anderson, Joseph: 59, 174, 215
Anderson, Marshal: 32
Anderson, William: 241
Andrus, Elisha: see "Bigfoot"
Angel Island: 17
Angels Camp: 190
Ansbro, Thomas: 15, 196
Anthony, Ellen: 314
Antone: 299
Apache Indians: 70, 152
"A Pardoned Lifer": 97
Ardaga, Sylvester: 164
Ardillero, Francisco: 132, 135
Ardinger, W.O: 178
Argrave, W.W: 39
Arizona: 19, 86, 116, 140, 148, 170, 184, 212, 225, 261
Arnett, ————: 67
Arroyo Burro Ranch: 270
Arthur, Ben: 317
Ashurst, John: 276

Astares, Jesus: 65
Atkins, Sam: 285
Auburn: 31, 32, 34, 35, 36, 38
Aull, Charles: bio sketch, 25-30; 96, 97, 116, 117, 129, 130, 139, 221
Austerman, Wayne: 9
Austin, Nevada: 244
Australia: 192, 243
Azoff, Alexander: 171, 172
Azusa Valley: 143

Bad Company: 323
Badge and Buckshot: 323
Bagley, J.W: 77, 78
Baker, Captain: 237
Baker, Charles: 133
Baker's ranch: 86
Bakersfield: 8, 15, 16, 68, 128, 210, 212, 304
Bancroft, Hubert H: 11
Bannack, Montana: 267
Banning, Phineas: 179
Barbour County, Ala: 285
Barcenas, Francisco: 67, 302
Barnes, George E: 160
Barron, George: 210
Barry, Richard: 319-320
Barter, Richard A: bio. sketch, 31-36
Barton, Sheriff James: 62, 133, 180, 227
Basque cattle buyers: 271
Bay State Ranche: 248
Beale Memorial Library: 8
Bealova, Jesus: 297
Bean, General Joshua: 177, 248
Bear River: 32
Bear Valley: 89, 90, 93, 137
Beard, Estle: 9
Beaver, Oscar: 122, 280
Becker, Charles: 201
Becker, Olive: 191
Beckwourth, Jim: 70
Bee, A.W: 34, 35
Beers, George: 164, 305
Behan, Sheriff John: 253

329

Belcher, Lewis: 74
Bell, Horace: 178, 180, 225, 227, 228, 270, 273, 286
Bell, Tom: 14; bio. sketch, 37-42; 43, 170, 257-58, 261, 263, 287
Bellingham, Wa: 222
Bells Corners, Canada: 120
Belmont: 236
Belt, George G: 42, 215, 218
Belton, Mo: 106
Ben Ali: 55
Benitez, Ana: 248
Bennett, Mrs. Mary: 205, 206
Bennett, Winston: 207
Benson, Robert: 285
Berkeley: 7, 186
Bernhard, Dr: 188
Berrigan, William: 140
Berry, Jack: 53
Berryessa, Encarnacion: 132
Besancon, Lorenzo A: 318
Bicuna, Blas: 304
"Big Dick": 173
Big Lake: 85
Big Oak Flat: 286
Big Oak Flat Road: 43
"Bigfoot," Elisha Andrus: 310
Bigler, Joseph: 89, 90
Bigler, Margaret: 93
Bilderain, Jesus: 162, 163
Billman murder case: 193
Bingham, C.E: 205
Black Bart: 11, 14, 15, 43, 47, 103, 118, 130, 184, 232, 292, 293, 299, 300; *see also* Bolton and Boles, Charles
"Black Bess": 91
"Black Jack," John Bowen: 236
Black Kid, The: bio. sketch, 43-47
"Black Knight of the Zayante": 206
Black, Sam: 281
Blackburn, Sheriff John: 267
Blanco, Miguel: 271, 272
Blasdel, Nevada Governor: 194
Bliven home: 112
Bliven, Clark: 107
Bliven, Jane: 107
Bliven ranch: 107
Bludworth, Charles: 205
Boessenecker, John: 7, 8, 323
Boesque, Bertha: 252
Bodie: 253
Bogard, Sheriff John: 56, 145, 146
Boggs, John: 34, 35, 36, 41, 258
Bojorques, Narciso: 66, 229, 230
Boles, Charles E: bio. sketch, 48-52; 184
Boles, David: 48
Boles, Robert: 48
Bolger, Pete: 280
Bolton, Charles E: 50, 51; *see also* Black Bart

Bonds, W: 173
Bonney case: 199
Booth, Gov. Newton: 16, 84, 102, 232, 305
Boot Hill: 156
Borax Lake: 85
Borgwardt, Sheriff: 108
Boston, Mass: 14, 235, 252
Bottellier, Joaquin: 204, 249
Boulder Creek: 171
Bounty hunters: 144, 153, 275, 281
Bovee, James: 15, 19
Bowen, John: *see* "Black Jack"
Bowers, Sheriff: 84
Bowery: 268
Bowles: 48
Brace, Philander: 192
Brady, Jack: bio. sketch, 53-58; 146
Brevoort, E: 178
Briarre, Frank: 96
Briggs, H.W: 174
British Columbia: 144, 223
British Consul at Panama: 194
Bronough, Sheriff William: 221
Brooklyn, N. Y: 101
Broughton, Sheriff Robert: 255
Brown, David: 20; bio. sketch, 59-63
Brown, Jim (alias, Stanton Jones): 221
Brown, Lodi: 310
Brown, Newton: 146
Brown of Calaveras: 285
Brown, Oscar: 53, 55
Brown, Sam: 15, 89, 295
Brown, Thomas: 286
Browne, Juanita: 9
Browning: 53, 55, 56
Brownstone's store: 68
Brownsville, Tx: 203
Bruce, James: 139
Budd, Governor James H: 222
Bullion Bend robbery: 215
Burgos, Luis: 227
Burke, Constable: 130
Burke, Frederick T: 15
Burke, Jim: 13
Burke, Martin: 245
Burns Creek: 249
Burns, James: 163, 165
Burns, Tom: 19, 20, 122, 124, 144, 188, 189, 233, 275
Bush, ——: 165
Bush, Charles: 164
Bustamente, Tomas Procopio: bio. sketch, 64-69; 231, 302, 303
Bustamente, Vicenta: 64
Butte, Montana: 140, 253
Byrd, Perry: 124
Byrd, Molly: 120
Byrnes, William Wallace: 11; bio. sketch, 70-75; 205

Cahuenga Pass: 127
Calaveras County: 14, 51, 89, 221, 246, 248, 257-59, 261, 295, 297, 299, 300
Calaveras County Museum and Archives: 8
Calderwood, Ralph "Scotty": 212
Caliente: 68, 69, 128
"California Billy" (alias, Bill Miner): 221
California mustangs: 271
California Ranch: 16, 27, 304
California Rangers: 23, 71, 204, 205, 249
California State Archives: 7, 22
California State University, Fresno: 8
California Volunteers: 22
Calle de los Negros: 142, 162
Calliaud, Eugene: 175, 217
Camargo, Juan: 67
Camargo, Texas: 203
Camp Babbitt: 216
Campo: 147, 148, 150, 151
Campo Seco: 257, 261, 320
Camptonville: 40, 258
Canada: 31
Canadian Pacific Railroad: 223
Cantatran, Aureillo: 69
Cantua Canyon: 304
Cantua Creek: 13, 64, 72
Cape Horn Mills: 280
Carico, Asa: 37
Carillo, Don Carlos: 270
Carillo, Don Ramon: 65
Carlisle, Robert: 64
Carr, Andy: 173
Carr, Bill: 59
Carr, "English Bob": 38
Carrillo, Joaquin: 204
Carrillo, Jose Antonio: 177
Carson City, Nev: 266, 267
Carson Valley: 70
Carter, William: 32
Carter, Tap: 209, 210
Casebier, Dennis: 9
Casey, James: 243
Casey, James P: bio. sketch, 76-82
Castaic Creek: 126, 127
Castillo, Mary: 7
Castle, Owen: 193
Catabo, Juan: 132, 133
Cavalry: 2nd Calif., 219; 6th U.S., 45; 7th U.S., 11, 120
Central Pacific Railroad: 15, 170
Ceres train robbery: 94, 103, 121, 170, 186, 280
Cerradel, Manuel: 65
Chamberlain, Sam: 59
Chandler, Robert: 7
Chapman, J.M. case: 199
Chapman, Major W.W: 204
Chappel, Jake: 192
Chavez gang: 15, 150

Chavez, Clodoveo: bio. sketch, 83-88; 148, 232, 303
Cheatham, Colonel: 320
"Cherokee Bob" (Henry J. Talbot): 8, 15, 22, 23, 37; bio. sketch, 285-290
Cherokee Indians: 285
"Cherokee Mary": 236
Cheyenne, Wyo: 209
Chicago: 94, 118, 184, 295
Chicago Park: 8
Chihuahua, Mexico: 143
Chilenos: 269, 286
Chinese: 45, 142, 163, 174, 194, 205, 216, 248, 249, 277, 278
Chinese burglars: 198
Chinese Camp: 27
Chinese companies: 276
Choisser, Lafayette: bio. sketch, 89-93
Choisser, Punch: 8
Choisser, Talleyrand: 89, 90
Cholame Valley: 106
Chowchilla Rangers: 90, 91, 92
Chowchilla River: 216
Civil War: 215, 229, 244
Clantons: 261
Clark, ———: 318
Clark, Sheriff Charles A: 257, 258, 295
Clark, Ed: 126
Clark, Captain H.H: 204
Clark, Sheriff John C: 90, 91, 92
Claudio, Captain: 205
Claveras, Manuel: 192
Clemens, Samuel: 21, 236
Cleveland, Jack: 262
Clifford, Pinkney: 61
Clipper Gap train robbery: 170, 292
Cloverdale: 310
Coalinga: 69
Coarsegold: 275
Coarsegold Gulch: 153
Coast range: 274
Coats family: 12
Cochise County, Az: 253
Coffeyville, Kan: 110
Coleman, Tom: 244
Coleman, William T: 80
Collins, John C. (alias, Patterson): 27, 28, 113-116
Collins, Sheriff James D: 104
Collis train robbery: 94, 95, 103, 121, 280, 281
Colorado: 106, 140, 221
Colorado River: 59
Colquhoun, Louis: 223
Colt gun factory: 197
Colusa County: 31, 82
Colvig, Clark: 86, 88
Colville mines: 289
"Comanche Jack": 285
Common Council of Los Angeles: 177
Confederates: 181-82, 199, 215, 218, 229, 154

Connell, Sam: 307
Connor, Ned: 37, 38, 41
Connor, Patrick E: 205
Contant, George C: 23, 29, 30; bio. sketch, 94-100;
    121, 138, 279, 280, 281
Contant, John: 279
Contra Costa County: 132, 286
Conway, Officer: 230
Coon, Police Judge Henry: 20
Cooper, Charles: 219
Copperopolis: 27
Cora, Charles: 80, 243
Corbett, John: 192
Corrales, Jose: 321
Cortez, Jose Luis: 258
Cota, Roma: 150
Cottonwood Station: 86
Coulter, Judge A.H: 298
Covelo: 313
Covelo cemetery: 317
Coyado, Jose: 298
Coyote Holes: 84, 304
Crandall, Mr. and Mrs. E.E: 165-166
Crespo, Jose: 143, 144
"Crime of the Century": 234
Crippen, Sheriff J.D: 90
Crittenden, Sheriff J.L: 274
Crooks, Sheriff A.D: 237
Cross Creek stage station: 109
Croten, Ill: 58
Crow, Vern: 8
Crowley, Chief Patrick: 201, 219
Cruickshanks, Dave: 9
Crumm, Jim: 27, 113, 221
Crutcher, Deputy Sheriff Bill: 35
Cuba: 200
Cummings, William: 28, 114, 117
Cunningham, Judy: 8
Cunningham, Thomas: 56; bio. sketch, 101-105; 232
"Curly Bill": 34
Cushing, Robert: 77, 78
Cynthia: 290

Dabeen, Palacio: 260
Dalton: 30
Dalton, Anthony: 96
Dalton brothers: 106-10, 121, 186
Dalton, Emmett: 112
Dalton, Grat: 110
Dalton, Jane: 108, 109-12
Dalton, Lewis: 106
Dalton Mountain: 110
Dalton, Mason Frakes: bio. sketch, 106-112
Daly, Charles: 133
Daniel, Pancho: 132, 135, 136
Davila, Fernando: 137
Davis, Constable, A.H: 25, 26
Davis, Cliff: 9

Davis, Capt. Jonathan R: 12
Davis, Kip: 9
Davis, Deputy Sheriff L.C: 27
Davisville: 54, 57
Deal, Capt. Sam: 31
Dean, Riley: 109, 110
de Bert, August: 303
Decatur, Ill: 48
De Ferrari, Carlo M: 9
de Guignè, Christian: 9
Delaney, Mickey: 119
Delaware County, N. Y: 181
del Carme, Jose: 21
Del Norte, Colo: 221
Delta: 293
DeLong, Martin: 225, 226, 227
del Valle, Don Ygnacio: 177, 179
DeMattos, Jack: 9
Den, Dr. Nicholas A: 270, 271
Denim, Susan: 205
Dennis, William: 218
Denson, Samuel: 240
Dickens, Charles: 199
Dickson, Billy: 33
Dillon, Richard: 9, 323
Dixon, Al: 174
Donahue iron foundry: 197
Doniphan, Col. A.W: 152
Doolin, Bill: 110
Doolin-Dalton gang: 111
Dorsey, Charles H: 28; bio. sketch, 113-119; 184
Dorsey, John: 59
Douglas, ———: 166
Downey, John G: 177
Downieville: 21
Dowst, Deputy Sheriff Al: 274
Drebellis, Louis: 182
Driscoll, Jim: 33, 36
Dry Creek: 247
Duane, "Dutch Charley": 77
Ducommun, Charles: 227
Duels: 159, 244
Duffield, Milton: 13
Dugan, Mark: 9
Duncan's Mills: 128
Dunlap, Deputy Sheriff: 165
Dunn, William J. "Shorty": 223
Durrant, Theodore: 200, 234
"Dutchman": 154
Dye, Joe: 162, 175

Earps: 11, 14, 253, 261
Edwards (alias, Bill Miner): 223
Edwards, Harold: 9
Edwards, Jeff: 9
Eiverson, Christian: 206, 207
"Elaine" (painting): 200
El Camino Real: 271

El Dorado County: 70, 74, 182, 185
El Monte: 136
El Paso, Tx: 143, 152, 153
Elder, Robert: 9
Elisabeth Owens: 273
Elker, C.G: 280
Elkhorn Ranch and stage station: 174, 216
Ellis, Supervisor: 281
England: 243
English, William: 189
Ensenada, Mexico, jail: 151
Ericson, George: 315
Espinosa, ———: 86
Espinosa, Jose: 132, 135
Estell, James M: 17, 18, 19, 287
Eugenio, Tal: 65
Eureka: 49
Eureka stage: 113
Evans, Christopher: 15, 19, 94, 103, 109; bio. sketch, 120-25; 140, 144, 145, 186, 187, 188, 233, 275, 279, 280, 281, 283, 293
Evans, Eva: 122, 123, 125, 138-140, 280, 283
Evans family: 96, 138
Evans, George: 205
Evans, Molly: 122, 123, 248, 283
Evans, Senator: 231
Evans, William: 186
Ewing, Dr. William: 286

Fair, J.D: 173
Farmersville: 208
Farnsworth brothers: 40, 263
Farnsworth, Miss Millie: 137
Farnum, Dustin: 100
Feliz, Jesus: 249
Feliz, Reyes: 248
Feliz, Rosa: 246, 248
Fellows, Dick: 27; bio. sketch, 126-31; 184
Fernandez, Juan (Spanish John): 38, 41, 42, 258
Ferry, Bob: 236
Field, Supreme Court Justice Stephen: 103, 255
Finn, Robert: 309
Firebaugh's Ferry: 40, 65, 84, 174, 303, 305
Fleeson, Capt. William; 74
Fleming, Jack: 9
Flemming, Wilbur: 288
Flinn, Charles J. (Charles Mortimer): 235
Flinn, Frank: 240
Flinn, William: 239
Florence, Id: 252, 290
Flores bandit gang: 271
Flores, Juan: bio. sketch, 132-36
Folly of a Life of Crime, The: 97, 100
Folsom: 32, 34, 38, 41, 264
Folsom State Prison: 8, 19, 28, 58, 82, 95, 97, 118, 125, 130, 131, 138-40, 281
Fontes, Andres: 133, 136
Forbes' Ranch: 247

Ford, Bill: 319, 321
Foreign Miners Tax Law: 318
Foreman's Ranche: 248
Forest Hill: 258
Fort Brown, Tx: 203
Fort Defiance: 124, 125
Fort Gunnybags: 80
Fort Hill Cemetery: 180
Forts: Jones, 293; Miller, 72, 73; Tejon, 102, 215, 304; Walla Walla, Wa., 289; Yuma, 86, 151
Foster, A.H: 43, 44
Foster, George: 236, 237
Foster, Stephen: 61, 63, 177
Fowler, Sen. Tom: 231
Franks, Sheriff: 129, 130
Franks, U. S. Marshal J.C: 254
Frazee, Ben: 113, 115
Fredericks, William: 29, 96; bio. sketch, 137-41
Fredonia, Dr.: 321
Freeman and Company Express: 193
Fremont, Gen. John C: 89
French, Dep. Sheriff: 92
Frenchman: 150, 164, 271, 298
Fresno: 53, 94, 95, 123-25, 144, 187, 274, 280, 293
Fresno Catholic Calvary Cemetery: 284
Fresno Chinatown: 276, 277, 278
Fresno City: 174
Fresno County: 19, 68, 72, 84, 110, 174, 188, 232, 275
Fresno County Jail: 145, 188, 283
Fresno Public Library: 7
Fresno River: 174
Frost family: 12

Galindo, Francisco: 302
Garcia, Anastacio: 301
Garcia, Gregoria: 318
Garcia, Manuel ("Three-fingered Jack"): 205
Gard, George E: 15, 56, 122; bio-sketch, 142-46; 162-64, 188-89, 275, 281, 293
Garibaldi Mine: 221
Garra Indian uprising: 242
Gaskill, Luman H. and Silas E: bio. sketch, 147-151
Geary, George: 317
Gentry, Al: 309
Gentry, Dr: 135
Gentry, Sheriff Robert: 307
Georgia: 223
Georgia state prison: 224
Gerterio, Romero: 275
Getman, William C: 178
Ghayer, Mrs: 34
Gibson, Frank: 164
Gibson, Mary: 169, 238, 239, 240
Gibson, "Scotty": 221
Gila River: 86, 152, 204
Gilroy: 174, 231, 303
Gladden, Solomon: 69

Glanton, John: 59
Glasgow, Scotland: 192
Glendale: 189, 191
Goddard, Francis: 135
Goff, Linda: 7
Gold Run: 139
Golden Era: 285
Golden Gate Park: 140
Golding, Aaron: 66
Gomez, Francisco: 164
Gomez, Manuel: 304
Gonzales, Pedro: 205
Gonzales, Ricardo: 143, 144
Gonzales, Romulo: 303, 304
Good behavior prison credits: 222
Gordon brothers: 292
Gordon, Jack: 8; bio. sketch, 152-56
Goshen train robbery: 120, 186, 170, 280
Goucher, George: 92, 93
Gould, Judge: 244
Graham, Will Hicks: 11, 15; bio. sketch, 157-61
Grammond, David: 182
Grangeville: 68
Granite Springs Station: 85
Grass Valley: 113, 139, 182
Gray, J.M: 288
Gray, William (alias, Gregg): 199
Great Northern Railroad: 223
Great Panoche Valley: 217
"Greek George": 164, 305
Green, Nat: 38
Green, Sam: 247
Greenhorn Crossing: 34
Greenhorn Mountain: 217
Grieves, Robert: 313
Griggs, Charles: 7
Grijalva, Desidera: 272
Gristy (Bill White): 32, 37
Groupie, Samuel: 154, 156
Grow, Charles: 91
Grub Gulch: 43, 47
Guaymas, Mexico: 69, 170
Guiterrez, Mrs: 125
Gunfighter, Man or Myth, The: 11
Gunfighters, Highwaymen and Vigilantes: 323
Gunn, John: 59

Hackett, George: 50, 184
Haight, Gov. Henry H: 169
Hale, John: 91
Hale, Warden William: 119, 210
Hall, Undersheriff William: 124, 189
Halpin, Pat: 178
Hamilton, Charley: 41
Hamlin, Jack: 285
Hammell, Kate: 142
Hampton, Joe: 27
Hanel, Mary: 8

Hanford: 68, 69, 123
Hanford, ———: 182
Hanlon, Bill: 119
Hannibal, Mo: 52
Hanover, Rita: 8
Hansen, ———: 151
Hardmount, Constable William: 301
Hardy brothers: 132, 133
Hare, E.C: 178
Harlin, Tom: 59
Harmen—Harms: 57
Harral, William: 293
Harrington, "Alkali Jim": 219, 221
Harris, ———: 154
Harris, Emil: 142, 143; bio. sketch, 162-67; 305
Harris, Jack: 172
Harris, Leonard: 15; bio. sketch, 168-72; 238, 280, 310
Harrison, Robert: 32
Harry Morse Agency: 122, 144
Harte, Bret: 285
Hart, G.W: 178
Hartley, Benjamin F: 162, 164, 305
Harvey, Judge Walter: 205
Haskill, N.R: 70, 71
Haswell, C.C: 108
Havilah: 160
Hawkins, Tom: 175, 217
Hawthorne's stage station: 174, 216
Hayden, Tom: 317
Hays, Jack: 17, 37, 74, 152, 241, 242
Hayes, Judge Benjamin: 177, 288
Hayes, Jr., L.H: 9
Healdsburg: 310
Heathen Chinee, The: 285
Heenan, John C: 243
Heenan-Sayers prize fight: 243
Heering, ———: 14
Heinlan, John: 15
Henlinger, Captain: 288
Henry, James: bio. sketch, 173-176; 215-217
Henshaw, Joshua: 153
Hensley, Sheriff John: 110
Herbert, Philemon T: 205
Hereford, T.S: 178
Harmen, Deputy Sheriff John: 275
Hermosillo, Mexico: 64, 69, 170, 273
Hernandez, Estanislaos: 83
Herrick, William: 14, 141
Hickey, Bill: 103, 170
Hickok, Wild Bill: 11, 12
Highbinders: 277
Higuerra, Jose: 301
Hill, Constable Warren: 281
Hill, Jim: 320
Hill, Sarah: 254
Hodges, Thomas (Tom Bell): 287
Hollister: 88

Holt, J.R: 164
Honolulu, Hawaii: 257
Hood, Mrs. Elisabeth: 40, 42
Hope, Dr. Alexander W: 60; bio. sketch, 177-180; 226, 227
Hopkins, Edward: 241, 243
Hopkins, Officer: 245
Hornitos: 92, 249
Host, Constable William: 314
Houx, John: 310
Howard, Bill: 292
Howard, William: 204
"Hounds": 268, 269
Hoyt's: 309
Hughes, Anne: 159
Hulse, Al: 208, 212, 214
Humboldt County: 312
Humboldt County, Nev: 291
Humboldt River, Nev: 291
Hume, James B: 13, 15, 23, 24, 26, 49, 50, 51, 52, 97, 118, 126, 130, 131, 146, 170; bio. sketch, 181-86; 196, 284, 291, 292, 293, 310, 311
Hunsaker, Sheriff William: 150
Hunter, Charlie: 223
Hunter, Edward: 178
Huntington Lake Power Company: 278
Huron: 108

Idaho: 23, 48, 289
Illinois: 90, 173, 208, 215
Illinois Central Railroad: 15
Indian Territory: 53, 106, 107, 109, 110, 112
Indian Wells: 164
Indiana: 28
Ingalls, Oklahoma: 111
Ingham County, Michigan: 219
Ingram, Captain Rufus H: 181
Inyo County: 120, 218, 260
Ireland: 101, 241
"Irish Maggy": 266
Isthmus of Panama: 205

Jackson: 248, 249
Jackson, Andrew: 187
Jackson, Annie Petter: 191
Jackson County, Mo: 106
Jackson, Frederick Eugene: 144; bio. sketch, 187-91; 275
Jackson, John: 59
Jackson, Joseph Henry: 11, 323
Jackson, Tom: 174, 199
James brothers: 11
Jefferson County, N. Y: 48
Jewel, John: 7
Jewett, Philo: 217
Jewett sheep camp: 175, 217
Jewish Home of Peace Cemetery: 167
J.M. Chapman case: 199

Johnson, David: 263
Johnson, Henry J: 15, 182; bio. sketch, 192-96
Johnson, John A: 59
Johnson, Undersheriff George: 35
Johnson, William: 57
Jones, John P: 74
Jones, Abe: 292
Jones Bar: 139
Jones, John: 178
Jones, Pat: 8
Jones, Stanton: see Brown, Jim
Jones' store: 84, 232, 304
Jordan's Museum: 250
Juanita, Tal: 65
Junction House stage station: 36
J.W.Chapman: 215

Kamloops, B. C: 223
Kansas, 106
Kaseburg, Howard: 8
Kasota Junction, Minn: 94
Kasota, Minnesota, train robbery: 121
Kay, Sheriff Eugene: 108, 109, 124
Keagle, Del: 102
Kearney, William "Wooley": 198
Keller, John: 9
Kelly, Mickey: 168
Kennedy, Lorrayne: 8
Kentucky: 113
Kern County: 68, 102, 184, 212, 218, 278
Kern River: 84, 153
Kern River Valley: 175
Kibbee, William C: 74
Kimball, Constable: 170, 310
King, James: 78, 82
King, Tom: 236
Kings River: 84, 304
Kingfisher, Okla: 110
Kingman, Az: 212
Kingston: 84, 232, 304
Klamath County, Oreg: 192
Klamath River: 236
Knight's Ferry: 41
Kraszewski, Miguel: 133

La Lista Blanca, Mexico: 65
Lagrange County, Ind: 181
Laird, E.G: 91, 92
Lameet, William: 199
Lang, William: 247
Lansing, Sheriff James: 168
Laporte: 50
Las Juntas: 16
Lash, David: 39
Lathrop: 103, 255
Latta, Frank: 9, 69
Laurel Hill Cemetery: 202
Lawler, Judge: 202

Lawrence, Joe: 311
Lawson, A.B: 170, 171
LeFevre, Eugene: 194
LeRoy, Billy: 221
Leadville, Colorado: 208
Lebanon, Ohio: 307
Lee, Archy: 199
Lee, Colonel Henry: 290
Lee, J.H: 309
Lees, Isaiah W: 13, 14, 15, 24, 27, 56, 58, 116, 140, 165, 192-94, 196; bio. sketch, 197-202; 234, 244, 245
Leggett, Thomas: 321
Leighton, Morgan: 230
Leiva, Abdon: 83, 84, 303, 304
Leiva, Rosario: 304
Lemon, George Frank: 159
Levy, Jim: 253
Lewis, Mary: 244
Lewiston, Id: 267, 290
Linares, Pio: 271, 272
Lincoln, Abraham: 156
Lincoln, Dr. A.L: 59
Little: 53
Little, William: 133, 178
Lillie, Chris: 241
Little Lake: 12
Little Lake (Inyo Co.): 85
Livermore Valley: 66, 230
Liverpool, England: 229
Lodi: 55
London, England: 9
Lone Pine: 260
Longview, Tx: 111
Lopez, ———: 84
Lopez, Cruz: 86, 148, 150
Lopez, Leonardo: 132, 135
Lopez, Pedro: 132
Lorenzano, Faustino: 302
Los Angeles: 16, 20, 59, 60-62, 65, 69, 84, 102, 112, 119, 127-28, 132, 133, 135, 142, 144-46, 161-62, 164-67, 177, 188, 189, 204, 218, 225, 227, 230, 232, 247, 255, 271, 285, 286, 288, 301, 305, 320
Los Angeles City Council: 164
Los Angeles County: 126, 179, 217
Los Angeles County Jail: 143
Los Angeles Police Force: 162, 164
Los Angeles Public Library: 8
Los Angeles Rangers: 178, 179, 180, 226
Los Angeles River: 225
Louisiana: 82
Louisiana Mounted Volunteers: 241
Louisville, Ky: 116
Love, Henry (Harry): 8, 14, 23, 71, 73, 153; bio. sketch, 203-07; 247, 249, 250
Lovin, Sheriff Henry: 212
Low, Gov. Frederick: 174, 216

Lowell, Mass: 257
Lower California: 148
Lucas, A.J: 165
Lugo, Maria Merced: 63
Lumley, Aubrey: 209
Lynching: 20, 21, 22, 150, 163, 174, 184, 215, 221, 246, 248, 258, 272, 301, 304, 321
Lynn, Mass: 240
Lynn, William: 210, 212
Lynn's Valley: 175, 217
Lyon, "Monte Jack": 38
Lyons, Early: 321
Lyttle, David Y: 126
Lyttle, George B. (Dick Fellows): 126, 130

McBride, Jack: 160
McCandless Gang: 12
McCardle, Deputy Sheriff Ed: 110
McCauley, Ed: 173
McCauley, Thomas: 173, 215
McConnell, Reason: 50, 190
McCormick, Dep. Sheriff: 258
McDonald, Dep. Sheriff Alexander: 57
McDonald, John: 164
McDougall, John: 288
McDowell, Gen. Irvin: 194
McFarlane, Robert: 208, 209
McGinnis, ———: 122
McGinnes, Andrew: 281
McGowan, Judge Edward: 271
McGrath, Roger: 323
McGuire, A.J. "Yank": 160
McGurley, A: 285
McKee, Frank: 309
McKinney, Andrew: 208
McKinney, James O: 15; bio. sketch, 208-14
McLennan, Constable: 298
McManus, G.L: 178
McMasters, Sherman: 253
McNabb, Jack: 244
McNish, Dep. Sheriff: 258
McPherson, Mrs. Thomas: 314

Madera: 100, 274
Maguire, George: 236
Mahoney, Lewis: 193
Mahoney, Ronald: 8
Maine: 235, 262
Majestic: 257
Mallard, Justice Joseph: 204
Malone, John J: 277
Maloney, Tom: 277
"Manilas": 132, 133
Mankato, Minn: 94, 279
Manning, Harry: 119
Maricopa: 210
Mariposa: 73, 90, 247, 298

Mariposa County: 8, 37, 71, 89, 92, 137, 142, 153, 156, 204, 216, 249, 259, 286, 297
Mariposa County Jail: 90
Mariposa Grant: 93
Marker, Thomas: 34
Markham, Gov. Henry: 210
Marple, ————: 70
Marin County: 17, 37, 38
Marshall, Green: 178
Marshall, Joe: 222
Martin, George: 35, 36
Martin, Greg: 9
Marvin, Judge John G: 247, 319
Maryland: 152, 215
Marysville: 32, 40, 53, 113, 291, 296
Mason-Henry gang: 154
Mason, John: 15, 174-76; bio-sketch, 215-218
Mathews, Constable: 298
Maupin, Howard: 296
Maxwell, J.W: 303
Mayfield: 130, 219
Mayfield, Ben: 217, 218
Mayfield, Bill: 262, 267, 290
Mayfield, Jeff: 153, 154
"Mayor of West Fresno": 277
Meade, U.S. Marshal William K.: 170
Meany, Sheriff A.J: 92
Meller County, Mo: 291
Melones Diggings: 286
Mendocino: 147
Mendocino City: 314
Mendocino County: 11, 12, 310, 312
Mendocino Mountains: 312
Merced: 91, 92, 171, 208, 209, 275
Merced County: 107, 112, 174, 175, 209, 217, 274
Merced River: 174, 215, 247
Merced River Canyon: 93
Metzer, Laren: 7
Metzler, Police Detective: 165
Mexican vaqueros: 148
Mexican War: 37, 70, 132, 152, 177, 203, 204, 241, 268
Mexican Yaqui Indian country: 146
Mexico: 39, 60, 69, 86, 150, 151, 212, 225, 227, 228, 247, 273, 288, 302
Michelson, Charles: 141
Michigan: 147, 223
Millard, Dr: 150
Milledgeville City Cemetery: 224
Milledgeville, Ga: 224
Miller, Bill: 27
Miller, Henry: 305
Miller, Jim: 59
Miller, "Joaquin": 281
Miller, William: 221
Millerton: 84, 216, 304
Milquitay Valley: 147

Milton: 27, 49, 50
Milwaukee, Wisconsin: 47
Miner, Ezra A., (Bill): 8, 14, 22, 27, 103; bio. sketch, 219-24; see also "California Billy"; Edwards; Morgan
Miner, Mrs. Harriet J: 219
Minnesota: 94, 280, 281
Mission Dolores: 77, 80, 157, 269
Mission Junction, Canada: 223
Mission San Jose: 229
Missouri: 53, 70, 208
Mitchell, Annie: 8
Mitchell, John: 34
Mitchell, Levi: 156
Mobile, Ala: 203
Modesto: 25, 120, 170, 280
Mojave Desert: 12, 84, 85, 304
Mokelumne Hill: 261, 297
Molino, Andres: 298
Molino, Santiago: 297
Montana: 32, 48, 262
Monteca, Clemente: 21
Montejos, Refugio: 84
Montello, Nev: 292
Monteras, ————: 304
Monterey: 67, 74, 196, 288, 289, 301, 302
Monterey County: 20, 84, 129
Monterey Mission: 288
Montgomery: 160
Montgomery, Sheriff: 115
Moore, A.D: 113
Moore, Ben: 41
Moore, B.F: 258
Moore's Flat: 113
Moore, George: 309
Morales, ————: 296
Morehead, J.C: 60
Morehouse, E.A: 178
Moreno, Atanacio 179; bio. sketch, 225-28
Moreno, Teodoro: 303, 304
Morgan, O: 178
Morgan, William A. (alias, Bill Miner): 224
Mormon Bar: 92
Mormon Gulch: 328
Mormon Station, Nev: 70, 71
Morrell, Ed: 124, 323
Morrisey, John: 243, 244
Morrison, Judge Murray: 78
Morrison, Judge R.N: 157, 159
Morse, Henry Nicholson (Harry): 14, 16, 23, 24, 50, 51, 67, 84, 102, 122, 144; bio. sketch, 229-234; 302, 304
Mortimer, Charles: 21, 169; bio. sketch, 235-40; 323
Moses: 287
Mosher, Dave: 210, 212
Mt. Ophir: 137
Mud springs: 230

Mug shots: 14
Muldoon, J.W: 266
Mulford, Sheriff: 258
Mulligan, Barney: 245
Mulligan, William (Billy): 12, 13; bio. sketch, 241-45
Muriati, Joaquin: 204, 249
Murphy, Captain: 96
Murphys: 246, 247
Murrieta, Joaquin: 11, 14, 15, 16, 23, 64, 69, 71, 72, 73, 74, 153, 204, 231; bio. sketch, 246-50; 302, 323
Mussel Slough Tragedy: 12, 15, 280
Myers, John: 264
Mylar, Isaac: 83

National Archives: 22
Naughton, Charles (alias, Chris Evans): 122
Navarra, Diego: 132
Neagle, David Butler: 103; bio. sketch, 252-256
Neagle, Emma: 252
Nebraska State Prison: 94
Nethercott, Fireman: 56
Nevada: 70, 74, 156, 160, 187, 188, 255, 291, 311
Nevada City: 28, 34, 39, 113, 116, 262, 264-66, 307, 311
Nevada County: 8, 28, 34, 35, 113, 184, 265, 310
Nevada State Prison: 182
New Idria: 17, 303
New Mexico: 140
New Orleans, La: 116, 203, 241
New York: 52, 69, 76, 147, 162, 168, 194, 200, 241, 318
New York City: 157, 159, 229, 243, 244, 268
New Westminister Penitentiary, Canada: 223
Newcomb, George: 110
Newell, Joe: 230
Newman, Maurice: 93
Newmark, Harris: 135
Newton, Adolph: 32
Nichols & Littlefield: 85
Niles Canyon: 64, 247, 250
Nome Lackee: 312
Noriega, Jose Antonio: 271
Norman, Sheriff Tom: 191
North, Hampton: 198
North Hollywood: 191
North San Juan: 307
Northwest Mounted Police: 223
Nowlin, W.L: 315
Nuenes: 65
Nugent, John: 152, 153
Nugent, Police Officer John: 192

Oakhurst, John: 285
Oakland: 172, 229, 234, 256, 286, 294
Oakland Ferry: 193
O'Brien, ———: 264
Ocomorenia, Joaquin: 204, 249
O.K. Corral: 12

Oklahoma: 186
Older, Fremont: 119
Oldham, Lancashire, England: 197
Oliphant, James: 297
Olive, John: 48
Olson, Monna: 9
Olson, Robert A: 9
O'Meara, Roger: 116, 118
Ontario, Canada: 274
Oregon: 139
Oregon Express: 56, 145
Orestimba: 154
Orestimba Creek: 247
Orizaba: 164, 230
Oroville: 39, 50
Ortega, Bartolo "Chano": 66
Ottawa, Canada: 120
Outcasts of Poker Flat, The: 285
Overall, Sheriff Dan: 209
Overend, John: 21
Overland Monthly: 285
Owen, Perris "Texas": 41
Owens, Bill: 15
Owens, Hugh "Bunty": 89, 295
Owens Valley: 160
Owensville: 161
Owsley, Barney: 290

Pacific Mail Steamship Company: 194
Pacific Republic: 215
Packard, City Marshal Jeff: 212
Packwood, ———: 313
Padillo, Isadore: 304
Paine, Mona: 8
Paiute Indians: 74, 177
Palmer, ———: 258
Palmer, George: 320
Panama: 235
Panama, Cal: 16
Panamint: 253
Pardee, Gov. George C: 82
Pares, Louis: 276
Paris Suertè: 14
Parkinson, ———: 288
Pascoe, Sheriff William H: 139, 141
Paso Robles: 107
Passmore, Sheriff Thomas: 260
Paterson, N. J: 197
Patterson (alias, John C. Collins): 28
Patterson, Dr: 188
Patton, Joseph: 74
Paul, Robert Havlin (Bob): 9, 14, 41, 170, 184; bio. sketch, 257-61; 296, 297, 298
Pedlar, Dr. A.J: 46
Pendergast, Senator: 231
Pennsylvania: 223
Peralta, Santos: 271
Pereda, Buenaventura: 200

Perkins, E.H: 189
Perkins, Elijah: 124
Perkins, Richard: 128
Perkins, W.W: 178
Perkins,William: 320
Petaluma: 147
Petersen, Mr: 288
Pfister, Conrad: 235
Pfleugardt, George: 133
Philadelphia: 157
Phillips, Jack: 38, 39, 164, 258
Phillips, John G: 178
Phillips and Weinshench store: 68
Phipps, John: 296
Phoenix, Az: 170
Phoenix Mills: 248
Pico, Andres: 133, 135
Pico, Don Pio: 270
Pima County, Arizona: 170, 261
Pinkerton, Allan: 15
Pinkerton, William: 13, 118, 202
Pinole Valley: 230
Pioche, Nev: 253
Pixley train robbery: 120, 170, 186, 280
Placer City: 31
Placer County: 32, 36, 219
Placerville: 12, 70, 181
Placerville-Nevada road: 181, 182
Platt, C.D: 165
Plattsburg, N. Y: 295
Plessis, New York: 48
Plumer, Jerimiah and Elisabeth: 262
Plumer, William Henry Handy: bio. sketch, 262-67; 290
Point Arena: 49
Point San Quentin: 17, 37, 73
Ponce, Naratto: 230
Pond, Arthur: 221
Pony Express: 14, 194
Pope, ————: 66
Port Huron, Mich: 274
Porterville: 209, 210
Porterville cemetery: 214
Portland, Ore: 125, 222
Posa Chanè: 16, 69, 84
Postal Department of the United States: 51
Potter, A.W: 309
Power, John A: bio. sketch, 268-73
Potter, Elijah: 74
Prassel, Frank R: 11
Pratt, Charlie: 311
Pratt, Mary: 8
Pratt, W.H. & R.H: 31
Prenel, Caroline: 239
Prescott, Az: 253
Prewitt, Bill: 59
Price, Sterling: 70
Princeton: 259

Prison escapes: 29-30, 33, 35, 38, 59, 94, 96, 109, 118, 124, 128, 130, 132, 139, 153, 209, 223, 236, 267, 286-87, 301
Private detectives: 14, 15, 19, 196
Probasco, Donati: 275
Procopio: 15
Prussia: 162
Pueblo de Murrieta: 246
Puente: 179
Pulgas Rancho: 288
Pullam, Captain B.F: 286
Purvis, Sheriff R.B: 104

Quebec, Canada: 31
Quiroz, Ramon: 25-26

Racine, Wisconsin: 280
Radcliffe, Fireman: 108
Radford, Dep. Sheriff: 293
Rady, Constable: 209
Rafael, Huero: 271, 272, 273
Raggio, Luis: 83, 86, 88
Railroad Flat: 298
Rains, John: 61, 65
Ramirez, ————: 40
Ramirez, Jesus: 319
Rancheria: 257
Rand, Justice of the Peace Jasper: 290
Rand, Thomas: 178
Rapelje, Harry: 278
Rapelje, Hiram Lee (Hi): 124, 144, 188, 189; bio. sketch, 274-78; 283
Rapelje, Zella: 278
Rattlesnake Bar: 31
Rattlesnake Dick (alias, Richard Barter): 14, 36
Rawlins, Wyo: 209
Raymond: 43
Red Bluff: 56, 187
Red Horse: 132
Redding: 56, 292, 293
Reddy, Patrick: 161
Rewards: 19, 28, 109, 115, 124, 128, 158, 184, 188, 194, 205, 216, 221, 227, 233, 249, 250, 263, 272, 281, 293, 304, 307, 309
Rhodes, ————: 12, 242
Rice, ————: 292
Rickards, Colin: 9
Richardson, General William H: 80
Riley, William: 266
Rio Grande: 152, 203, 204
Ripon: 103
Robbers Record: 292
Robbins, Orlando: 290
Roberts, Harry: 86, 88
Roberts, Marshal L.T: 302
Roberts, William: 7
Robinson, ————: 174
Robinson, E.G: 216

Robles, Nieves: 271, 272
Rocky Mountains: 152
Rodgers, Sheriff John: 25
Rodriguez, Nicanora: 32
Rodundo, Tomas (alias, Procopio Bustamente): 67
Rogers, John: 175, 176
Rogers, Sheriff William H: 181, 182
Rogues Gallery: 104, 202, 235
Rolf, Frank H: 27
Rome, Tenn: 37, 42
Ronquel, Ignacio: 304
Rosa, Joseph G: 9, 11
Roscoe: 145
Rose, George: 236, 237, 239
Rosenthal, ————: 39
Roseville: 49
Ross, Aaron Y: 292
Ross, F.N: 299
Ross, George: 119
Ross, Mary A: 74
Ross, Willie: 90, 91, 92, 93
Round Valley: 312, 313
Rowell, Dr: 279
Rowland, Sheriff William: 164, 232, 305
Rubottom, Billy: 136
Rucker, ————: 286
Ruddle, Allen: 204, 247
Rugg, George: 184
Ruggles, Charley and John: 21, 293
Russian River: 154

Sacramento: 19, 32, 53-55, 57, 118, 139, 168, 172, 209, 219, 221, 222, 235, 238, 239, 245, 258, 262, 292
Sacramento County Hospital: 74
Sacramento County Jail: 168, 239, 240
Sacramento Court of Sessions: 31
Sacramento-Nevada City road: 40
Sacramento railroad hospital: 279
Sacramento Valley: 312
Saguache County, Colo: 221
Said, Elkanah: 297
Saint Louis, Mo: 27, 116
Saint Louis University: 70
Salinas jail: 305
Saline County, Ill: 89
Salmon River: 289
Salt Lake City: 48, 140, 239, 252
Samora, Joseph: 7
Sampson, ————: 56
Sampson's Flat: 122
San Andreas: 51, 219, 248, 300
San Antonio: 295, 296
San Bernardino: 64, 97, 147, 164, 175, 176, 217
San Buenaventura: 204
San Diego: 21, 59, 60, 147, 150
San Fernando stage station: 126

San Francisco: 7, 11, 14, 17-22, 27, 32, 37, 50, 53-57, 67, 76, 77, 86, 92, 100, 101, 104, 116, 119, 123, 130, 140, 144, 146, 152, 156, 161, 162, 165, 184, 188, 192, 194, 197, 200-202, 204, 205, 210, 215, 219, 229, 232, 235, 236, 242-44, 252, 254, 255, 257, 261, 268, 269, 271, 272, 277, 285, 300, 302, 305
San Francisco Bay: 37, 132, 288
San Francisco city jail: 141, 237
San Francisco police: 165, 192, 130
San Gabriel: 136, 247, 248, 288
San Jacinto: 147
San Joaquin county: 56, 232
San Joaquin Hills: 133
San Joaquin River: 27, 40, 42, 72, 84, 103, 232, 247, 258
San Joaquin Valley: 94, 106, 120, 170, 174, 186, 187, 210, 215, 279, 280, 291, 304
San Jose: 14, 74, 130, 142, 153, 206, 219, 288, 305
San Jose de Guadalupe, Mexico: 64
San Jose jail: 130
San Juan Bautista: 83, 86, 88, 249, 303
San Juan Capistrano: 133
San Leandro: 67
San Lorenzo Valley: 206
San Luis Gonzaga Ranch: 204, 247
San Luis Obispo: 69, 107, 128, 129, 132, 271
San Luis Obispo County: 120
San Mateo: 130
San Miguel: 106, 107
San Quentin State Prison: 19, 21, 22, 26, 27, 28, 31, 35, 36, 42, 51, 53, 67, 69, 89, 90, 91, 93, 104, 109, 113, 116-19, 127, 128, 132, 133, 141, 160, 164, 165, 168-70, 173, 184, 185, 194, 208, 210, 215, 219, 222, 227, 235, 237, 264, 265, 286, 289, 290, 295, 297, 301, 302, 311
Sanchez, Lewis: 65
Sanchez, Tomas: 177
Sanchez estate: 74
Sands, ————: 258
Sanford, W.T.B: 177, 178
Santa Ana Mountains: 133
Santa Barbara: 130, 132, 255, 268, 269, 270, 271, 288
Santa Clara: 130, 206, 236
Santa Clara Mission Cemetery: 207, 306
Santa Clara ranch: 151
Santa Clara Valley: 129, 174, 215
Santa Cruz: 22, 128, 174, 205, 239, 302
Santa Cruz County: 171
Santa Cruz County Treasury: 237
Santa Fe, N. M: 70, 203
Santa Fe Railroad: 278
Santiago Canyon: 133
Santos, Jose: 132
Sapato China Creek: 232
Scannell, David: 80, 243
Schell, E.M: 288
Schlagel, George: 104

Schmidt, William: 28
Scobie, James: 84
Scott, Sheriff Jay: 124, 187, 275, 276, 293
Scott, Judge Jonathan R: 135
Scott Valley: 293
Scotland Yard: 14
Sea Bird: 289
Sears, Tom: 210
Secrest, Dr. James: 8
Secrest, Jr., William B: 8
Secrest, Shirley: 8
Senate, Jesus: 225, 227
Sepulveda, Juan: 177
Sequoia: 281
Servan, Froilan: 272
Shadley, Marshal Lafe: 111
Shanks, ————: 236
Sharon-Hill divorce: 254
Sharon, Sen. William: 254
Shasta: 21, 32
Shasta County: 32, 56, 137, 179, 187, 292, 293
Shattuck, Bill: 168
Shaw's Flat: 173
Sherman, ————: 236
Sherman, William T: 78
Shine: John H: 48, 49
Shinn, Charles Howard: 11
Shinn, George: 118
Shirley, Warden Paul: 28
Shoemaker, ————: 139
Shortridge, James F: 56
Shovel Creek: 293
Shuler, Deputy: 258
Sierra Nevada: 12, 262
Silvas, Santiago: 132, 135
Simi Pass: 135
Sing Sing prison: 76, 244
Siskiyou County: 275
Siskiyou Public Library: 8
Skinner, Cyrus: 32, 37, 38, 262, 265, 267
Skinner, George: 32, 37, 38
Smith, ————: 221
Smith, Bill: 15
Smith, Ely: 178
Smith, Henderson: 59
Smith, Jim: 37, 38, 170
Smith, Sheriff Jim: 84
Smith, T.J: 8
Smith, Thomas "Pegleg": 70
Smith, Detective Will: 103, 108, 121, 122, 280
Snake River country: 289
Snelling: 208
Soap Lake: 302
Soher, Mrs. Adolph: 300
Soledad: 84, 126, 230
Sonoma County: 302
Sonora: 13, 27, 49, 50, 241, 246, 286, 288, 318, 320, 321

Sonora, Mexico: 69, 144, 148, 179, 246
Sontag, John: 15, 19, 103, 120-24, 144, 186-88, 233, 275; bio. sketch, 279-84; 293
Sontag, Mary: 279, 281, 284, 295
Soto, Juan: 231, 302
South America: 157
Southern Express train: 223
Southern Pacific Railroad: 15, 56, 94, 97, 108, 120, 145, 146, 170, 186, 188, 255, 261, 279, 281, 293, 303
Spanish Consul at San Francisco: 200
Special Police: 192, 237
Speck, Alex: 285
Spencer, Carrie: 237-40
Sprague, George: 171
Stanislaus County: 25, 104, 321
Stanislaus mines: 206
Stanislaus River: 49
Stanley, John Q.A: 178, 180
Star City, Nev: 291
Stearns, Abel: 177
Stephenson's California Regiment: 268
Stern, Dr. Norton B: 9
Steuben County Indiana: 147
Stewart, ————: 37
Stewart, Dep. Sheriff George: 293
Stewart, Senator William: 253, 255
Stockton: 42, 53, 55, 74, 101, 103, 104, 215, 221, 231, 247, 269, 321
Stockton Asylum: 75
Stockton Fire Department: 101
Stockton jail: 103
Stone, Capt. Appleton W: 51
Stone Corral: 122, 144, 145, 284
"Stones, The": 18
Sullivan, James: 118-19
Sullivan, James "Yankee": 241, 243
Sunol: 230, 302
Sunol Valley: 231
Supreme Court: 221
Sutherland, John: 84, 291, 304
Sutton, Smith: 40
Sycamore: 27
Sylvester, John: 72

Talbot, Henry J. ("Cherokee Bob"): bio. sketch, 285-290
Tailholt: 153, 154, 156
Taylor, Gen. Zachary: 203, 204
Taylor, George: 34, 35, 36
Tecate: 150
Tecate Valley: 148
Tehama County: 56
Tejada, Jesus: 231
Tejon Canyon: 217, 218
Tejon Pass: 68, 247, 248, 305
Temple, John: 60, 63
Tennessee: 157

Tennessee's Partner: 285
Terry, David S: 93, 103, 254, 255
Texas: 23, 59, 153, 154, 203, 205
"Texas": 175
Thacker, Eugene: 187, 294
Thacker, John Nelson: 56, 103, 104, 122, 144, 146, 184, 186, 188, 275; bio. sketch, 291-94
Thacker, Sarah: 294
The Dalles, Oregon: 289
The 25th Man: 323
Thomas, Constable Harry: 303
Thompson, James: 135
Thompson, Robert: 162
Thorn, Benjamin Kent: 14, 50, 89, 186, 257-61; bio. sketch, 295-300
Thorn, Charles H. (alias, Charles Dorsey): 113, 116
Thornpen, John: 60
Three-fingered Jack: 72, 73, 250
Thurman, Ormistead: 182, 185
Thurman, Sheriff: 45
Tibbet, Bert: 212, 214
Tibbet, Lawrence: 214
Tibbet, Rebecca: 214
Tibbet, William: 212, 214
Toll House: 275
Tom Bell's gang: 257, 258, 261, 263
Tombstone, Az: 12, 170, 184, 253, 261
Tompkins, E.O: 265
Tompkins, State Senator: 231
Tompkins, William: 210
Tovey, Mike: 186
Treher, Charles "Dutch Jake": 182
Tres Pinos, 84, 232, 274, 303, 306
Trinity Center: 32
Trinity County: 8, 312, 315
Trinity Mountains: 38
Tucson, Az: 152, 170, 261, 273
Tuggle, Troy: 8
Tulare County: 8, 12, 19, 110, 144, 154, 212, 218, 258
Tulare Lake: 153, 154, 174, 215
Tung, Leong: 277
Tuolumne County: 27, 105, 113, 173, 243, 246, 255, 286, 318, 321
Turcott, Abraham: 119
Turnerville: 248
Tuttletown: 105
Twain, Mark: 199
Twist, Sheriff William: 270
Tryon, George C: 258, 259

Union Bar: 48
Union City, Ind: 116
United States Court in Los Angeles: 144
United States Feature Film Company: 100
Ures, Mexico: 64
Ury, Henry (Jack Brady): 58
Utah: 70, 177, 209

Valencia, Antonio: 248
Valentine, ————: 287
Valentine, John J: 131
Valenzuela, Francisco: 64
Valenzuela, Jesus: 272, 273
Valenzuela, Joaquin: 204, 205, 249, 272
Valenzuela, Juan: 132
Vallejo, General Mariano: 17
Valley Springs: 190
Van brothers: 315
Van Hagen, J.B: 33, 34
Vanderbilt, Cornelius: 146
Varelas, Antonio: 132, 133, 135
Vasquez, Fedoro: 150
Vasquez, Tiburcio: 8, 11, 15, 16, 67, 68, 83, 84, 88, 102, 164, 207, 232, 280; bio. sketch, 301-306
Vedder, John: 264
Vedder, Lucinda: 264
Veith, Anton: 46
Venard, Stephen: 15, 170, 182; bio. sketch, 307-311
Verdi, Nev: 15
Vermont: 203
Viela, Francisco: 15
Vigilantes: 11, 17, 20, 21, 22, 33, 67, 80, 90, 135, 160, 174, 192, 198, 243, 244, 258, 267, 269, 272, 320
Villa Grove, Colo: 221
Vincennes, Ind: 312
Virginia: 152, 177
Virginia City, Nev: 74, 244, 252, 253
Visalia: 84, 94, 95, 120, 122-25, 138, 139, 144, 145, 162, 174, 186-88, 208-10, 216, 260, 279-81, 283, 302
Visalia jail: 109
Visitacion Valley murder: 199
Vogan, John: 299

Wabau: 17, 18, 37
Walker (alias, Skinner brothers): 32, 38
Walker, William: 157, 159
Wall, Isaac: 288
Walla Walla Valley Pioneer and Historical Soc: 8
Walla Walla, Wash: 285, 289
Wallis, Judge H.W: 321
Ward, ————: 151
Warnock, William R: 194
Warren, City Marshal William C: 162
Warren County, Oh: 142
Washington, Cal: 54
Washington, DC: 48
Washington (state): 23
Washoe County, Nev: 74, 267
Wathen, John David: bio. sketch, 312-317
Watkins, ————: 287
Watson, Judge John H: 153
Watson, Tom: 59
Watsonville: 119
Wawona: 47

INDEX

Waynesville, Oh: 307
Weaverville Public Library: 8
Webster, Jim: 33, 263
Webster, Marcus: 59
Weeks, Charles: 303
Weller, Gov. John B: 289
Wells Fargo and Company: 14, 15, 26-28, 34, 45, 49, 50, 56, 97, 127, 143, 144, 146, 170, 182, 184, 185, 187-89, 191, 193, 194, 196, 260, 261, 281, 291, 293, 309, 310
Wells Fargo Bank: 7
Wells Fargo box: 137, 219, 221, 303
Wells Fargo Detective: 323
Wells Fargo detectives: 122
Wells Fargo History Room: 7
Wells, Judge Alexander: 77, 198
Wesson, Dep. Sheriff: 297
West Fresno: 277
West, William B: 210
Western Peace Officer, The: 11
Whalen, Constable Jack: 225
Wheatland: 56, 145
Whimtown: 173
White and Courtney: 248
White, Bill: 32, 37, 38, 39, 40, 41, 287
White, Clarence: 314, 315, 316
White, Dep. Sheriff John J: 275
White, Eph: 184
White, Frankie: 315
White, George E: 312-14, 316
White Pine Mining District, Nev: 252
White Sulphur, Ga: 223
White's Bridge: 27
Whitehead, ———: 264
Whitlock, Dep. Sheriff: 27
Whitman, Mayor Elias B: 289
Whittacker, ———: 168
Wiggen, Charles: 235, 236, 239
Wilcox, Assemblyman: 13
Wildy, H.H: 151
Wiley, ———: 37
Wilkes County, Ga: 285
Williams, Charles: 297
Williams, Frank: 30, 96
Williams, George: 104
Williams, Henry: 53, 55
Williams, Isaac: 179
Williams, Jack (alias, Shanks): 309
Williams, Jakey: 290
Williams, Lewis: 168
Williams (alias, Skinner brothers): 32
Williams, Ca: 82

Williamson, Thomas: 288
Williamson (alias, Skinner brothers): 32, 37
Willis, John: 210
Willoughby, Bill: 290
Willow Springs: 230
Wilson, Benjamin D: 177, 178
Wilson, Hy: 30
Wilson, John: 320
Wilson, Vic: 122, 281
Winchell, E.C: 216
Wing Chong Co: 142
Winston, J.B: 178
Winters, ———: 104
Witty, Dep. Sheriff George: 103, 109, 121, 122, 189
Wood, Constable O.B: 66
Woodland: 27
Woodman, D.T: 317
Woods, G.W: 73
Woods, Richard (alias, Dick Barter): 33
Woolsey, King: 86
World War I: 278
Worthington, Henry G: 153, 156
Worthington, Peter: 152, 156
Work, George: bio. sketch, 318-21
Wren, Lee: 210
Wright, Aleck: 33, 36
Wright, W.W: 263, 307
Wyalusing, Wisc: 187
Wylacki Indians: 312
Wyoming: 140

Yankee Blade: 205
Yankee Jims: 219
Yaqui Camp: 248, 296
Yaqui Indian country: 146
Ybarra, Pedro: 296
Yolla Bolly country: 11, 312
Yorba ranch: 135
Yosemite: 11, 43, 44, 46, 274, 275
Young, Jim: 122, 281
Young, Tom: 73
Younger, Adeline: 106
Yreka: 8, 236, 293
Yuba County: 258, 265
Yuba River: 295
Yuma, Az: 86, 147
Yuma Indians: 59
Yuma road: 150

Zacatecas, Mexico: 143
Zemitis, Sibylle: 7